OUT ON THE WIRE

ALSO BY JESSICA ABEL

La Perdida

Mirror, Window

Soundtrack

BY JESSICA ABEL AND MATT MADDEN

Drawing Words & Writing Pictures

Mastering Comics

OUT ON THE WIRE

The Storytelling Secrets
of the
New Masters of Radio

JESSICA ABEL

Foreword by Ira Glass

B\D\W\Y

BROADWAY BOOKS

New York

Published in the United States by Broadway Books, an imprint of the
Crown Publishing Group, a division of Penguin Random House LLC,
New York.
www.crownpublishing.com

BROADWAY BOOKS and its logo, B \ D \ W \ Y, are trademarks of
Penguin Random House LLC.

Background drawing assistance by Matt Madden

This work received the support of the *Cité internationale de la bande dessinée
et de l'image*, in the form of an author residency at the Maison des auteurs
(Angoulême, France).

la **cité** internationale
de la bande dessinée
et de l'image

Library of Congress cataloging-in-publication data is available upon request.

ISBN 978-0-385-34843-0
eBook ISBN 978-0-385-34844-7

Printed in the United States of America

Cover illustration by Jessica Abel

10 9 8 7 6

First Edition

Contents

Acknowledgments

The list of people I need to thank for helping me bring forth this book into the world is long, and probably incomplete. It starts, of course, with all the producers, reporters, editors, and staff I talked to from the various shows I love. I have done my best to mention them by name in the Show Guide (page 222). But let me just say again, my sincere and fervent thanks to all of them, and most particularly those who carved out large chunks of time to allow me into their whole creative process: the staffs of *Snap Judgment* and *Planet Money*, as well as Jay Allison, who invited me into his Woods Hole, Massachusetts, home and shared his family table with me. I also want to acknowledge the crucial help provided by Sean Cole, who read the manuscript and saved me from a few very embarrassing blunders.

On my personal "staff" is a long list of studio assistants who have pitched in on this project by logging and transcribing tape, preparing pages, working up backgrounds, drawing panel borders, and all the other boring but necessary prep labor that goes into making comics. Thank you: Kou Chen, Li-Or Zatzman, Justine Sarlat, Bastien Nerre, Ryan Brewer, and Dido Drachman. Also, my thanks to Mebina Tudlahar for transcription and logging. On my trip to Oakland, I was so pleased to have a chance to stay with my old friends Dee Hoover and Steve Beal. Reconnecting with them made it possible for me to concentrate on *Snap* on that visit.

I interviewed several people who, for reasons of length, don't appear in the final book. Thanks to Daniel Alarcón of *Radio Ambulante*—the first show in Spanish (possibly the first in any language other than English?) to use this model of narrative journalism for radio. It's fantastic. And also sometimes in English (www.radioambulante.org/en). I also spoke to the very talented Ari Daniel Shapiro, who reports on science, and had lots of very cool things to say about how he makes science come alive (www.aridanielshapiro.wordpress.com). My thanks go also to Eben Mannes and Robb Jacobson for talking to me about their *Radiolab* remix experiences.

This book, quite literally, would not exist without Ira Glass and his sharp newspaper-clipping skills back in 1995. Thanks to Ira for coming up with the whole idea of radio comics, and getting me involved on the ground floor. Our work together has been an inspiration to me. Thanks also to Seth Lind, who has shepherded *Radio: An Illustrated Guide* for several years, and was instrumental in getting me started on this book.

For their help with *Radio: An Illustrated Guide*, my thanks go to the 1999-era staff of *This American Life*, and in particular Ira, Todd Bachmann, and Elizabeth Meister, for all their help and patience; as well as to Eric Nuzum for his generosity with his time and knowledge about computer editing; and to Brett Leveridge for help with photo reference.

I would probably still be thinking about what approach to take in these pages if it were not for my agent, Bob Mecoy. Thanks for making me do this.

My wonderful editor Meagan Stacey is the best one could hope for. Super-smart, cheerful, helpful, and ever willing to dive back in, again, to the dirty details; I feel incredibly lucky to have worked with her. Between Meagan and Domenica Alioto, I have always felt in safe hands. My thanks go also to Nancy Ethiel, who is my other best editor, as well as being my mother. She taught me well, and is still always there for me.

Matt Madden has redefined "helpmeet" in my personal dictionary. This is a man who can be the perfect partner, care for our kids, *and* edit the hell out of a weird comic book about radio, all at the same time. He even gets a chance to make his own comics, sometimes. Thanks and love to Matt for being a part of this book, and my life, at every stage.

Finally, thanks—for all you do—to the creative radio people who keep proliferating and creating ever more awesome audio. I am inspired by your work every day.

Foreword
by Ira Glass

I find myself lately living in a world I never imagined would exist. When I learned to make radio stories like the ones I make today, you could fit everyone who made these sorts of stories into a minivan. Now we're an army. Our ranks have been growing for a while but just in the last year, it feels like some new beachhead's been conquered and a flood of new podcasts has arrived, filled with stories that have surprising plotlines and humor and emotion and interesting, original ideas.

And these podcasts are finding audiences. One measure of just how much things have changed: When *This American Life* went on the air in 1995, it took us four years to get to a million listeners. In 2014, our spinoff *Serial* got there in four weeks. NPR's show *Invisibilia* got there even faster: over two million listeners per episode in four weeks. And as people continue to find these shows on the Internet, the numbers just keep climbing. At this point, each episode of *Invisibilia* has been downloaded by five million people. For *Serial*, the number's over seven million. Finally this year we seem to have left the era when telling someone about a podcast got you blank stares or a confused "HOW do you hear one of those things?"

If you picked up this book hoping to learn how to make stories like this yourself, let me be the first one to say Welcome! The water's warm! Jump on in!

If you picked up this book as a fan of these shows, to get a look behind the scenes, an enthusiastic Hello! to you as well. Please know that all of us in this comic book look cuter in these pages than we do in real life. I've read that being in the movies makes anyone look ten pounds heavier. Apparently comics lighten you by twelve or fifteen pounds. And in the comics, I and my colleagues agree, our skin has never looked better.

Jessica Abel has done a spectacular job capturing what our jobs are like. Frankly, I find it astonishing that an outsider could come into our radio offices and so thoroughly suss out the key things a person would need to know to make great work. So many parts of this book blow my mind, they're so well done. First and foremost: the chunk of this book that starts on page 47 about how to tell if a story idea is worth pursuing, and how to focus a story so it'll be great. People say so many smart things in that section that I'd never heard before, things I wanted to try out immediately. This book is a first-rate field manual for anyone thinking of joining our radio army.

If you're even vaguely considering this yourself, my advice is: start now. Don't wait for permission. Don't wait till you get a job doing this. Don't wait for inspiration to strike. Don't wait till you're at a better place in your life. Just start. You'll find it's simpler than you might think and as engrossing as you could ever hope for. And where to start? Well you should choose whatever feels right to you but the most basic radio piece you can make is an interview with someone who has some story to tell. For that kind of piece, you don't need to figure out how to write or perform your narration. You don't need narration! (All my early stories were non-narrated interviews for that very reason.) If you want to spend a little money, spring for a mic to plug into your smartphone and get a proper recording. Edit and mix the sound on GarageBand or whatever free software you like. You can strategize what to ask, do the interview, and structure the tape you get—go through all the steps of making that piece—in a week or two. Play it for a friend and have them critique and then make changes. Then play it for another friend and make more changes. Then try another story, and another. Rinse, repeat, get better, post to the Internet. Maybe pitch a story to some show you like.

In 1998 when Jessica Abel first came to Chicago to hang out and draw that first short comic book about our show, my coworkers and I all thought we were far along into our radio journey together, old hands at our craft. After all, we'd been making *This American Life* for three years! What else was there to learn? At that point we'd already succeeded beyond our expectations and gone as far as we could imagine anyone going, with our audience that was less than a million people and our barely existent internet presence. We had no idea other people would someday take up gear and join us on the battlefield making these sorts of stories. We didn't think of ourselves as the advance guard for the crowd that's now formed alongside us. But lately there's so much great audio being made, it's hard keeping up with it all. People are trying new things, expressing their personalities, documenting stuff nobody had gotten to till now. More than ever, it feels like there's so much to invent and discover. It feels like we're just at the beginning.

Preface

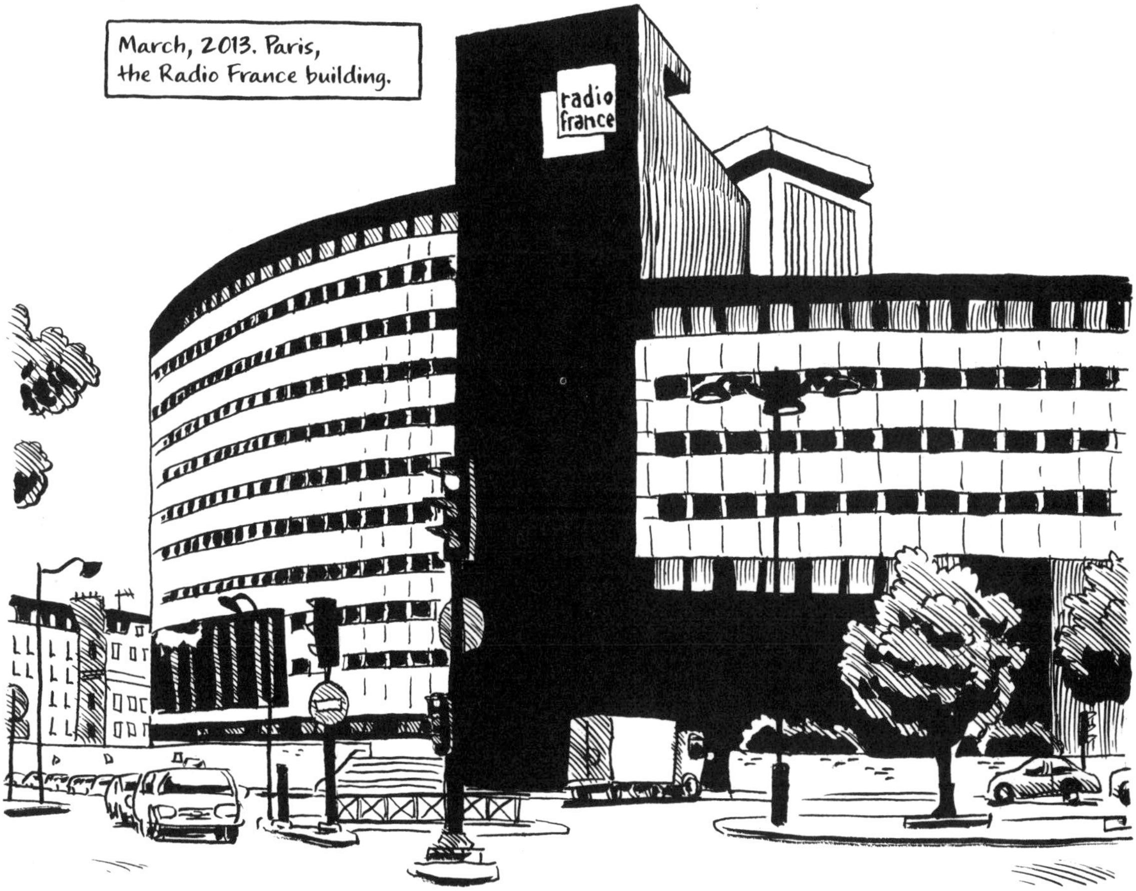
March, 2013. Paris, the Radio France building.
radio france

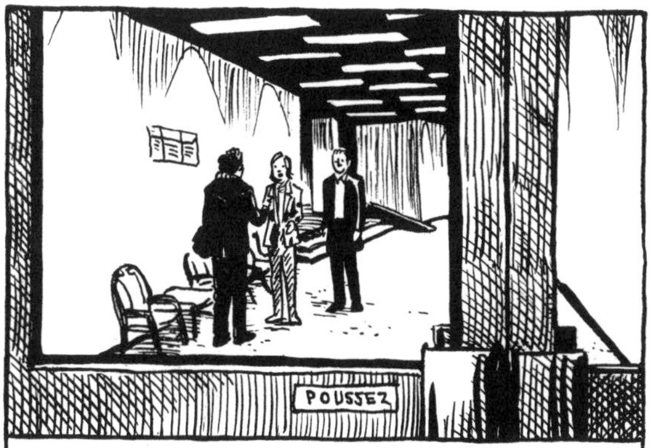
POUSSEZ
Thomas Baumgartner, the host of *L'Atelier du son* on Radio France, found out about my comics about radio and was intrigued. He asked me in for an interview.

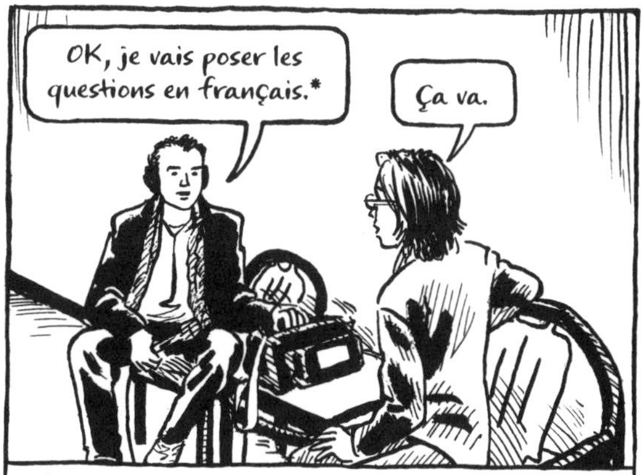
OK, je vais poser les questions en français.*
Ça va.
I'd been living in France for nine months at this point. Long enough to understand questions in French, not long enough to answer them.

*OK, I'm going to ask you the questions in French.

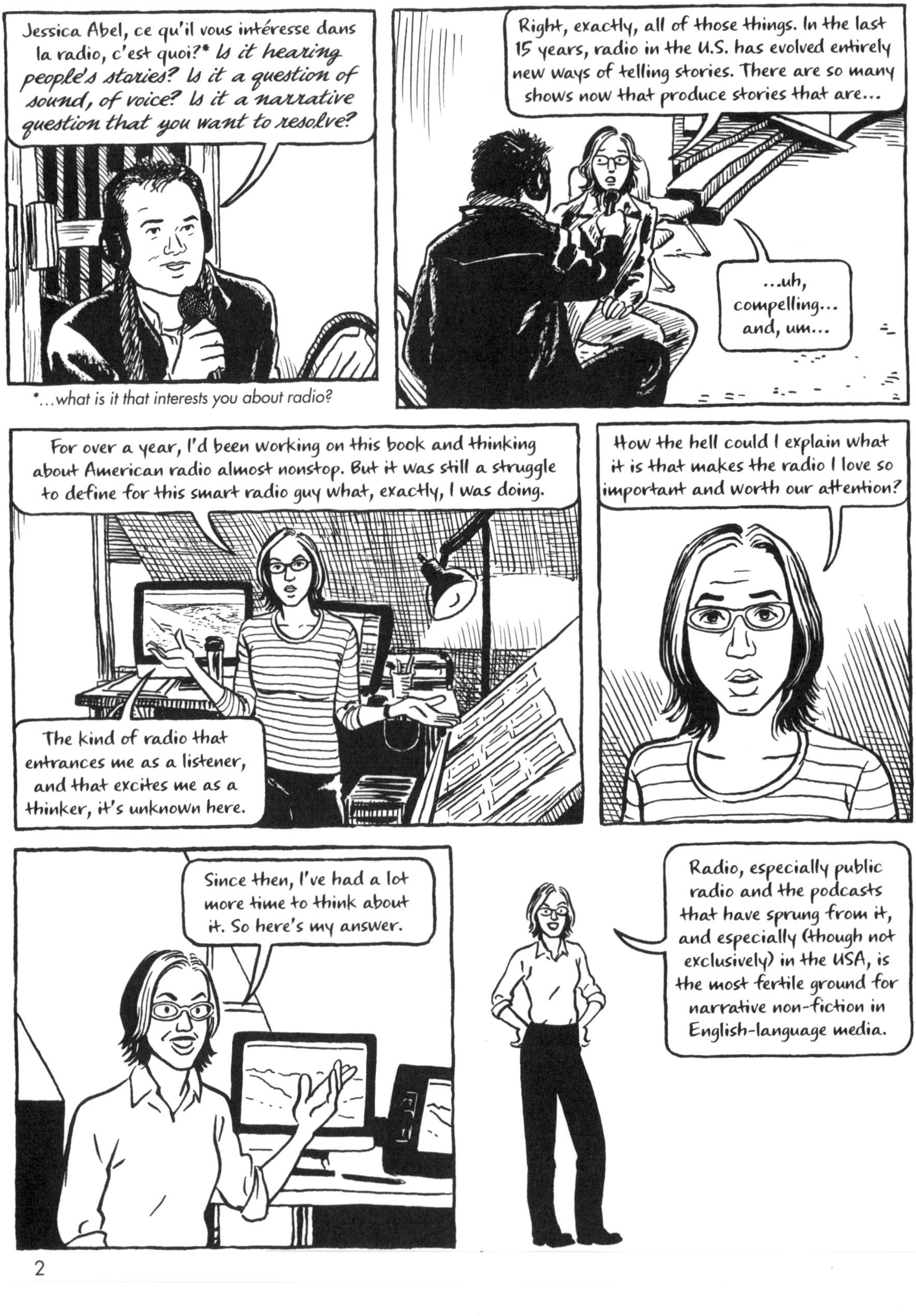
Jessica Abel, ce qu'il vous intéresse dans la radio, c'est quoi?* *Is it hearing people's stories? Is it a question of sound, of voice? Is it a narrative question that you want to resolve?*
*...what is it that interests you about radio?
Right, exactly, all of those things. In the last 15 years, radio in the U.S. has evolved entirely new ways of telling stories. There are so many shows now that produce stories that are...
...uh, compelling... and, um...
For over a year, I'd been working on this book and thinking about American radio almost nonstop. But it was still a struggle to define for this smart radio guy what, exactly, I was doing.
The kind of radio that entrances me as a listener, and that excites me as a thinker, it's unknown here.
How the hell could I explain what it is that makes the radio I love so important and worth our attention?
Since then, I've had a lot more time to think about it. So here's my answer.
Radio, especially public radio and the podcasts that have sprung from it, and especially (though not exclusively) in the USA, is the most fertile ground for narrative non-fiction in English-language media.

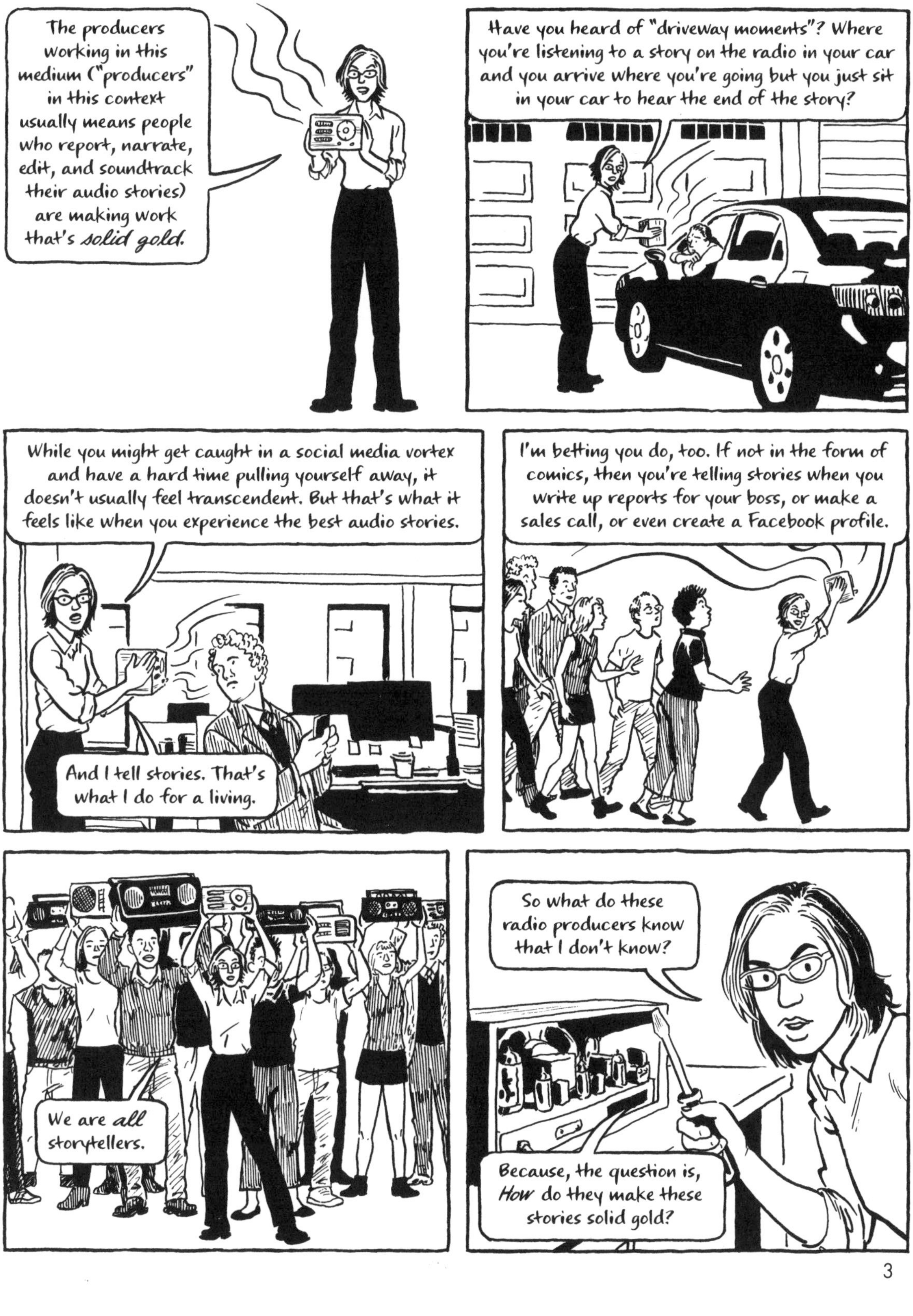
The producers working in this medium ("producers" in this context usually means people who report, narrate, edit, and soundtrack their audio stories) are making work that's *solid gold.*
Have you heard of "driveway moments"? Where you're listening to a story on the radio in your car and you arrive where you're going but you just sit in your car to hear the end of the story?
While you might get caught in a social media vortex and have a hard time pulling yourself away, it doesn't usually feel transcendent. But that's what it feels like when you experience the best audio stories.
And I tell stories. That's what I do for a living.
I'm betting you do, too. If not in the form of comics, then you're telling stories when you write up reports for your boss, or make a sales call, or even create a Facebook profile.
We are *all* storytellers.
So what do these radio producers know that I don't know?
Because, the question is, *How* do they make these stories solid gold?

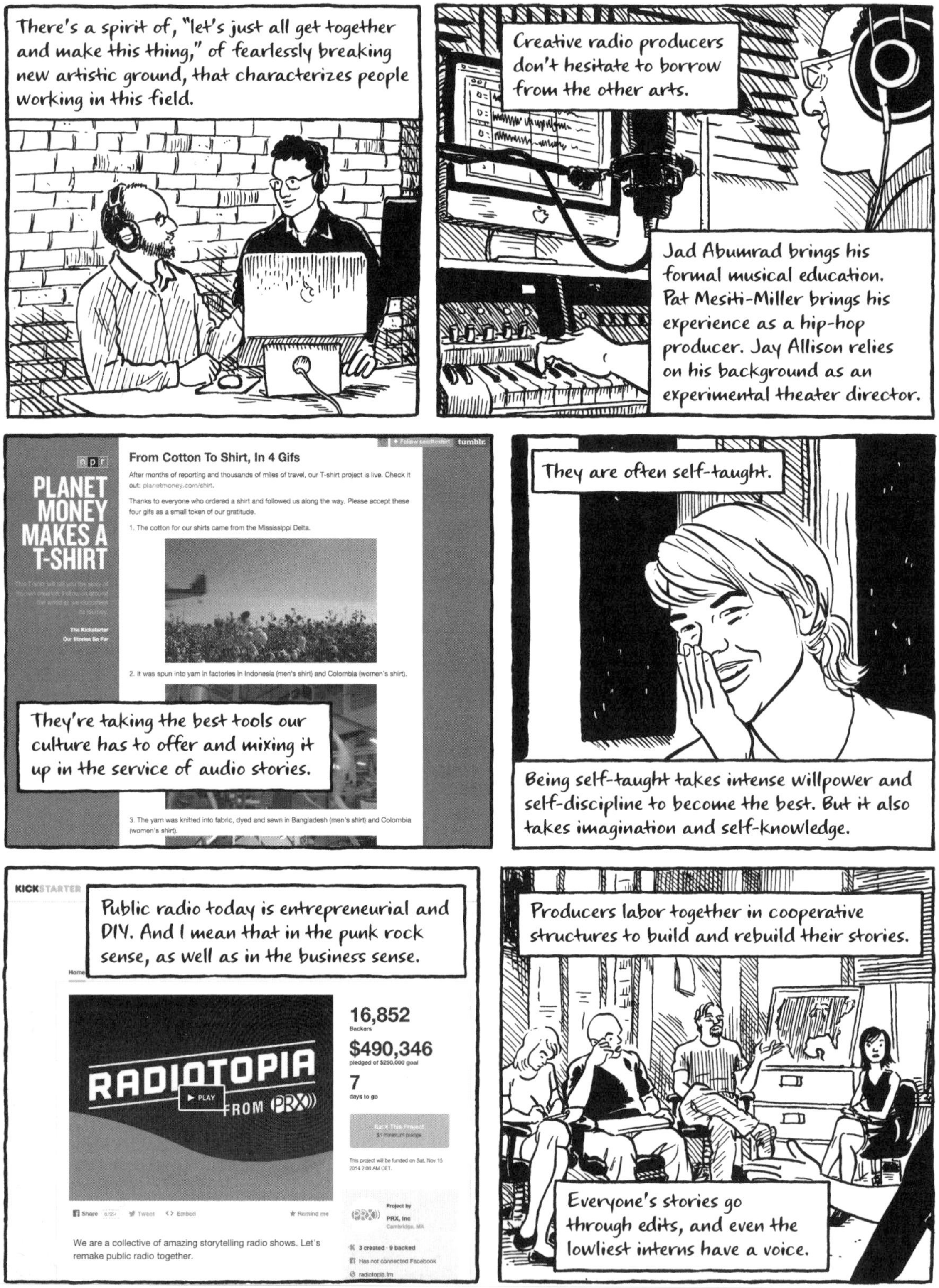

There's a spirit of, "let's just all get together and make this thing," of fearlessly breaking new artistic ground, that characterizes people working in this field.
Creative radio producers don't hesitate to borrow from the other arts.
Jad Abumrad brings his formal musical education. Pat Mesiti-Miller brings his experience as a hip-hop producer. Jay Allison relies on his background as an experimental theater director.
npr
PLANET MONEY MAKES A T-SHIRT
From Cotton To Shirt, In 4 Gifs
After months of reporting and thousands of miles of travel, our T-shirt project is live. Check it out: planetmoney.com/shirt.
Thanks to everyone who ordered a shirt and followed us along the way. Please accept these four gifs as a small token of our gratitude.
1. The cotton for our shirts came from the Mississippi Delta.
2. It was spun into yarn in factories in Indonesia (men's shirt) and Colombia (women's shirt).
3. The yarn was knitted into fabric, dyed and sewn in Bangladesh (men's shirt) and Colombia (women's shirt).
tumblr.
They're taking the best tools our culture has to offer and mixing it up in the service of audio stories.
They are often self-taught.
Being self-taught takes intense willpower and self-discipline to become the best. But it also takes imagination and self-knowledge.
KICKSTARTER
Public radio today is entrepreneurial and DIY. And I mean that in the punk rock sense, as well as in the business sense.
RADIOTOPIA
FROM PRX
16,852
Backers
$490,346
pledged of $250,000 goal
7
days to go
We are a collective of amazing storytelling radio shows. Let's remake public radio together.
Producers labor together in cooperative structures to build and rebuild their stories.
Everyone's stories go through edits, and even the lowliest interns have a voice.

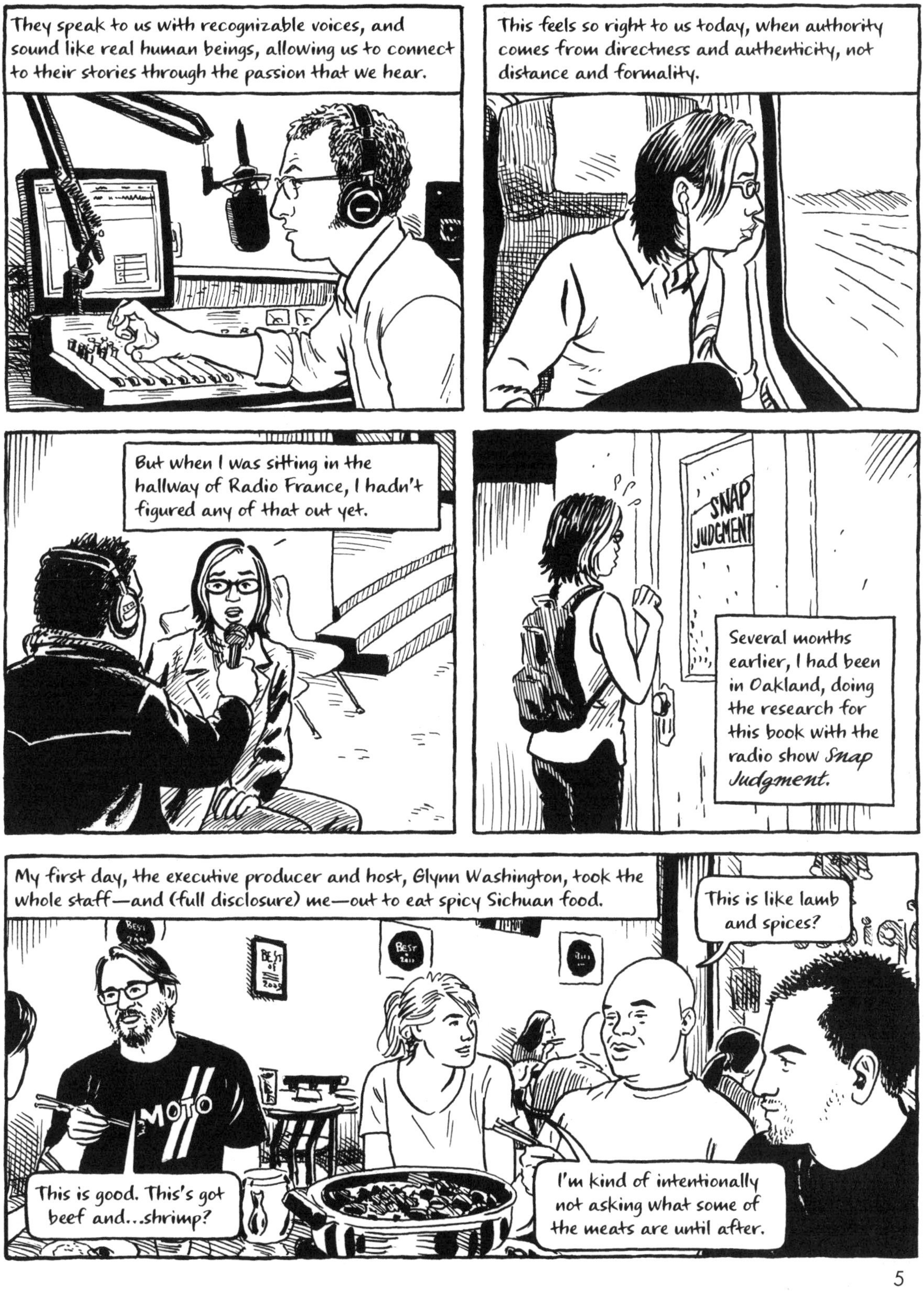
They speak to us with recognizable voices, and sound like real human beings, allowing us to connect to their stories through the passion that we hear.
This feels so right to us today, when authority comes from directness and authenticity, not distance and formality.
But when I was sitting in the hallway of Radio France, I hadn't figured any of that out yet.
SNAP JUDGMENT
Several months earlier, I had been in Oakland, doing the research for this book with the radio show *Snap Judgment*.
My first day, the executive producer and host, Glynn Washington, took the whole staff—and (full disclosure) me—out to eat spicy Sichuan food.
This is like lamb and spices?
MOTO
This is good. This's got beef and...shrimp?
I'm kind of intentionally not asking what some of the meats are until after.

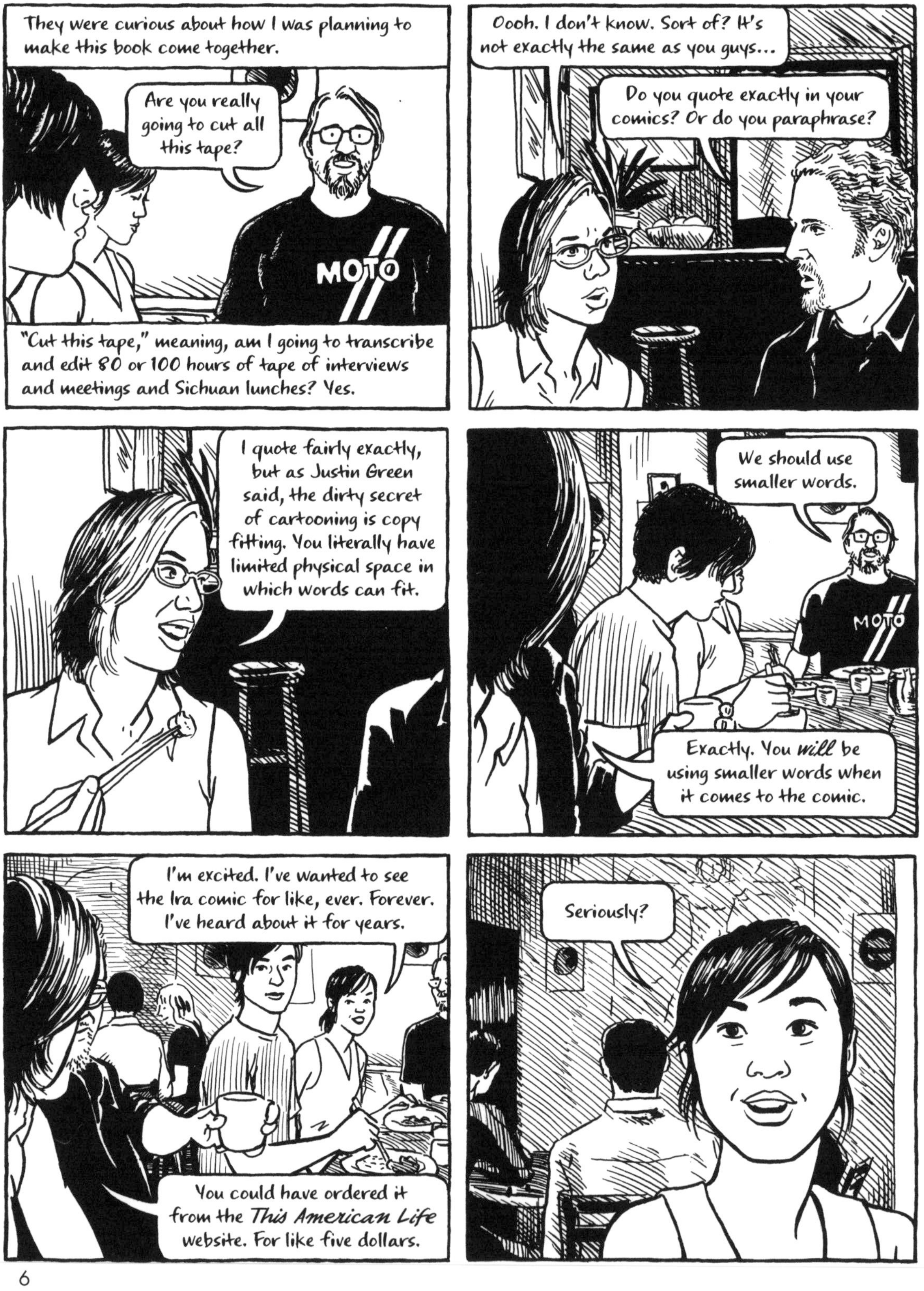
They were curious about how I was planning to make this book come together.
Are you really going to cut all this tape?
MOTO
"Cut this tape," meaning, am I going to transcribe and edit 80 or 100 hours of tape of interviews and meetings and Sichuan lunches? Yes.
Oooh. I don't know. Sort of? It's not exactly the same as you guys...
Do you quote exactly in your comics? Or do you paraphrase?
I quote fairly exactly, but as Justin Green said, the dirty secret of cartooning is copy fitting. You literally have limited physical space in which words can fit.
We should use smaller words.
MOTO
Exactly. You *will* be using smaller words when it comes to the comic.
I'm excited. I've wanted to see the Ira comic for like, ever. Forever. I've heard about it for years.
You could have ordered it from the *This American Life* website. For like five dollars.
Seriously?

OK, yeah, so this is not the first time I've made a comic book about radio.

Back in 1998, I was living in Mexico City.

What time is it?

I'm a cartoonist. If you ever want to picture what it's like to be a cartoonist, you can start by imagining incredibly long hours hunched over a drawing table.

And for most cartoonists, it therefore involves listening to radio—hours and hours and hours of radio.

It's 1:15.

So. Mexico. 1998. 56.6-baud dialup internet service (when it wasn't on the fritz).

beedleeedleeoop eeee-awnh e-eee-awnh EGgsshhhh

Buffering.

Oh lord, the buffering.

Of course, I could have just listened to music and not tested the primitive capabilities of RealAudio, but I was an addict of this new show, *This American Life*.

I'm Ira Glass.

Brrrring

I'd been listening to it since it launched on local Chicago public radio WBEZ as *Your Radio Playhouse* back in 1996. Sure, I'd moved to Mexico, but I was not about to give that up.

Bueno?

7

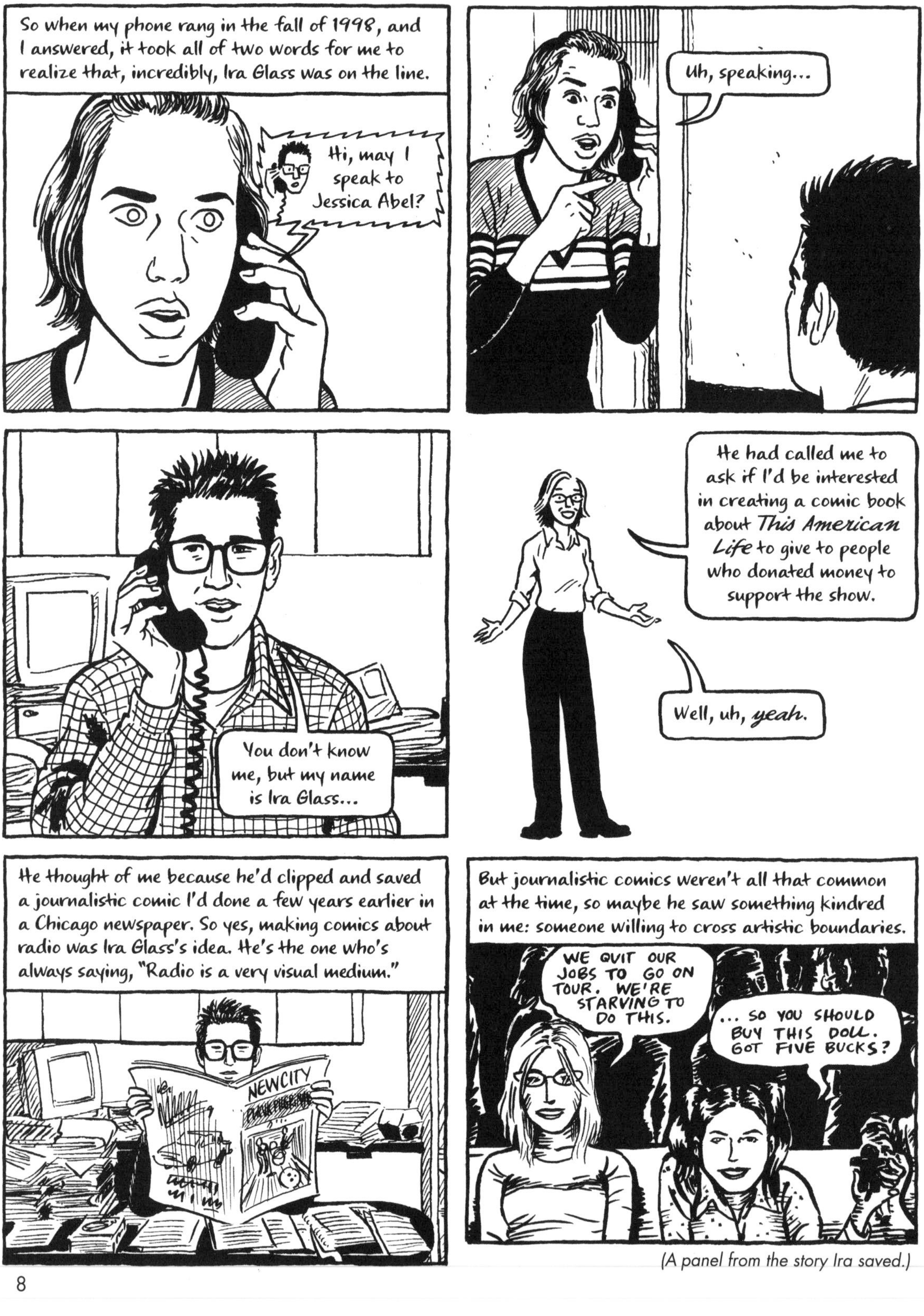
So when my phone rang in the fall of 1998, and I answered, it took all of two words for me to realize that, incredibly, Ira Glass was on the line.
Hi, may I speak to Jessica Abel?
Uh, speaking...
You don't know me, but my name is Ira Glass...
He had called me to ask if I'd be interested in creating a comic book about *This American Life* to give to people who donated money to support the show.
Well, uh, *yeah.*
He thought of me because he'd clipped and saved a journalistic comic I'd done a few years earlier in a Chicago newspaper. So yes, making comics about radio was Ira Glass's idea. He's the one who's always saying, "Radio is a very visual medium."
NEWCITY
But journalistic comics weren't all that common at the time, so maybe he saw something kindred in me: someone willing to cross artistic boundaries.
WE QUIT OUR JOBS TO GO ON TOUR. WE'RE STARVING TO DO THIS.
... SO YOU SHOULD BUY THIS DOLL. GOT FIVE BUCKS?

(A panel from the story Ira saved.)

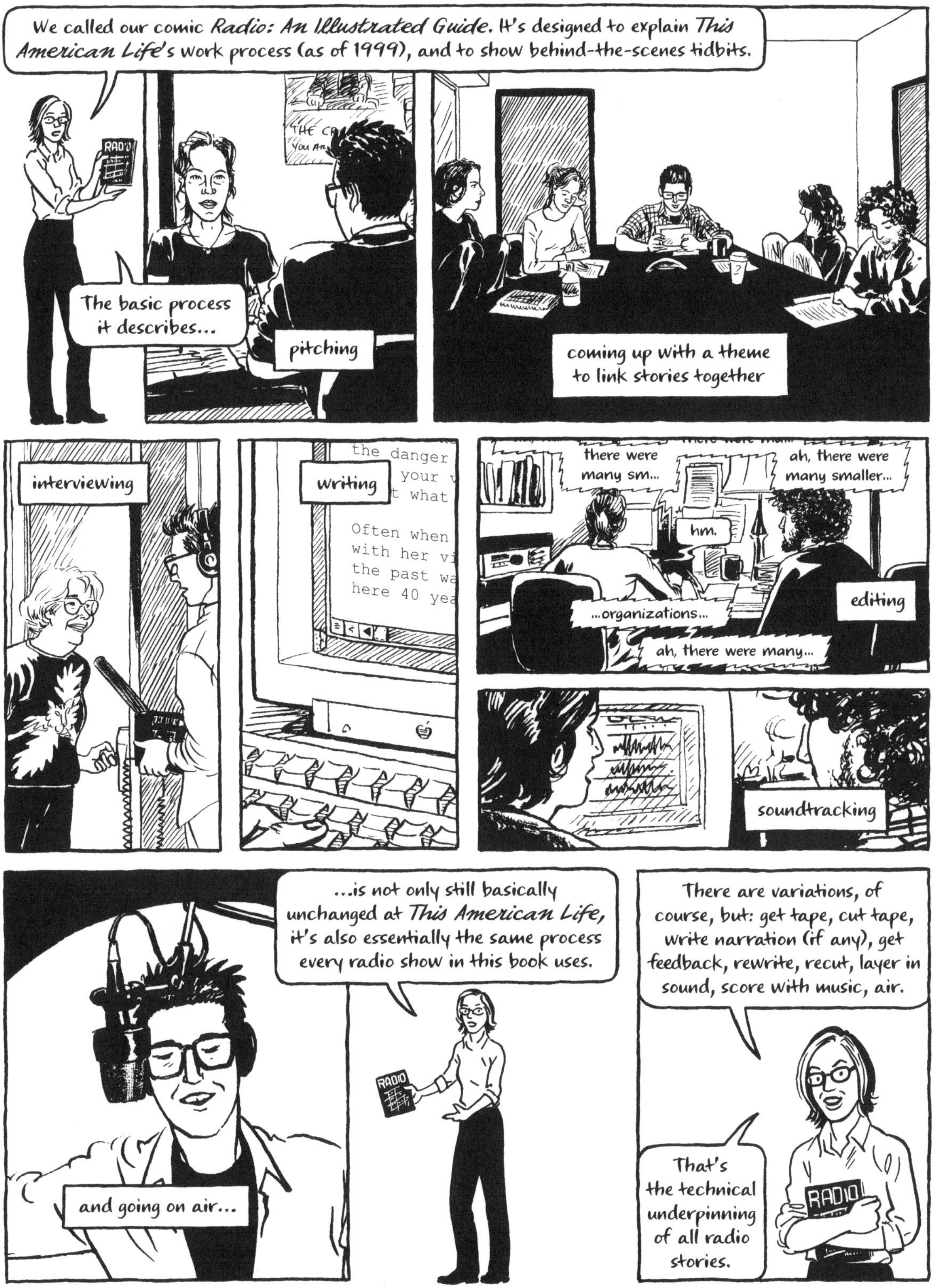

We called our comic *Radio: An Illustrated Guide*. It's designed to explain *This American Life*'s work process (as of 1999), and to show behind-the-scenes tidbits.
The basic process it describes...
pitching
coming up with a theme to link stories together
interviewing
writing
there were many sm...
ah, there were many smaller...
hm.
...organizations...
ah, there were many...
editing
soundtracking
and going on air...
...is not only still basically unchanged at *This American Life*, it's also essentially the same process every radio show in this book uses.
RADIO
There are variations, of course, but: get tape, cut tape, write narration (if any), get feedback, rewrite, recut, layer in sound, score with music, air.
That's the technical underpinning of all radio stories.
RADIO

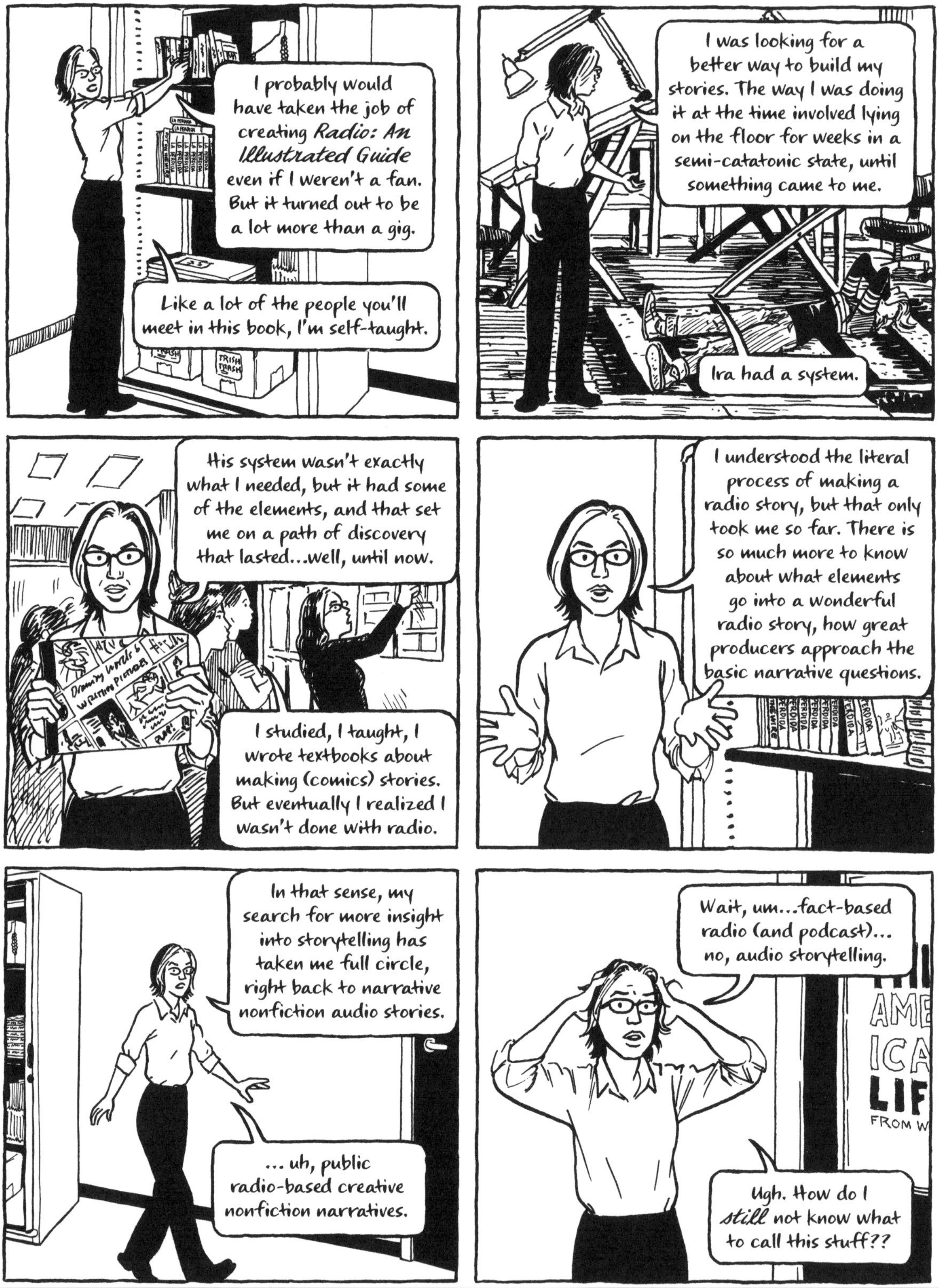
I probably would have taken the job of creating *Radio: An Illustrated Guide* even if I weren't a fan. But it turned out to be a lot more than a gig.
Like a lot of the people you'll meet in this book, I'm self-taught.
I was looking for a better way to build my stories. The way I was doing it at the time involved lying on the floor for weeks in a semi-catatonic state, until something came to me.
Ira had a system.
His system wasn't exactly what I needed, but it had some of the elements, and that set me on a path of discovery that lasted...well, until now.
I studied, I taught, I wrote textbooks about making (comics) stories. But eventually I realized I wasn't done with radio.
I understood the literal process of making a radio story, but that only took me so far. There is so much more to know about what elements go into a wonderful radio story, how great producers approach the basic narrative questions.
In that sense, my search for more insight into storytelling has taken me full circle, right back to narrative nonfiction audio stories.
... uh, public radio-based creative nonfiction narratives.
Wait, um...fact-based radio (and podcast)... no, audio storytelling.
Ugh. How do I *still* not know what to call this stuff??

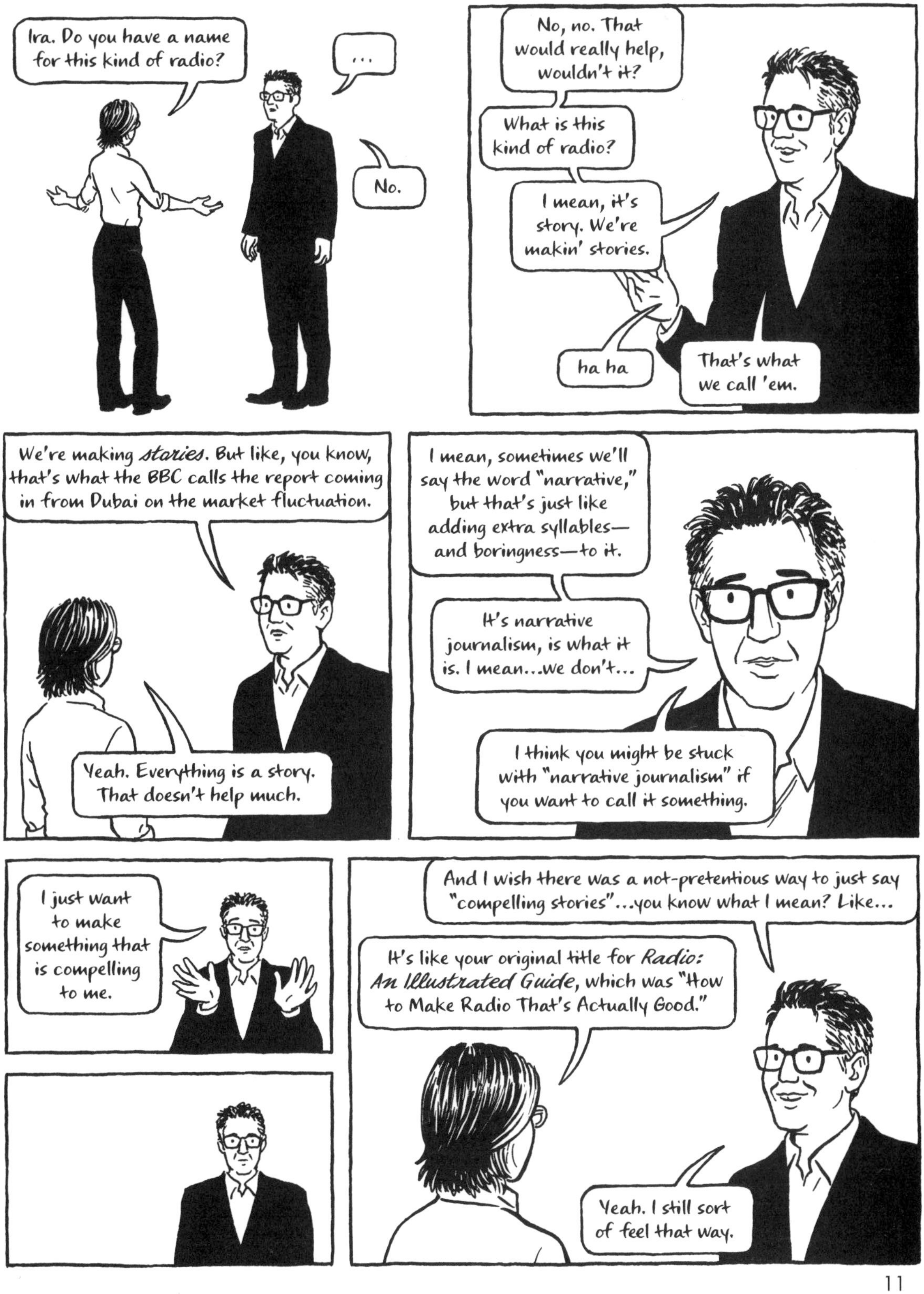
Ira. Do you have a name for this kind of radio?
...
No.
No, no. That would really help, wouldn't it?
What is this kind of radio?
I mean, it's story. We're makin' stories.
ha ha
That's what we call 'em.
We're making *stories*. But like, you know, that's what the BBC calls the report coming in from Dubai on the market fluctuation.
Yeah. Everything is a story. That doesn't help much.
I mean, sometimes we'll say the word "narrative," but that's just like adding extra syllables—and boringness—to it.
It's narrative journalism, is what it is. I mean...we don't...
I think you might be stuck with "narrative journalism" if you want to call it something.
I just want to make something that is compelling to me.
And I wish there was a not-pretentious way to just say "compelling stories"...you know what I mean? Like...
It's like your original title for *Radio: An Illustrated Guide*, which was "How to Make Radio That's Actually Good."
Yeah. I still sort of feel that way.

(excerpt from)

Radio: An Illustrated Guide

by Jessica Abel and Ira Glass

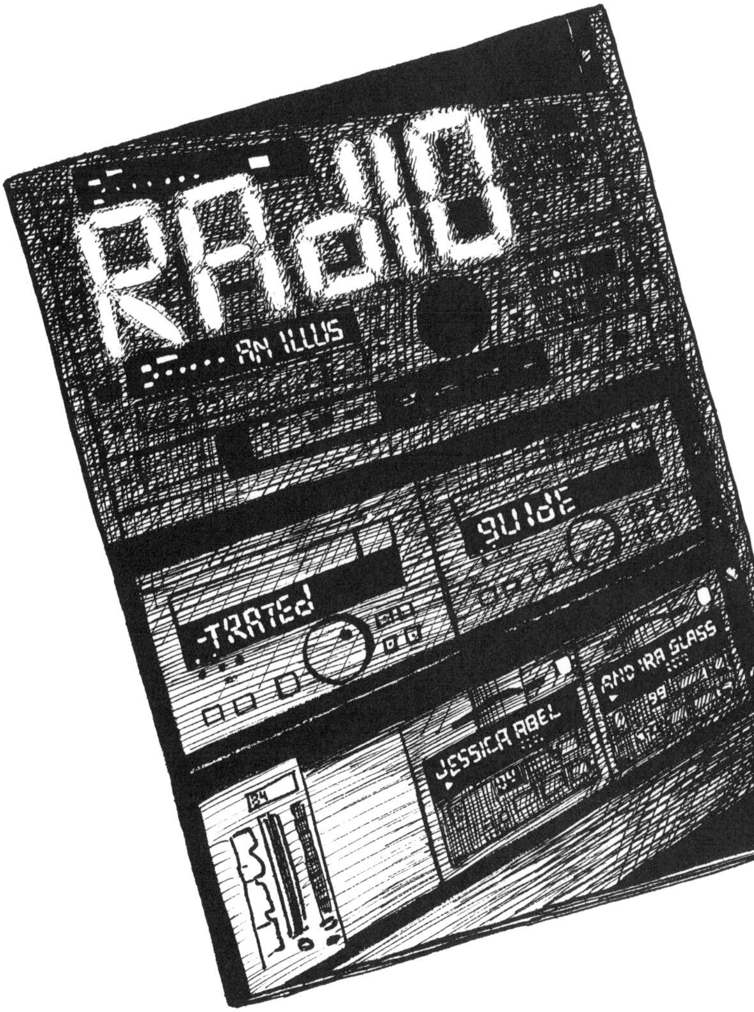
RAdIO
AN ILLUS
-TRATEd
GUIdE
JESSICA ABEL
AND IRA GLASS

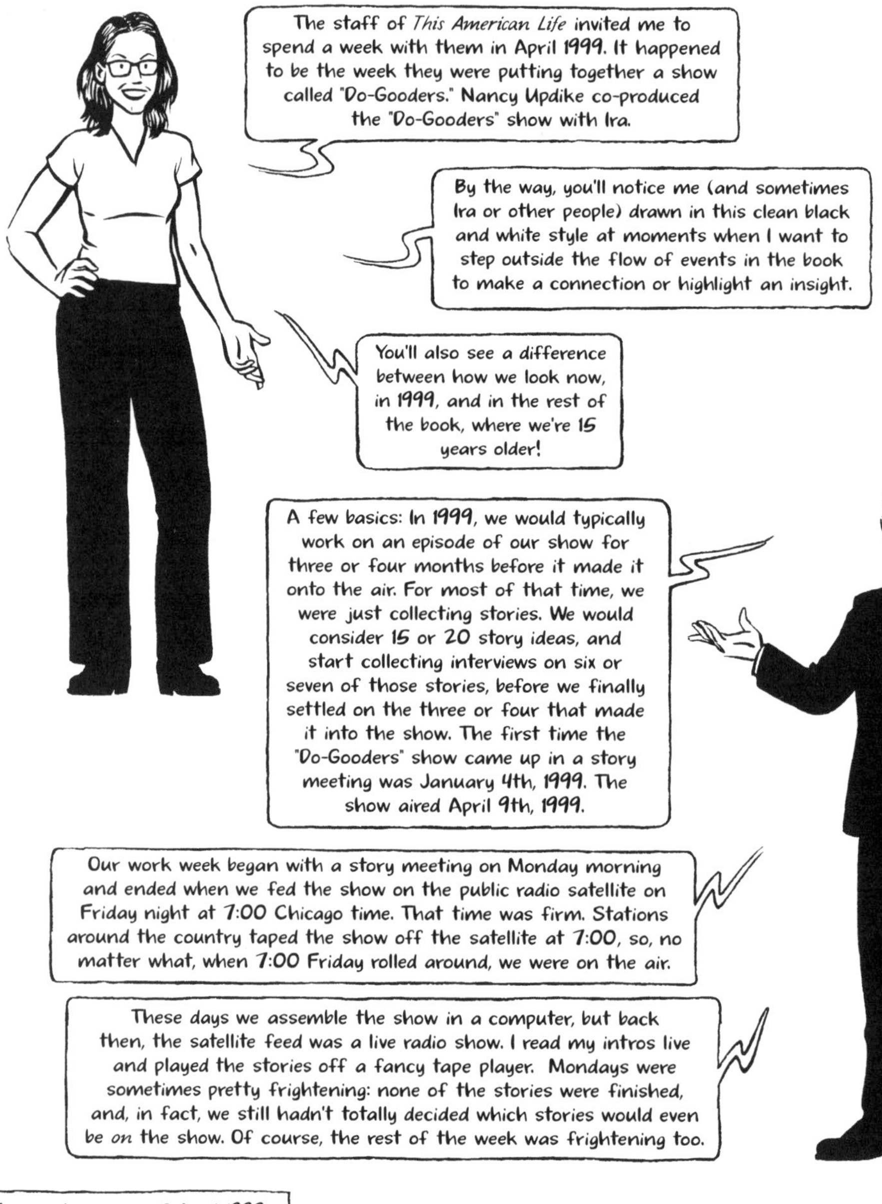
The staff of *This American Life* invited me to spend a week with them in April 1999. It happened to be the week they were putting together a show called "Do-Gooders." Nancy Updike co-produced the "Do-Gooders" show with Ira.
By the way, you'll notice me (and sometimes Ira or other people) drawn in this clean black and white style at moments when I want to step outside the flow of events in the book to make a connection or highlight an insight.
You'll also see a difference between how we look now, in 1999, and in the rest of the book, where we're 15 years older!
A few basics: In 1999, we would typically work on an episode of our show for three or four months before it made it onto the air. For most of that time, we were just collecting stories. We would consider 15 or 20 story ideas, and start collecting interviews on six or seven of those stories, before we finally settled on the three or four that made it into the show. The first time the "Do-Gooders" show came up in a story meeting was January 4th, 1999. The show aired April 9th, 1999.
Our work week began with a story meeting on Monday morning and ended when we fed the show on the public radio satellite on Friday night at 7:00 Chicago time. That time was firm. Stations around the country taped the show off the satellite at 7:00, so, no matter what, when 7:00 Friday rolled around, we were on the air.
These days we assemble the show in a computer, but back then, the satellite feed was a live radio show. I read my intros live and played the stories off a fancy tape player. Mondays were sometimes pretty frightening: none of the stories were finished, and, in fact, we still hadn't totally decided which stories would even be *on* the show. Of course, the rest of the week was frightening too.

The producers as of April 1999.

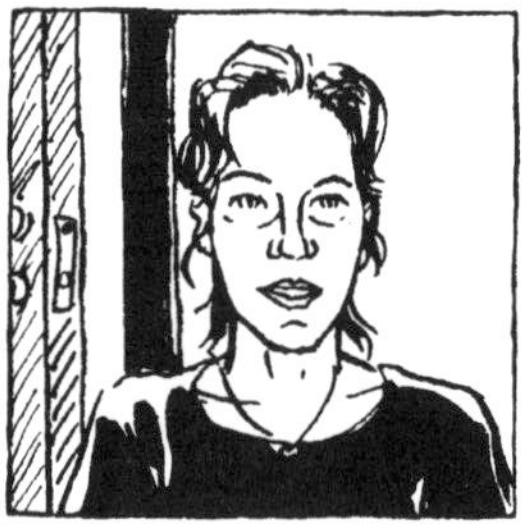
NANCY UPDIKE

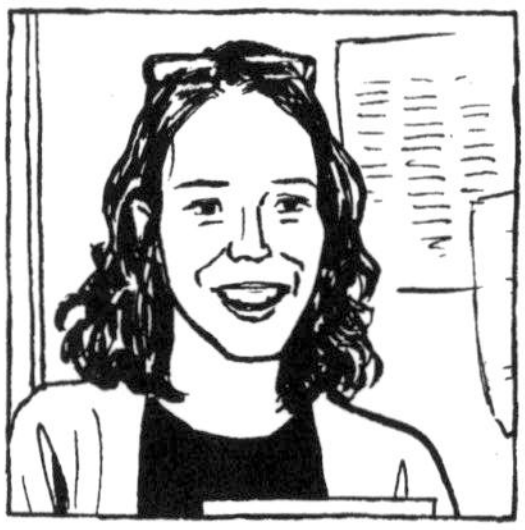
JULIE SNYDER

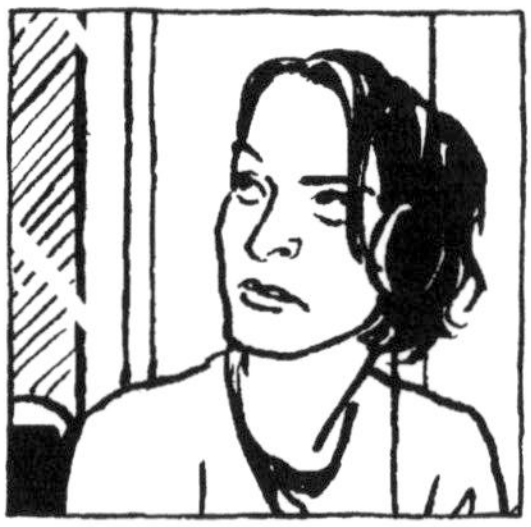
ALIX ("Elise") SPIEGEL

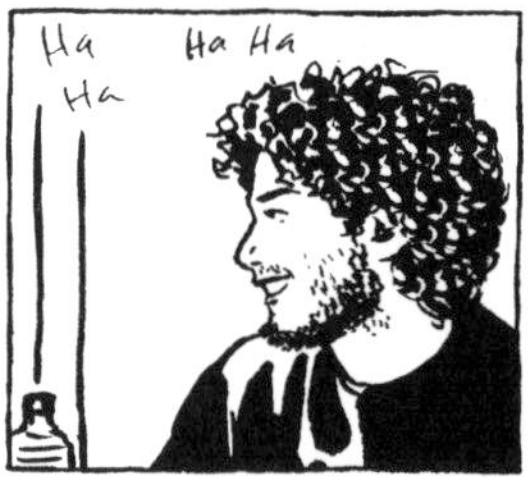
Ha Ha Ha
Ha
JORGE JUST
(Production Intern)

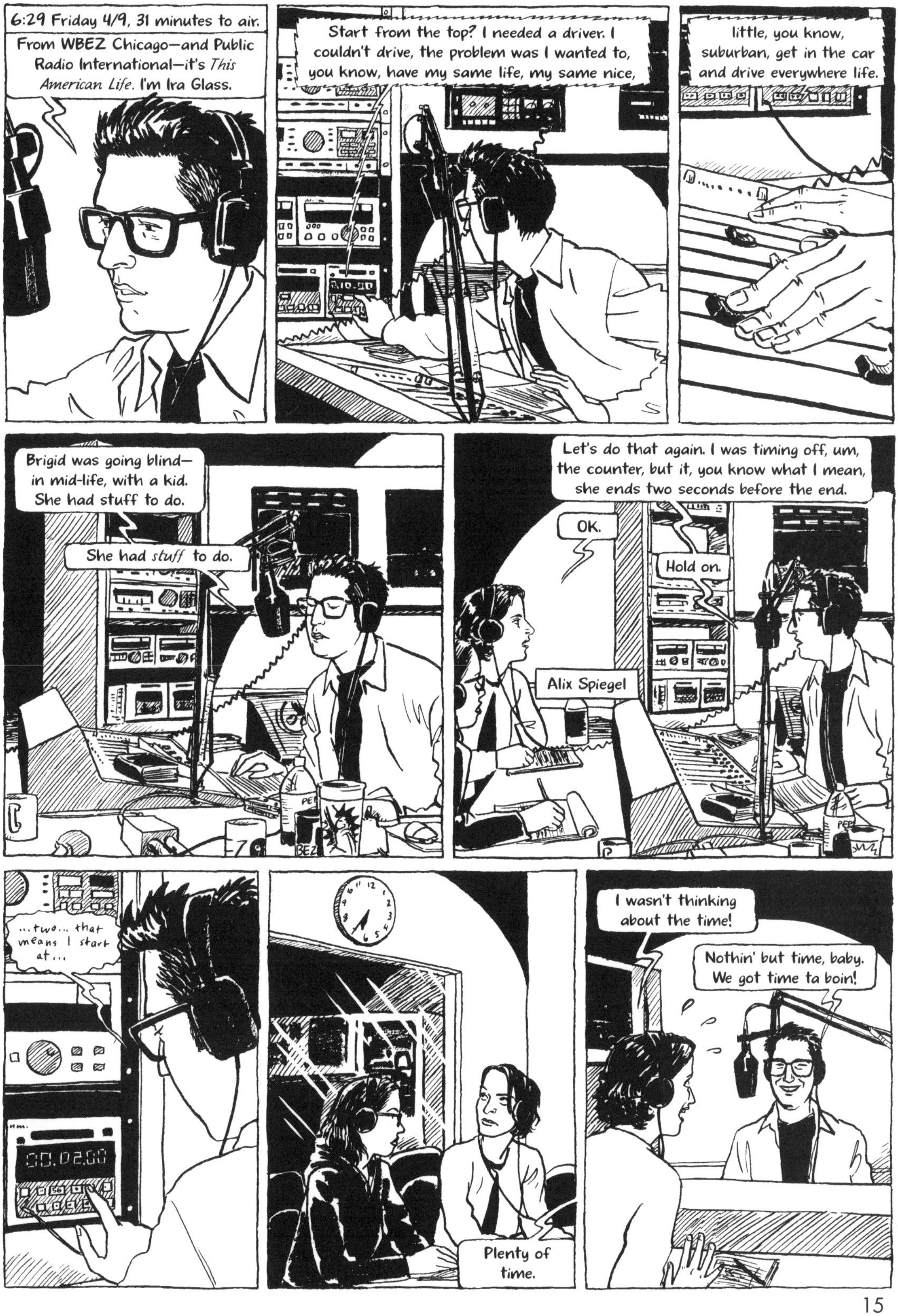
6:29 Friday 4/9, 31 minutes to air.
From WBEZ Chicago—and Public Radio International—it's *This American Life*. I'm Ira Glass.
Start from the top? I needed a driver. I couldn't drive, the problem was I wanted to, you know, have my same life, my same nice,
little, you know, suburban, get in the car and drive everywhere life.
Brigid was going blind—in mid-life, with a kid. She had stuff to do.
She had *stuff* to do.
Let's do that again. I was timing off, um, the counter, but it, you know what I mean, she ends two seconds before the end.
OK.
Hold on.
Alix Spiegel
...two... that means I start at...
Plenty of time.
I wasn't thinking about the time!
Nothin' but time, baby. We got time ta boin!

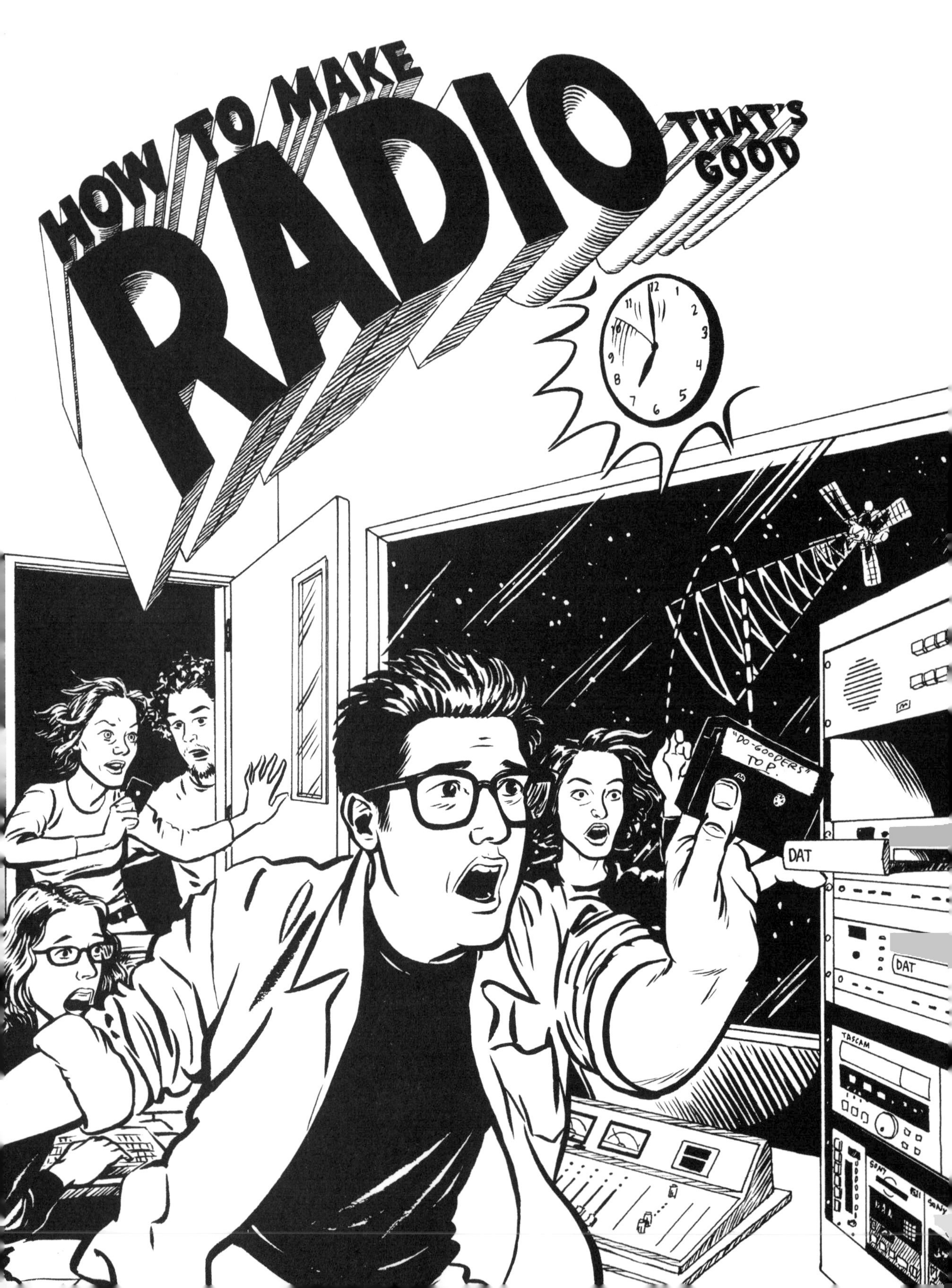
HOW TO MAKE RADIO THAT'S GOOD
"DO-GOODERS" TOP.
DAT
DAT
TASCAM
SONY
SONY

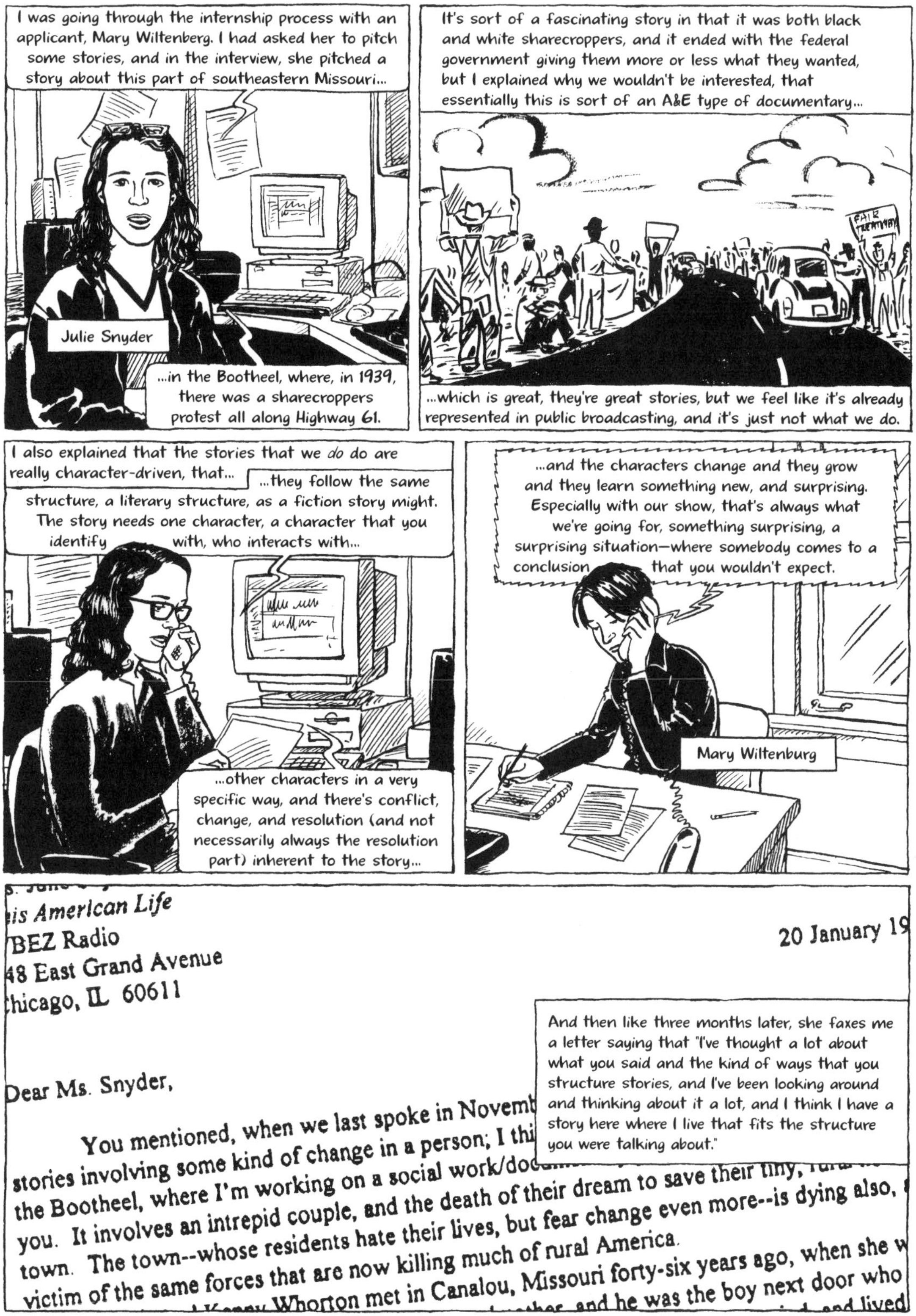
I was going through the internship process with an applicant, Mary Wiltenberg. I had asked her to pitch some stories, and in the interview, she pitched a story about this part of southeastern Missouri...
Julie Snyder
...in the Bootheel, where, in 1939, there was a sharecroppers protest all along Highway 61.
It's sort of a fascinating story in that it was both black and white sharecroppers, and it ended with the federal government giving them more or less what they wanted, but I explained why we wouldn't be interested, that essentially this is sort of an A&E type of documentary...
FAIR TREATMENT
...which is great, they're great stories, but we feel like it's already represented in public broadcasting, and it's just not what we do.
I also explained that the stories that we *do* do are really character-driven, that...
...they follow the same structure, a literary structure, as a fiction story might. The story needs one character, a character that you identify with, who interacts with...
...other characters in a very specific way, and there's conflict, change, and resolution (and not necessarily always the resolution part) inherent to the story...
...and the characters change and they grow and they learn something new, and surprising. Especially with our show, that's always what we're going for, something surprising, a surprising situation—where somebody comes to a conclusion that you wouldn't expect.
Mary Wiltenburg
is American Life
BEZ Radio
48 East Grand Avenue
hicago, IL 60611
20 January 19
Dear Ms. Snyder,
You mentioned, when we last spoke in Novemb
stories involving some kind of change in a person; I thi
the Bootheel, where I'm working on a social work/doc
you. It involves an intrepid couple, and the death of their dream to save their tiny,
town. The town--whose residents hate their lives, but fear change even more--is dying also,
victim of the same forces that are now killing much of rural America.
Kenny Whorton met in Canalou, Missouri forty-six years ago, when she w
and he was the boy next door who
And then like three months later, she faxes me a letter saying that "I've thought a lot about what you said and the kind of ways that you structure stories, and I've been looking around and thinking about it a lot, and I think I have a story here where I live that fits the structure you were talking about."

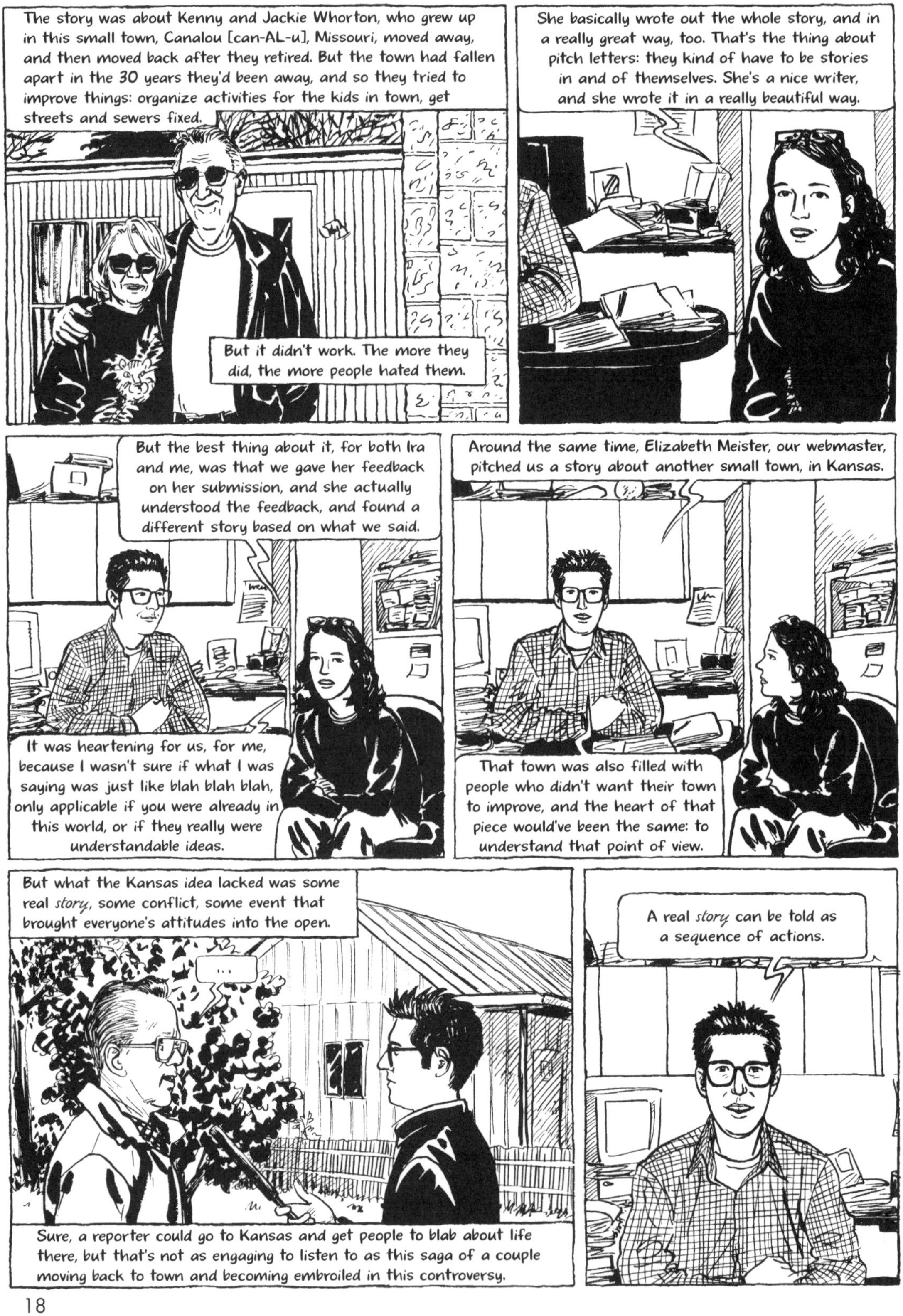
The story was about Kenny and Jackie Whorton, who grew up in this small town, Canalou [can-AL-u], Missouri, moved away, and then moved back after they retired. But the town had fallen apart in the 30 years they'd been away, and so they tried to improve things: organize activities for the kids in town, get streets and sewers fixed.
But it didn't work. The more they did, the more people hated them.
She basically wrote out the whole story, and in a really great way, too. That's the thing about pitch letters: they kind of have to be stories in and of themselves. She's a nice writer, and she wrote it in a really beautiful way.
But the best thing about it, for both Ira and me, was that we gave her feedback on her submission, and she actually understood the feedback, and found a different story based on what we said.
It was heartening for us, for me, because I wasn't sure if what I was saying was just like blah blah blah, only applicable if you were already in this world, or if they really were understandable ideas.
Around the same time, Elizabeth Meister, our webmaster, pitched us a story about another small town, in Kansas.
That town was also filled with people who didn't want their town to improve, and the heart of that piece would've been the same: to understand that point of view.
But what the Kansas idea lacked was some real *story*, some conflict, some event that brought everyone's attitudes into the open.
...
Sure, a reporter could go to Kansas and get people to blab about life there, but that's not as engaging to listen to as this saga of a couple moving back to town and becoming embroiled in this controversy.
A real *story* can be told as a sequence of actions.

FOR EXAMPLE...

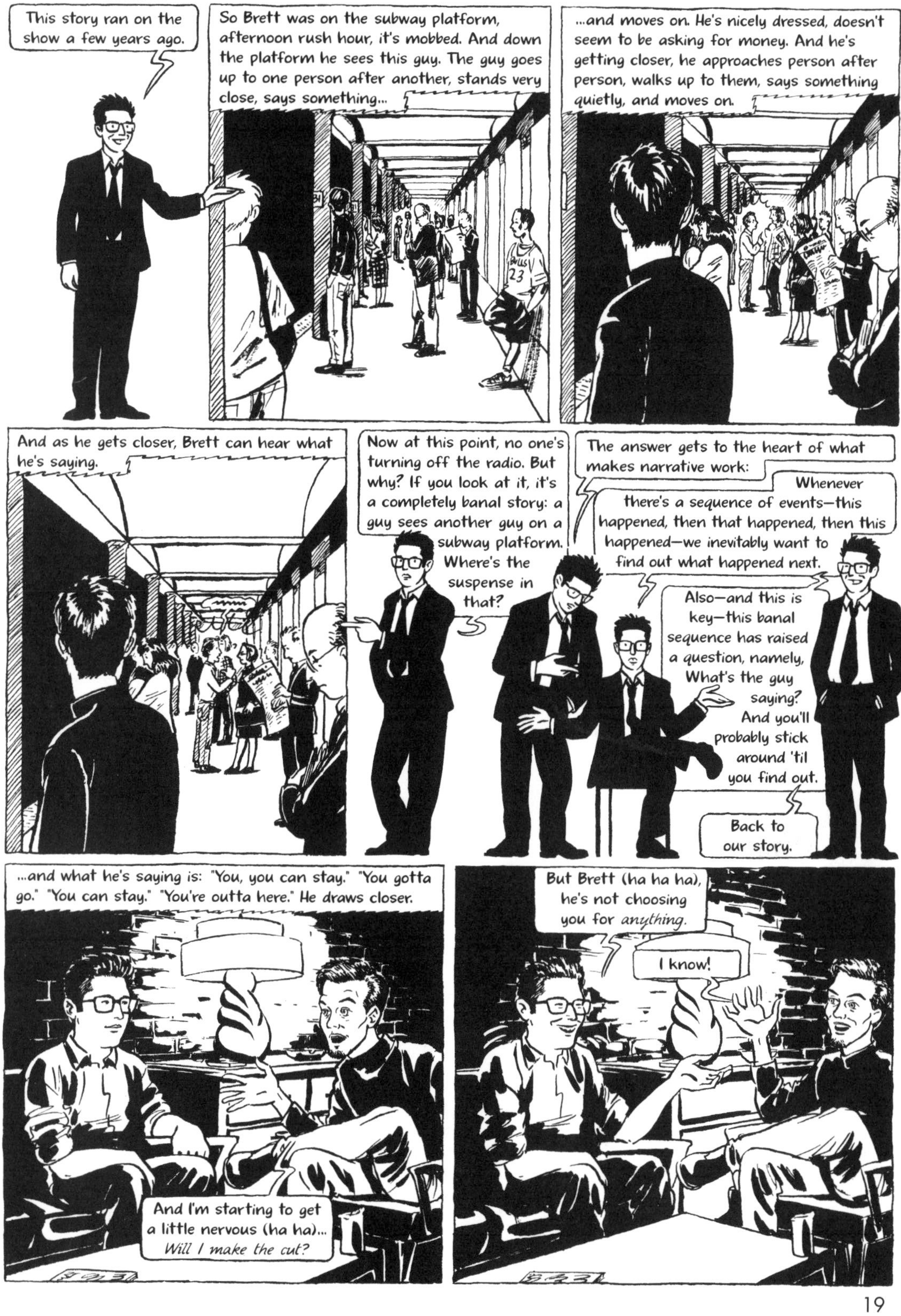

This story ran on the show a few years ago.
So Brett was on the subway platform, afternoon rush hour, it's mobbed. And down the platform he sees this guy. The guy goes up to one person after another, stands very close, says something...
...and moves on. He's nicely dressed, doesn't seem to be asking for money. And he's getting closer, he approaches person after person, walks up to them, says something quietly, and moves on.
BULLS 23
And as he gets closer, Brett can hear what he's saying.
Now at this point, no one's turning off the radio. But why? If you look at it, it's a completely banal story: a guy sees another guy on a subway platform. Where's the suspense in that?
The answer gets to the heart of what makes narrative work:
Whenever there's a sequence of events—this happened, then that happened, then this happened—we inevitably want to find out what happened next.
Also—and this is key—this banal sequence has raised a question, namely, What's the guy saying? And you'll probably stick around 'til you find out.
Back to our story.
...and what he's saying is: "You, you can stay." "You gotta go." "You can stay." "You're outta here." He draws closer.
And I'm starting to get a little nervous (ha ha)... *Will I make the cut?*
But Brett (ha ha ha), he's not choosing you for *anything*.
I know!

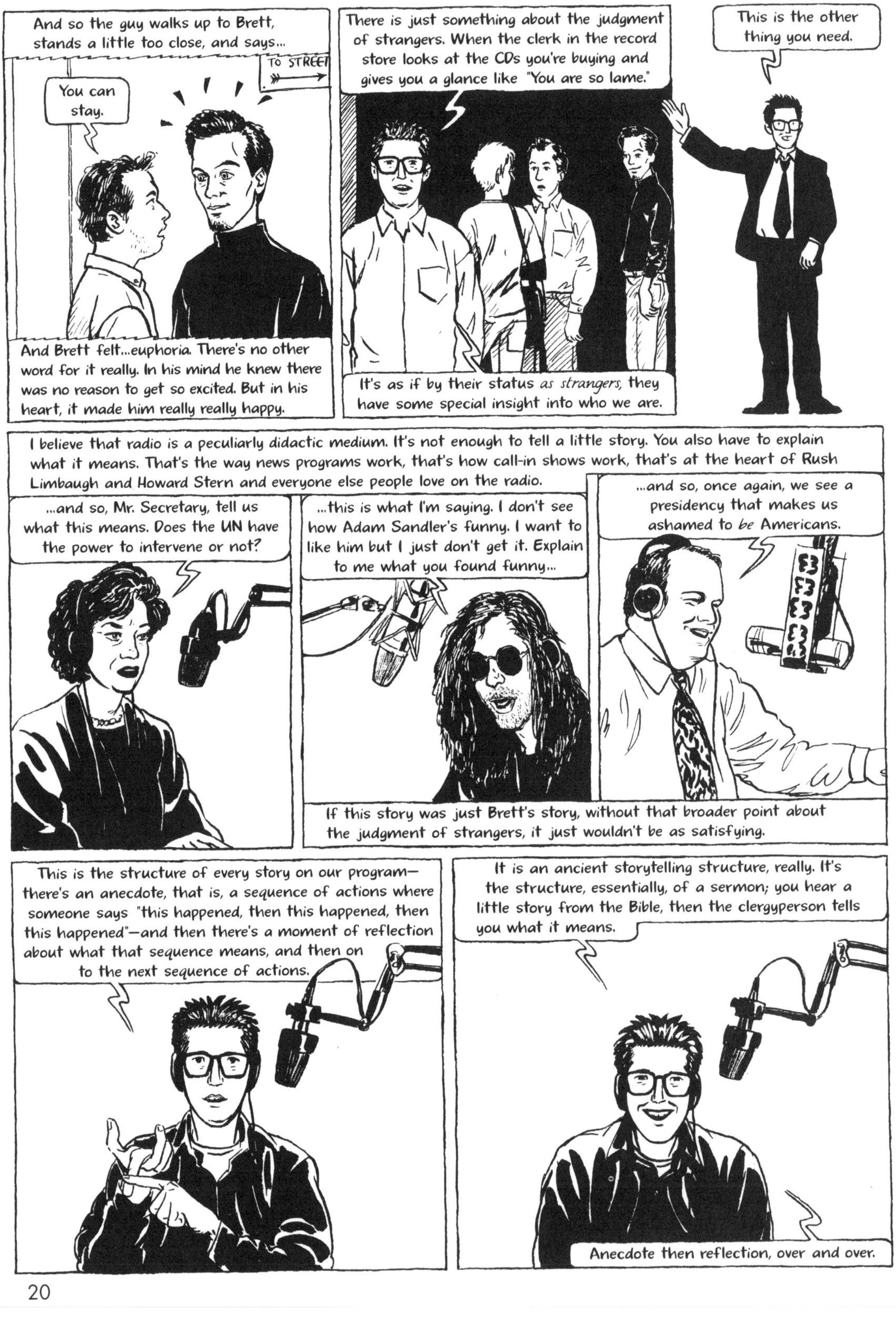
And so the guy walks up to Brett, stands a little too close, and says...
TO STREET
You can stay.
And Brett felt...euphoria. There's no other word for it really. In his mind he knew there was no reason to get so excited. But in his heart, it made him really really happy.
There is just something about the judgment of strangers. When the clerk in the record store looks at the CDs you're buying and gives you a glance like "You are so lame."
It's as if by their status *as strangers,* they have some special insight into who we are.
This is the other thing you need.
I believe that radio is a peculiarly didactic medium. It's not enough to tell a little story. You also have to explain what it means. That's the way news programs work, that's how call-in shows work, that's at the heart of Rush Limbaugh and Howard Stern and everyone else people love on the radio.
...and so, Mr. Secretary, tell us what this means. Does the UN have the power to intervene or not?
...this is what I'm saying. I don't see how Adam Sandler's funny. I want to like him but I just don't get it. Explain to me what you found funny...
...and so, once again, we see a presidency that makes us ashamed to *be* Americans.
If this story was just Brett's story, without that broader point about the judgment of strangers, it just wouldn't be as satisfying.
This is the structure of every story on our program—there's an anecdote, that is, a sequence of actions where someone says "this happened, then this happened, then this happened"—and then there's a moment of reflection about what that sequence means, and then on to the next sequence of actions.
It is an ancient storytelling structure, really. It's the structure, essentially, of a sermon; you hear a little story from the Bible, then the clergyperson tells you what it means.
Anecdote then reflection, over and over.

THINGS COME TOGETHER, OR: GLOMMING ON

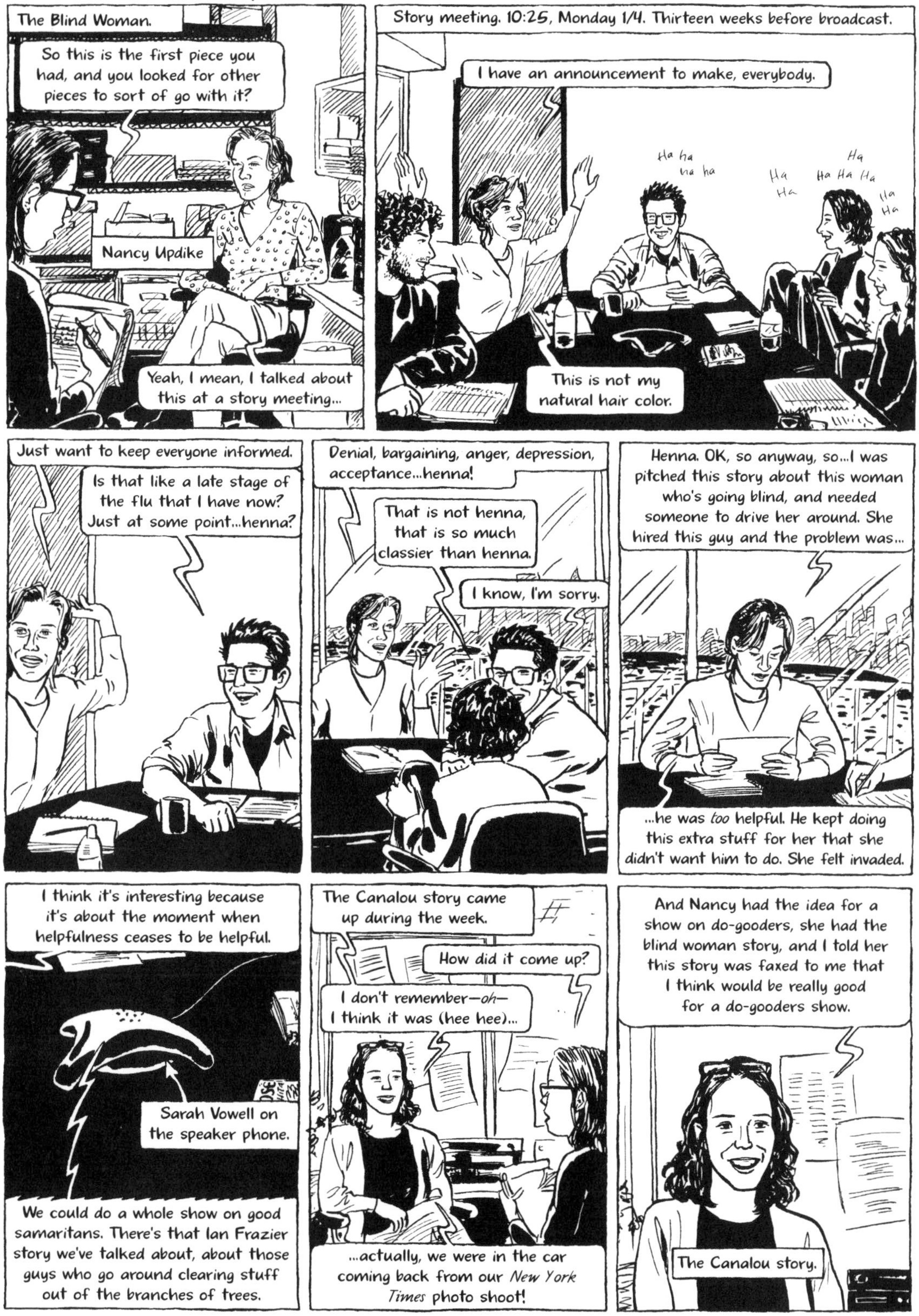

The Blind Woman.
So this is the first piece you had, and you looked for other pieces to sort of go with it?
Nancy Updike
Yeah, I mean, I talked about this at a story meeting...
Story meeting. 10:25, Monday 1/4. Thirteen weeks before broadcast.
I have an announcement to make, everybody.
Ha ha ha ha
Ha Ha
Ha Ha Ha Ha
Ha Ha
This is not my natural hair color.
Just want to keep everyone informed.
Is that like a late stage of the flu that I have now? Just at some point...henna?
Denial, bargaining, anger, depression, acceptance...henna!
That is not henna, that is so much classier than henna.
I know, I'm sorry.
Henna. OK, so anyway, so...I was pitched this story about this woman who's going blind, and needed someone to drive her around. She hired this guy and the problem was...
...he was *too* helpful. He kept doing this extra stuff for her that she didn't want him to do. She felt invaded.
I think it's interesting because it's about the moment when helpfulness ceases to be helpful.
Sarah Vowell on the speaker phone.
We could do a whole show on good samaritans. There's that Ian Frazier story we've talked about, about those guys who go around clearing stuff out of the branches of trees.
The Canalou story came up during the week.
How did it come up?
I don't remember—*oh*— I think it was (hee hee)...
...actually, we were in the car coming back from our *New York Times* photo shoot!
And Nancy had the idea for a show on do-gooders, she had the blind woman story, and I told her this story was faxed to me that I think would be really good for a do-gooders show.
The Canalou story.

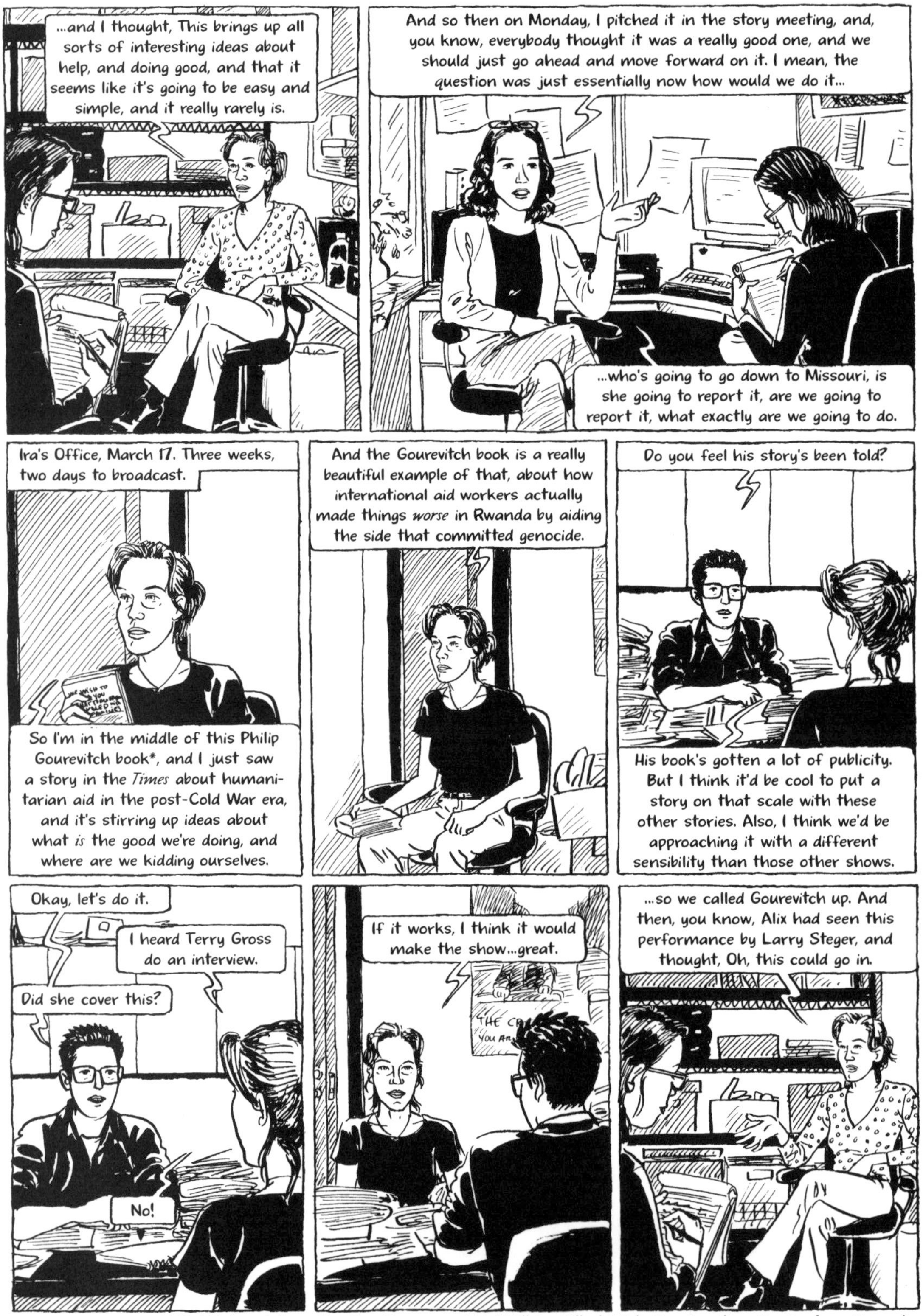
...and I thought, This brings up all sorts of interesting ideas about help, and doing good, and that it seems like it's going to be easy and simple, and it really rarely is.
And so then on Monday, I pitched it in the story meeting, and, you know, everybody thought it was a really good one, and we should just go ahead and move forward on it. I mean, the question was just essentially now how would we do it...
...who's going to go down to Missouri, is she going to report it, are we going to report it, what exactly are we going to do.
Ira's Office, March 17. Three weeks, two days to broadcast.
So I'm in the middle of this Philip Gourevitch book*, and I just saw a story in the *Times* about humanitarian aid in the post-Cold War era, and it's stirring up ideas about what *is* the good we're doing, and where are we kidding ourselves.
And the Gourevitch book is a really beautiful example of that, about how international aid workers actually made things *worse* in Rwanda by aiding the side that committed genocide.
Do you feel his story's been told?
His book's gotten a lot of publicity. But I think it'd be cool to put a story on that scale with these other stories. Also, I think we'd be approaching it with a different sensibility than those other shows.
Okay, let's do it.
I heard Terry Gross do an interview.
Did she cover this?
No!
If it works, I think it would make the show...great.
...so we called Gourevitch up. And then, you know, Alix had seen this performance by Larry Steger, and thought, Oh, this could go in.

*We Wish to Inform You That Tomorrow We Will Be Killed With Our Families: Stories from Rwanda. *Farrar, Straus and Giroux, 1998.*

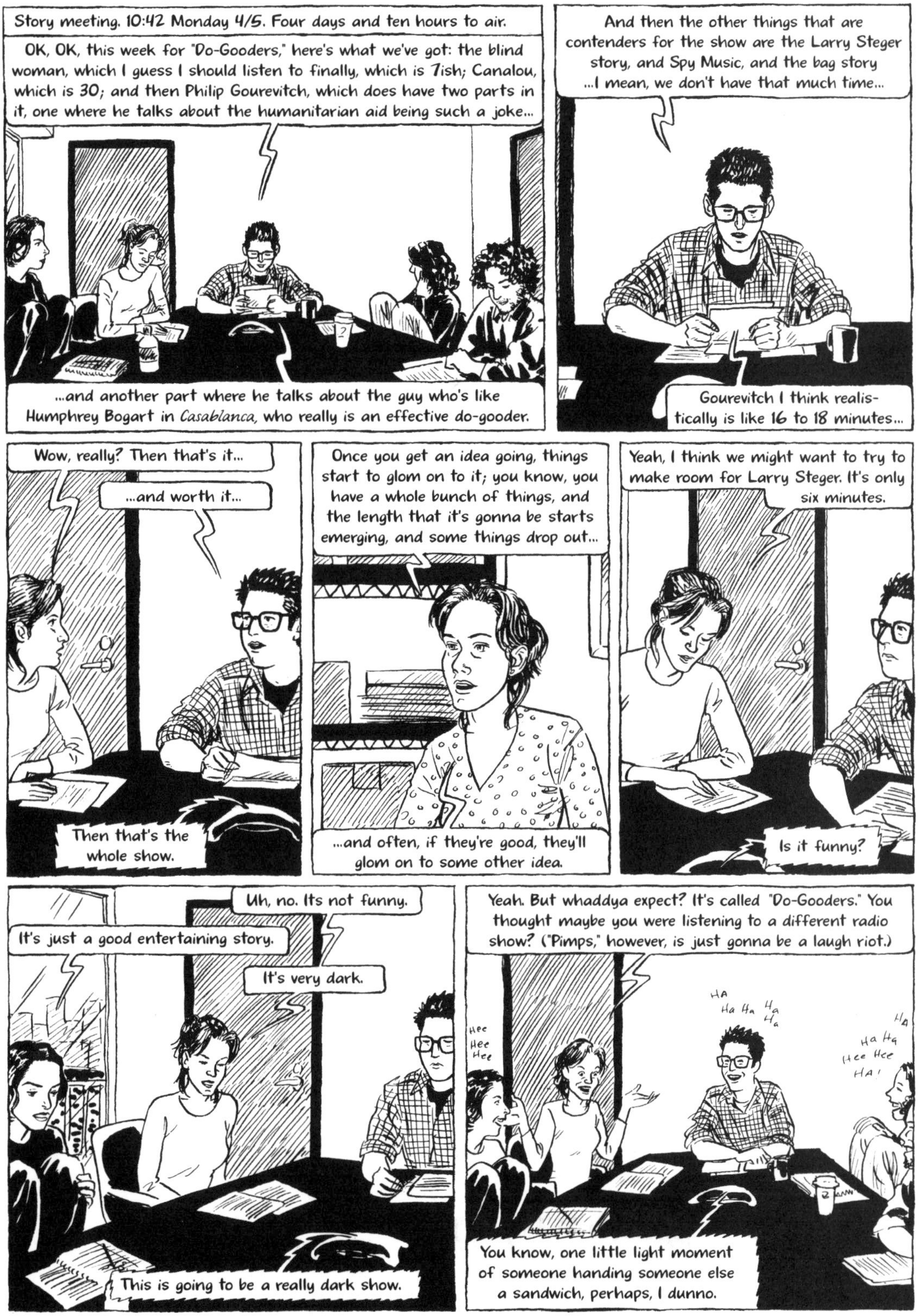
Story meeting. 10:42 Monday 4/5. Four days and ten hours to air.
OK, OK, this week for "Do-Gooders," here's what we've got: the blind woman, which I guess I should listen to finally, which is 7ish; Canalou, which is 30; and then Philip Gourevitch, which does have two parts in it, one where he talks about the humanitarian aid being such a joke...
...and another part where he talks about the guy who's like Humphrey Bogart in *Casablanca,* who really is an effective do-gooder.
And then the other things that are contenders for the show are the Larry Steger story, and Spy Music, and the bag story ...I mean, we don't have that much time...
Gourevitch I think realistically is like 16 to 18 minutes...
Wow, really? Then that's it...
...and worth it...
Then that's the whole show.
Once you get an idea going, things start to glom on to it; you know, you have a whole bunch of things, and the length that it's gonna be starts emerging, and some things drop out...
...and often, if they're good, they'll glom on to some other idea.
Yeah, I think we might want to try to make room for Larry Steger. It's only six minutes.
Is it funny?
Uh, no. Its not funny.
It's just a good entertaining story.
It's very dark.
This is going to be a really dark show.
Yeah. But whaddya expect? It's called "Do-Gooders." You thought maybe you were listening to a different radio show? ("Pimps," however, is just gonna be a laugh riot.)
Hee Hee Hee
Ha Ha Ha Ha Ha
Ha Ha Ha Hee Hee Ha!
You know, one little light moment of someone handing someone else a sandwich, perhaps, I dunno.

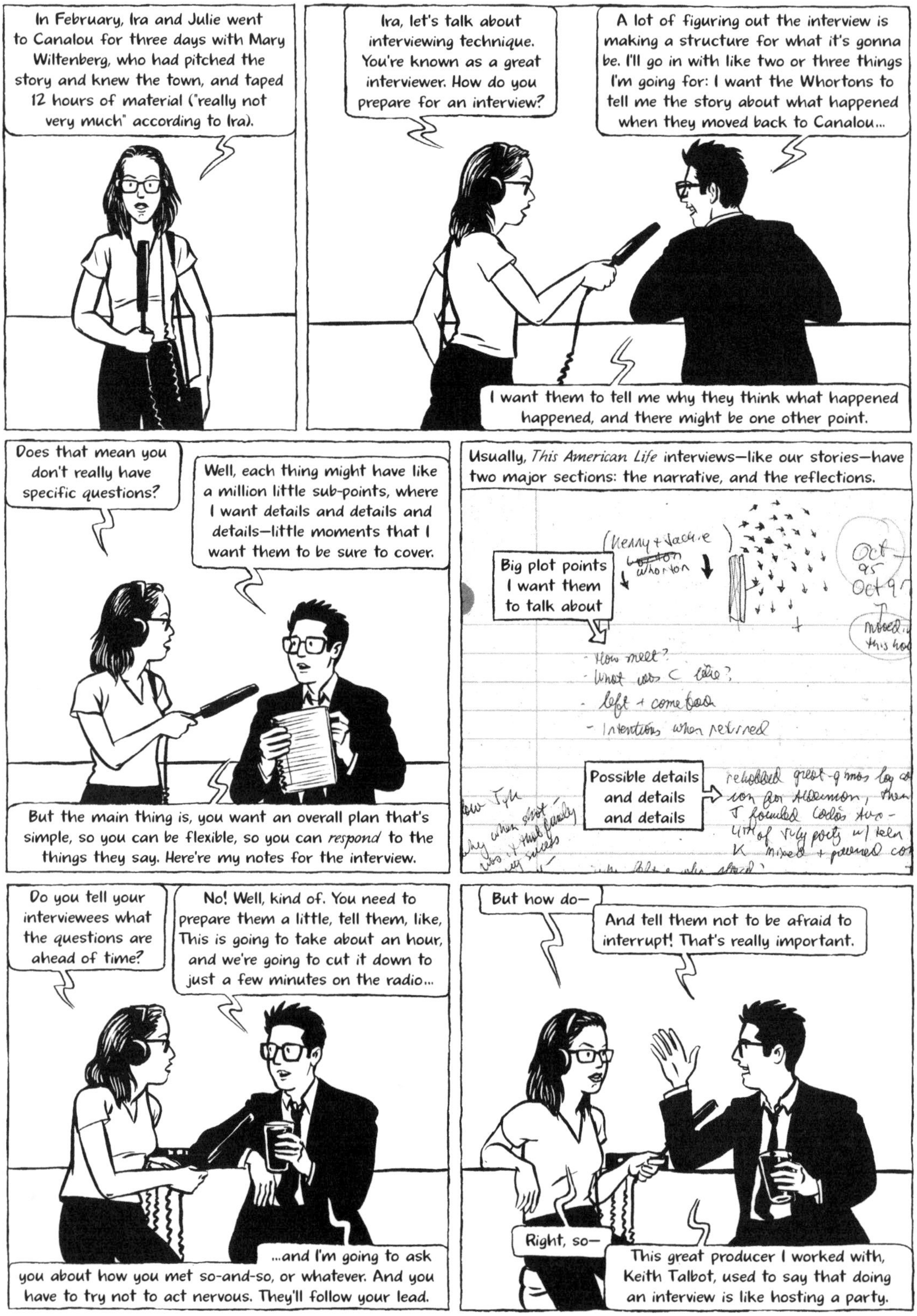
In February, Ira and Julie went to Canalou for three days with Mary Wiltenberg, who had pitched the story and knew the town, and taped 12 hours of material ("really not very much" according to Ira).
Ira, let's talk about interviewing technique. You're known as a great interviewer. How do you prepare for an interview?
A lot of figuring out the interview is making a structure for what it's gonna be. I'll go in with like two or three things I'm going for: I want the Whortons to tell me the story about what happened when they moved back to Canalou...
I want them to tell me why they think what happened happened, and there might be one other point.
Does that mean you don't really have specific *questions*?
Well, each thing might have like a million little sub-points, where I want details and details and details—little moments that I want them to be sure to cover.
But the main thing is, you want an overall plan that's simple, so you can be flexible, so you can *respond* to the things they say. Here're my notes for the interview.
Usually, *This American Life* interviews—like our stories—have two major sections: the narrative, and the reflections.
Big plot points I want them to talk about
Possible details and details and details
Do you tell your interviewees what the questions are ahead of time?
No! Well, kind of. You need to prepare them a little, tell them, like, This is going to take about an hour, and we're going to cut it down to just a few minutes on the radio...
...and I'm going to ask you about how you met so-and-so, or whatever. And you have to try not to act nervous. They'll follow your lead.
But how do—
And tell them not to be afraid to interrupt! That's really important.
Right, so—
This great producer I worked with, Keith Talbot, used to say that doing an interview is like hosting a party.

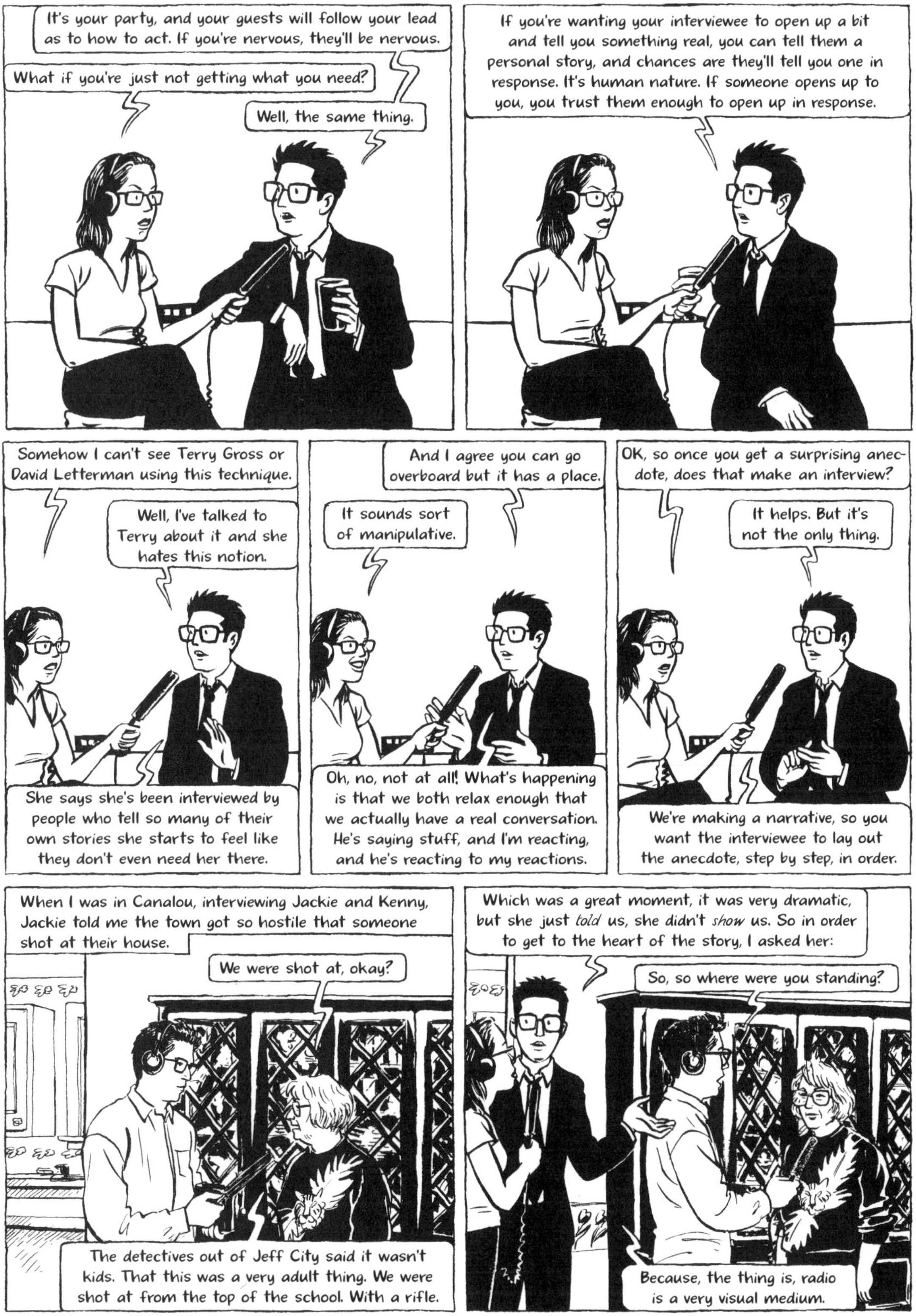

It's your party, and your guests will follow your lead as to how to act. If you're nervous, they'll be nervous.
What if you're just not getting what you need?
Well, the same thing.
If you're wanting your interviewee to open up a bit and tell you something real, you can tell them a personal story, and chances are they'll tell you one in response. It's human nature. If someone opens up to you, you trust them enough to open up in response.
Somehow I can't see Terry Gross or David Letterman using this technique.
Well, I've talked to Terry about it and she hates this notion.
She says she's been interviewed by people who tell so many of their own stories she starts to feel like they don't even need her there.
And I agree you can go overboard but it has a place.
It sounds sort of manipulative.
Oh, no, not at all! What's happening is that we both relax enough that we actually have a real conversation. He's saying stuff, and I'm reacting, and he's reacting to my reactions.
OK, so once you get a surprising anecdote, does that make an interview?
It helps. But it's not the only thing.
We're making a narrative, so you want the interviewee to lay out the anecdote, step by step, in order.
When I was in Canalou, interviewing Jackie and Kenny, Jackie told me the town got so hostile that someone shot at their house.
We were shot at, okay?
The detectives out of Jeff City said it wasn't kids. That this was a very adult thing. We were shot at from the top of the school. With a rifle.
Which was a great moment, it was very dramatic, but she just *told* us, she didn't *show* us. So in order to get to the heart of the story, I asked her:
So, so where were you standing?
Because, the thing is, radio is a very visual medium.

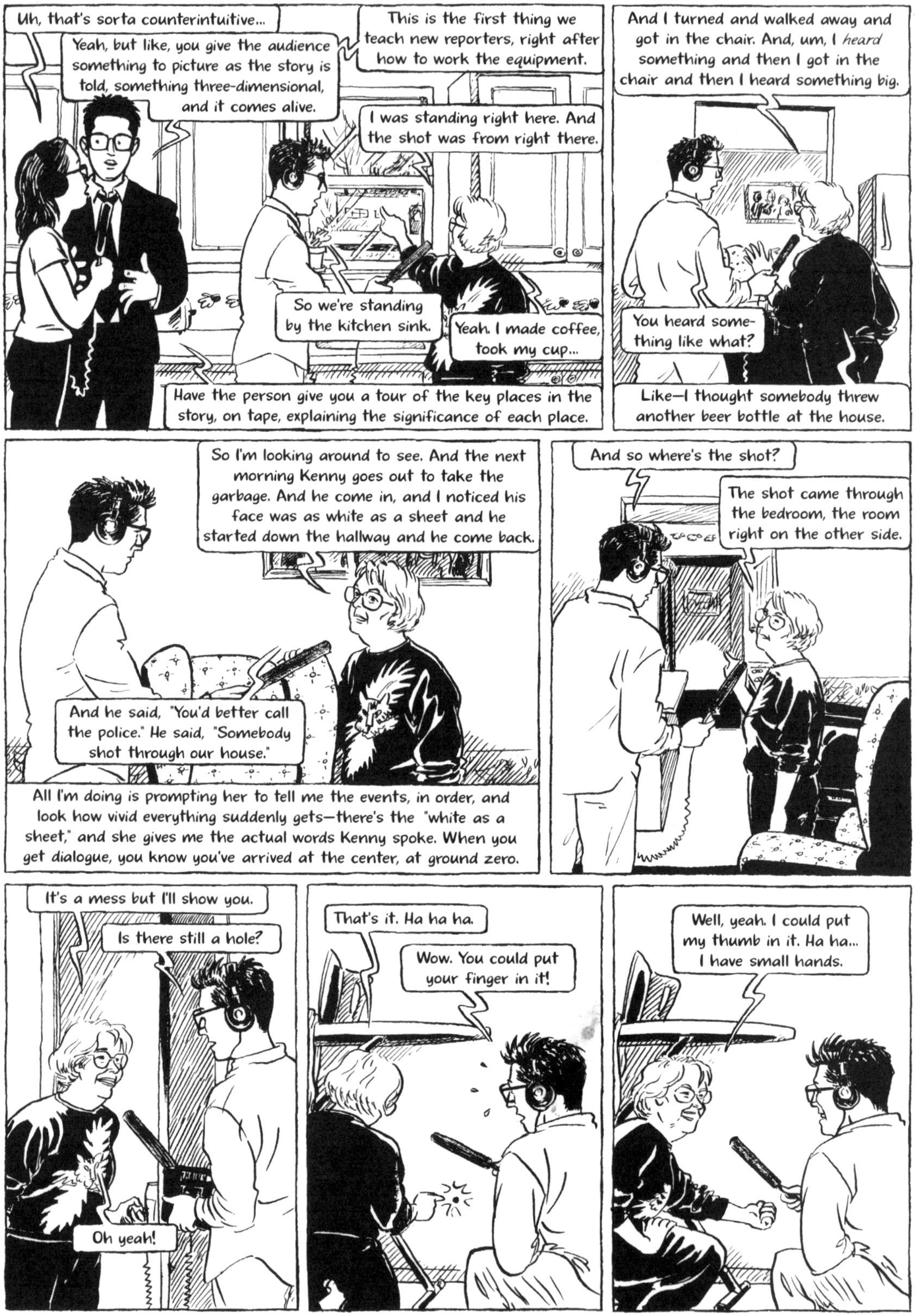
Uh, that's sorta counterintuitive...
Yeah, but like, you give the audience something to picture as the story is told, something three-dimensional, and it comes alive.
This is the first thing we teach new reporters, right after how to work the equipment.
I was standing right here. And the shot was from right there.
So we're standing by the kitchen sink.
Yeah. I made coffee, took my cup...
Have the person give you a tour of the key places in the story, on tape, explaining the significance of each place.
And I turned and walked away and got in the chair. And, um, I *heard* something and then I got in the chair and then I heard something big.
You heard something like what?
Like—I thought somebody threw another beer bottle at the house.
So I'm looking around to see. And the next morning Kenny goes out to take the garbage. And he come in, and I noticed his face was as white as a sheet and he started down the hallway and he come back.
And he said, "You'd better call the police." He said, "Somebody shot through our house."
All I'm doing is prompting her to tell me the events, in order, and look how vivid everything suddenly gets—there's the "white as a sheet," and she gives me the actual words Kenny spoke. When you get dialogue, you know you've arrived at the center, at ground zero.
And so where's the shot?
The shot came through the bedroom, the room right on the other side.
It's a mess but I'll show you.
Is there still a hole?
Oh yeah!
That's it. Ha ha ha.
Wow. You could put your finger in it!
Well, yeah. I could put my thumb in it. Ha ha... I have small hands.

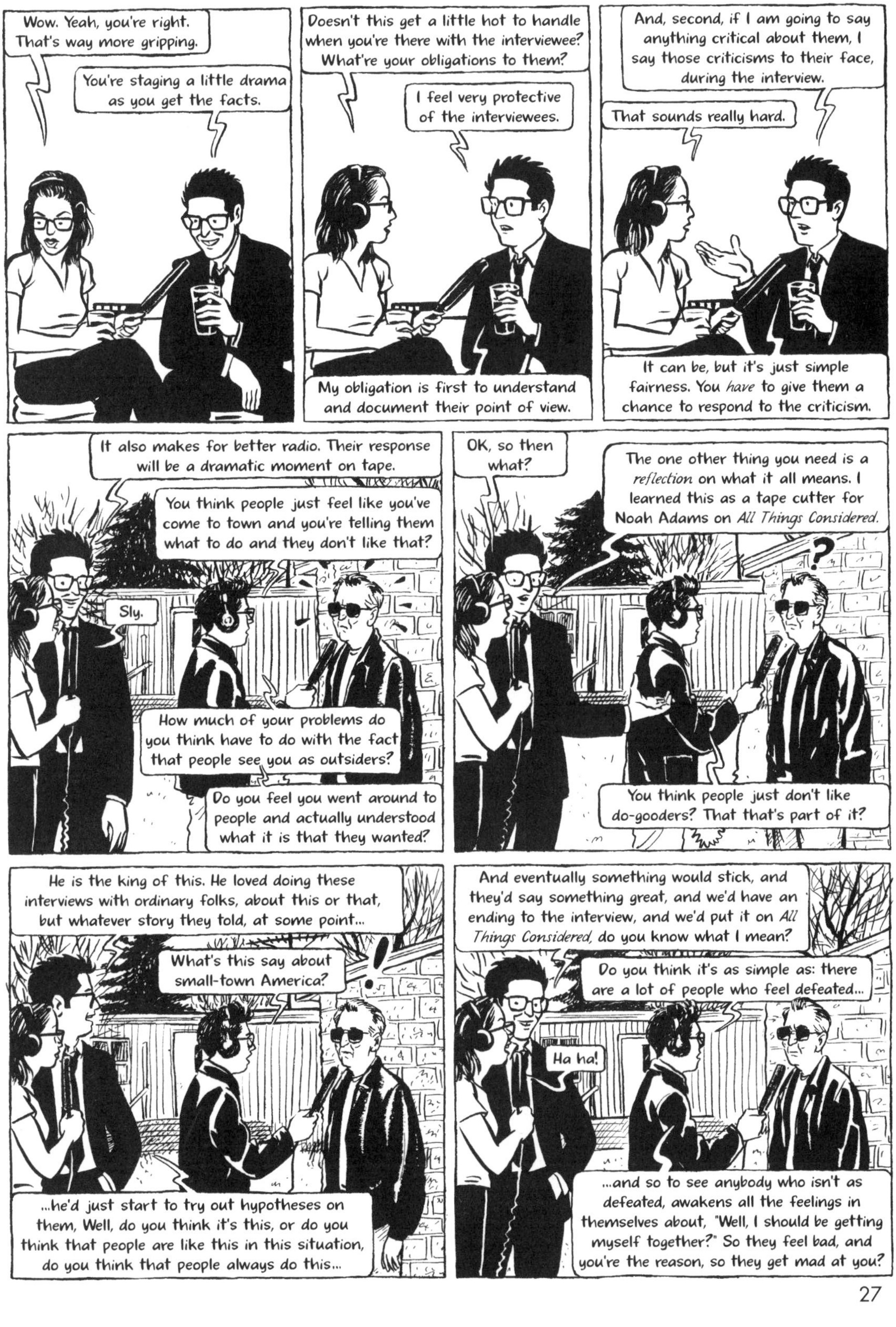
Wow. Yeah, you're right. That's way more gripping.
You're staging a little drama as you get the facts.
Doesn't this get a little hot to handle when you're there with the interviewee? What're your obligations to them?
I feel very protective of the interviewees.
My obligation is first to understand and document their point of view.
And, second, if I am going to say anything critical about them, I say those criticisms to their face, during the interview.
That sounds really hard.
It can be, but it's just simple fairness. You *have* to give them a chance to respond to the criticism.
It also makes for better radio. Their response will be a dramatic moment on tape.
You think people just feel like you've come to town and you're telling them what to do and they don't like that?
Sly.
How much of your problems do you think have to do with the fact that people see you as outsiders?
Do you feel you went around to people and actually understood what it is that they wanted?
OK, so then what?
The one other thing you need is a *reflection* on what it all means. I learned this as a tape cutter for Noah Adams on *All Things Considered.*
?
You think people just don't like do-gooders? That that's part of it?
He is the king of this. He loved doing these interviews with ordinary folks, about this or that, but whatever story they told, at some point...
What's this say about small-town America?
!
...he'd just start to try out hypotheses on them, Well, do you think it's this, or do you think that people are like this in this situation, do you think that people always do this...
And eventually something would stick, and they'd say something great, and we'd have an ending to the interview, and we'd put it on *All Things Considered,* do you know what I mean?
Do you think it's as simple as: there are a lot of people who feel defeated...
Ha ha!
...and so to see anybody who isn't as defeated, awakens all the feelings in themselves about, "Well, I should be getting myself together?" So they feel bad, and you're the reason, so they get mad at you?

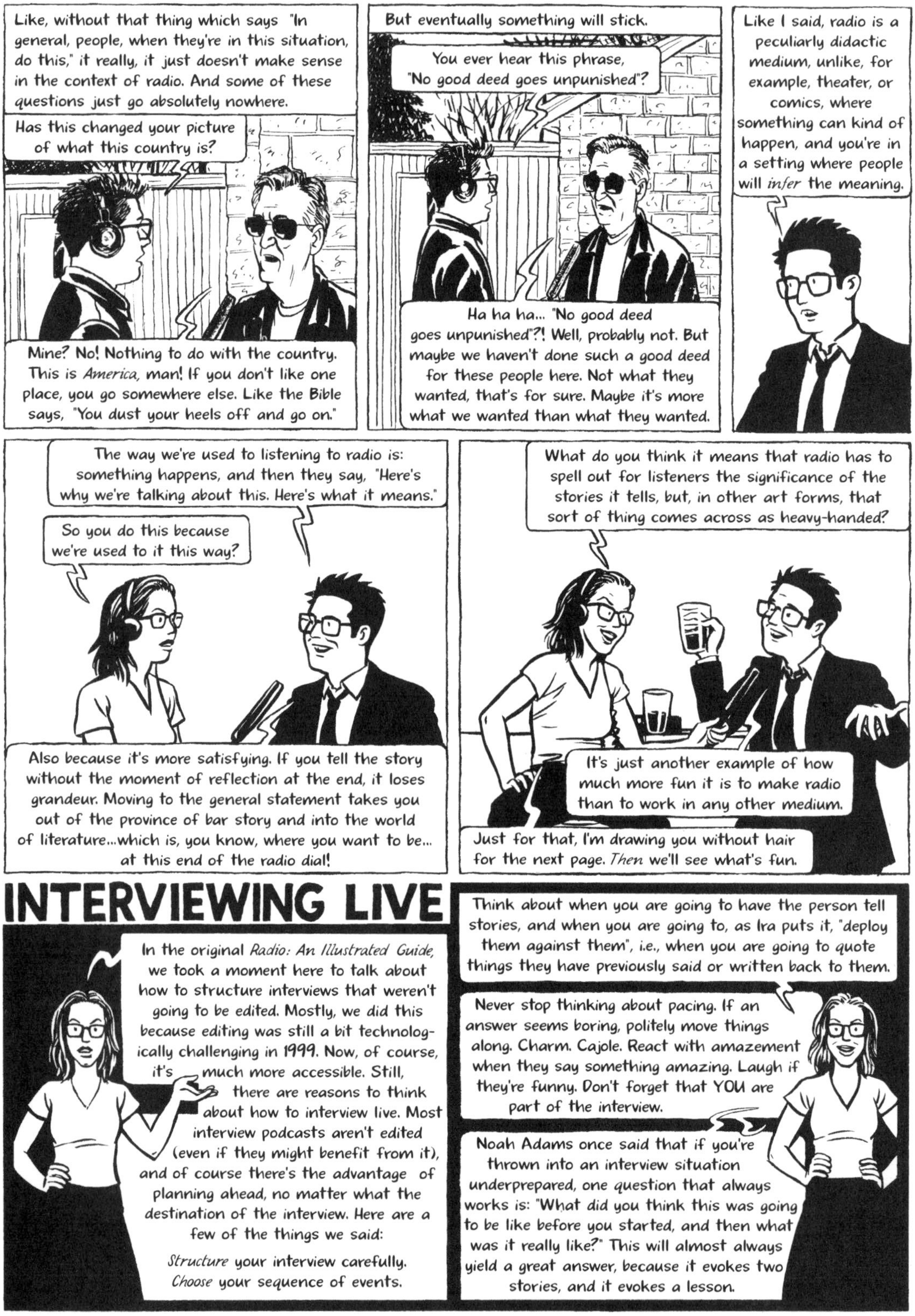

Like, without that thing which says "In general, people, when they're in this situation, do this," it really, it just doesn't make sense in the context of radio. And some of these questions just go absolutely nowhere.
Has this changed your picture of what this country is?
Mine? No! Nothing to do with the country. This is *America*, man! If you don't like one place, you go somewhere else. Like the Bible says, "You dust your heels off and go on."
But eventually something will stick.
You ever hear this phrase, "No good deed goes unpunished"?
Ha ha ha... "No good deed goes unpunished"?! Well, probably not. But maybe we haven't done such a good deed for these people here. Not what they wanted, that's for sure. Maybe it's more what we wanted than what they wanted.
Like I said, radio is a peculiarly didactic medium, unlike, for example, theater, or comics, where something can kind of happen, and you're in a setting where people will *infer* the meaning.
The way we're used to listening to radio is: something happens, and then they say, "Here's why we're talking about this. Here's what it means."
So you do this because we're used to it this way?
Also because it's more satisfying. If you tell the story without the moment of reflection at the end, it loses grandeur. Moving to the general statement takes you out of the province of bar story and into the world of literature...which is, you know, where you want to be... at this end of the radio dial!
What do you think it means that radio has to spell out for listeners the significance of the stories it tells, but, in other art forms, that sort of thing comes across as heavy-handed?
It's just another example of how much more fun it is to make radio than to work in any other medium.
Just for that, I'm drawing you without hair for the next page. *Then* we'll see what's fun.
INTERVIEWING LIVE
In the original *Radio: An Illustrated Guide*, we took a moment here to talk about how to structure interviews that weren't going to be edited. Mostly, we did this because editing was still a bit technologically challenging in 1999. Now, of course, it's much more accessible. Still, there are reasons to think about how to interview live. Most interview podcasts aren't edited (even if they might benefit from it), and of course there's the advantage of planning ahead, no matter what the destination of the interview. Here are a few of the things we said:
Structure your interview carefully. *Choose* your sequence of events.
Think about when you are going to have the person tell stories, and when you are going to, as Ira puts it, "deploy them against them", i.e., when you are going to quote things they have previously said or written back to them.
Never stop thinking about pacing. If an answer seems boring, politely move things along. Charm. Cajole. React with amazement when they say something amazing. Laugh if they're funny. Don't forget that YOU are part of the interview.
Noah Adams once said that if you're thrown into an interview situation underprepared, one question that always works is: "What did you think this was going to be like before you started, and then what was it really like?" This will almost always yield a great answer, because it evokes two stories, and it evokes a lesson.

WRITING: GETTING YOUR STORY STRAIGHT

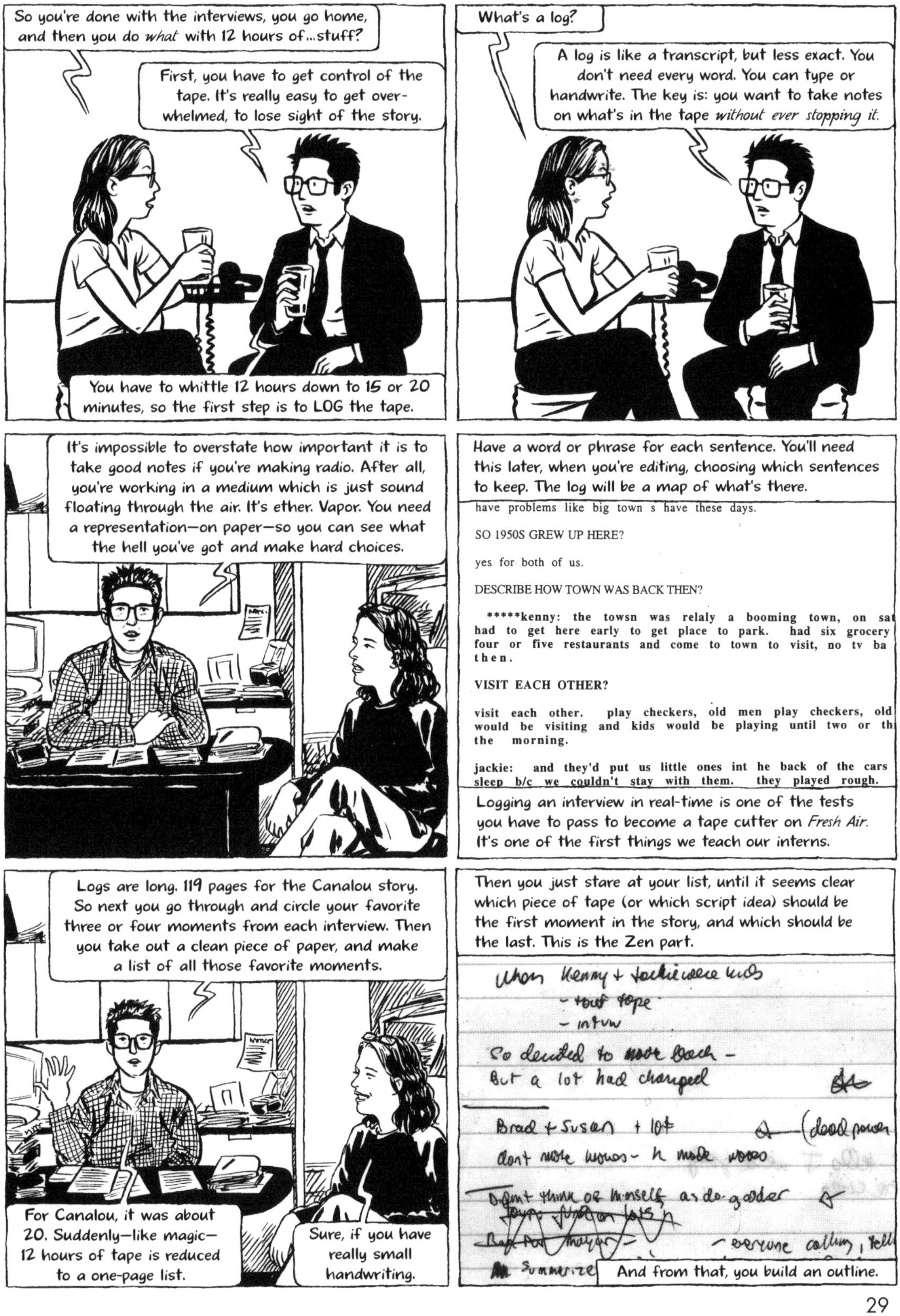

So you're done with the interviews, you go home, and then you do *what* with 12 hours of...stuff?
First, you have to get control of the tape. It's really easy to get over-whelmed, to lose sight of the story.
You have to whittle 12 hours down to 15 or 20 minutes, so the first step is to LOG the tape.
What's a log?
A log is like a transcript, but less exact. You don't need every word. You can type or handwrite. The key is: you want to take notes on what's in the tape *without ever stopping it.*
It's impossible to overstate how important it is to take good notes if you're making radio. After all, you're working in a medium which is just sound floating through the air. It's ether. Vapor. You need a representation—on paper—so you can see what the hell you've got and make hard choices.
Have a word or phrase for each sentence. You'll need this later, when you're editing, choosing which sentences to keep. The log will be a map of what's there.
have problems like big town s have these days.
SO 1950S GREW UP HERE?
yes for both of us.
DESCRIBE HOW TOWN WAS BACK THEN?
*****kenny: the towsn was relaly a booming town, on sat had to get here early to get place to park. had six grocery four or five restaurants and come to town to visit, no tv ba then.
VISIT EACH OTHER?
visit each other. play checkers, old men play checkers, old would be visiting and kids would be playing until two or th the morning.
jackie: and they'd put us little ones int he back of the cars sleep b/c we couldn't stay with them. they played rough.
Logging an interview in real-time is one of the tests you have to pass to become a tape cutter on *Fresh Air.* It's one of the first things we teach our interns.
Logs are long. 119 pages for the Canalou story. So next you go through and circle your favorite three or four moments from each interview. Then you take out a clean piece of paper, and make a list of all those favorite moments.
For Canalou, it was about 20. Suddenly—like magic—12 hours of tape is reduced to a one-page list.
Sure, if you have really small handwriting.
Then you just stare at your list, until it seems clear which piece of tape (or which script idea) should be the first moment in the story, and which should be the last. This is the Zen part.
So decided to move back -
But a lot had changed
Brad + Susan + lot
Summarize
And from that, you build an outline.

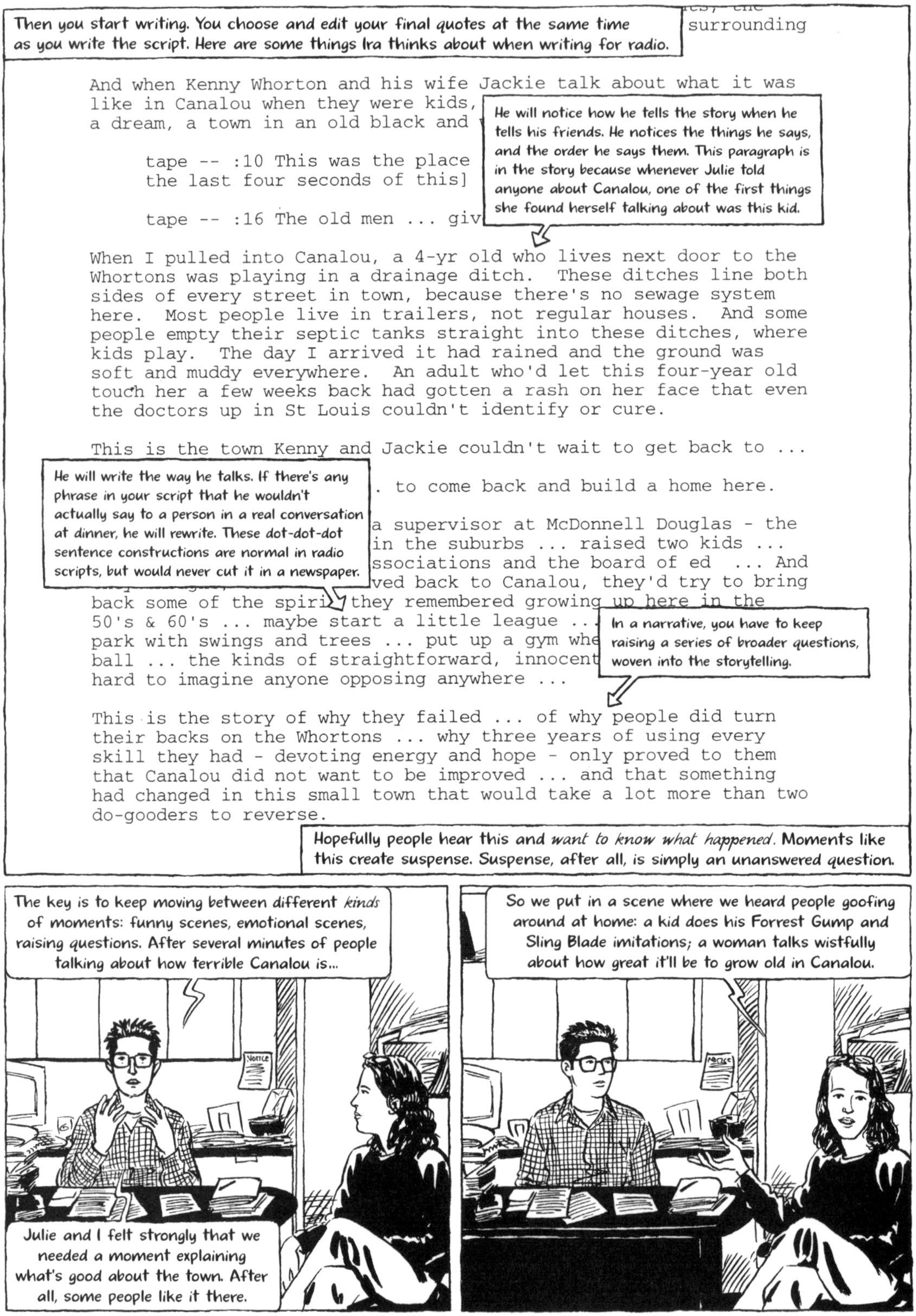
Then you start writing. You choose and edit your final quotes at the same time as you write the script. Here are some things Ira thinks about when writing for radio.
surrounding
And when Kenny Whorton and his wife Jackie talk about what it was like in Canalou when they were kids,
a dream, a town in an old black and
He will notice how he tells the story when he tells his friends. He notices the things he says, and the order he says them. This paragraph is in the story because whenever Julie told anyone about Canalou, one of the first things she found herself talking about was this kid.
tape -- :10 This was the place
the last four seconds of this]
tape -- :16 The old men ... giv
When I pulled into Canalou, a 4-yr old who lives next door to the Whortons was playing in a drainage ditch. These ditches line both sides of every street in town, because there's no sewage system here. Most people live in trailers, not regular houses. And some people empty their septic tanks straight into these ditches, where kids play. The day I arrived it had rained and the ground was soft and muddy everywhere. An adult who'd let this four-year old touch her a few weeks back had gotten a rash on her face that even the doctors up in St Louis couldn't identify or cure.
This is the town Kenny and Jackie couldn't wait to get back to ...
He will write the way he talks. If there's any phrase in your script that he wouldn't actually say to a person in a real conversation at dinner, he will rewrite. These dot-dot-dot sentence constructions are normal in radio scripts, but would never cut it in a newspaper.
. to come back and build a home here.
a supervisor at McDonnell Douglas - the
in the suburbs ... raised two kids ...
ssociations and the board of ed ... And
ved back to Canalou, they'd try to bring
back some of the spiri they remembered growing up here in the
50's & 60's ... maybe start a little league ...
park with swings and trees ... put up a gym whe
ball ... the kinds of straightforward, innocent
hard to imagine anyone opposing anywhere ...
In a narrative, you have to keep raising a series of broader questions, woven into the storytelling.
This is the story of why they failed ... of why people did turn their backs on the Whortons ... why three years of using every skill they had - devoting energy and hope - only proved to them that Canalou did not want to be improved ... and that something had changed in this small town that would take a lot more than two do-gooders to reverse.
Hopefully people hear this and *want to know what happened*. Moments like this create suspense. Suspense, after all, is simply an unanswered question.
The key is to keep moving between different *kinds* of moments: funny scenes, emotional scenes, raising questions. After several minutes of people talking about how terrible Canalou is...
NOTICE
Julie and I felt strongly that we needed a moment explaining what's good about the town. After all, some people like it there.
So we put in a scene where we heard people goofing around at home: a kid does his Forrest Gump and Sling Blade imitations; a woman talks wistfully about how great it'll be to grow old in Canalou.
NOTICE

Once you have a first draft, you run the whole thing by someone else. You read them the script and play the quotes. They critique. On our show, I edit the producers' stories, and they edit mine.

That transition to the last scene makes no sense. The tape's pretty but I have no idea why I'm hearing it.

I know, I know.

You know what the point of this scene is? In order to do good of any kind, you have to have a vision of the way you want things...There's a ruthlessness to changing anything...

Hold it—let me type this into the script...

...to imposing your will on what the world is...And the danger of having a vision is that your vision can cloud your eyes about what is...

will on what the world is...A the danger of having a visi that your vision can cloud about what is...

Often when I talked to Jack with her vision of Canalou the past was to her ... Peo here 40 years saw the town

TAPING AN INTERVIEW

Radio reporters need to follow certain rules to record broadcast-quality tape.

1) A decent microphone, a digital recorder, and a set of headphones are essential. But you have lots of options. You can make a broadcast-quality recording on your iPhone. The key is having a decent microphone. Built-in mics won't cut it. (And yes, they make good cheap mics to use with an iPhone.) Up-to-date, specific recommendations can be found on Transom.org.

2) Location location location. You need quiet. No noisy fans, no music or TV playing in the background, no street noise, nothing that'll make it hard to edit later. Avoid echoey rooms. A carpeted living room is ideal. And wear headphones so you can be sure the recording's OK.

NO

YES

Shall we do our interview in this restaurant?

Shall we do our interview in my hotel room?

PARADE OUTSIDE

HEAVY DRAPES

MARIACHI BAND

SOUND ABSORBING MATERIAL

ECHOEY FLOOR

CARPET

3) Get in close. The single biggest factor in making a good recording is proper mic placement. You can make cheap equipment sound good if you do this right. Hold the mic 3-4 inches *below* the interviewee's mouth, just below the chin. Yes, you'll feel weird getting this close to a stranger's face. *But you must.* Be brave! Now Ira will demonstrate the cartooning skills that inspired him to hire Jessica for this job:

Ira © 1999

Keep the mic below the mouth: if it's 4" away, but directly in front of the mouth, the air coming out of the interviewee's mouth will make annoying "p-pops."

Why is it so important to get close? Make a recording with the mic 4", 8", and 12" from your mouth. Listen. When the mic's closer, your recordings sound richer, with more frequencies present, with less of the hum of the room.

...

4) More mic placement. When you ask a question, point the mic back at yourself. Otherwise, the question won't be loud enough on tape. At the end of the interview, record a half minute of room sound, without anyone talking; you'll need this for editing.

EDITING: THE INVISIBLE ART

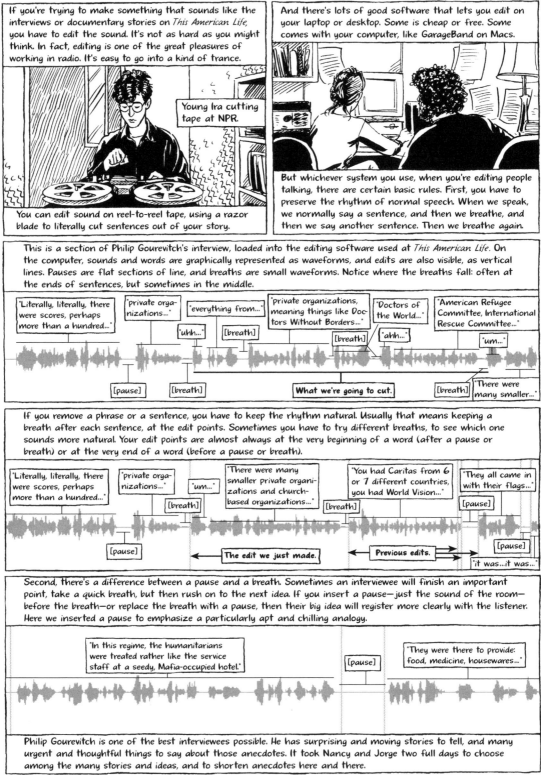

If you're trying to make something that sounds like the interviews or documentary stories on *This American Life,* you have to edit the sound. It's not as hard as you might think. In fact, editing is one of the great pleasures of working in radio. It's easy to go into a kind of trance.

Young Ira cutting tape at NPR.

You can edit sound on reel-to-reel tape, using a razor blade to literally cut sentences out of your story.

And there's lots of good software that lets you edit on your laptop or desktop. Some is cheap or free. Some comes with your computer, like GarageBand on Macs.

But whichever system you use, when you're editing people talking, there are certain basic rules. First, you have to preserve the rhythm of normal speech. When we speak, we normally say a sentence, and then we breathe, and then we say another sentence. Then we breathe again.

This is a section of Philip Gourevitch's interview, loaded into the editing software used at *This American Life.* On the computer, sounds and words are graphically represented as waveforms, and edits are also visible, as vertical lines. Pauses are flat sections of line, and breaths are small waveforms. Notice where the breaths fall: often at the ends of sentences, but sometimes in the middle.

"Literally, literally, there were scores, perhaps more than a hundred..."
"private organizations..."
"everything from..."
"private organizations, meaning things like Doctors Without Borders..."
"Doctors of the World..."
"American Refugee Committee, International Rescue Committee..."
"uhh..."
[breath]
[breath]
"ahh..."
"um..."
[pause]
[breath]
What we're going to cut.
[breath]
"There were many smaller..."

If you remove a phrase or a sentence, you have to keep the rhythm natural. Usually that means keeping a breath after each sentence, at the edit points. Sometimes you have to try different breaths, to see which one sounds more natural. Your edit points are almost always at the very beginning of a word (after a pause or breath) or at the very end of a word (before a pause or breath).

"Literally, literally, there were scores, perhaps more than a hundred..."
"private organizations..."
"um..."
[breath]
"There were many smaller private organizations and church-based organizations..."
[breath]
"You had Caritas from 6 or 7 different countries, you had World Vision..."
"They all came in with their flags..."
[pause]
[pause]
The edit we just made.
Previous edits.
[pause]
"it was...it was..."

Second, there's a difference between a pause and a breath. Sometimes an interviewee will finish an important point, take a quick breath, but then rush on to the next idea. If you insert a pause—just the sound of the room—before the breath—or replace the breath with a pause, then their big idea will register more clearly with the listener. Here we inserted a pause to emphasize a particularly apt and chilling analogy.

"In this regime, the humanitarians were treated rather like the service staff at a seedy, Mafia-occupied hotel."
[pause]
"They were there to provide: food, medicine, housewares..."

Philip Gourevitch is one of the best interviewees possible. He has surprising and moving stories to tell, and many urgent and thoughtful things to say about those anecdotes. It took Nancy and Jorge two full days to choose among the many stories and ideas, and to shorten anecdotes here and there.

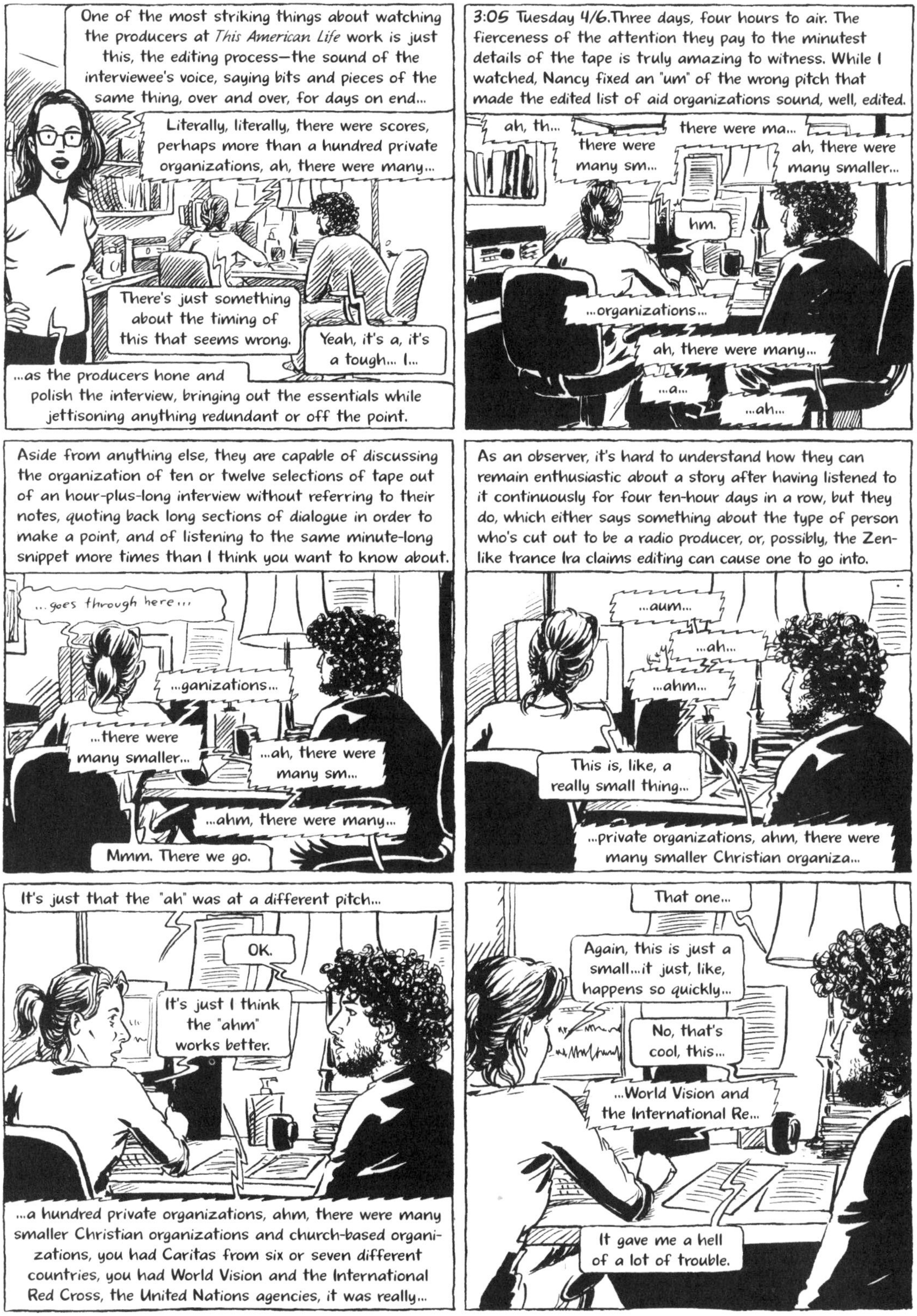
One of the most striking things about watching the producers at *This American Life* work is just this, the editing process—the sound of the interviewee's voice, saying bits and pieces of the same thing, over and over, for days on end...
Literally, literally, there were scores, perhaps more than a hundred private organizations, ah, there were many...
There's just something about the timing of this that seems wrong.
Yeah, it's a, it's a tough... I...
...as the producers hone and polish the interview, bringing out the essentials while jettisoning anything redundant or off the point.
3:05 Tuesday 4/6. Three days, four hours to air. The fierceness of the attention they pay to the minutest details of the tape is truly amazing to witness. While I watched, Nancy fixed an "um" of the wrong pitch that made the edited list of aid organizations sound, well, edited.
ah, th...
there were many sm...
there were ma...
ah, there were many smaller...
hm.
...organizations...
ah, there were many...
...a...
...ah...
Aside from anything else, they are capable of discussing the organization of ten or twelve selections of tape out of an hour-plus-long interview without referring to their notes, quoting back long sections of dialogue in order to make a point, and of listening to the same minute-long snippet more times than I think you want to know about.
...goes through here...
...ganizations...
...there were many smaller...
...ah, there were many sm...
...ahm, there were many...
Mmm. There we go.
As an observer, it's hard to understand how they can remain enthusiastic about a story after having listened to it continuously for four ten-hour days in a row, but they do, which either says something about the type of person who's cut out to be a radio producer, or, possibly, the Zen-like trance Ira claims editing can cause one to go into.
...aum...
...ah...
...ahm...
This is, like, a really small thing...
...private organizations, ahm, there were many smaller Christian organiza...
It's just that the "ah" was at a different pitch...
OK.
It's just I think the "ahm" works better.
...a hundred private organizations, ahm, there were many smaller Christian organizations and church-based organizations, you had Caritas from six or seven different countries, you had World Vision and the International Red Cross, the United Nations agencies, it was really...
That one...
Again, this is just a small...it just, like, happens so quickly...
No, that's cool, this...
...World Vision and the International Re...
It gave me a hell of a lot of trouble.

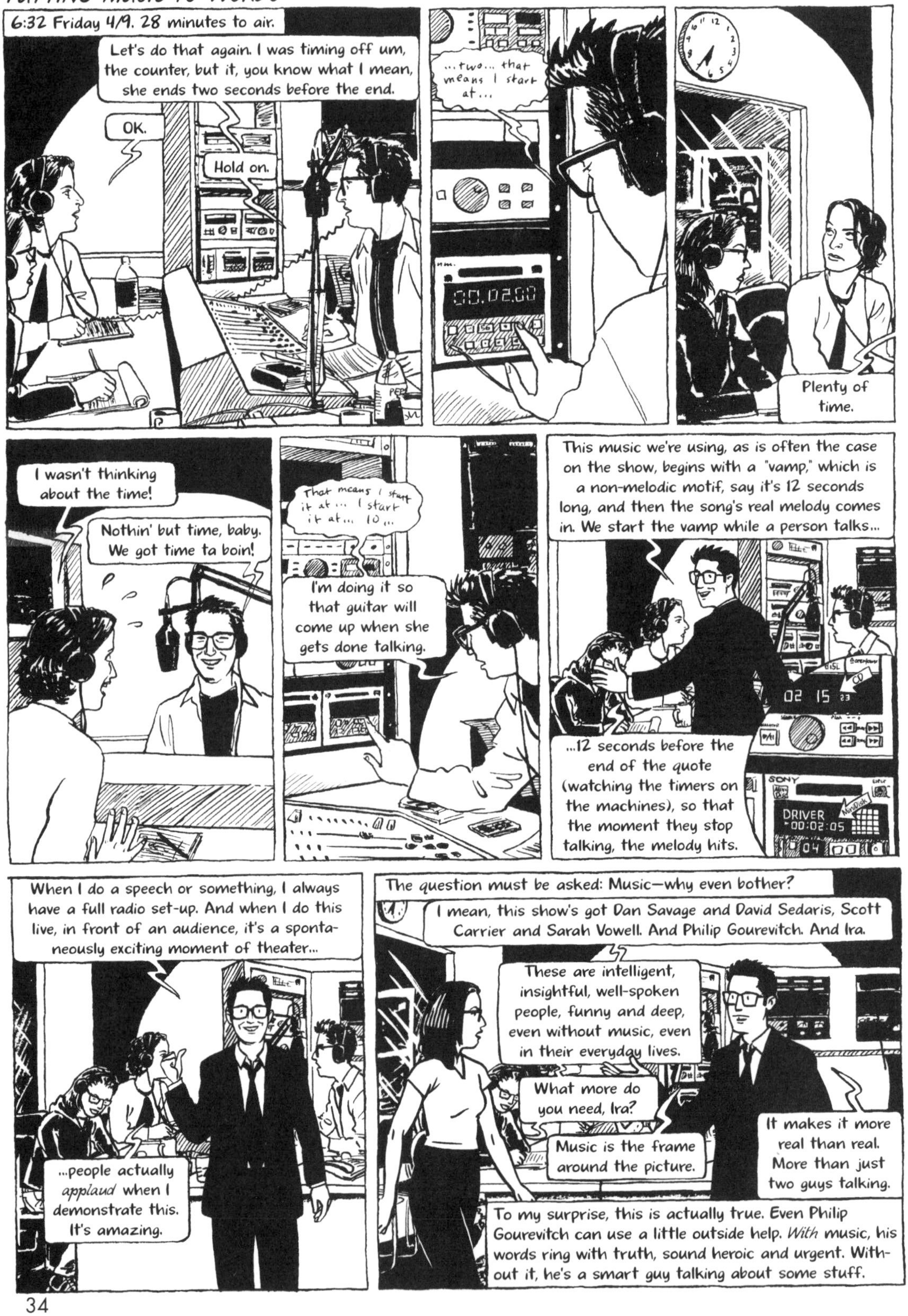
6:32 Friday 4/9. 28 minutes to air.
Let's do that again. I was timing off um, the counter, but it, you know what I mean, she ends two seconds before the end.
OK.
Hold on.
...two... that means I start at...
Plenty of time.
I wasn't thinking about the time!
Nothin' but time, baby. We got time ta boin!
That means I start it at... I start it at... 10...
I'm doing it so that guitar will come up when she gets done talking.
This music we're using, as is often the case on the show, begins with a "vamp," which is a non-melodic motif, say it's 12 seconds long, and then the song's real melody comes in. We start the vamp while a person talks...
...12 seconds before the end of the quote (watching the timers on the machines), so that the moment they stop talking, the melody hits.
When I do a speech or something, I always have a full radio set-up. And when I do this live, in front of an audience, it's a spontaneously exciting moment of theater...
...people actually *applaud* when I demonstrate this. It's amazing.
The question must be asked: Music—why even bother?
I mean, this show's got Dan Savage and David Sedaris, Scott Carrier and Sarah Vowell. And Philip Gourevitch. And Ira.
These are intelligent, insightful, well-spoken people, funny and deep, even without music, even in their everyday lives.
What more do you need, Ira?
Music is the frame around the picture.
It makes it more real than real. More than just two guys talking.
To my surprise, this is actually true. Even Philip Gourevitch can use a little outside help. *With* music, his words ring with truth, sound heroic and urgent. Without it, he's a smart guy talking about some stuff.

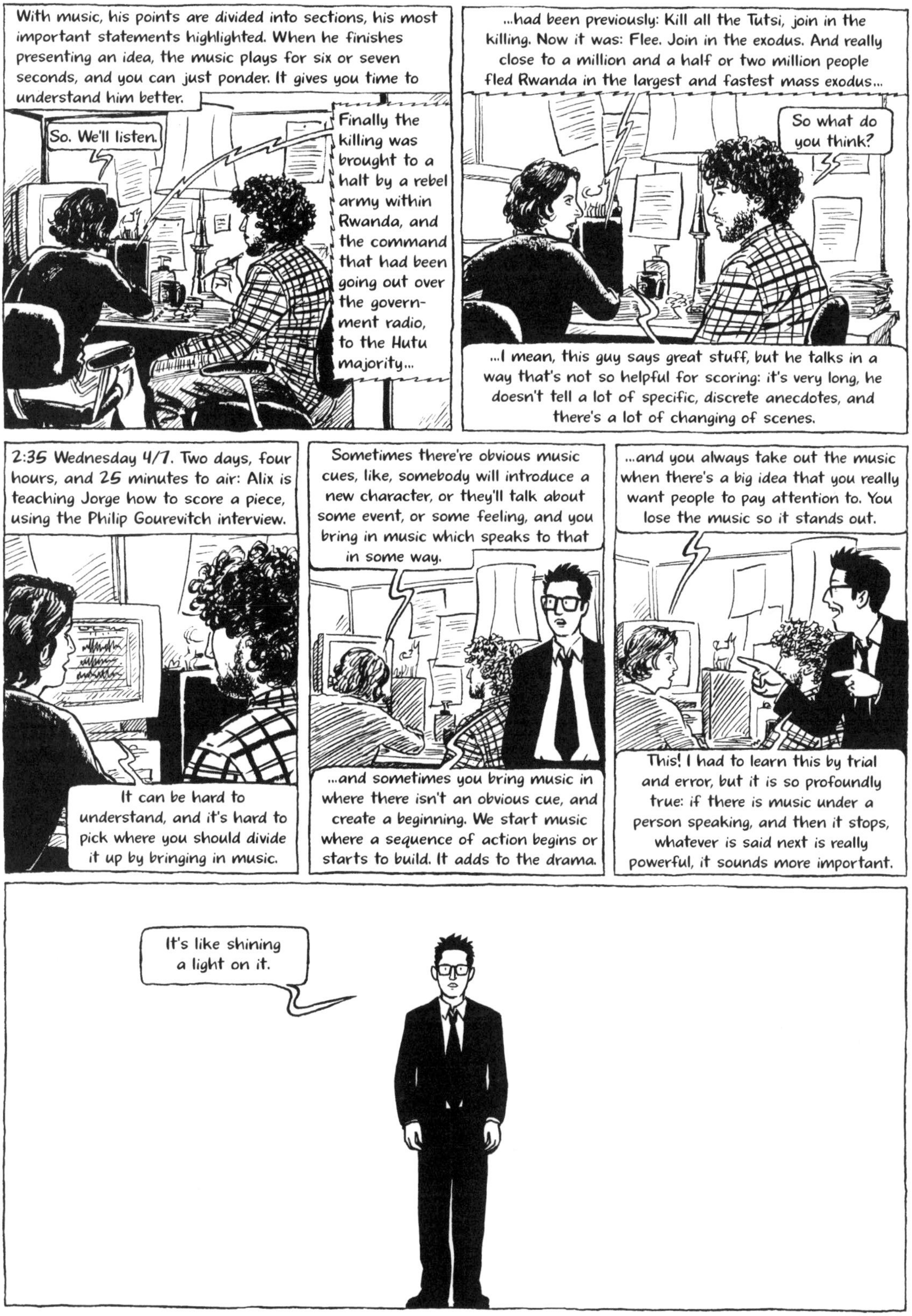
With music, his points are divided into sections, his most important statements highlighted. When he finishes presenting an idea, the music plays for six or seven seconds, and you can just ponder. It gives you time to understand him better.
So. We'll listen.
Finally the killing was brought to a halt by a rebel army within Rwanda, and the command that had been going out over the government radio, to the Hutu majority...
...had been previously: Kill all the Tutsi, join in the killing. Now it was: Flee. Join in the exodus. And really close to a million and a half or two million people fled Rwanda in the largest and fastest mass exodus...
So what do you think?
...I mean, this guy says great stuff, but he talks in a way that's not so helpful for scoring: it's very long, he doesn't tell a lot of specific, discrete anecdotes, and there's a lot of changing of scenes.
2:35 Wednesday 4/7. Two days, four hours, and 25 minutes to air: Alix is teaching Jorge how to score a piece, using the Philip Gourevitch interview.
It can be hard to understand, and it's hard to pick where you should divide it up by bringing in music.
Sometimes there're obvious music cues, like, somebody will introduce a new character, or they'll talk about some event, or some feeling, and you bring in music which speaks to that in some way.
...and sometimes you bring music in where there isn't an obvious cue, and create a beginning. We start music where a sequence of action begins or starts to build. It adds to the drama.
...and you always take out the music when there's a big idea that you really want people to pay attention to. You lose the music so it stands out.
This! I had to learn this by trial and error, but it is so profoundly true: if there is music under a person speaking, and then it stops, whatever is said next is really powerful, it sounds more important.
It's like shining a light on it.

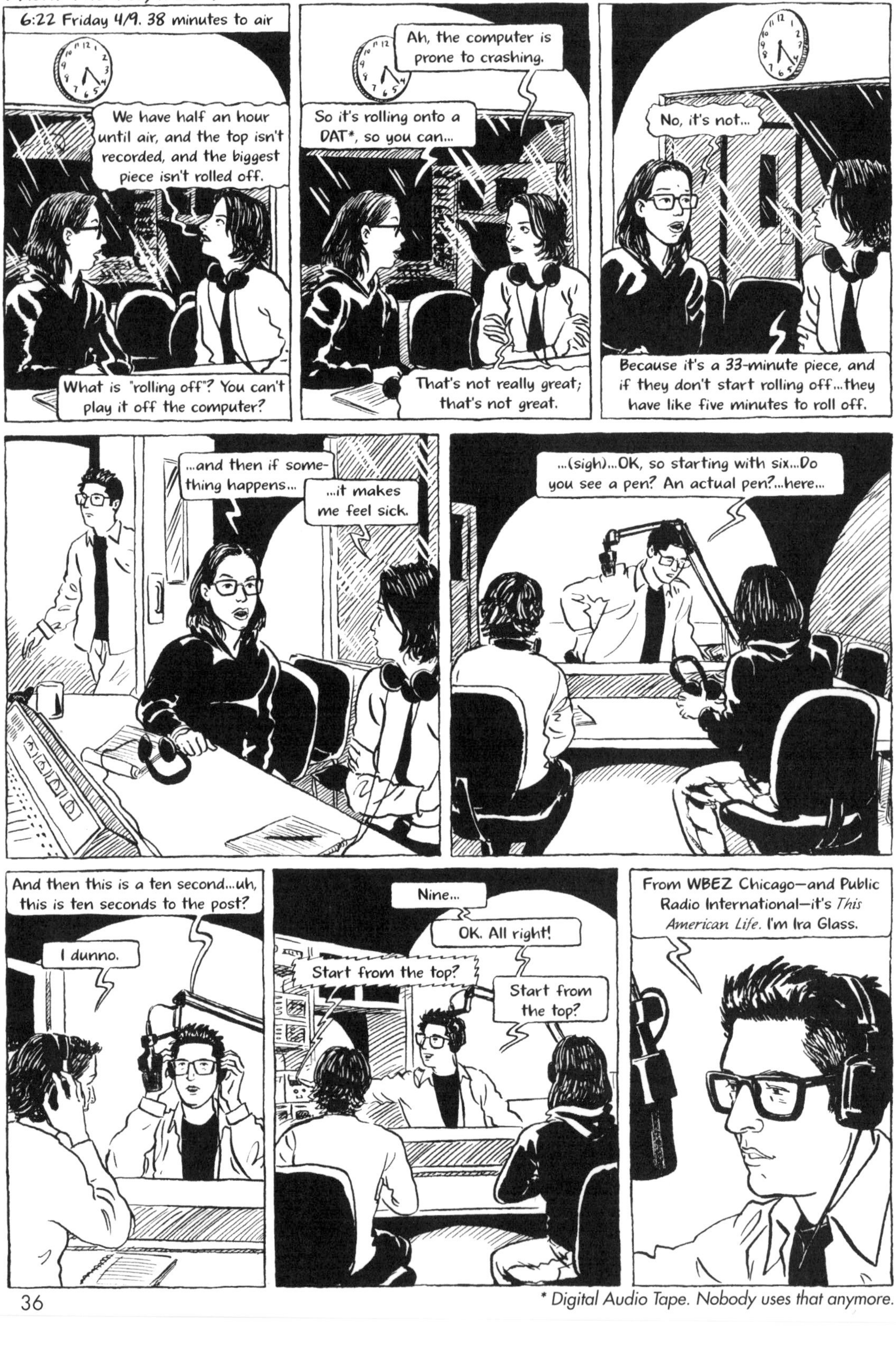
6:22 Friday 4/9. 38 minutes to air
We have half an hour until air, and the top isn't recorded, and the biggest piece isn't rolled off.
What is "rolling off"? You can't play it off the computer?
Ah, the computer is prone to crashing.
So it's rolling onto a DAT*, so you can...
That's not really great; that's not great.
No, it's not...
Because it's a 33-minute piece, and if they don't start rolling off...they have like five minutes to roll off.
...and then if something happens...
...it makes me feel sick.
...(sigh)...OK, so starting with six...Do you see a pen? An actual pen?...here...
And then this is a ten second...uh, this is ten seconds to the post?
I dunno.
Nine...
OK. All right!
Start from the top?
Start from the top?
From WBEZ Chicago—and Public Radio International—it's *This American Life*. I'm Ira Glass.

* Digital Audio Tape. Nobody uses that anymore.

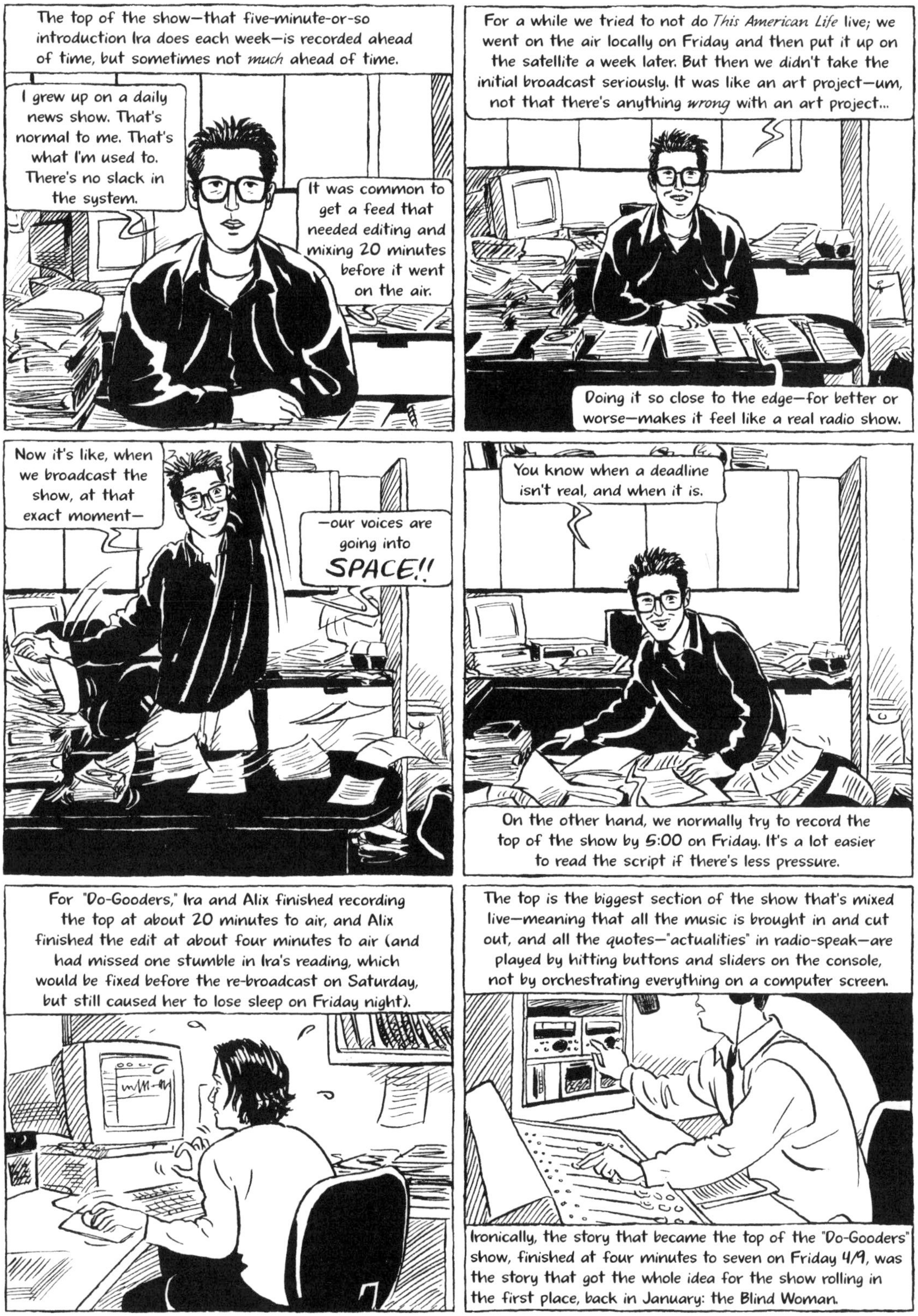

The top of the show—that five-minute-or-so introduction Ira does each week—is recorded ahead of time, but sometimes not *much* ahead of time.
I grew up on a daily news show. That's normal to me. That's what I'm used to. There's no slack in the system.
It was common to get a feed that needed editing and mixing 20 minutes before it went on the air.
For a while we tried to not do *This American Life* live; we went on the air locally on Friday and then put it up on the satellite a week later. But then we didn't take the initial broadcast seriously. It was like an art project—um, not that there's anything *wrong* with an art project...
Doing it so close to the edge—for better or worse—makes it feel like a real radio show.
Now it's like, when we broadcast the show, at that exact moment—
—our voices are going into SPACE!!
You know when a deadline isn't real, and when it is.
On the other hand, we normally try to record the top of the show by 5:00 on Friday. It's a lot easier to read the script if there's less pressure.
For "Do-Gooders," Ira and Alix finished recording the top at about 20 minutes to air, and Alix finished the edit at about four minutes to air (and had missed one stumble in Ira's reading, which would be fixed before the re-broadcast on Saturday, but still caused her to lose sleep on Friday night).
The top is the biggest section of the show that's mixed live—meaning that all the music is brought in and cut out, and all the quotes—"actualities" in radio-speak—are played by hitting buttons and sliders on the console, not by orchestrating everything on a computer screen.
Ironically, the story that became the top of the "Do-Gooders" show, finished at four minutes to seven on Friday 4/9, was the story that got the whole idea for the show rolling in the first place, back in January: the Blind Woman.

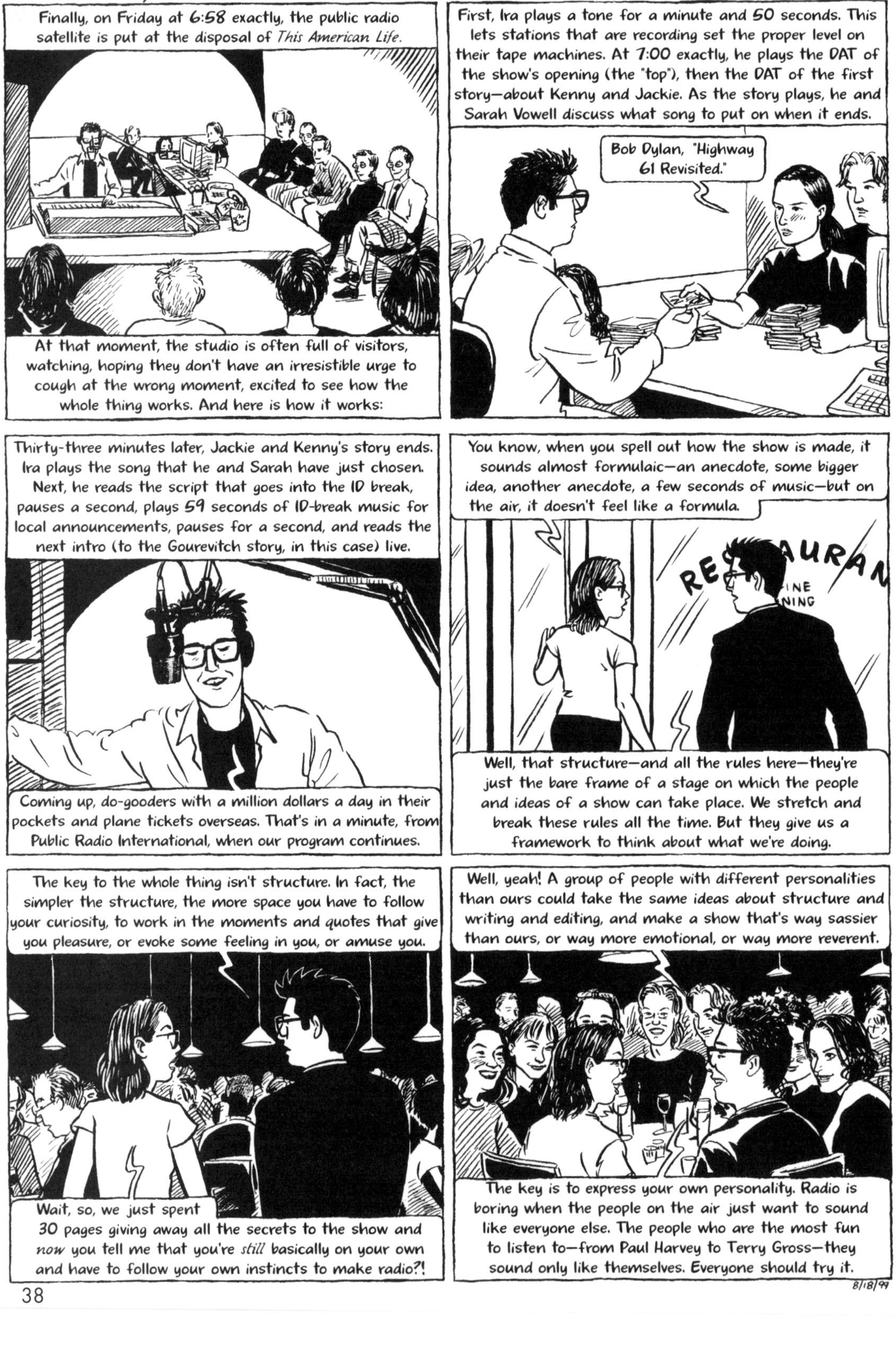
Finally, on Friday at 6:58 exactly, the public radio satellite is put at the disposal of *This American Life.*
At that moment, the studio is often full of visitors, watching, hoping they don't have an irresistible urge to cough at the wrong moment, excited to see how the whole thing works. And here is how it works:
First, Ira plays a tone for a minute and 50 seconds. This lets stations that are recording set the proper level on their tape machines. At 7:00 exactly, he plays the DAT of the show's opening (the "top"), then the DAT of the first story—about Kenny and Jackie. As the story plays, he and Sarah Vowell discuss what song to put on when it ends.
Bob Dylan, "Highway 61 Revisited."
Thirty-three minutes later, Jackie and Kenny's story ends. Ira plays the song that he and Sarah have just chosen. Next, he reads the script that goes into the ID break, pauses a second, plays 59 seconds of ID-break music for local announcements, pauses for a second, and reads the next intro (to the Gourevitch story, in this case) live.
Coming up, do-gooders with a million dollars a day in their pockets and plane tickets overseas. That's in a minute, from Public Radio International, when our program continues.
You know, when you spell out how the show is made, it sounds almost formulaic—an anecdote, some bigger idea, another anecdote, a few seconds of music—but on the air, it doesn't feel like a formula.
RESTAURAN
INE
NING
Well, that structure—and all the rules here—they're just the bare frame of a stage on which the people and ideas of a show can take place. We stretch and break these rules all the time. But they give us a framework to think about what we're doing.
The key to the whole thing isn't structure. In fact, the simpler the structure, the more space you have to follow your curiosity, to work in the moments and quotes that give you pleasure, or evoke some feeling in you, or amuse you.
Wait, so, we just spent 30 pages giving away all the secrets to the show and *now* you tell me that you're *still* basically on your own and have to follow your own instincts to make radio?!
Well, yeah! A group of people with different personalities than ours could take the same ideas about structure and writing and editing, and make a show that's way sassier than ours, or way more emotional, or way more reverent.
The key is to express your own personality. Radio is boring when the people on the air just want to sound like everyone else. The people who are the most fun to listen to—from Paul Harvey to Terry Gross—they sound only like themselves. Everyone should try it.
8/18/99

BACK IN THE PRESENT DAY

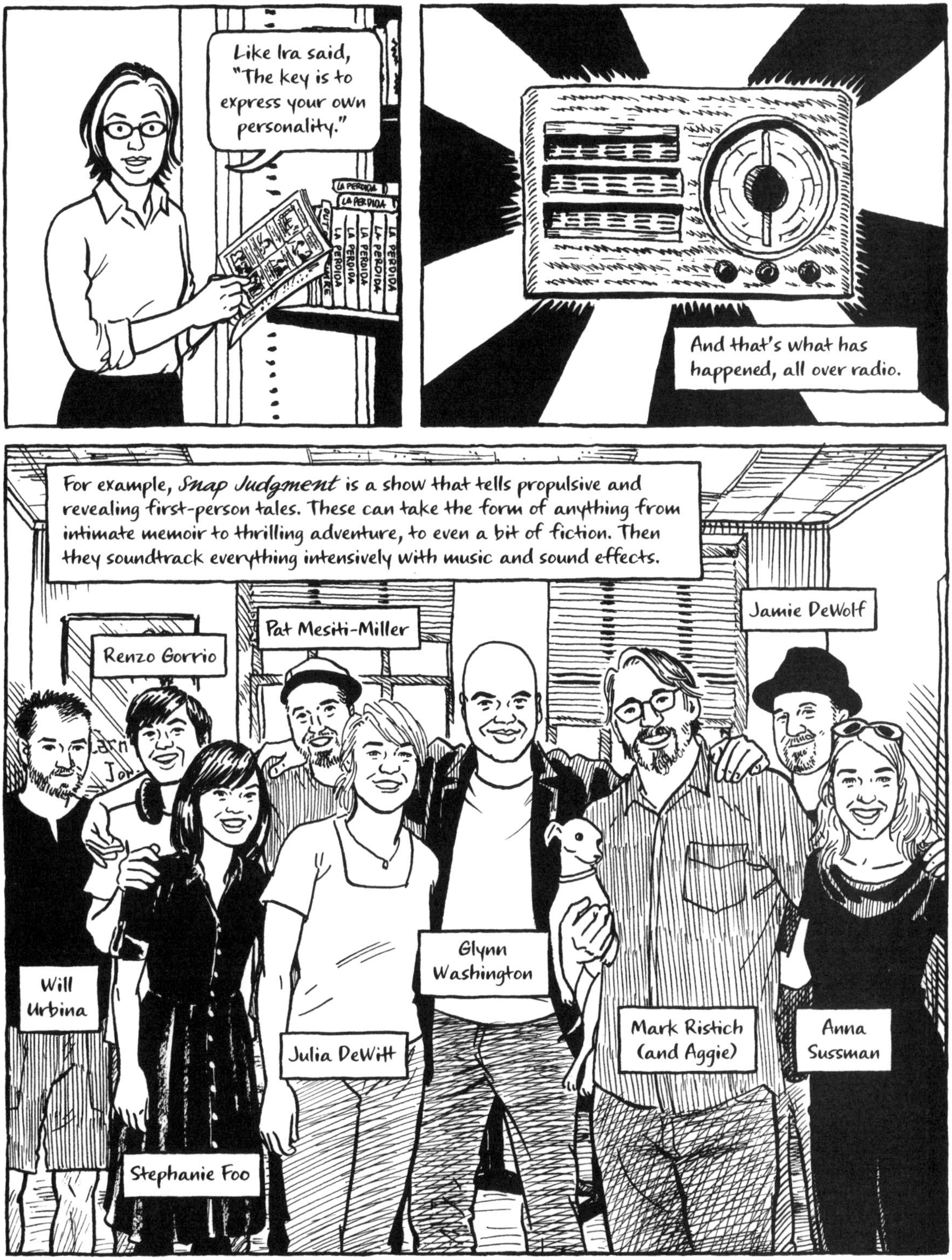
Like Ira said, "The key is to express your own personality."
LA PERDIDA
And that's what has happened, all over radio.
For example, *Snap Judgment* is a show that tells propulsive and revealing first-person tales. These can take the form of anything from intimate memoir to thrilling adventure, to even a bit of fiction. Then they soundtrack everything intensively with music and sound effects.
Pat Mesiti-Miller
Jamie DeWolf
Renzo Gorrio
Will Urbina
Glynn Washington
Julia DeWitt
Mark Ristich (and Aggie)
Anna Sussman
Stephanie Foo

The people pictured in the following pages are those that I've interviewed or mentioned by name in this book. They are not by any means all who are involved in producing these shows. They're also not all still at the same shows since I interviewed them. Please see Notes, page 211 for details.

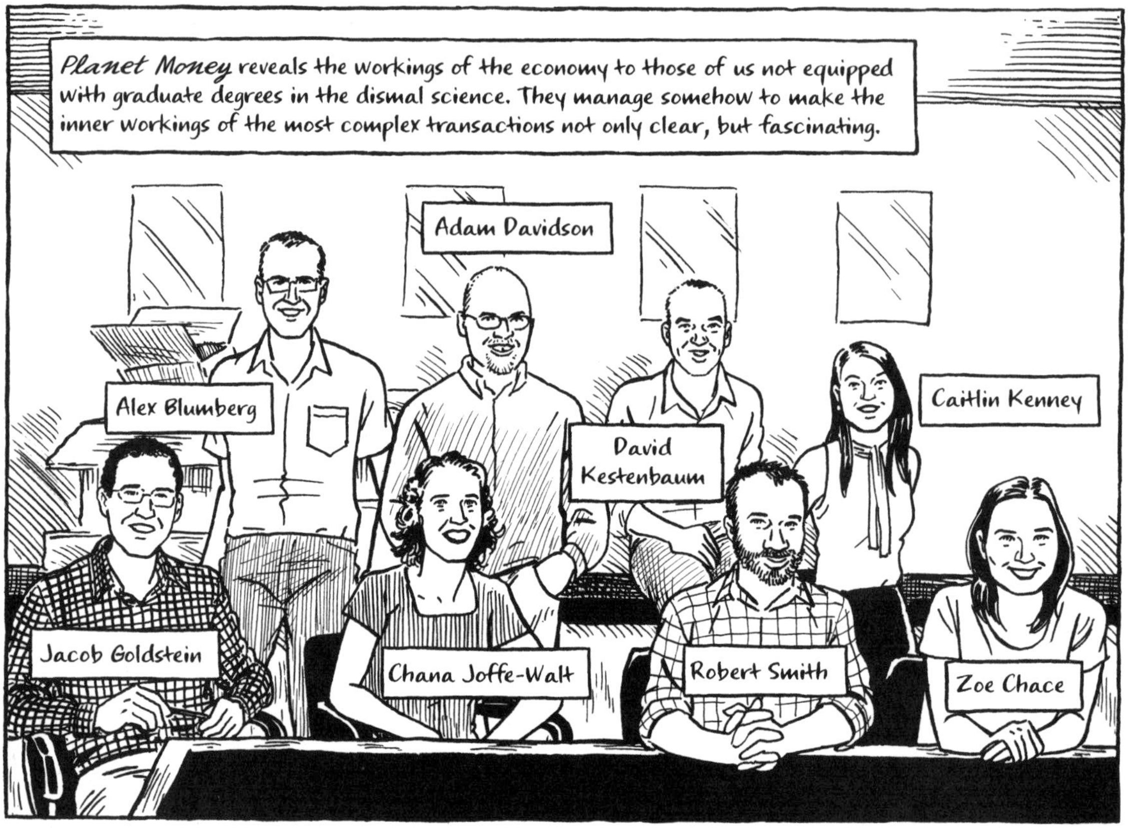
Planet Money reveals the workings of the economy to those of us not equipped with graduate degrees in the dismal science. They manage somehow to make the inner workings of the most complex transactions not only clear, but fascinating.
Adam Davidson
Alex Blumberg
Caitlin Kenney
David Kestenbaum
Jacob Goldstein
Chana Joffe-Walt
Robert Smith
Zoe Chace

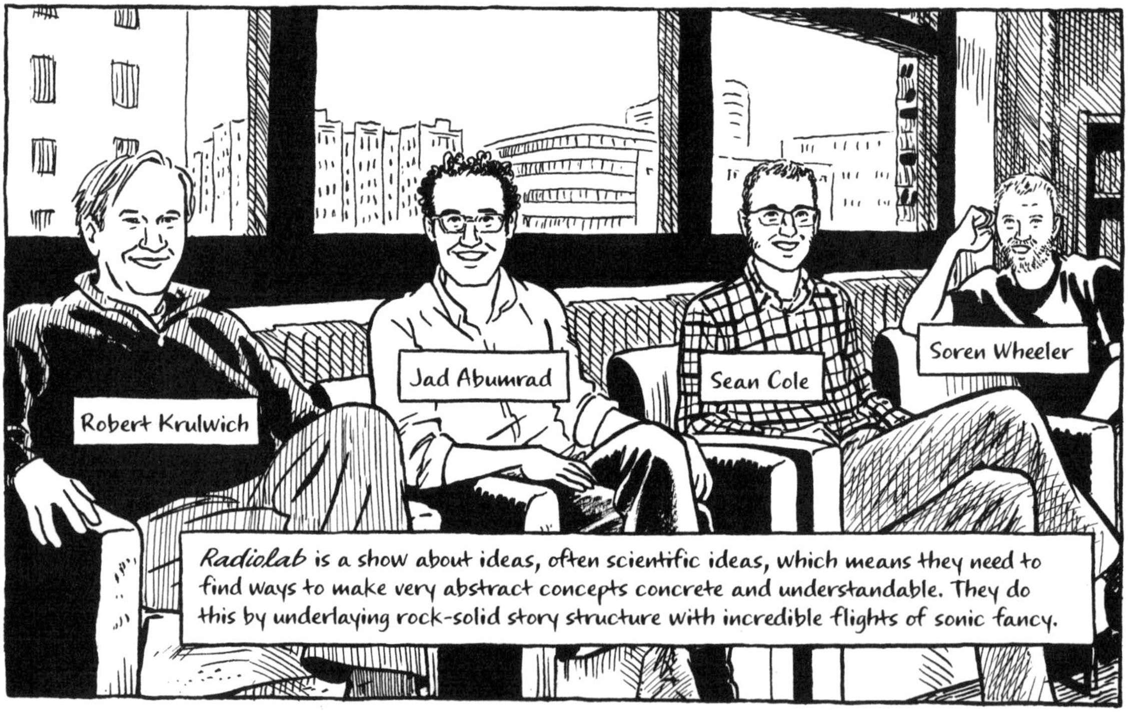
Soren Wheeler
Jad Abumrad
Sean Cole
Robert Krulwich
Radiolab is a show about ideas, often scientific ideas, which means they need to find ways to make very abstract concepts concrete and understandable. They do this by underlaying rock-solid story structure with incredible flights of sonic fancy.

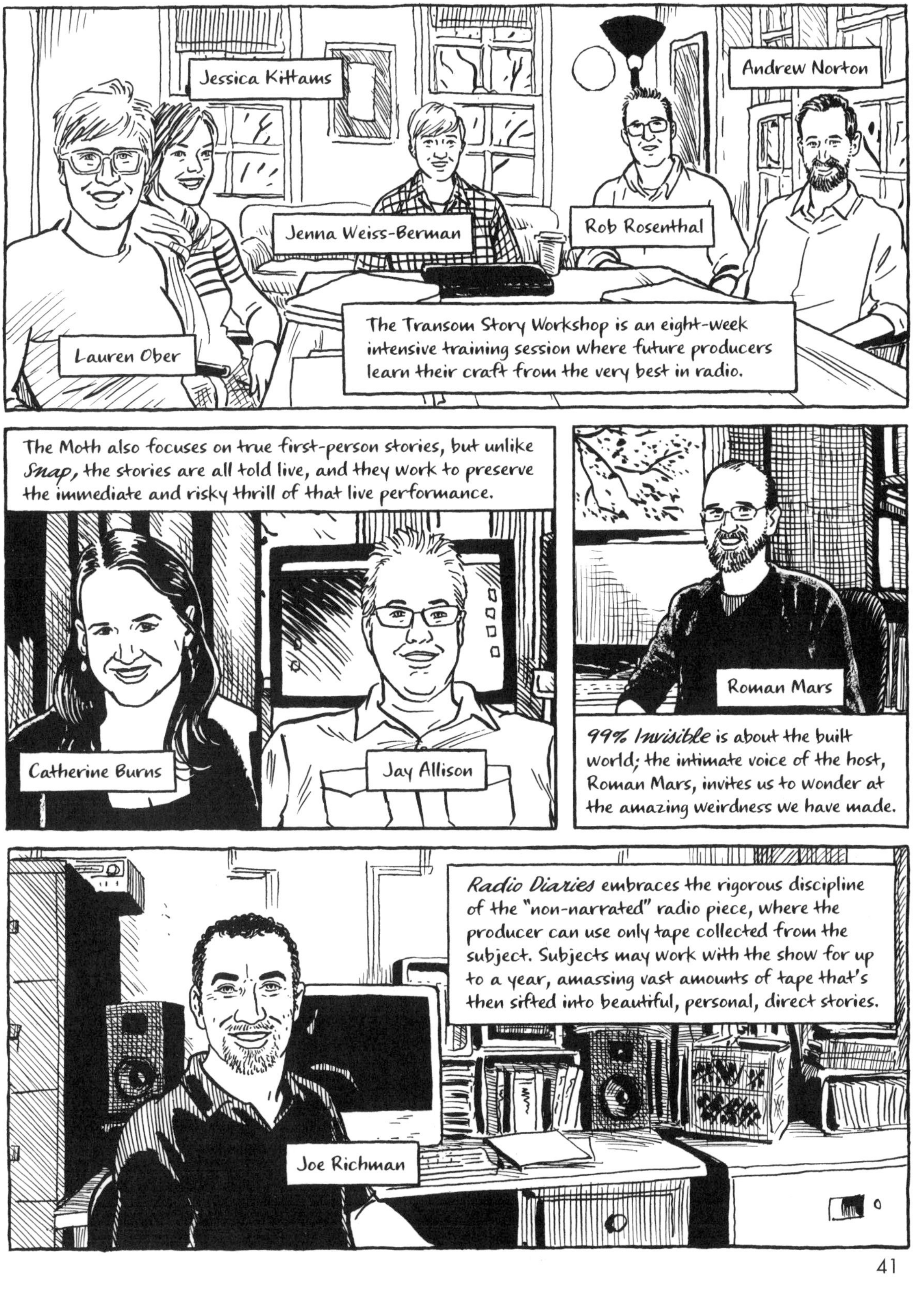

Jessica Kittams
Andrew Norton
Jenna Weiss-Berman
Rob Rosenthal
Lauren Ober
The Transom Story Workshop is an eight-week intensive training session where future producers learn their craft from the very best in radio.
The Moth also focuses on true first-person stories, but unlike *Snap,* the stories are all told live, and they work to preserve the immediate and risky thrill of that live performance.
Catherine Burns
Jay Allison
Roman Mars
99% Invisible is about the built world; the intimate voice of the host, Roman Mars, invites us to wonder at the amazing weirdness we have made.
Radio Diaries embraces the rigorous discipline of the "non-narrated" radio piece, where the producer can use only tape collected from the subject. Subjects may work with the show for up to a year, amassing vast amounts of tape that's then sifted into beautiful, personal, direct stories.
Joe Richman

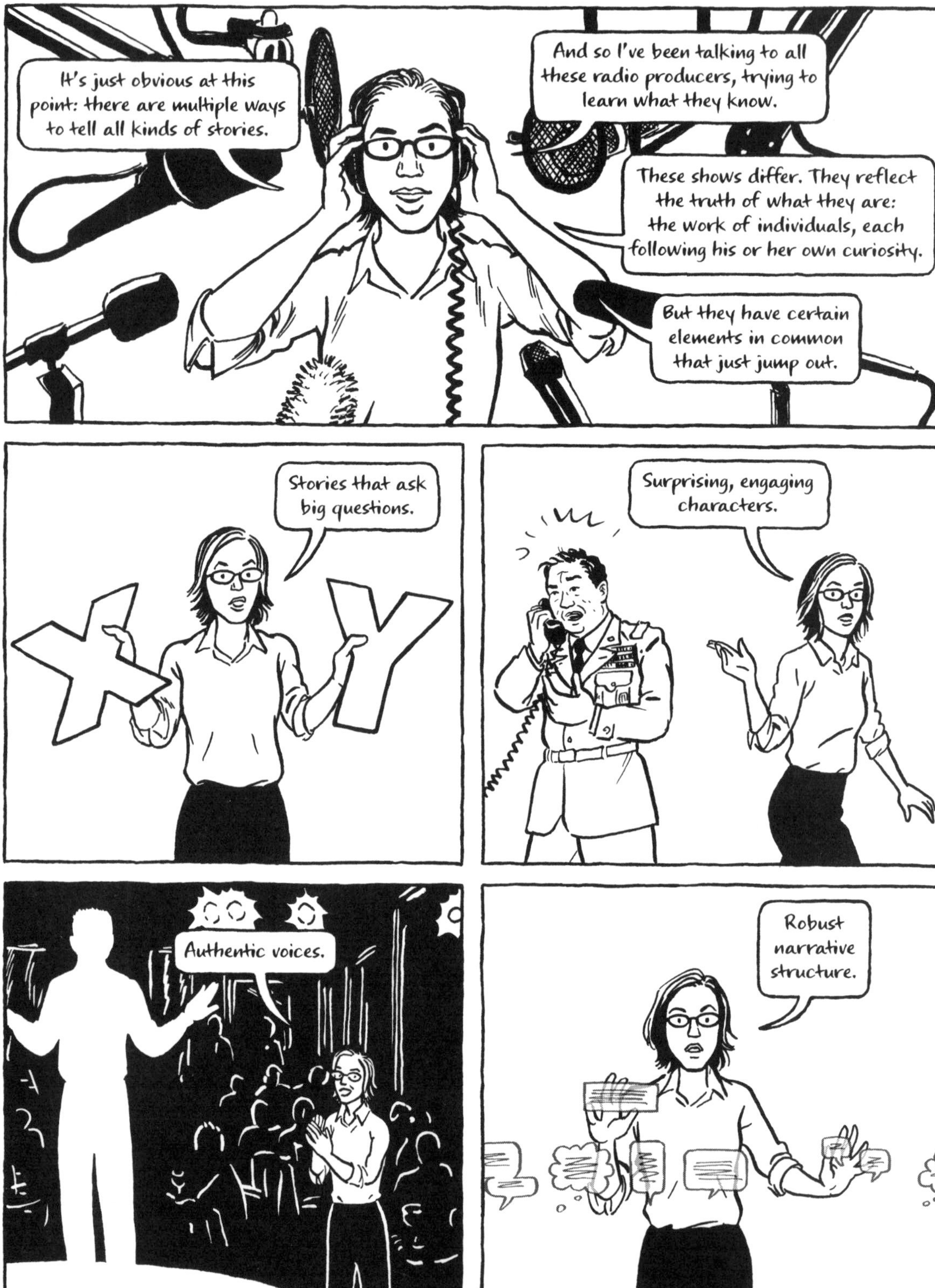
It's just obvious at this point: there are multiple ways to tell all kinds of stories.
And so I've been talking to all these radio producers, trying to learn what they know.
These shows differ. They reflect the truth of what they are: the work of individuals, each following his or her own curiosity.
But they have certain elements in common that just jump out.
Stories that ask big questions.
Surprising, engaging characters.
Authentic voices.
Robust narrative structure.

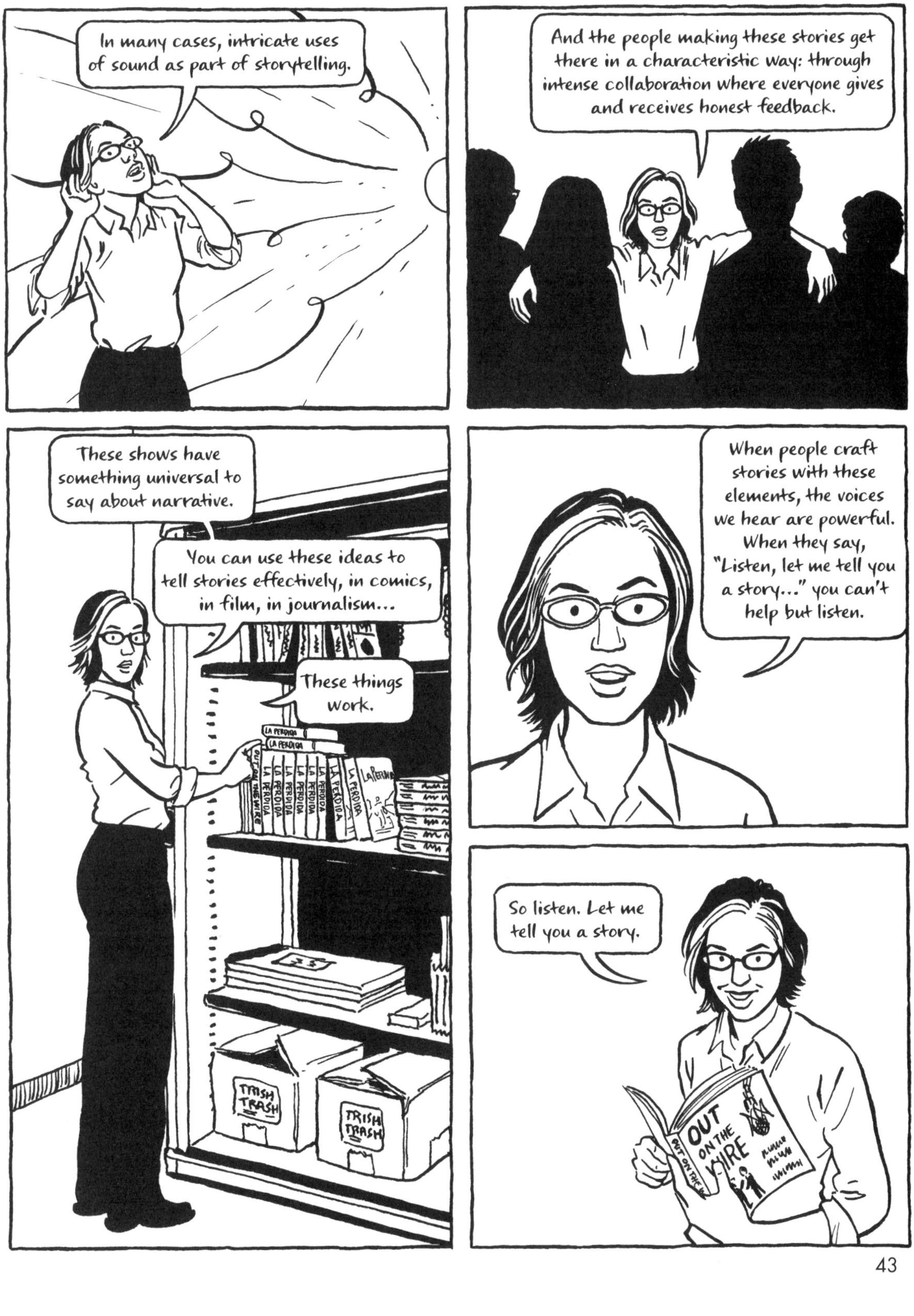
In many cases, intricate uses of sound as part of storytelling.
And the people making these stories get there in a characteristic way: through intense collaboration where everyone gives and receives honest feedback.
These shows have something universal to say about narrative.
You can use these ideas to tell stories effectively, in comics, in film, in journalism...
These things work.
LA PERDIDA
OUT ON THE WIRE
TRISH TRASH
When people craft stories with these elements, the voices we hear are powerful. When they say, "Listen, let me tell you a story..." you can't help but listen.
So listen. Let me tell you a story.
OUT ON THE WIRE

AMUSE YOURSELF:
Ideas

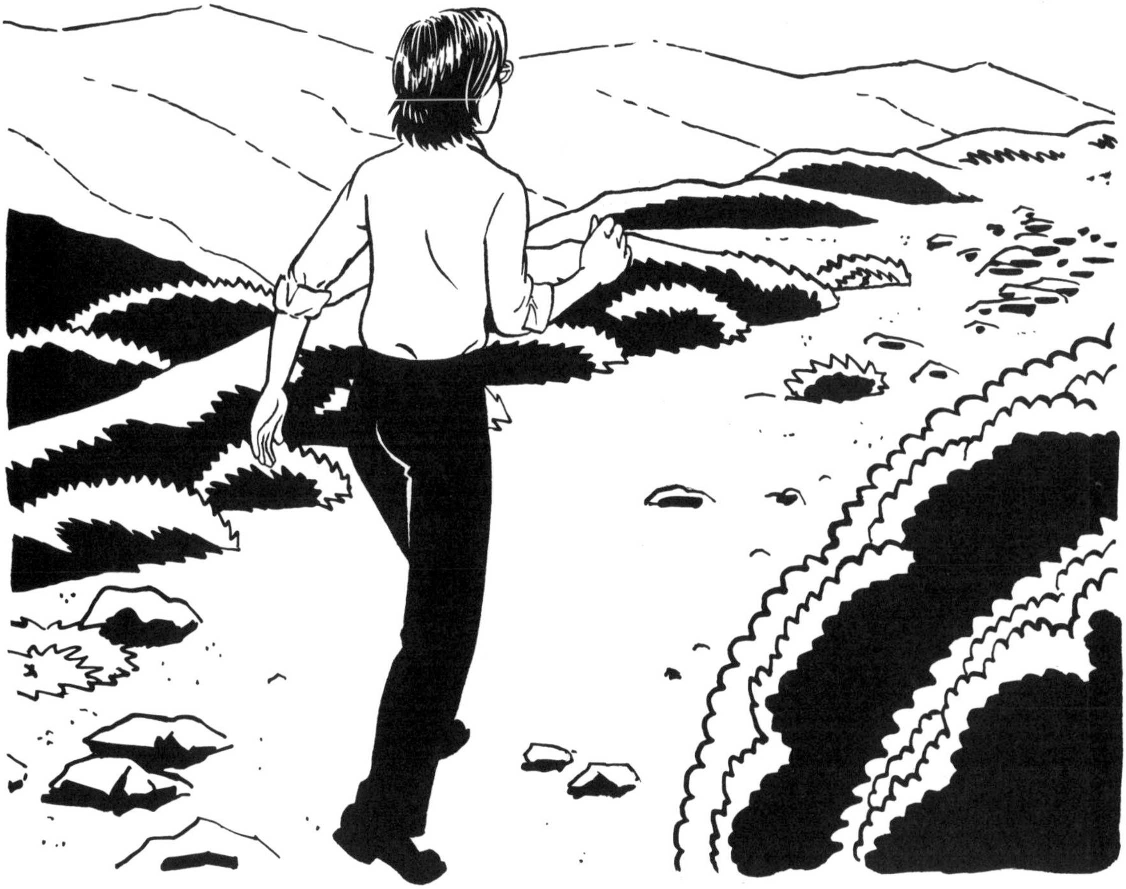

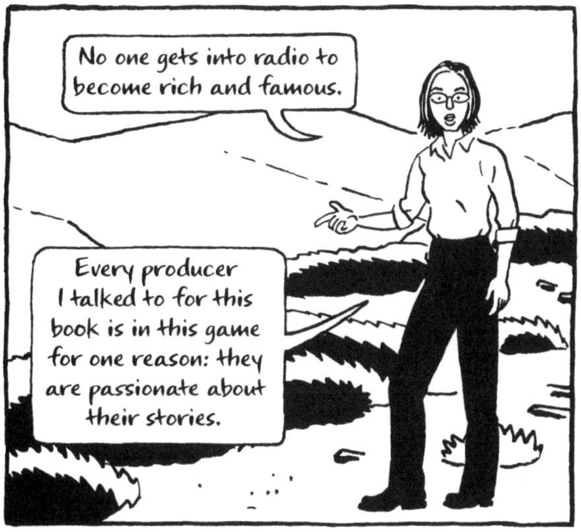
No one gets into radio to become rich and famous.
Every producer I talked to for this book is in this game for one reason: they are passionate about their stories.

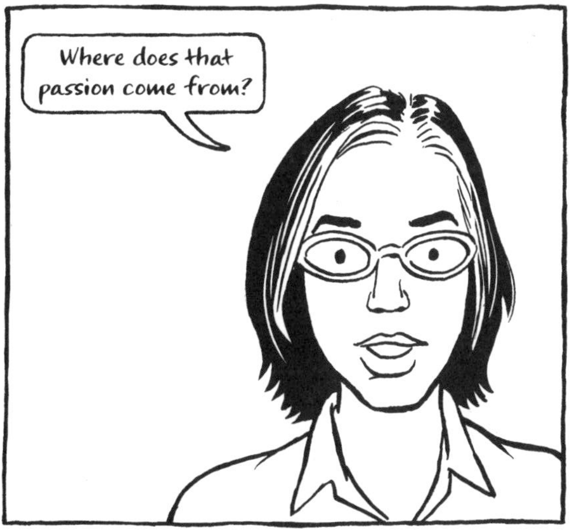
Where does that passion come from?

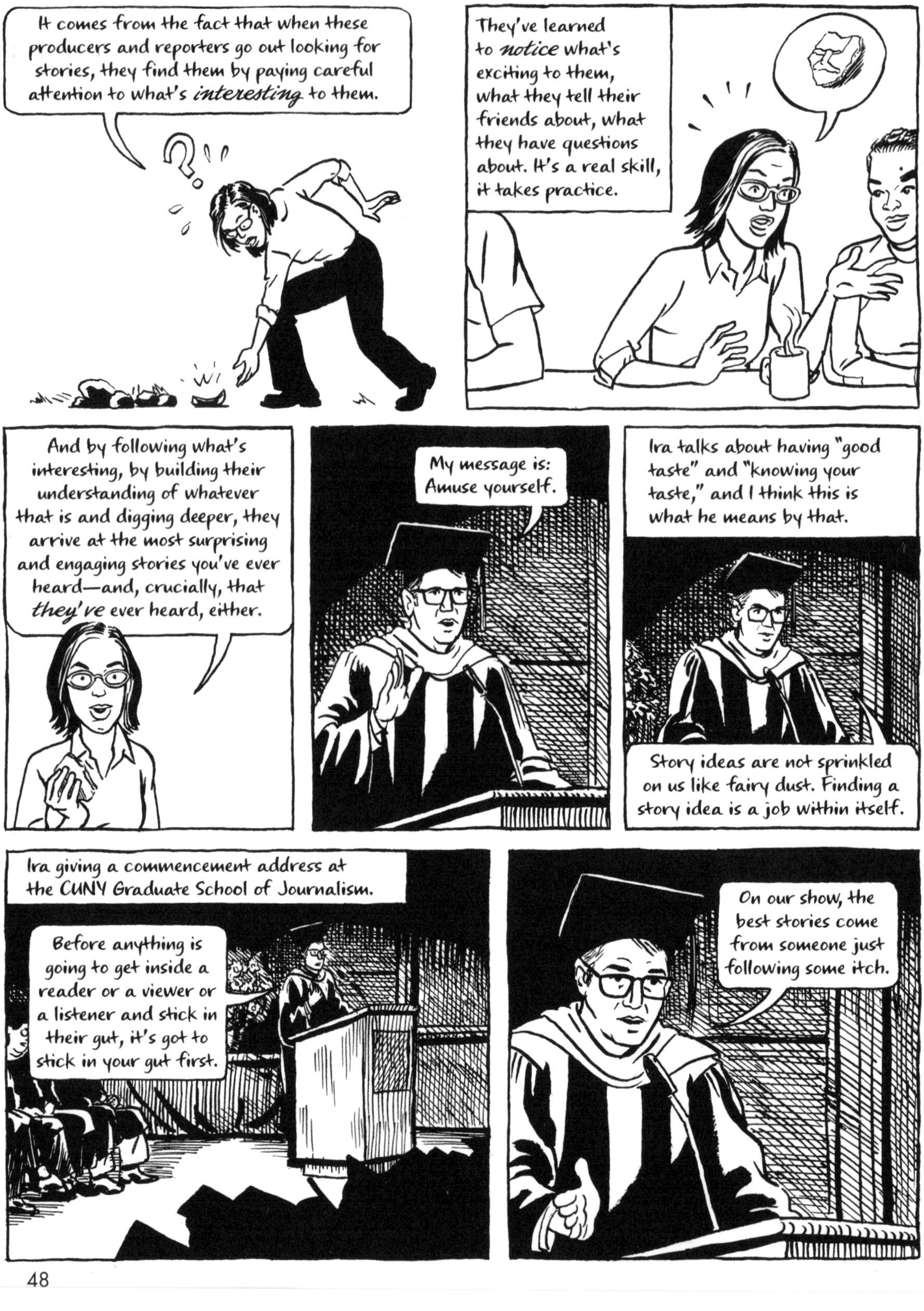
It comes from the fact that when these producers and reporters go out looking for stories, they find them by paying careful attention to what's *interesting* to them.
They've learned to *notice* what's exciting to them, what they tell their friends about, what they have questions about. It's a real skill, it takes practice.
And by following what's interesting, by building their understanding of whatever that is and digging deeper, they arrive at the most surprising and engaging stories you've ever heard—and, crucially, that *they've* ever heard, either.
My message is: Amuse yourself.
Ira talks about having "good taste" and "knowing your taste," and I think this is what he means by that.
Story ideas are not sprinkled on us like fairy dust. Finding a story idea is a job within itself.
Ira giving a commencement address at the CUNY Graduate School of Journalism.
Before anything is going to get inside a reader or a viewer or a listener and stick in their gut, it's got to stick in your gut first.
On our show, the best stories come from someone just following some itch.

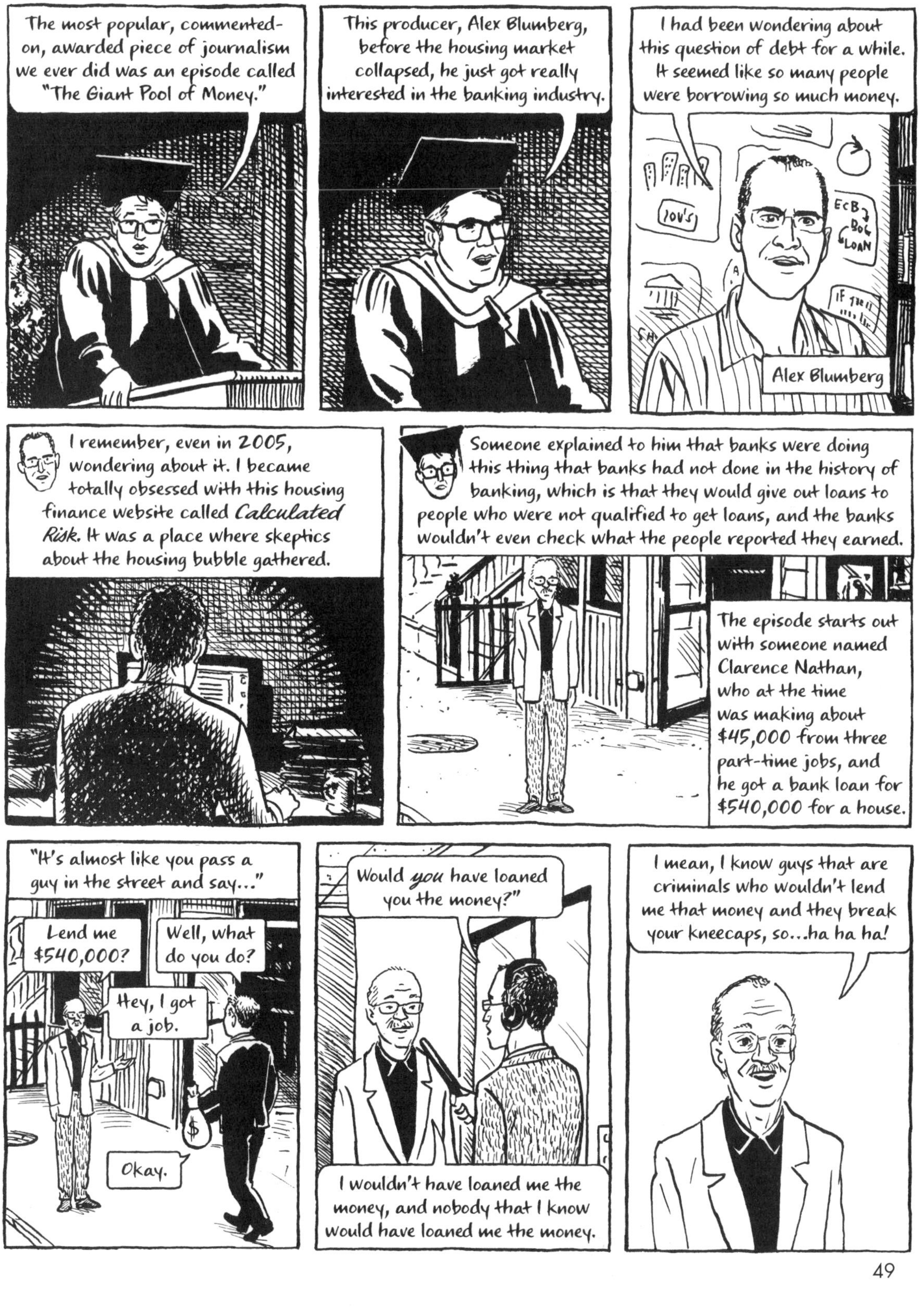
The most popular, commented-on, awarded piece of journalism we ever did was an episode called "The Giant Pool of Money."
This producer, Alex Blumberg, before the housing market collapsed, he just got really interested in the banking industry.
I had been wondering about this question of debt for a while. It seemed like so many people were borrowing so much money.
Alex Blumberg
I remember, even in 2005, wondering about it. I became totally obsessed with this housing finance website called *Calculated Risk*. It was a place where skeptics about the housing bubble gathered.
Someone explained to him that banks were doing this thing that banks had not done in the history of banking, which is that they would give out loans to people who were not qualified to get loans, and the banks wouldn't even check what the people reported they earned.
The episode starts out with someone named Clarence Nathan, who at the time was making about $45,000 from three part-time jobs, and he got a bank loan for $540,000 for a house.
"It's almost like you pass a guy in the street and say..."
Lend me $540,000?
Well, what do you do?
Hey, I got a job.
Okay.
Would *you* have loaned you the money?"
I wouldn't have loaned me the money, and nobody that I know would have loaned me the money.
I mean, I know guys that are criminals who wouldn't lend me that money and they break your kneecaps, so...ha ha ha!

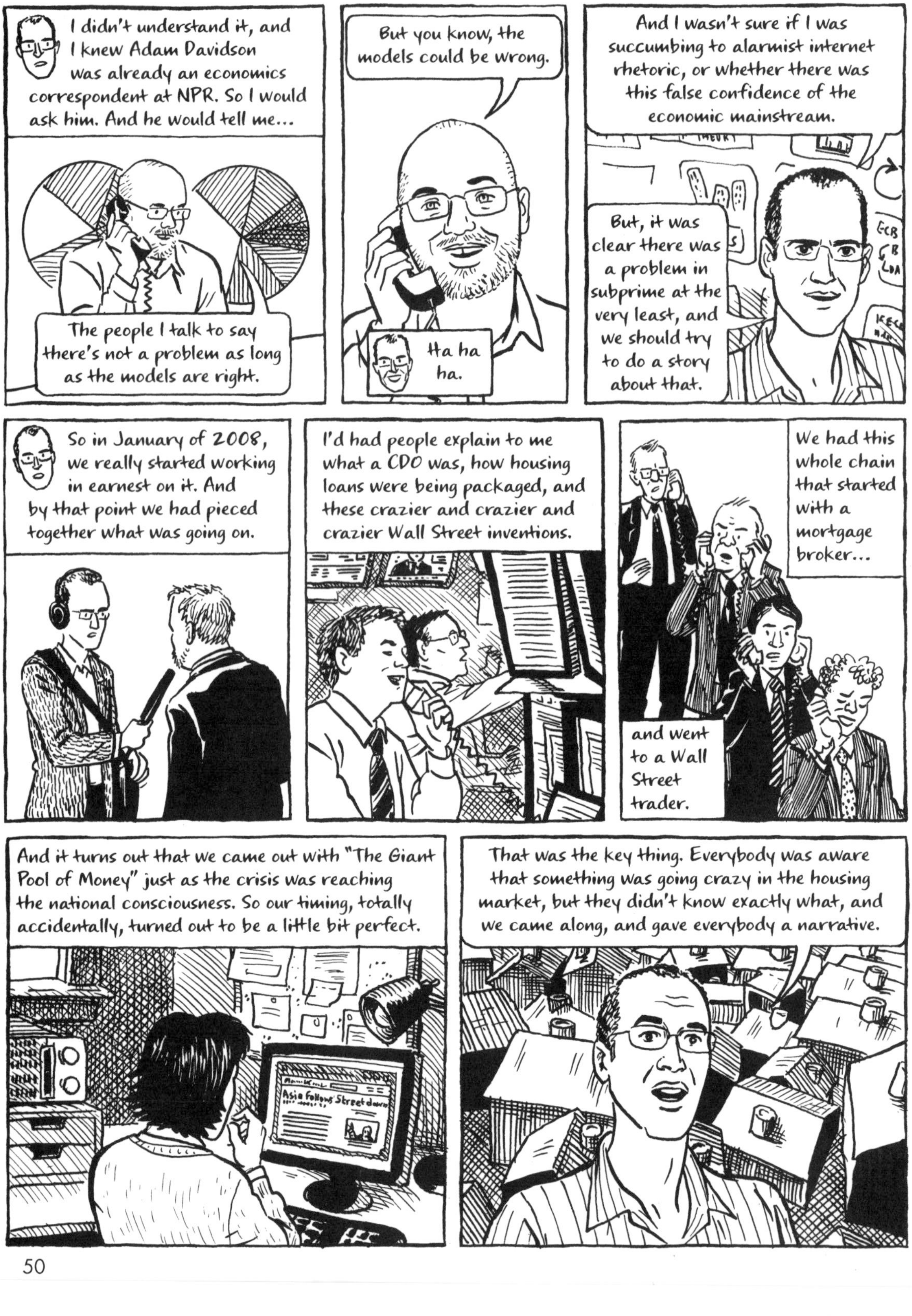
I didn't understand it, and I knew Adam Davidson was already an economics correspondent at NPR. So I would ask him. And he would tell me...
The people I talk to say there's not a problem as long as the models are right.
But you know, the models could be wrong.
Ha ha ha.
And I wasn't sure if I was succumbing to alarmist internet rhetoric, or whether there was this false confidence of the economic mainstream.
But, it was clear there was a problem in subprime at the very least, and we should try to do a story about that.
So in January of 2008, we really started working in earnest on it. And by that point we had pieced together what was going on.
I'd had people explain to me what a CDO was, how housing loans were being packaged, and these crazier and crazier and crazier Wall Street inventions.
We had this whole chain that started with a mortgage broker...
and went to a Wall Street trader.
And it turns out that we came out with "The Giant Pool of Money" just as the crisis was reaching the national consciousness. So our timing, totally accidentally, turned out to be a little bit perfect.
That was the key thing. Everybody was aware that something was going crazy in the housing market, but they didn't know exactly what, and we came along, and gave everybody a narrative.

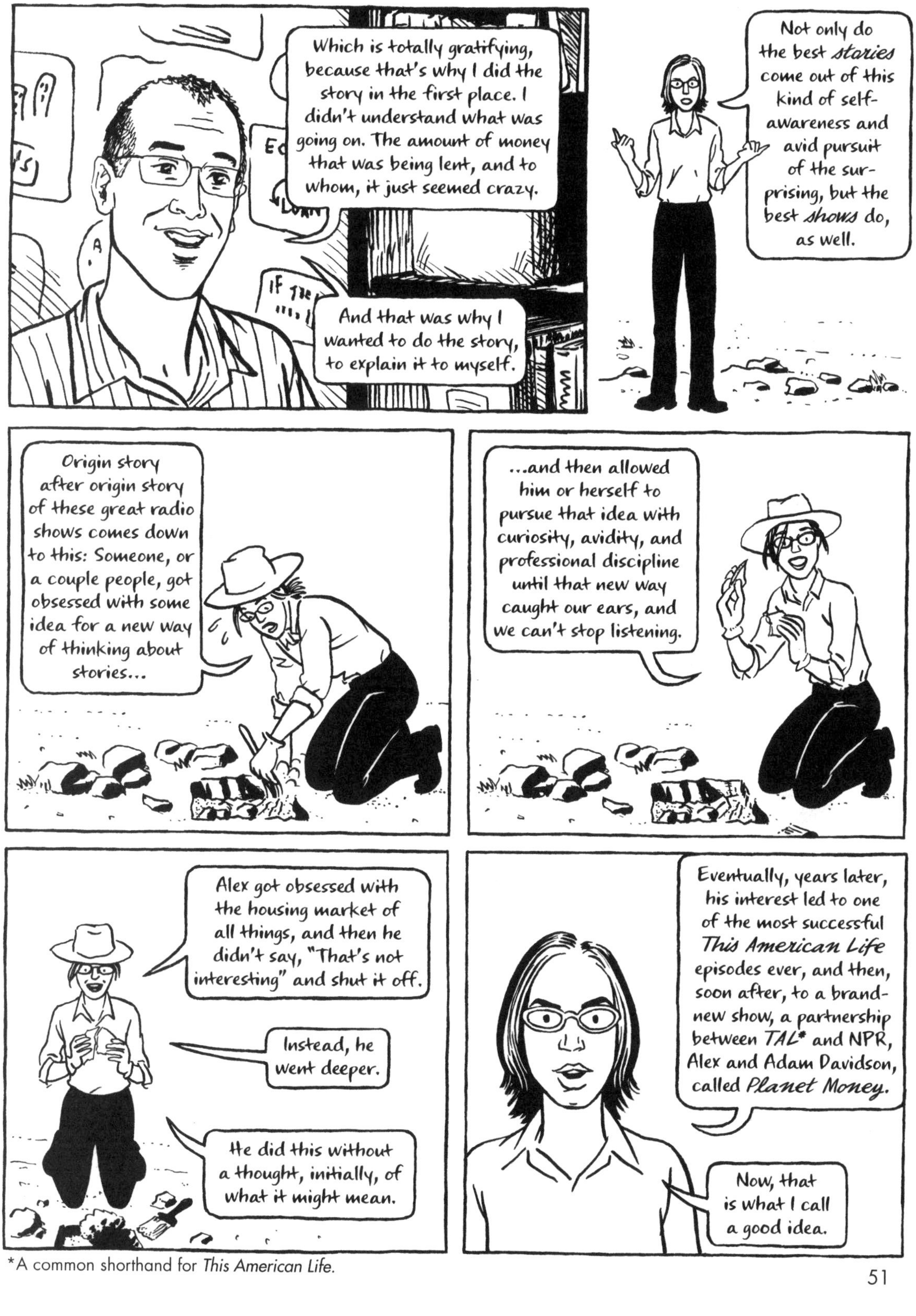
Which is totally gratifying, because that's why I did the story in the first place. I didn't understand what was going on. The amount of money that was being lent, and to whom, it just seemed crazy.
And that was why I wanted to do the story, to explain it to myself.
Not only do the best *stories* come out of this kind of self-awareness and avid pursuit of the surprising, but the best *shows* do, as well.
Origin story after origin story of these great radio shows comes down to this: Someone, or a couple people, got obsessed with some idea for a new way of thinking about stories...
...and then allowed him or herself to pursue that idea with curiosity, avidity, and professional discipline until that new way caught our ears, and we can't stop listening.
Alex got obsessed with the housing market of all things, and then he didn't say, "That's not interesting" and shut it off.
Instead, he went deeper.
He did this without a thought, initially, of what it might mean.
Eventually, years later, his interest led to one of the most successful *This American Life* episodes ever, and then, soon after, to a brand-new show, a partnership between *TAL** and NPR, Alex and Adam Davidson, called *Planet Money*.
Now, that is what I call a good idea.

*A common shorthand for *This American Life*.

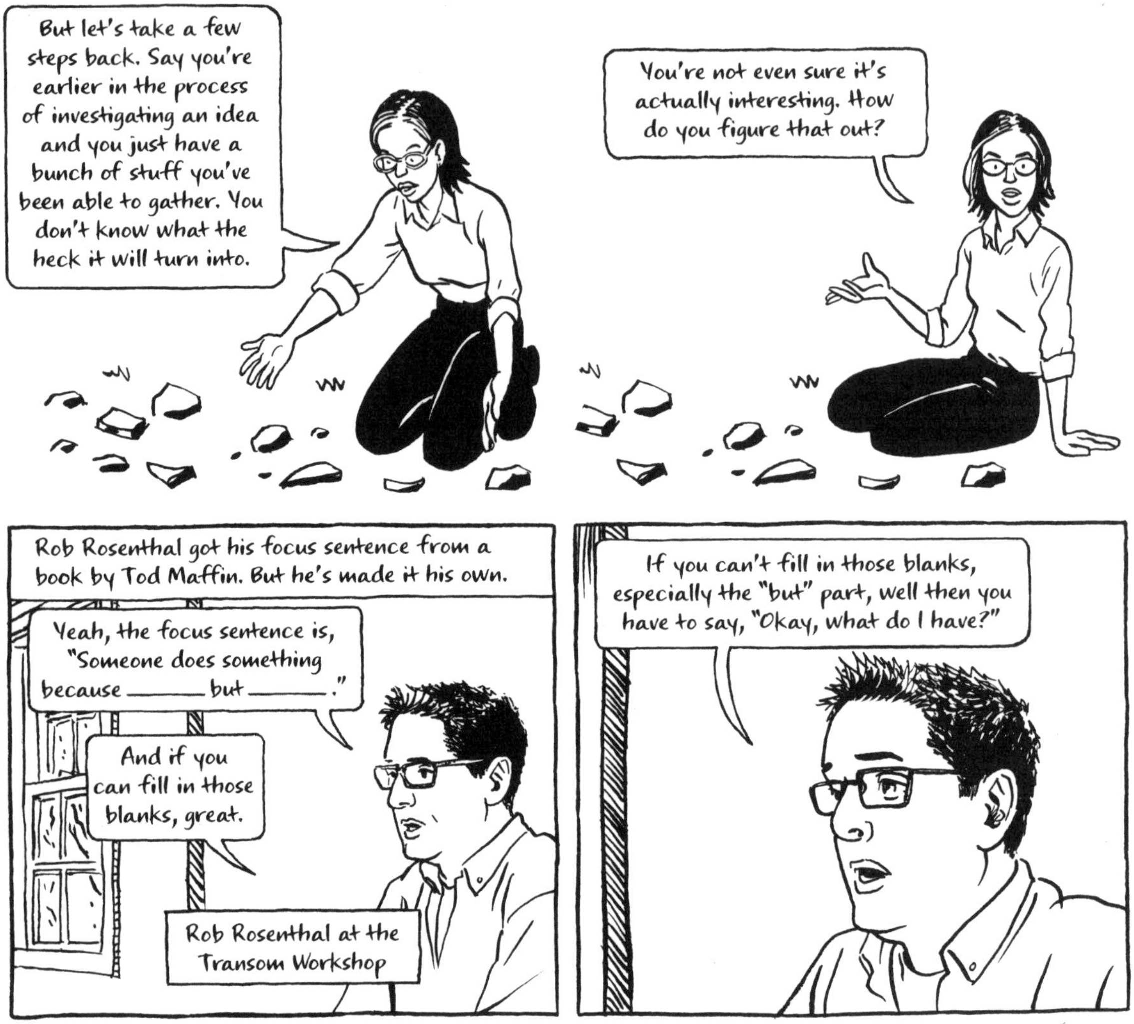
But let's take a few steps back. Say you're earlier in the process of investigating an idea and you just have a bunch of stuff you've been able to gather. You don't know what the heck it will turn into.
You're not even sure it's actually interesting. How do you figure that out?
Rob Rosenthal got his focus sentence from a book by Tod Maffin. But he's made it his own.
Yeah, the focus sentence is, "Someone does something because _____ but _____."
And if you can fill in those blanks, great.
Rob Rosenthal at the Transom Workshop
If you can't fill in those blanks, especially the "but" part, well then you have to say, "Okay, what do I have?"

The focus sentence:

A character in motion. Doing something.

Somebody does something

because_______________

A motivation for doing that thing.

but _______________.

A challenge to overcome.

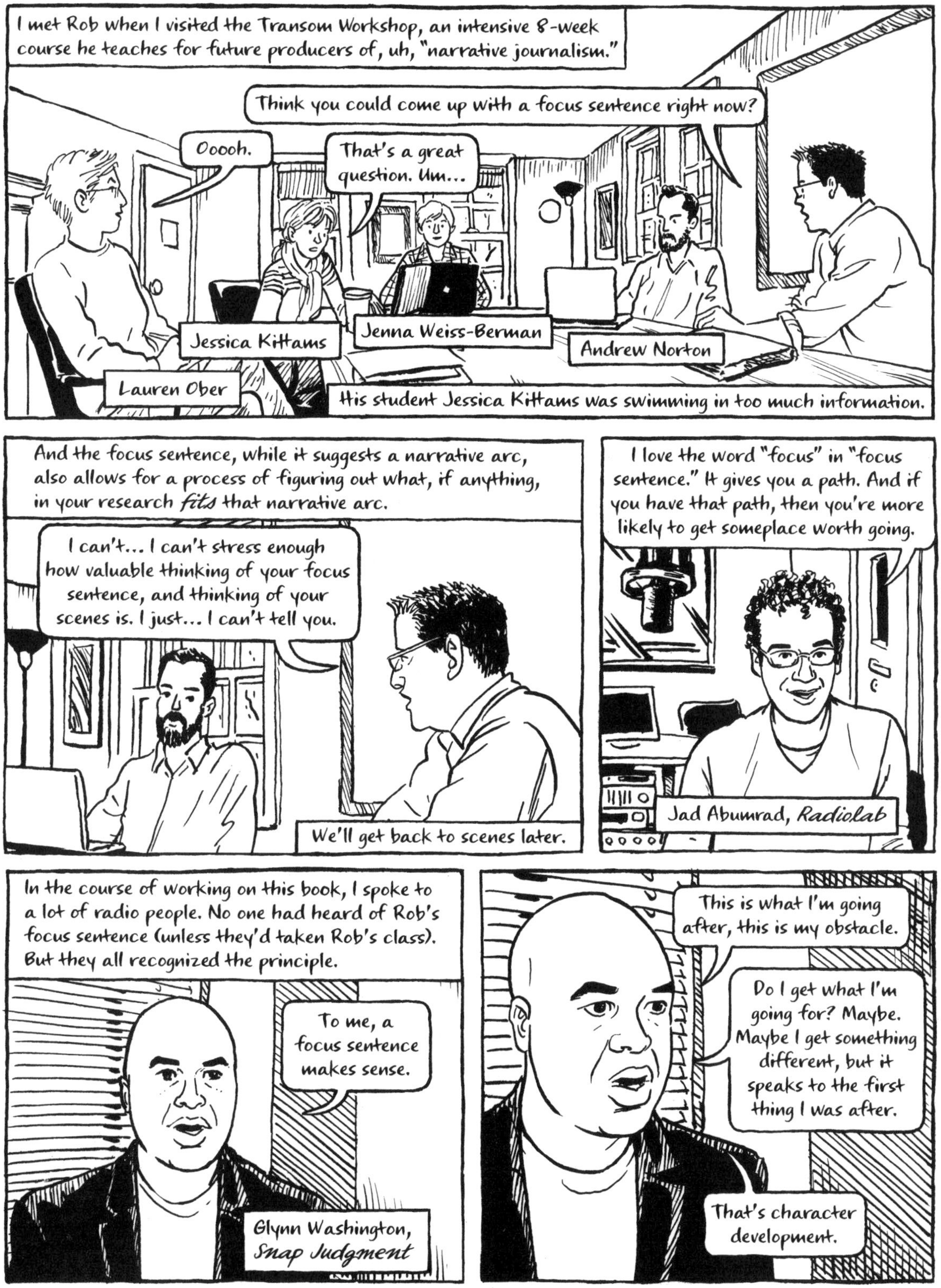
I met Rob when I visited the Transom Workshop, an intensive 8-week course he teaches for future producers of, uh, "narrative journalism."
Think you could come up with a focus sentence right now?
Ooooh.
That's a great question. Um...
Jessica Kittams
Jenna Weiss-Berman
Andrew Norton
Lauren Ober
His student Jessica Kittams was swimming in too much information.
And the focus sentence, while it suggests a narrative arc, also allows for a process of figuring out what, if anything, in your research *fits* that narrative arc.
I can't... I can't stress enough how valuable thinking of your focus sentence, and thinking of your scenes is. I just... I can't tell you.
We'll get back to scenes later.
I love the word "focus" in "focus sentence." It gives you a path. And if you have that path, then you're more likely to get someplace worth going.
Jad Abumrad, *Radiolab*
In the course of working on this book, I spoke to a lot of radio people. No one had heard of Rob's focus sentence (unless they'd taken Rob's class). But they all recognized the principle.
To me, a focus sentence makes sense.
Glynn Washington, *Snap Judgment*
This is what I'm going after, this is my obstacle.
Do I get what I'm going for? Maybe. Maybe I get something different, but it speaks to the first thing I was after.
That's character development.

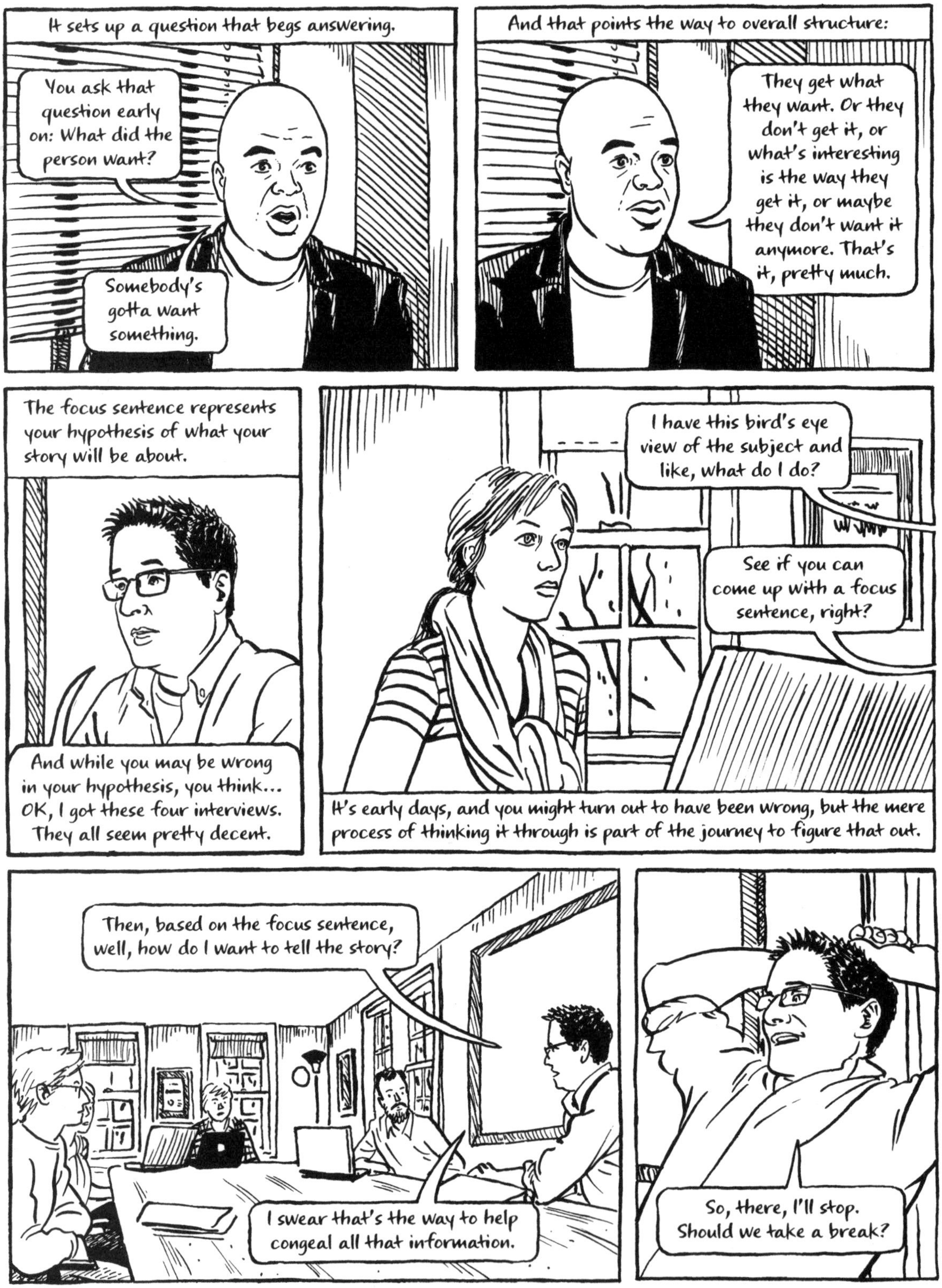
It sets up a question that begs answering.
You ask that question early on: What did the person want?
Somebody's gotta want something.
And that points the way to overall structure:
They get what they want. Or they don't get it, or what's interesting is the way they get it, or maybe they don't want it anymore. That's it, pretty much.
The focus sentence represents your hypothesis of what your story will be about.
And while you may be wrong in your hypothesis, you think... OK, I got these four interviews. They all seem pretty decent.
I have this bird's eye view of the subject and like, what do I do?
See if you can come up with a focus sentence, right?
It's early days, and you might turn out to have been wrong, but the mere process of thinking it through is part of the journey to figure that out.
Then, based on the focus sentence, well, how do I want to tell the story?
I swear that's the way to help congeal all that information.
So, there, I'll stop. Should we take a break?

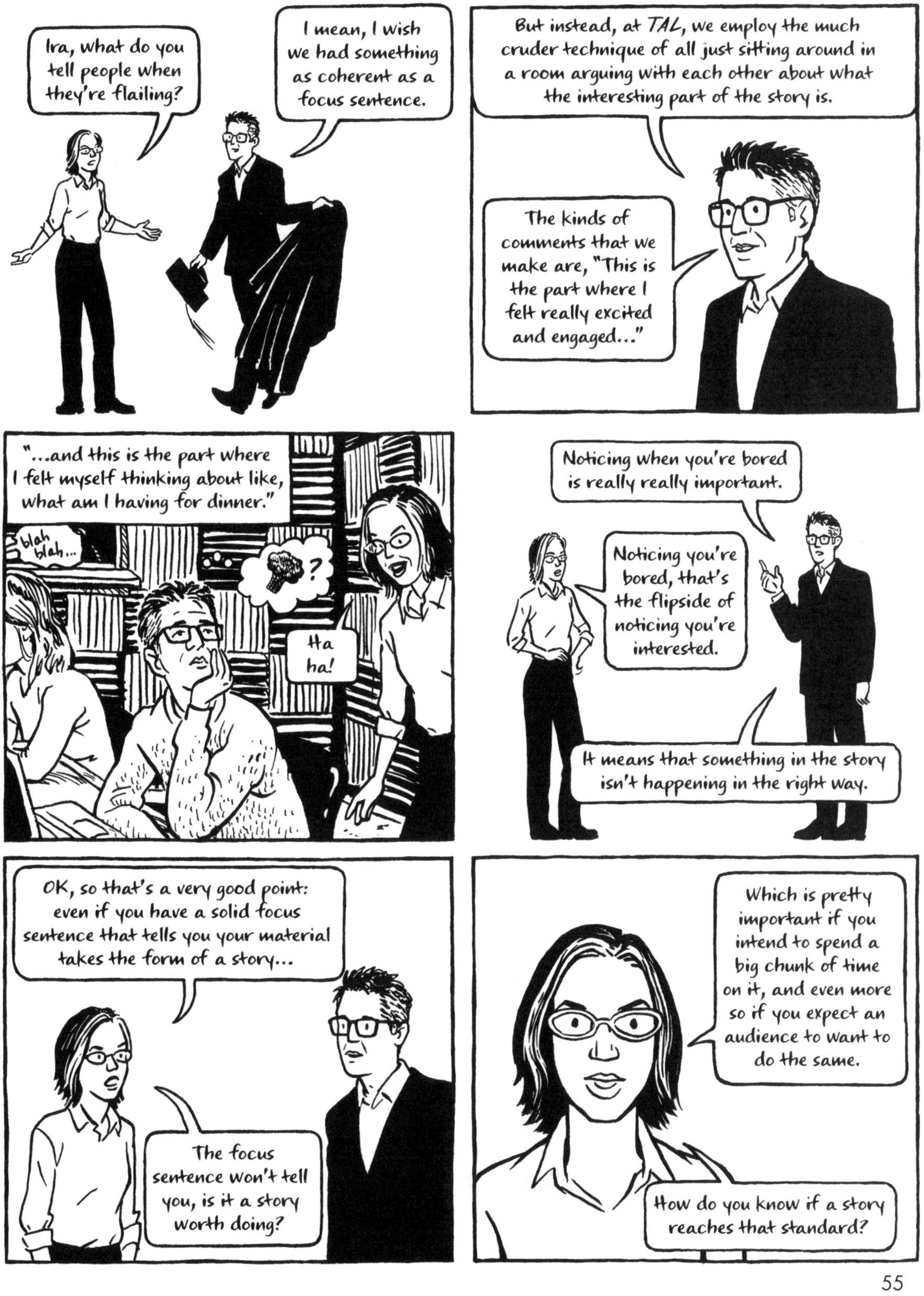
Ira, what do you tell people when they're flailing?
I mean, I wish we had something as coherent as a focus sentence.
But instead, at TAL, we employ the much cruder technique of all just sitting around in a room arguing with each other about what the interesting part of the story is.
The kinds of comments that we make are, "This is the part where I felt really excited and engaged..."
"...and this is the part where I felt myself thinking about like, what am I having for dinner."
blah blah...
?
Ha ha!
Noticing when you're bored is really really important.
Noticing you're bored, that's the flipside of noticing you're interested.
It means that something in the story isn't happening in the right way.
OK, so that's a very good point: even if you have a solid focus sentence that tells you your material takes the form of a story...
The focus sentence won't tell you, is it a story worth doing?
Which is pretty important if you intend to spend a big chunk of time on it, and even more so if you expect an audience to want to do the same.
How do you know if a story reaches that standard?

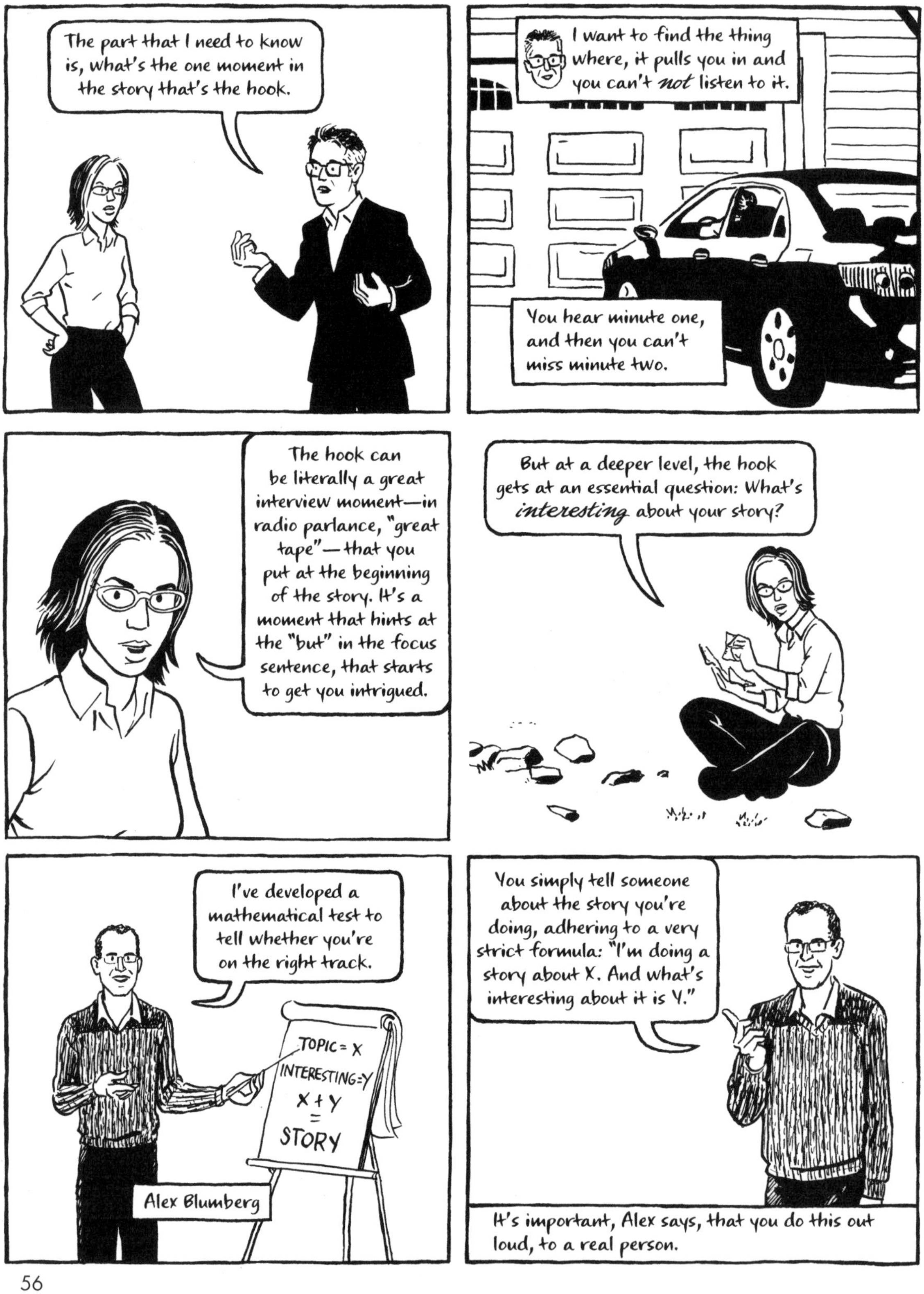
The part that I need to know is, what's the one moment in the story that's the hook.
I want to find the thing where, it pulls you in and you can't *not* listen to it.
You hear minute one, and then you can't miss minute two.
The hook can be literally a great interview moment—in radio parlance, "great tape"—that you put at the beginning of the story. It's a moment that hints at the "but" in the focus sentence, that starts to get you intrigued.
But at a deeper level, the hook gets at an essential question: What's *interesting* about your story?
I've developed a mathematical test to tell whether you're on the right track.
TOPIC = X
INTERESTING = Y
X + Y = STORY
Alex Blumberg
You simply tell someone about the story you're doing, adhering to a very strict formula: "I'm doing a story about X. And what's interesting about it is Y."
It's important, Alex says, that you do this out loud, to a real person.

I'm doing a story about X. ⇐ Topic
And what's interesting about it is Y. ⇐ Story

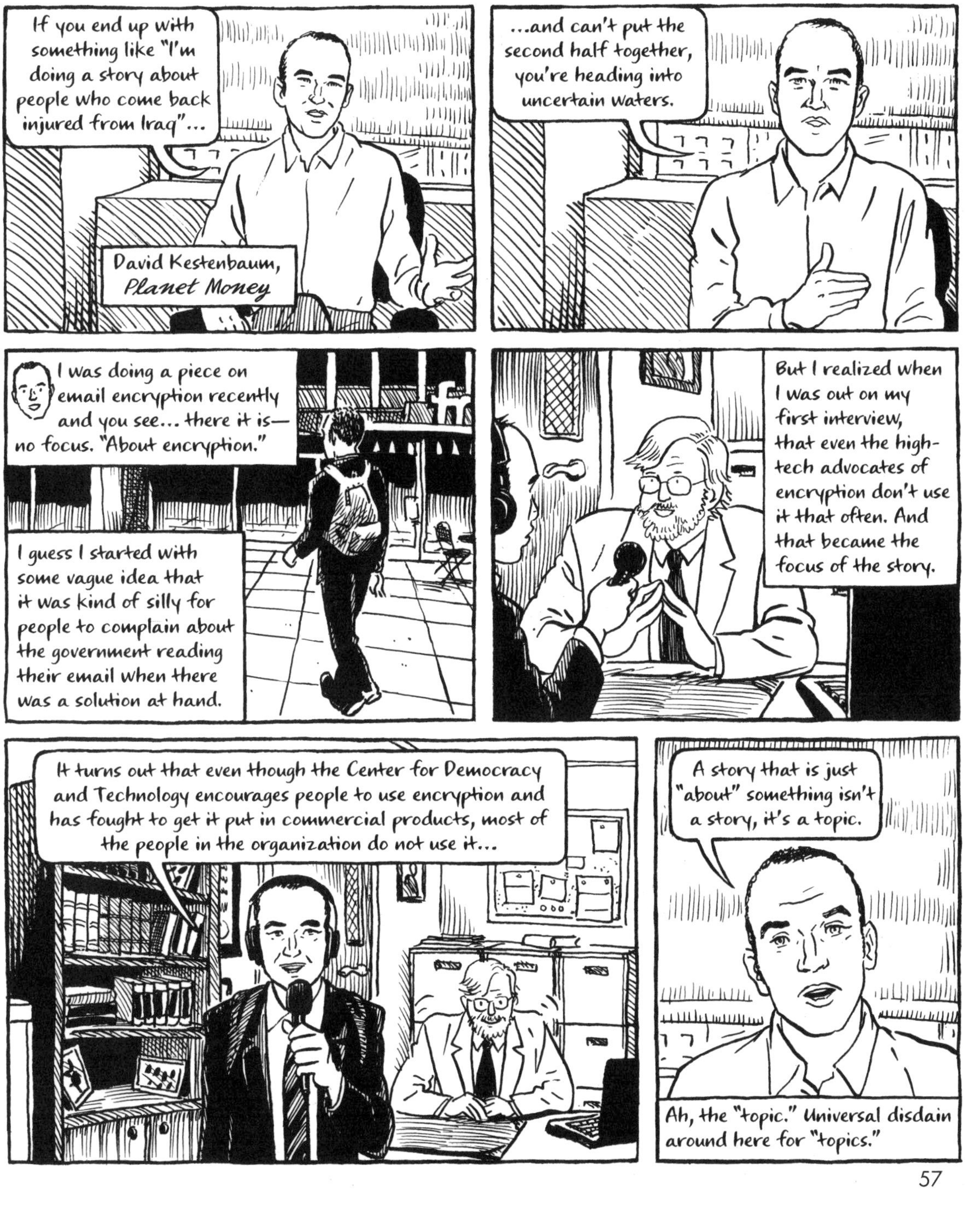
If you end up with something like "I'm doing a story about people who come back injured from Iraq"...
David Kestenbaum, *Planet Money*
...and can't put the second half together, you're heading into uncertain waters.
I was doing a piece on email encryption recently and you see... there it is— no focus. "About encryption."
I guess I started with some vague idea that it was kind of silly for people to complain about the government reading their email when there was a solution at hand.
But I realized when I was out on my first interview, that even the high-tech advocates of encryption don't use it that often. And that became the focus of the story.
It turns out that even though the Center for Democracy and Technology encourages people to use encryption and has fought to get it put in commercial products, most of the people in the organization do not use it...
A story that is just "about" something isn't a story, it's a topic.
Ah, the "topic." Universal disdain around here for "topics."

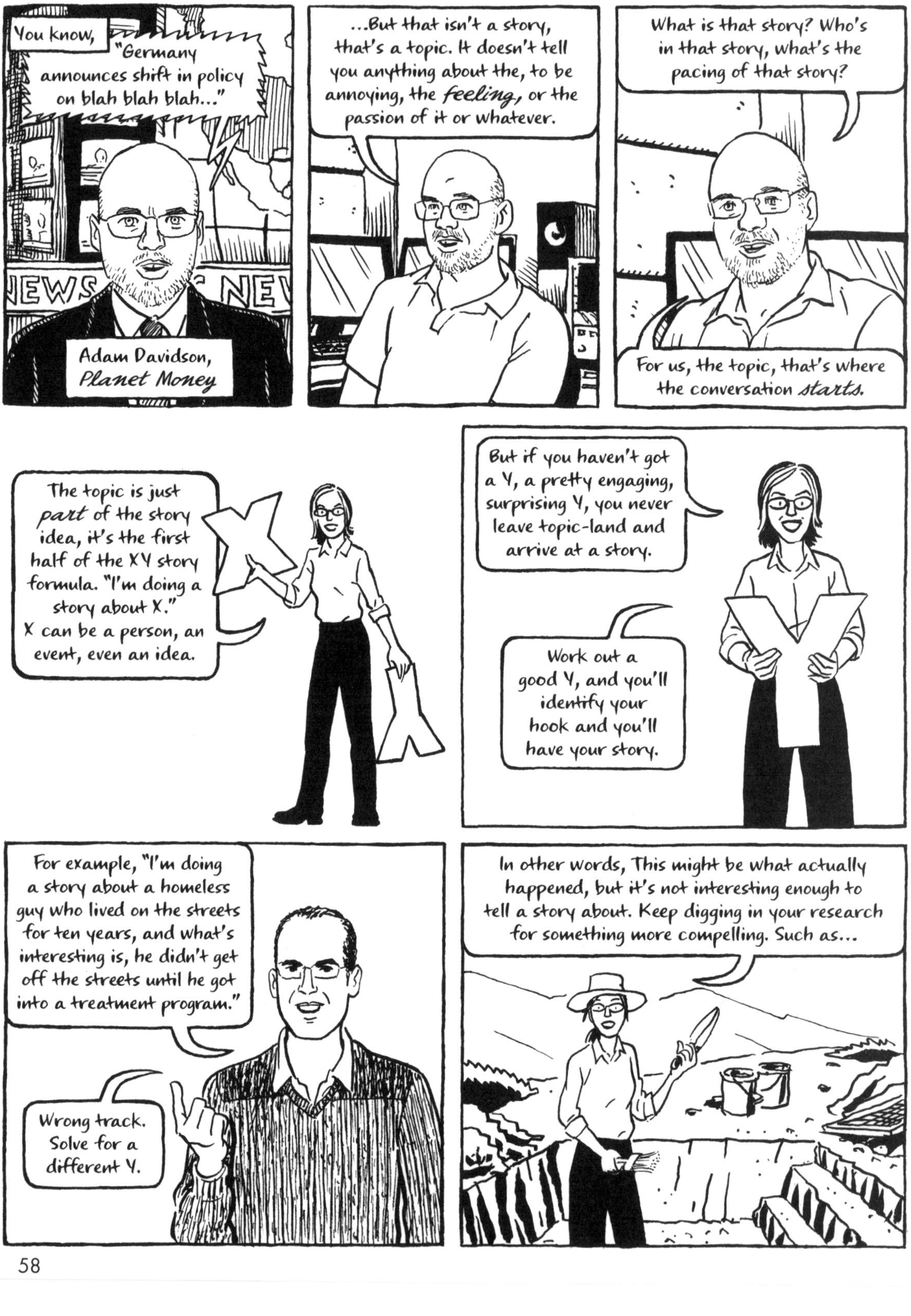
You know,
"Germany announces shift in policy on blah blah blah..."
Adam Davidson, *Planet Money*
...But that isn't a story, that's a topic. It doesn't tell you anything about the, to be annoying, the *feeling*, or the passion of it or whatever.
What is that story? Who's in that story, what's the pacing of that story?
For us, the topic, that's where the conversation *starts*.
The topic is just *part* of the story idea, it's the first half of the XY story formula. "I'm doing a story about X." X can be a person, an event, even an idea.
But if you haven't got a Y, a pretty engaging, surprising Y, you never leave topic-land and arrive at a story.
Work out a good Y, and you'll identify your hook and you'll have your story.
For example, "I'm doing a story about a homeless guy who lived on the streets for ten years, and what's interesting is, he didn't get off the streets until he got into a treatment program."
Wrong track. Solve for a different Y.
In other words, This might be what actually happened, but it's not interesting enough to tell a story about. Keep digging in your research for something more compelling. Such as...

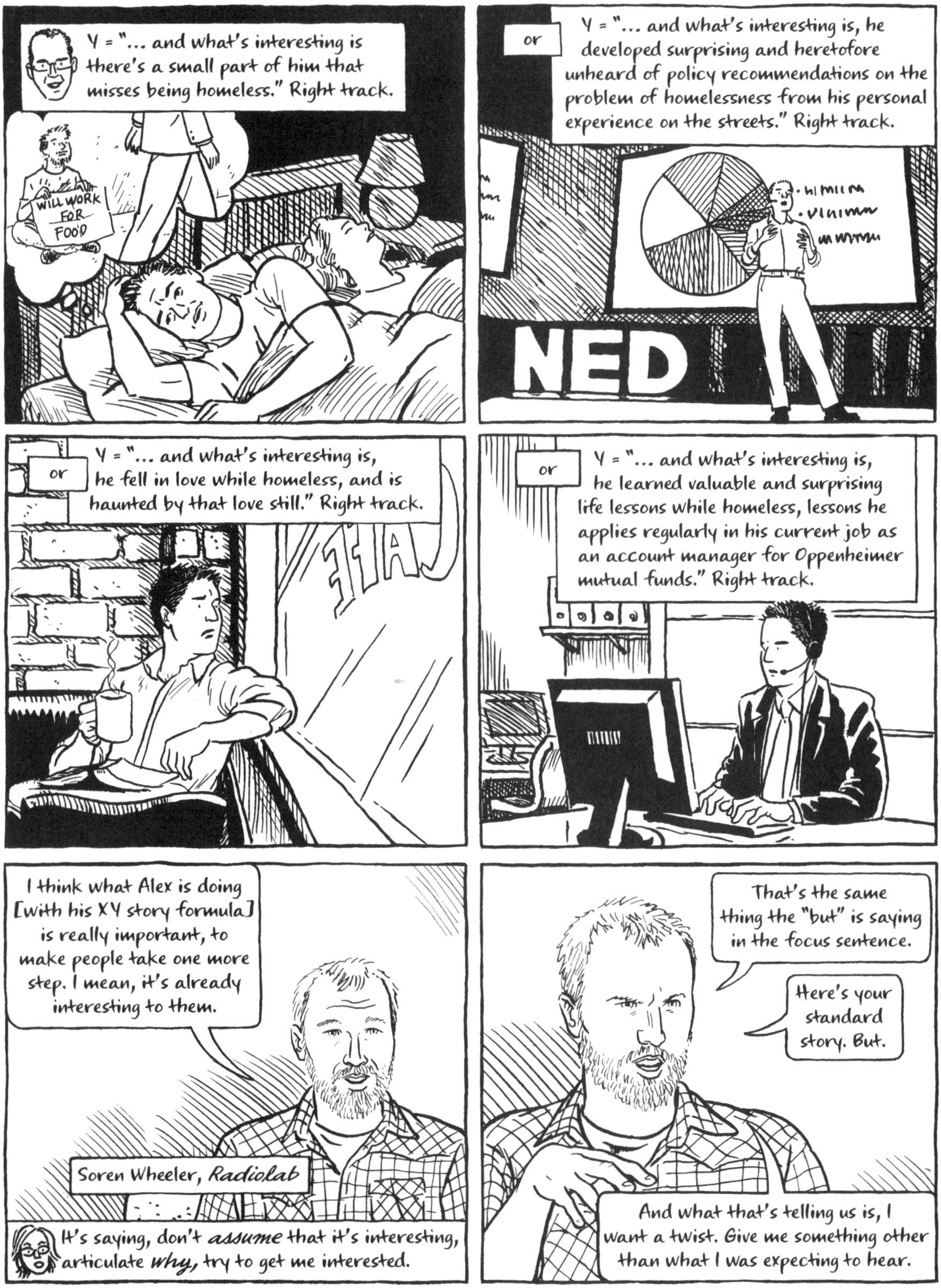
Y = "... and what's interesting is there's a small part of him that misses being homeless." Right track.
WILL WORK FOR FOOD
or
Y = "... and what's interesting is, he developed surprising and heretofore unheard of policy recommendations on the problem of homelessness from his personal experience on the streets." Right track.
NED
or
Y = "... and what's interesting is, he fell in love while homeless, and is haunted by that love still." Right track.
or
Y = "... and what's interesting is, he learned valuable and surprising life lessons while homeless, lessons he applies regularly in his current job as an account manager for Oppenheimer mutual funds." Right track.
I think what Alex is doing [with his XY story formula] is really important, to make people take one more step. I mean, it's already interesting to them.
Soren Wheeler, *Radiolab*
It's saying, don't *assume* that it's interesting, articulate *why*, try to get me interested.
That's the same thing the "but" is saying in the focus sentence.
Here's your standard story. But.
And what that's telling us is, I want a twist. Give me something other than what I was expecting to hear.

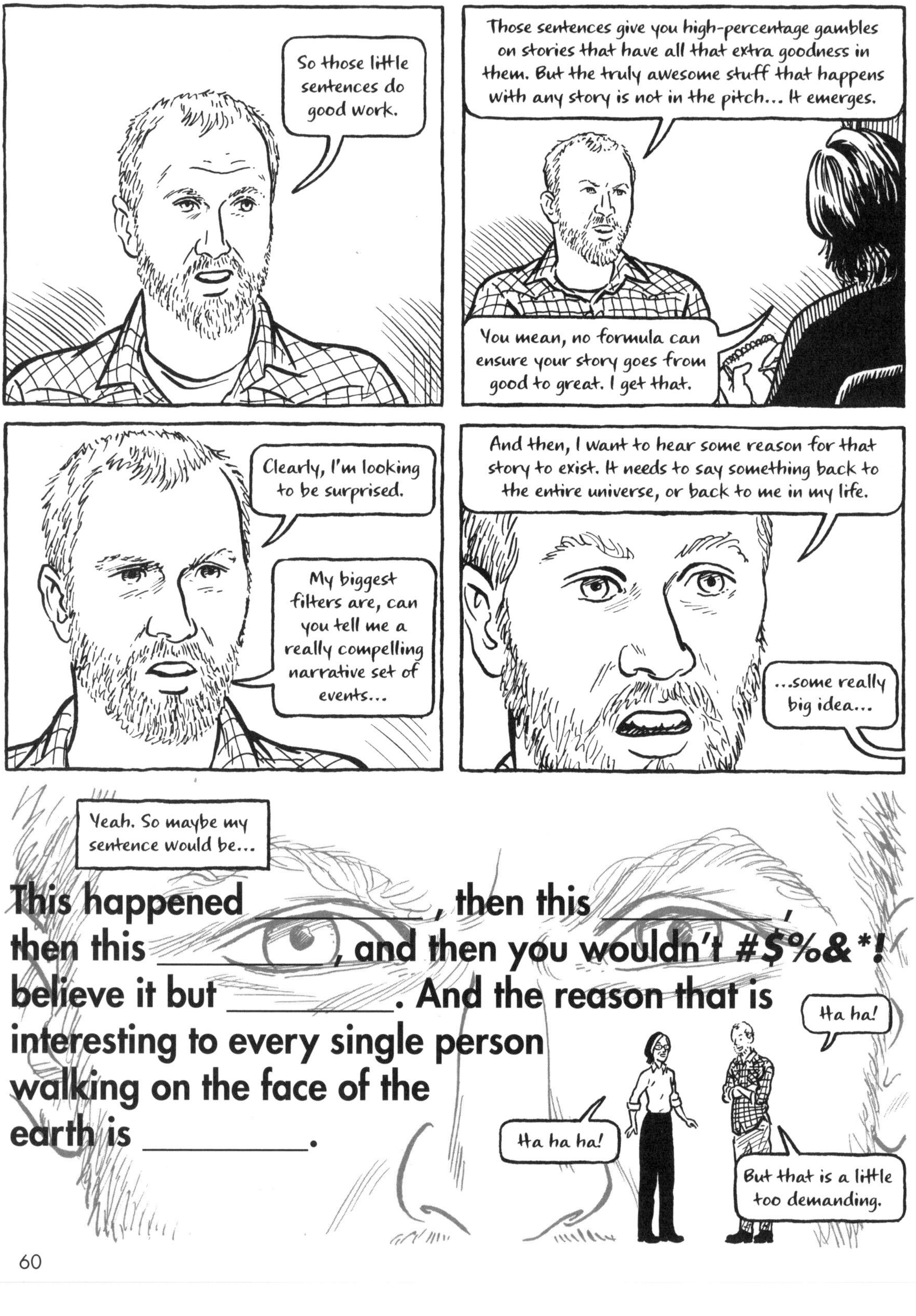

So those little sentences do good work.
Those sentences give you high-percentage gambles on stories that have all that extra goodness in them. But the truly awesome stuff that happens with any story is not in the pitch... It emerges.
You mean, no formula can ensure your story goes from good to great. I get that.
Clearly, I'm looking to be surprised.
My biggest filters are, can you tell me a really compelling narrative set of events...
And then, I want to hear some reason for that story to exist. It needs to say something back to the entire universe, or back to me in my life.
...some really big idea...
Yeah. So maybe my sentence would be...
This happened ________, then this ________, then this ________, and then you wouldn't #$%&*! believe it but ________. And the reason that is interesting to every single person walking on the face of the earth is ________.
Ha ha!
Ha ha ha!
But that is a little too demanding.

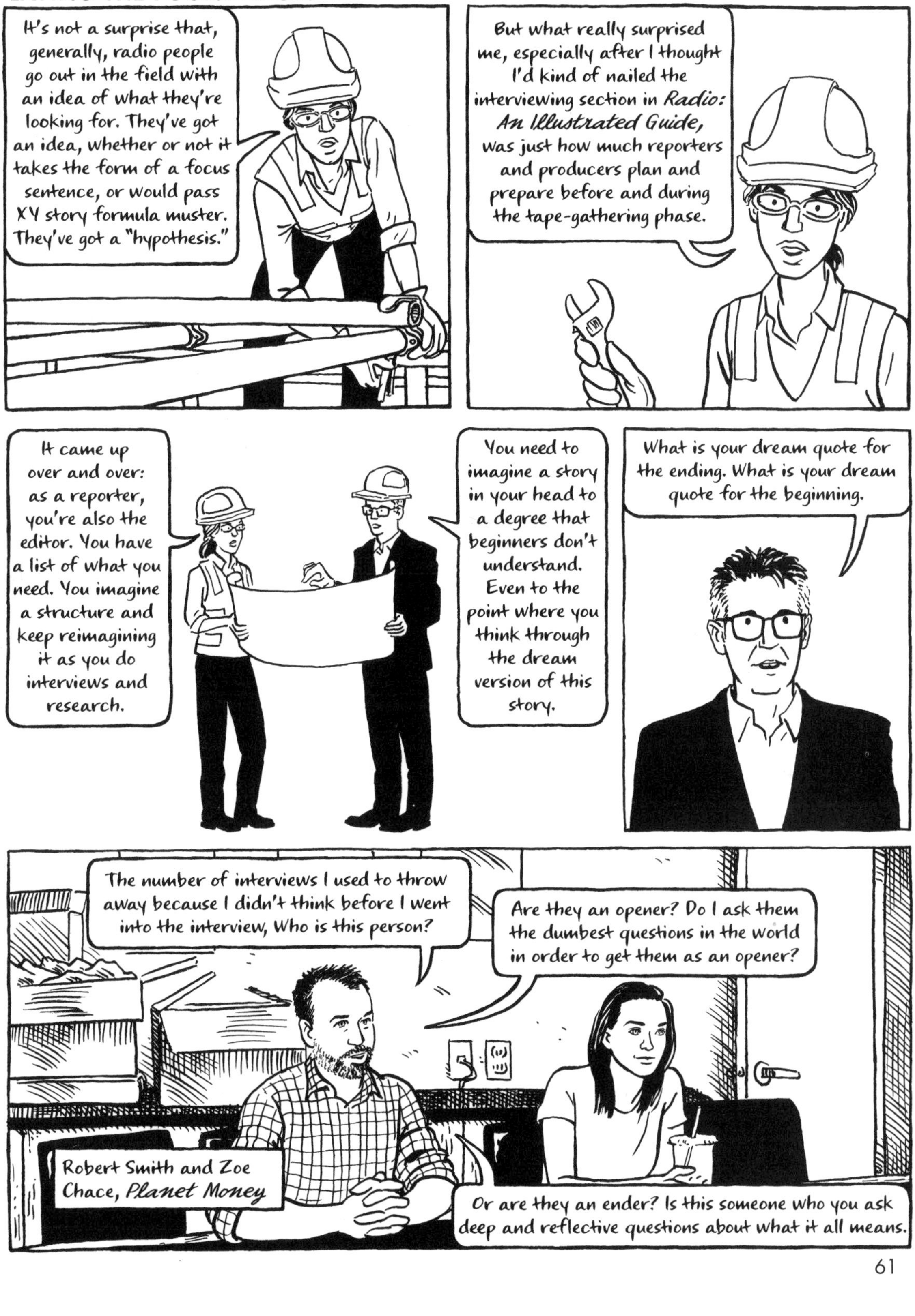
It's not a surprise that, generally, radio people go out in the field with an idea of what they're looking for. They've got an idea, whether or not it takes the form of a focus sentence, or would pass XY story formula muster. They've got a "hypothesis."
But what really surprised me, especially after I thought I'd kind of nailed the interviewing section in *Radio: An Illustrated Guide,* was just how much reporters and producers plan and prepare before and during the tape-gathering phase.
It came up over and over: as a reporter, you're also the editor. You have a list of what you need. You imagine a structure and keep reimagining it as you do interviews and research.
You need to imagine a story in your head to a degree that beginners don't understand. Even to the point where you think through the dream version of this story.
What is your dream quote for the ending. What is your dream quote for the beginning.
The number of interviews I used to throw away because I didn't think before I went into the interview, Who is this person?
Are they an opener? Do I ask them the dumbest questions in the world in order to get them as an opener?
Robert Smith and Zoe Chace, *Planet Money*
Or are they an ender? Is this someone who you ask deep and reflective questions about what it all means.

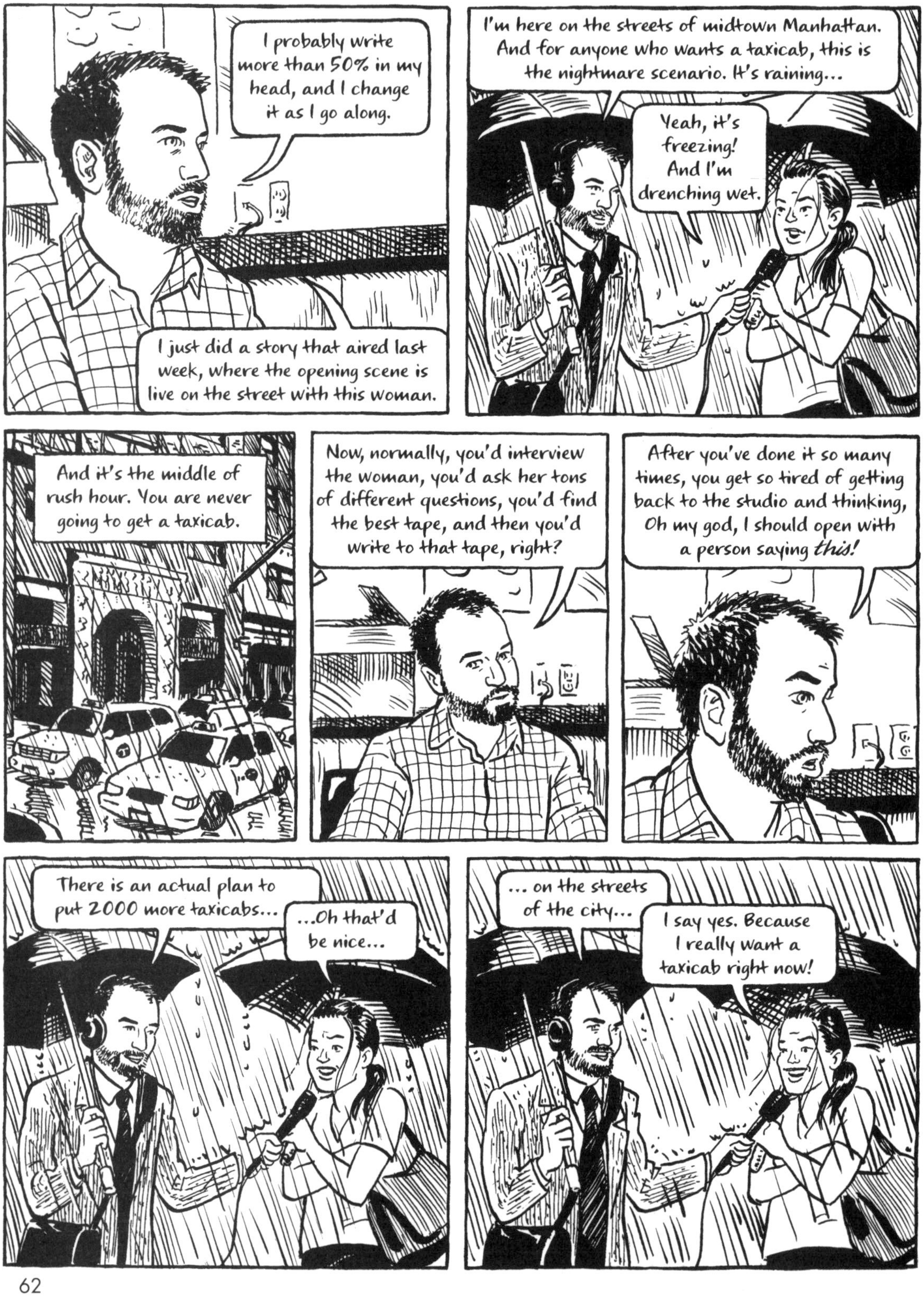
I probably write more than 50% in my head, and I change it as I go along.
I just did a story that aired last week, where the opening scene is live on the street with this woman.
I'm here on the streets of midtown Manhattan. And for anyone who wants a taxicab, this is the nightmare scenario. It's raining...
Yeah, it's freezing! And I'm drenching wet.
And it's the middle of rush hour. You are never going to get a taxicab.
Now, normally, you'd interview the woman, you'd ask her tons of different questions, you'd find the best tape, and then you'd write to that tape, right?
After you've done it so many times, you get so tired of getting back to the studio and thinking, Oh my god, I should open with a person saying *this!*
There is an actual plan to put 2000 more taxicabs...
...Oh that'd be nice...
... on the streets of the city...
I say yes. Because I really want a taxicab right now!

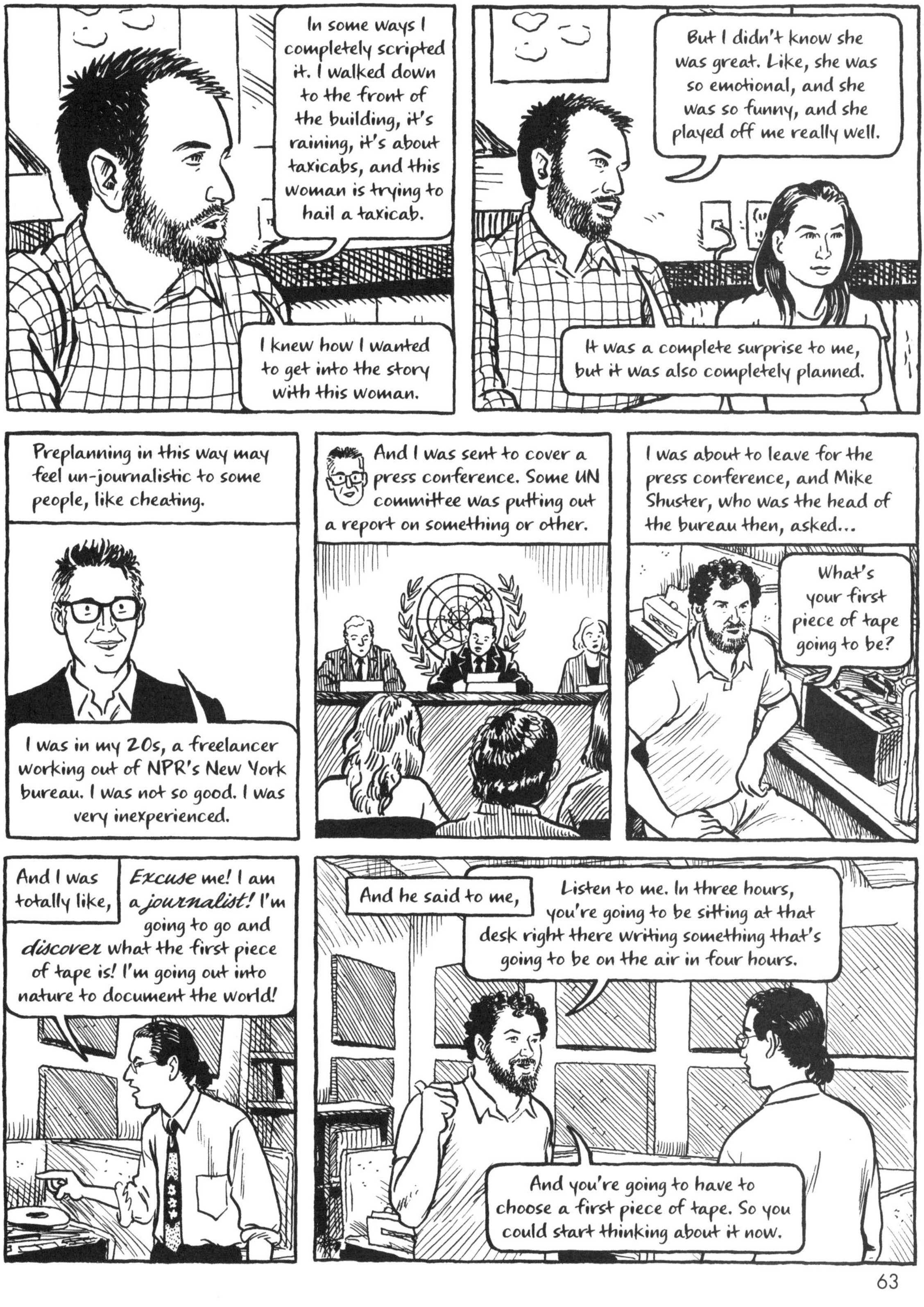

In some ways I completely scripted it. I walked down to the front of the building, it's raining, it's about taxicabs, and this woman is trying to hail a taxicab.
I knew how I wanted to get into the story with this woman.
But I didn't know she was great. Like, she was so emotional, and she was so funny, and she played off me really well.
It was a complete surprise to me, but it was also completely planned.
Preplanning in this way may feel un-journalistic to some people, like cheating.
I was in my 20s, a freelancer working out of NPR's New York bureau. I was not so good. I was very inexperienced.
And I was sent to cover a press conference. Some UN committee was putting out a report on something or other.
I was about to leave for the press conference, and Mike Shuster, who was the head of the bureau then, asked...
What's your first piece of tape going to be?
And I was totally like,
Excuse me! I am a *journalist!* I'm going to go and *discover* what the first piece of tape is! I'm going out into nature to document the world!
And he said to me,
Listen to me. In three hours, you're going to be sitting at that desk right there writing something that's going to be on the air in four hours.
And you're going to have to choose a first piece of tape. So you could start thinking about it now.

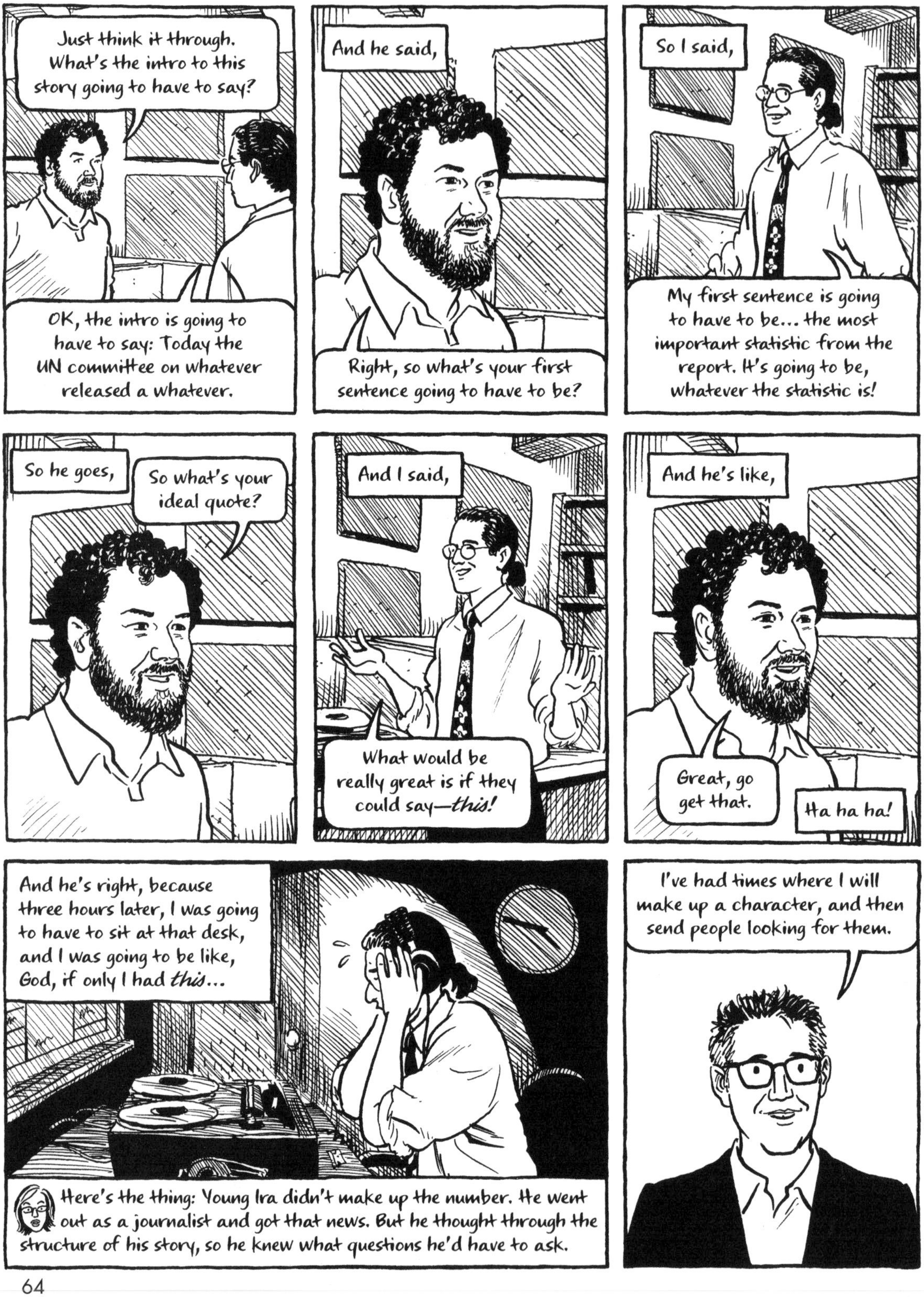
Just think it through. What's the intro to this story going to have to say?
OK, the intro is going to have to say: Today the UN committee on whatever released a whatever.
And he said,
Right, so what's your first sentence going to have to be?
So I said,
My first sentence is going to have to be... the most important statistic from the report. It's going to be, whatever the statistic is!
So he goes,
So what's your ideal quote?
And I said,
What would be really great is if they could say—*this!*
And he's like,
Great, go get that.
Ha ha ha!
And he's right, because three hours later, I was going to have to sit at that desk, and I was going to be like, God, if only I had *this*...
Here's the thing: Young Ira didn't make up the number. He went out as a journalist and got that news. But he thought through the structure of his story, so he knew what questions he'd have to ask.
I've had times where I will make up a character, and then send people looking for them.

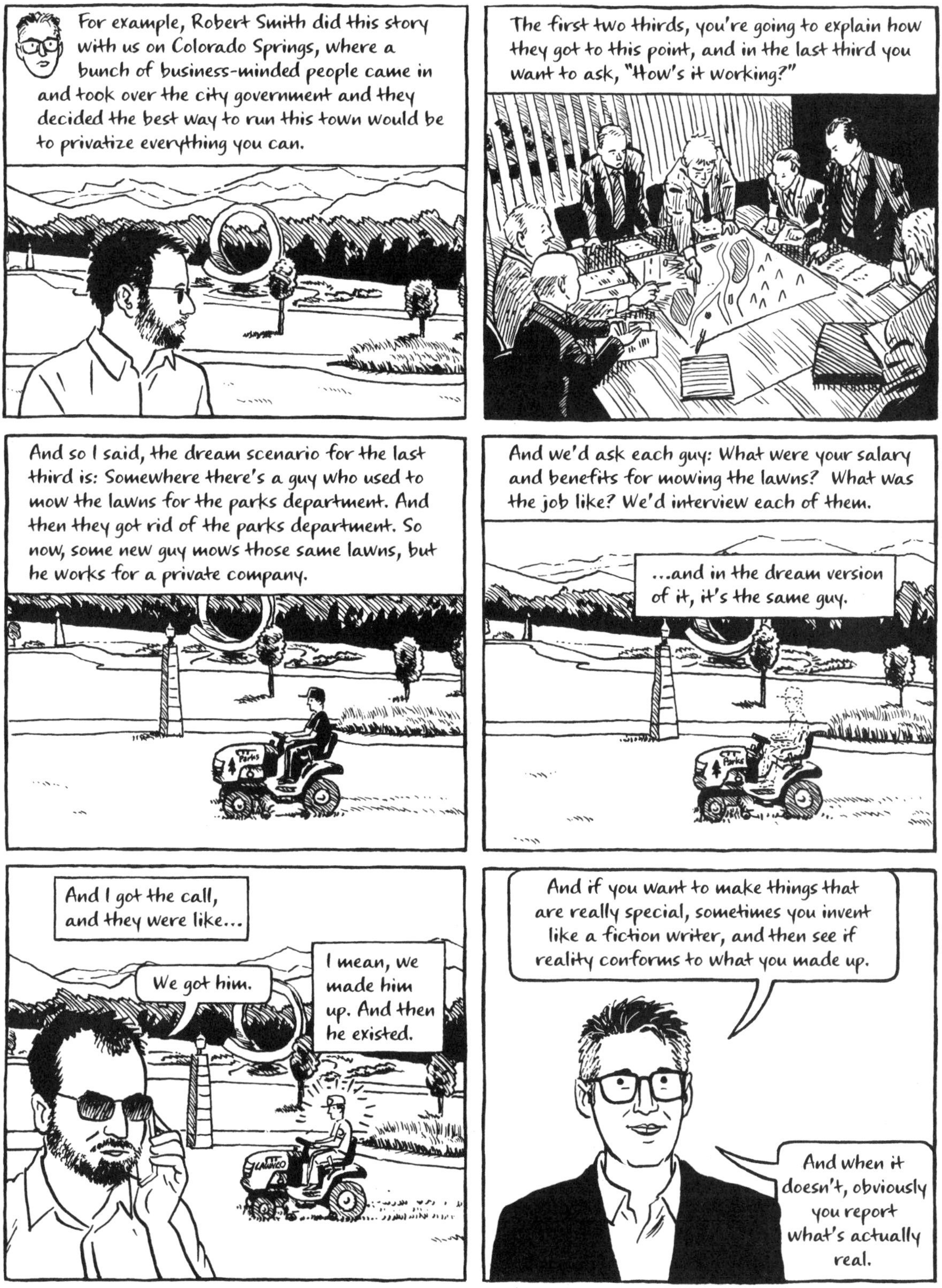
For example, Robert Smith did this story with us on Colorado Springs, where a bunch of business-minded people came in and took over the city government and they decided the best way to run this town would be to privatize everything you can.
The first two thirds, you're going to explain how they got to this point, and in the last third you want to ask, "How's it working?"
And so I said, the dream scenario for the last third is: Somewhere there's a guy who used to mow the lawns for the parks department. And then they got rid of the parks department. So now, some new guy mows those same lawns, but he works for a private company.
Parks
And we'd ask each guy: What were your salary and benefits for mowing the lawns? What was the job like? We'd interview each of them.
...and in the dream version of it, it's the same guy.
Parks
And I got the call, and they were like...
We got him.
I mean, we made him up. And then he existed.
LAWNCO
And if you want to make things that are really special, sometimes you invent like a fiction writer, and then see if reality conforms to what you made up.
And when it doesn't, obviously you report what's actually real.

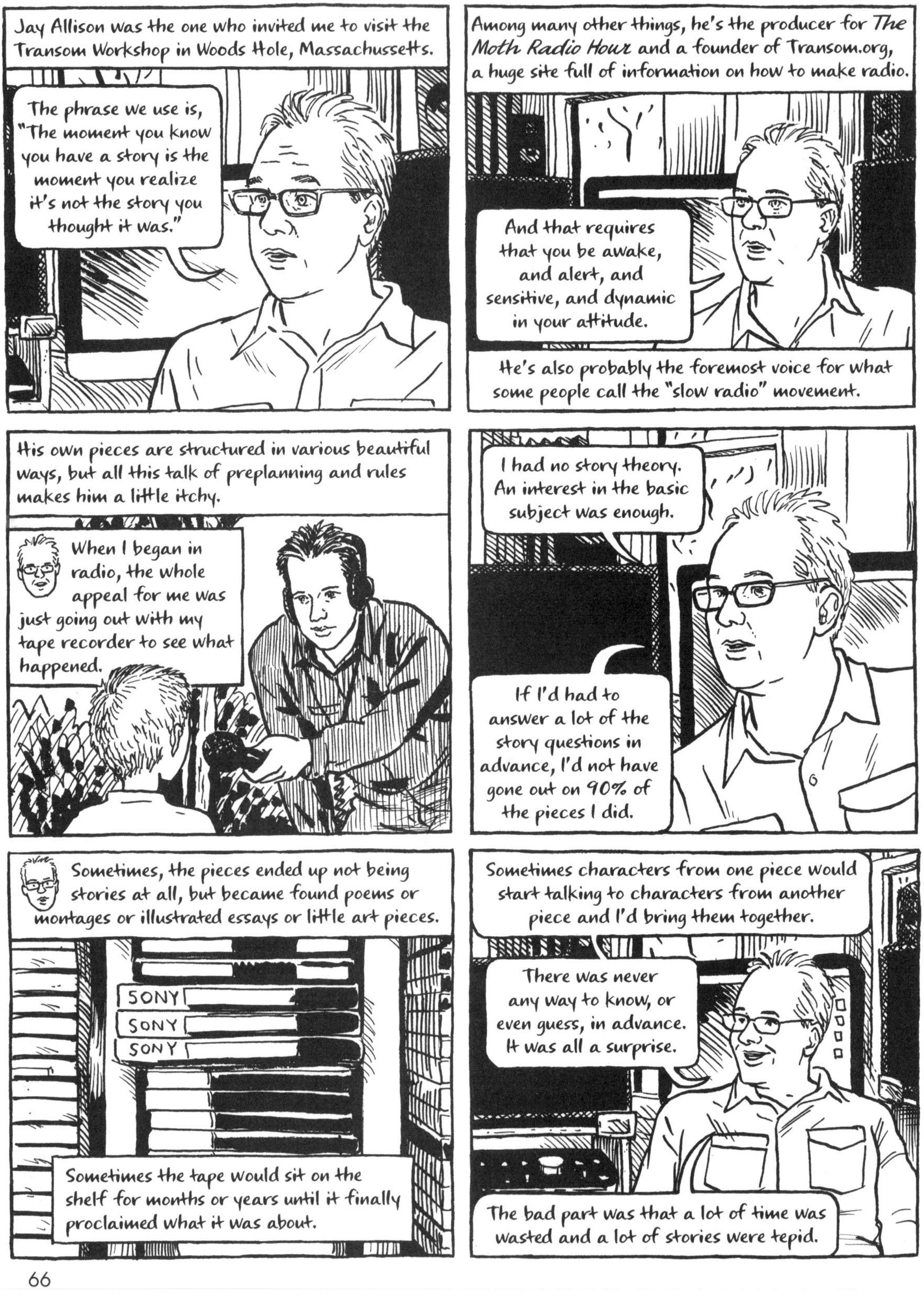
Jay Allison was the one who invited me to visit the Transom Workshop in Woods Hole, Massachussetts.
The phrase we use is, "The moment you know you have a story is the moment you realize it's not the story you thought it was."
Among many other things, he's the producer for *The Moth Radio Hour* and a founder of Transom.org, a huge site full of information on how to make radio.
And that requires that you be awake, and alert, and sensitive, and dynamic in your attitude.
He's also probably the foremost voice for what some people call the "slow radio" movement.
His own pieces are structured in various beautiful ways, but all this talk of preplanning and rules makes him a little itchy.
When I began in radio, the whole appeal for me was just going out with my tape recorder to see what happened.
I had no story theory. An interest in the basic subject was enough.
If I'd had to answer a lot of the story questions in advance, I'd not have gone out on 90% of the pieces I did.
Sometimes, the pieces ended up not being stories at all, but became found poems or montages or illustrated essays or little art pieces.
SONY
SONY
SONY
Sometimes the tape would sit on the shelf for months or years until it finally proclaimed what it was about.
Sometimes characters from one piece would start talking to characters from another piece and I'd bring them together.
There was never any way to know, or even guess, in advance. It was all a surprise.
The bad part was that a lot of time was wasted and a lot of stories were tepid.

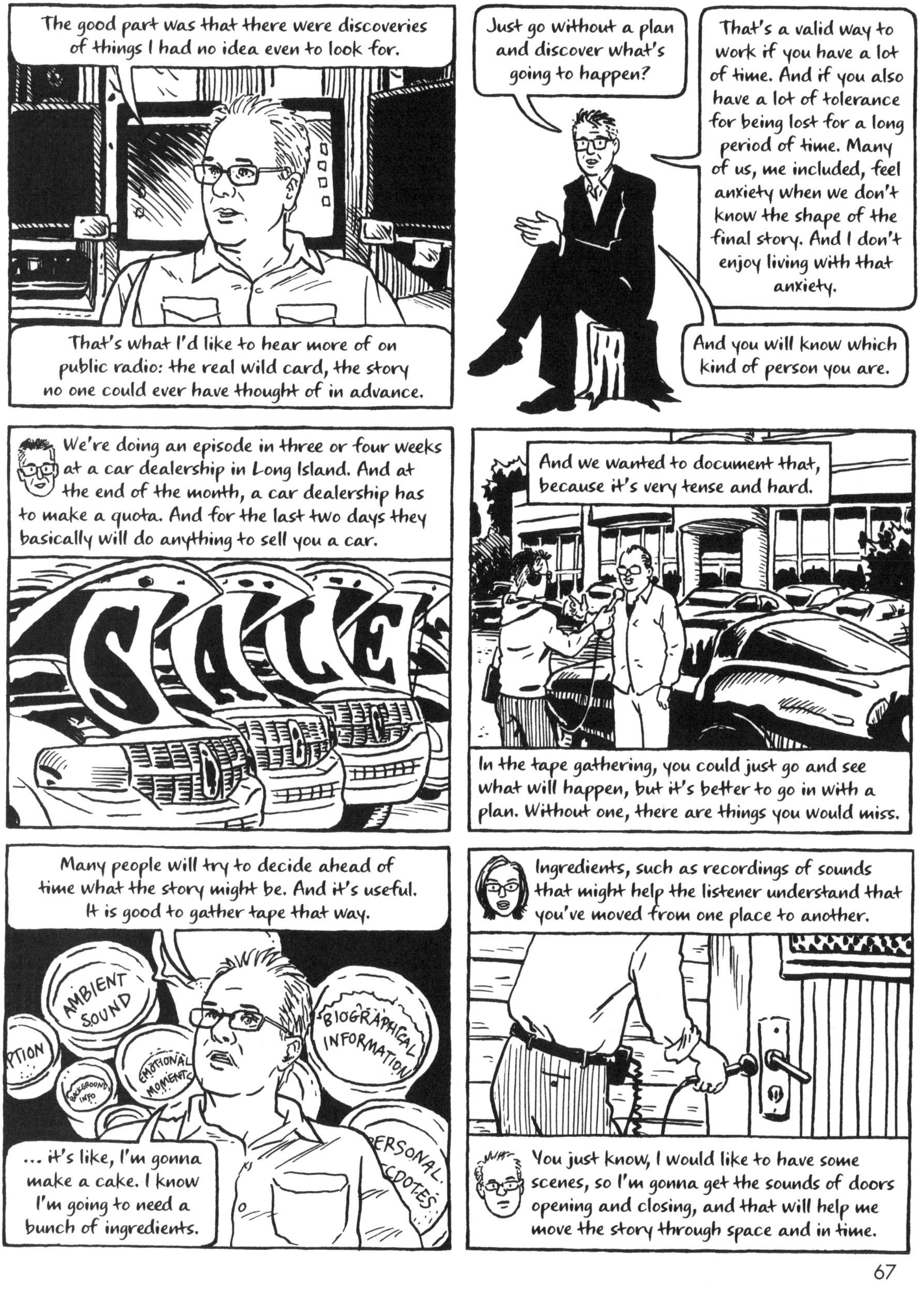

The good part was that there were discoveries of things I had no idea even to look for.
That's what I'd like to hear more of on public radio: the real wild card, the story no one could ever have thought of in advance.
Just go without a plan and discover what's going to happen?
That's a valid way to work if you have a lot of time. And if you also have a lot of tolerance for being lost for a long period of time. Many of us, me included, feel anxiety when we don't know the shape of the final story. And I don't enjoy living with that anxiety.
And you will know which kind of person you are.
We're doing an episode in three or four weeks at a car dealership in Long Island. And at the end of the month, a car dealership has to make a quota. And for the last two days they basically will do anything to sell you a car.
SALE
And we wanted to document that, because it's very tense and hard.
In the tape gathering, you could just go and see what will happen, but it's better to go in with a plan. Without one, there are things you would miss.
Many people will try to decide ahead of time what the story might be. And it's useful. It is good to gather tape that way.
AMBIENT SOUND
BIOGRAPHICAL INFORMATION
EMOTIONAL MOMENTS
BACKGROUND INFO
... it's like, I'm gonna make a cake. I know I'm going to need a bunch of ingredients.
Ingredients, such as recordings of sounds that might help the listener understand that you've moved from one place to another.
You just know, I would like to have some scenes, so I'm gonna get the sounds of doors opening and closing, and that will help me move the story through space and in time.

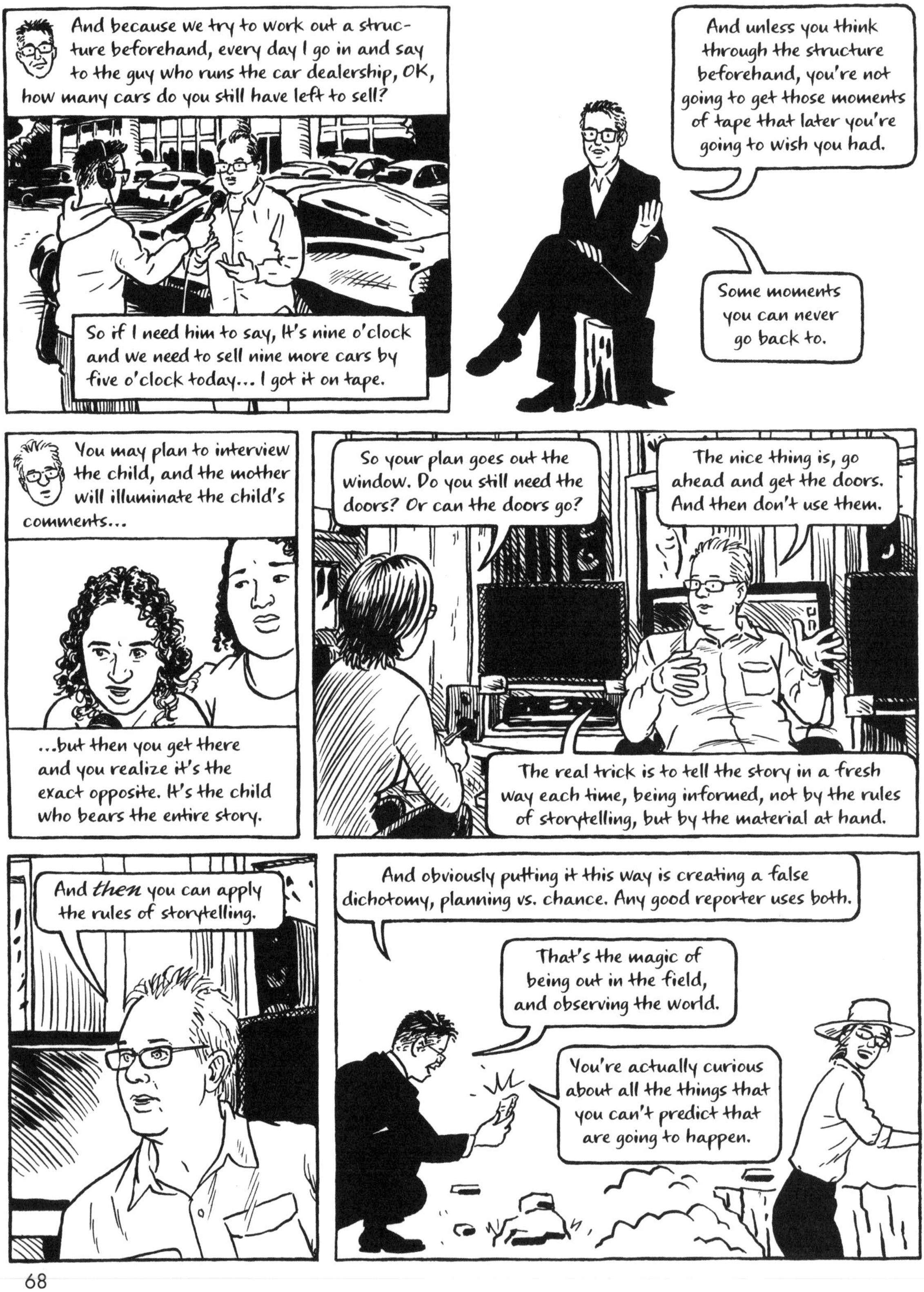
And because we try to work out a structure beforehand, every day I go in and say to the guy who runs the car dealership, OK, how many cars do you still have left to sell?
So if I need him to say, It's nine o'clock and we need to sell nine more cars by five o'clock today... I got it on tape.
And unless you think through the structure beforehand, you're not going to get those moments of tape that later you're going to wish you had.
Some moments you can never go back to.
You may plan to interview the child, and the mother will illuminate the child's comments...
...but then you get there and you realize it's the exact opposite. It's the child who bears the entire story.
So your plan goes out the window. Do you still need the doors? Or can the doors go?
The nice thing is, go ahead and get the doors. And then don't use them.
The real trick is to tell the story in a fresh way each time, being informed, not by the rules of storytelling, but by the material at hand.
And *then* you can apply the rules of storytelling.
And obviously putting it this way is creating a false dichotomy, planning vs. chance. Any good reporter uses both.
That's the magic of being out in the field, and observing the world.
You're actually curious about all the things that you can't predict that are going to happen.

THE (EVEN) BIGGER PICTURE

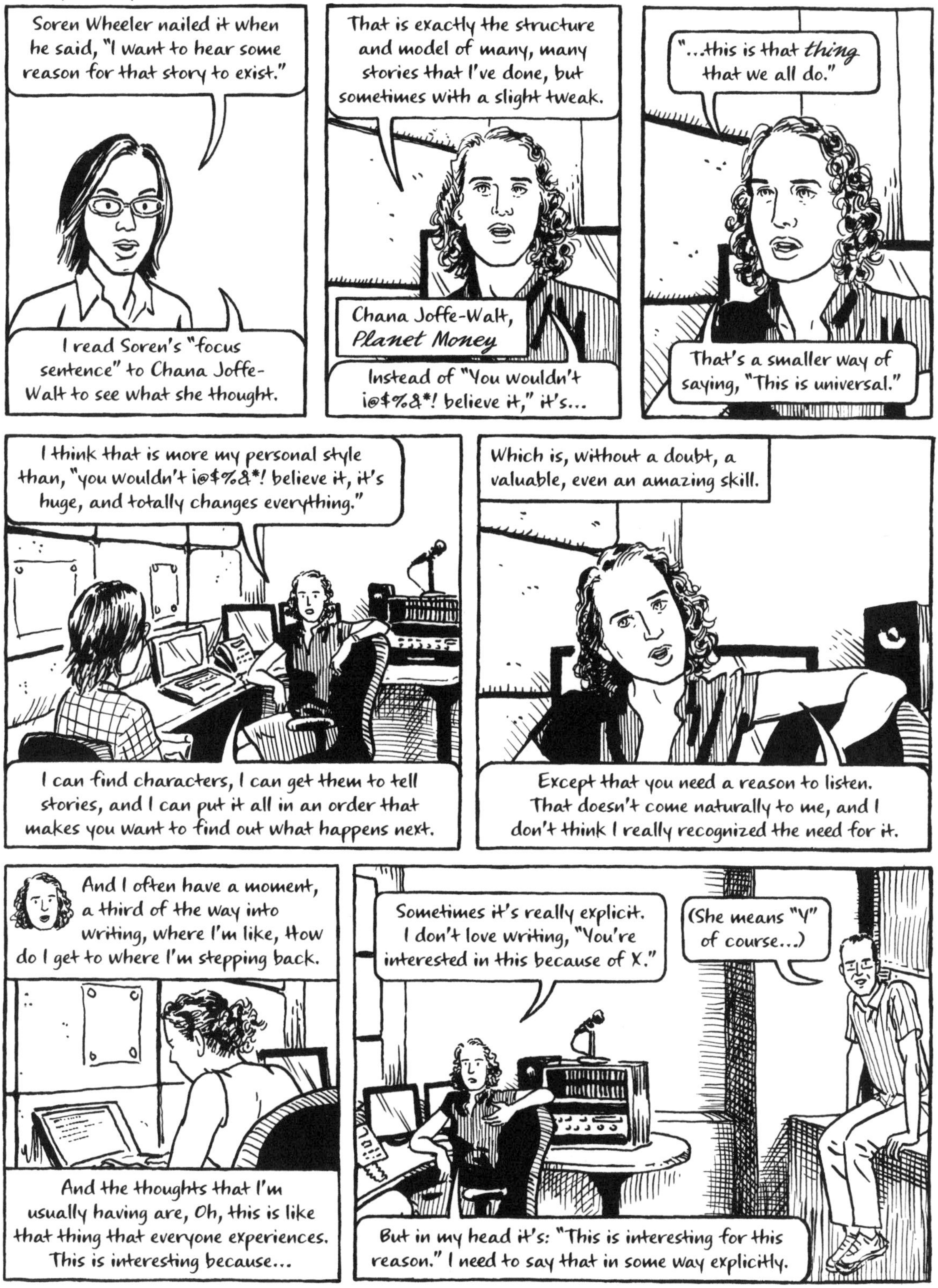
Soren Wheeler nailed it when he said, "I want to hear some reason for that story to exist."
I read Soren's "focus sentence" to Chana Joffe-Walt to see what she thought.
That is exactly the structure and model of many, many stories that I've done, but sometimes with a slight tweak.
Chana Joffe-Walt, *Planet Money*
Instead of "You wouldn't i@$%&*! believe it," it's...
"...this is that *thing* that we all do."
That's a smaller way of saying, "This is universal."
I think that is more my personal style than, "you wouldn't i@$%&*! believe it, it's huge, and totally changes everything."
I can find characters, I can get them to tell stories, and I can put it all in an order that makes you want to find out what happens next.
Which is, without a doubt, a valuable, even an amazing skill.
Except that you need a reason to listen. That doesn't come naturally to me, and I don't think I really recognized the need for it.
And I often have a moment, a third of the way into writing, where I'm like, How do I get to where I'm stepping back.
And the thoughts that I'm usually having are, Oh, this is like that thing that everyone experiences. This is interesting because...
Sometimes it's really explicit. I don't love writing, "You're interested in this because of X."
(She means "Y" of course...)
But in my head it's: "This is interesting for this reason." I need to say that in some way explicitly.

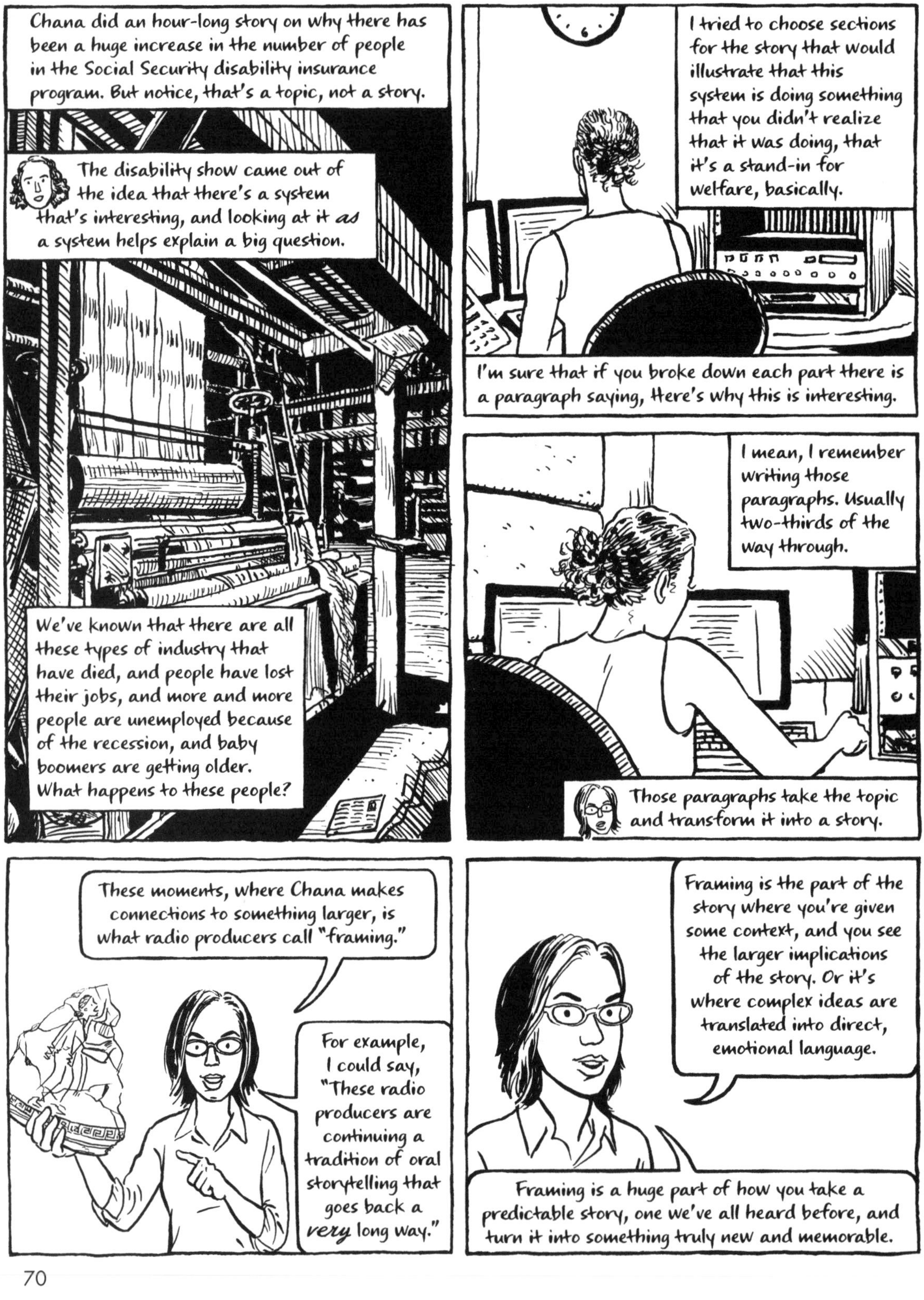

Chana did an hour-long story on why there has been a huge increase in the number of people in the Social Security disability insurance program. But notice, that's a topic, not a story.
The disability show came out of the idea that there's a system that's interesting, and looking at it *as* a system helps explain a big question.
We've known that there are all these types of industry that have died, and people have lost their jobs, and more and more people are unemployed because of the recession, and baby boomers are getting older. What happens to these people?
I tried to choose sections for the story that would illustrate that this system is doing something that you didn't realize that it was doing, that it's a stand-in for welfare, basically.
I'm sure that if you broke down each part there is a paragraph saying, Here's why this is interesting.
I mean, I remember writing those paragraphs. Usually two-thirds of the way through.
Those paragraphs take the topic and transform it into a story.
These moments, where Chana makes connections to something larger, is what radio producers call "framing."
For example, I could say, "These radio producers are continuing a tradition of oral storytelling that goes back a *very* long way."
Framing is the part of the story where you're given some context, and you see the larger implications of the story. Or it's where complex ideas are translated into direct, emotional language.
Framing is a huge part of how you take a predictable story, one we've all heard before, and turn it into something truly new and memorable.

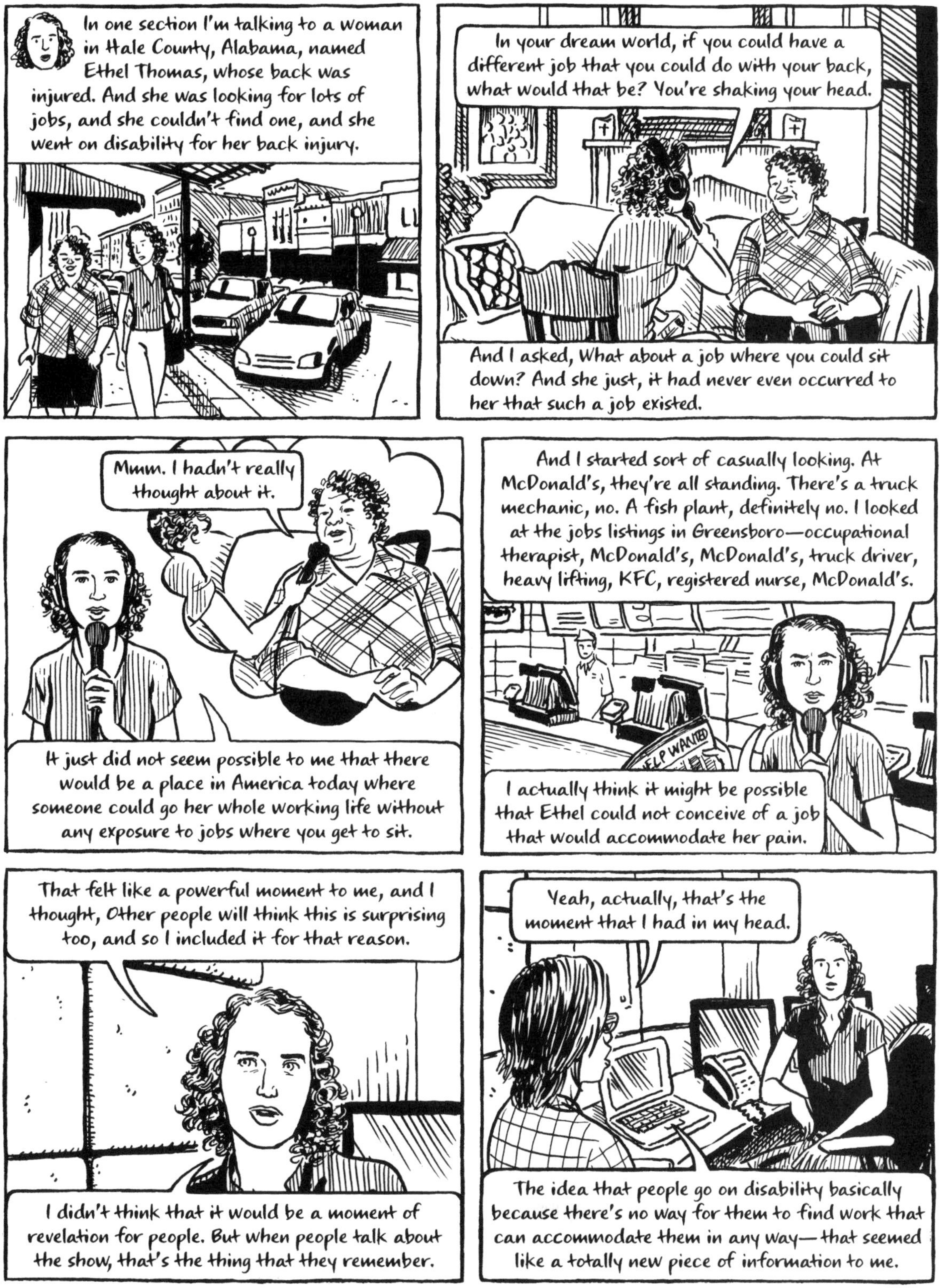
In one section I'm talking to a woman in Hale County, Alabama, named Ethel Thomas, whose back was injured. And she was looking for lots of jobs, and she couldn't find one, and she went on disability for her back injury.
In your dream world, if you could have a different job that you could do with your back, what would that be? You're shaking your head.
And I asked, What about a job where you could sit down? And she just, it had never even occurred to her that such a job existed.
Mmm. I hadn't really thought about it.
It just did not seem possible to me that there would be a place in America today where someone could go her whole working life without any exposure to jobs where you get to sit.
And I started sort of casually looking. At McDonald's, they're all standing. There's a truck mechanic, no. A fish plant, definitely no. I looked at the jobs listings in Greensboro—occupational therapist, McDonald's, McDonald's, truck driver, heavy lifting, KFC, registered nurse, McDonald's.
I actually think it might be possible that Ethel could not conceive of a job that would accommodate her pain.
That felt like a powerful moment to me, and I thought, Other people will think this is surprising too, and so I included it for that reason.
I didn't think that it would be a moment of revelation for people. But when people talk about the show, that's the thing that they remember.
Yeah, actually, that's the moment that I had in my head.
The idea that people go on disability basically because there's no way for them to find work that can accommodate them in any way—that seemed like a totally new piece of information to me.

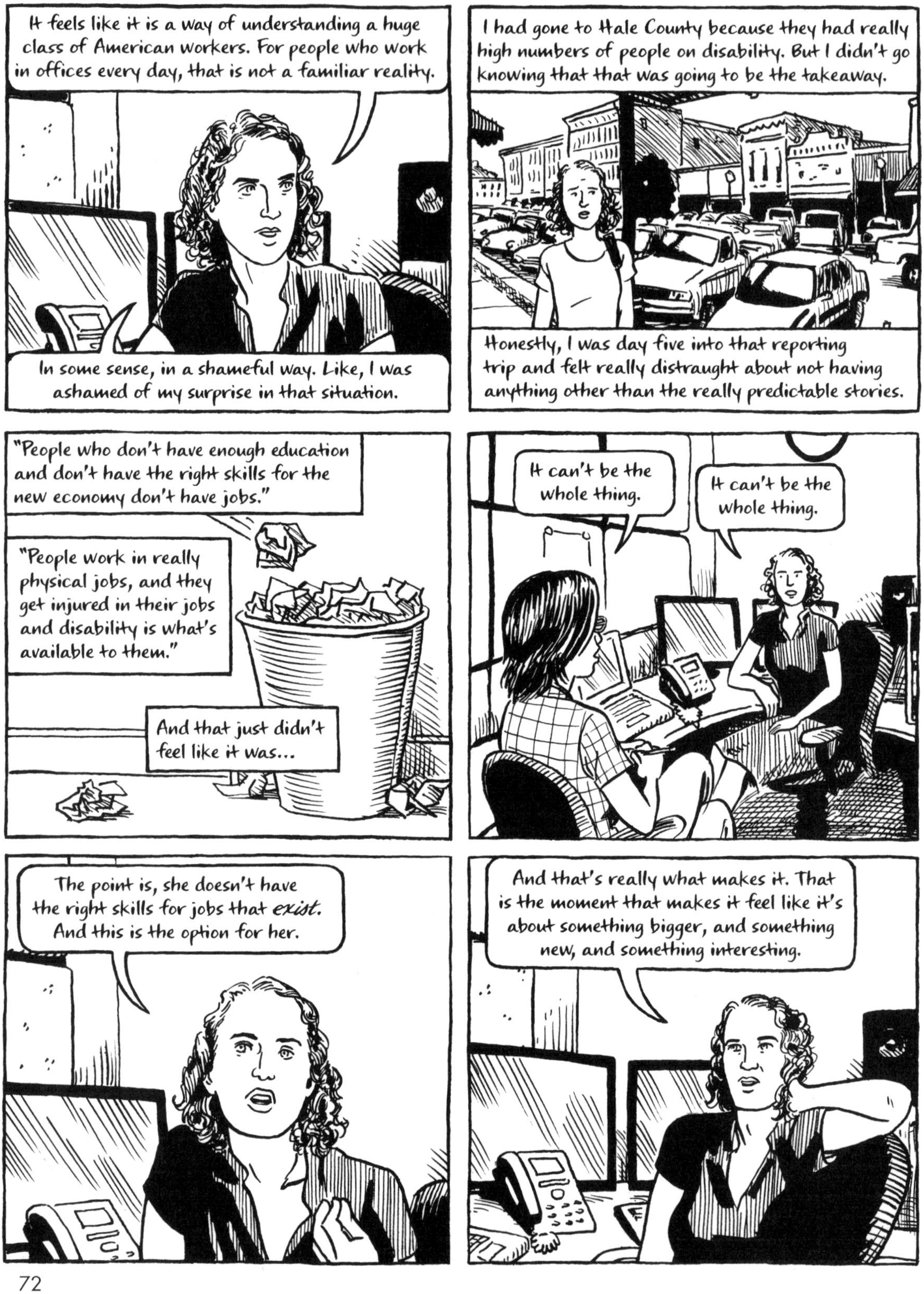
It feels like it is a way of understanding a huge class of American workers. For people who work in offices every day, that is not a familiar reality.
In some sense, in a shameful way. Like, I was ashamed of my surprise in that situation.
I had gone to Hale County because they had really high numbers of people on disability. But I didn't go knowing that that was going to be the takeaway.
Honestly, I was day five into that reporting trip and felt really distraught about not having anything other than the really predictable stories.
"People who don't have enough education and don't have the right skills for the new economy don't have jobs."
"People work in really physical jobs, and they get injured in their jobs and disability is what's available to them."
And that just didn't feel like it was...
It can't be the whole thing.
It can't be the whole thing.
The point is, she doesn't have the right skills for jobs that *exist*. And this is the option for her.
And that's really what makes it. That is the moment that makes it feel like it's about something bigger, and something new, and something interesting.

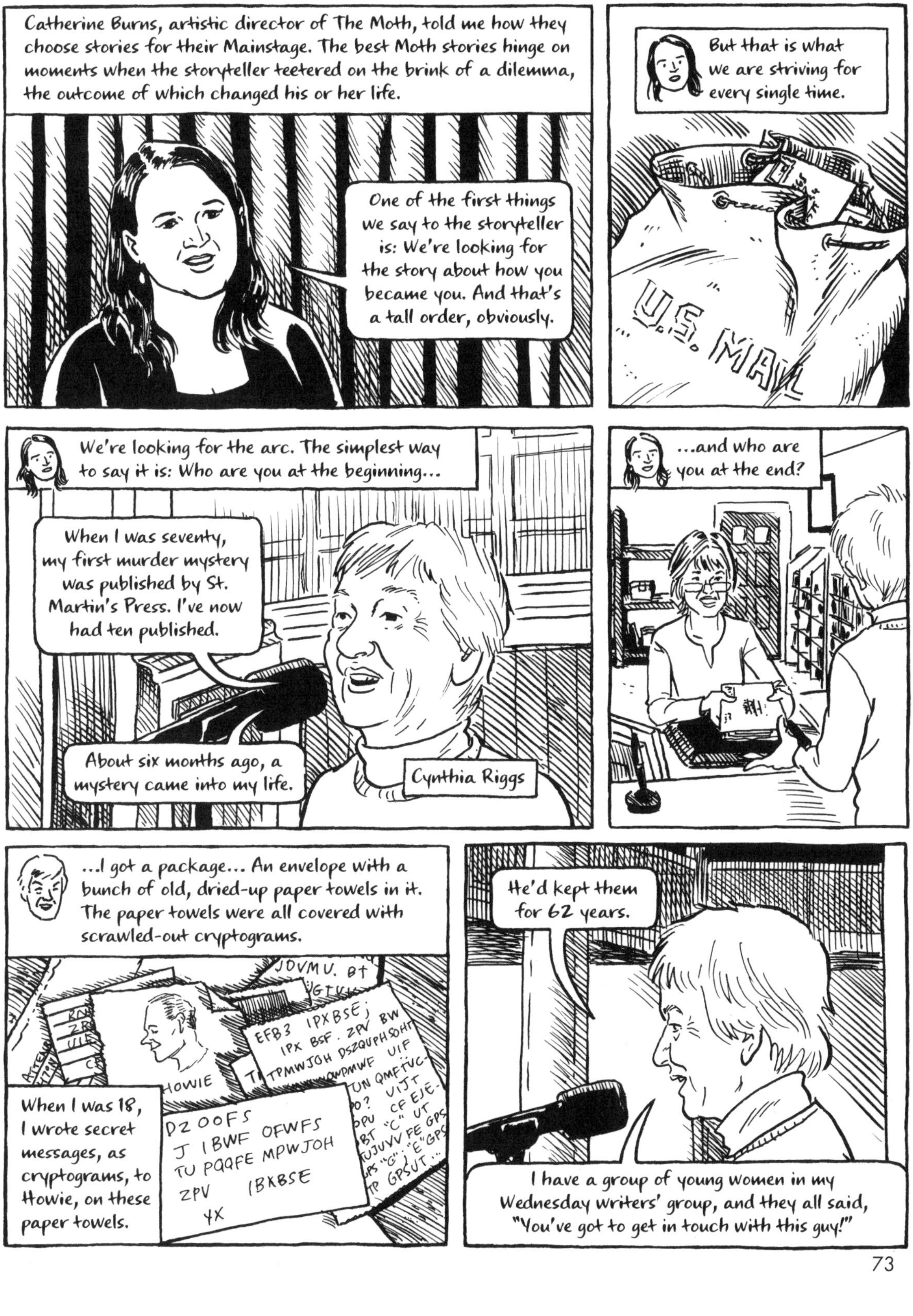
Catherine Burns, artistic director of The Moth, told me how they choose stories for their Mainstage. The best Moth stories hinge on moments when the storyteller teetered on the brink of a dilemma, the outcome of which changed his or her life.
One of the first things we say to the storyteller is: We're looking for the story about how you became you. And that's a tall order, obviously.
But that is what we are striving for every single time.
U.S. MAIL
We're looking for the arc. The simplest way to say it is: Who are you at the beginning...
When I was seventy, my first murder mystery was published by St. Martin's Press. I've now had ten published.
About six months ago, a mystery came into my life.
Cynthia Riggs
...and who are you at the end?
...I got a package... An envelope with a bunch of old, dried-up paper towels in it. The paper towels were all covered with scrawled-out cryptograms.
HOWIE
EFB3 IPXBSE;
IPX BSF. ZPV BW
DZ OOFS
J IBWF OFWFS
TU PQQFE MPWJOH
ZPV IBXBSE
YX
When I was 18, I wrote secret messages, as cryptograms, to Howie, on these paper towels.
He'd kept them for 62 years.
I have a group of young women in my Wednesday writers' group, and they all said, "You've got to get in touch with this guy!"

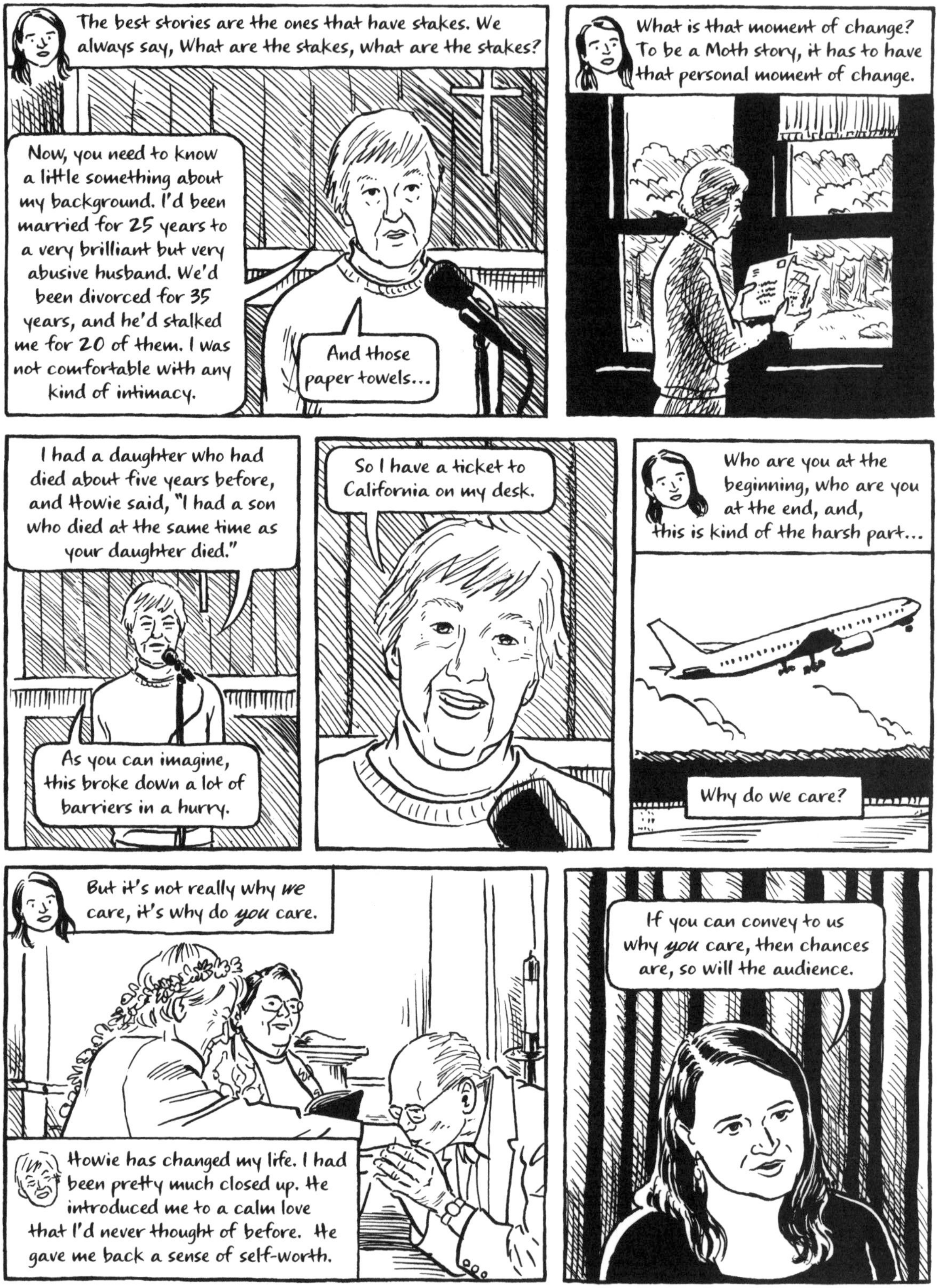
The best stories are the ones that have stakes. We always say, What are the stakes, what are the stakes?
Now, you need to know a little something about my background. I'd been married for 25 years to a very brilliant but very abusive husband. We'd been divorced for 35 years, and he'd stalked me for 20 of them. I was not comfortable with any kind of intimacy.
And those paper towels...
What is that moment of change? To be a Moth story, it has to have that personal moment of change.
I had a daughter who had died about five years before, and Howie said, "I had a son who died at the same time as your daughter died."
As you can imagine, this broke down a lot of barriers in a hurry.
So I have a ticket to California on my desk.
Who are you at the beginning, who are you at the end, and, this is kind of the harsh part...
Why do we care?
But it's not really why *we* care, it's why do *you* care.
Howie has changed my life. I had been pretty much closed up. He introduced me to a calm love that I'd never thought of before. He gave me back a sense of self-worth.
If you can convey to us why *you* care, then chances are, so will the audience.

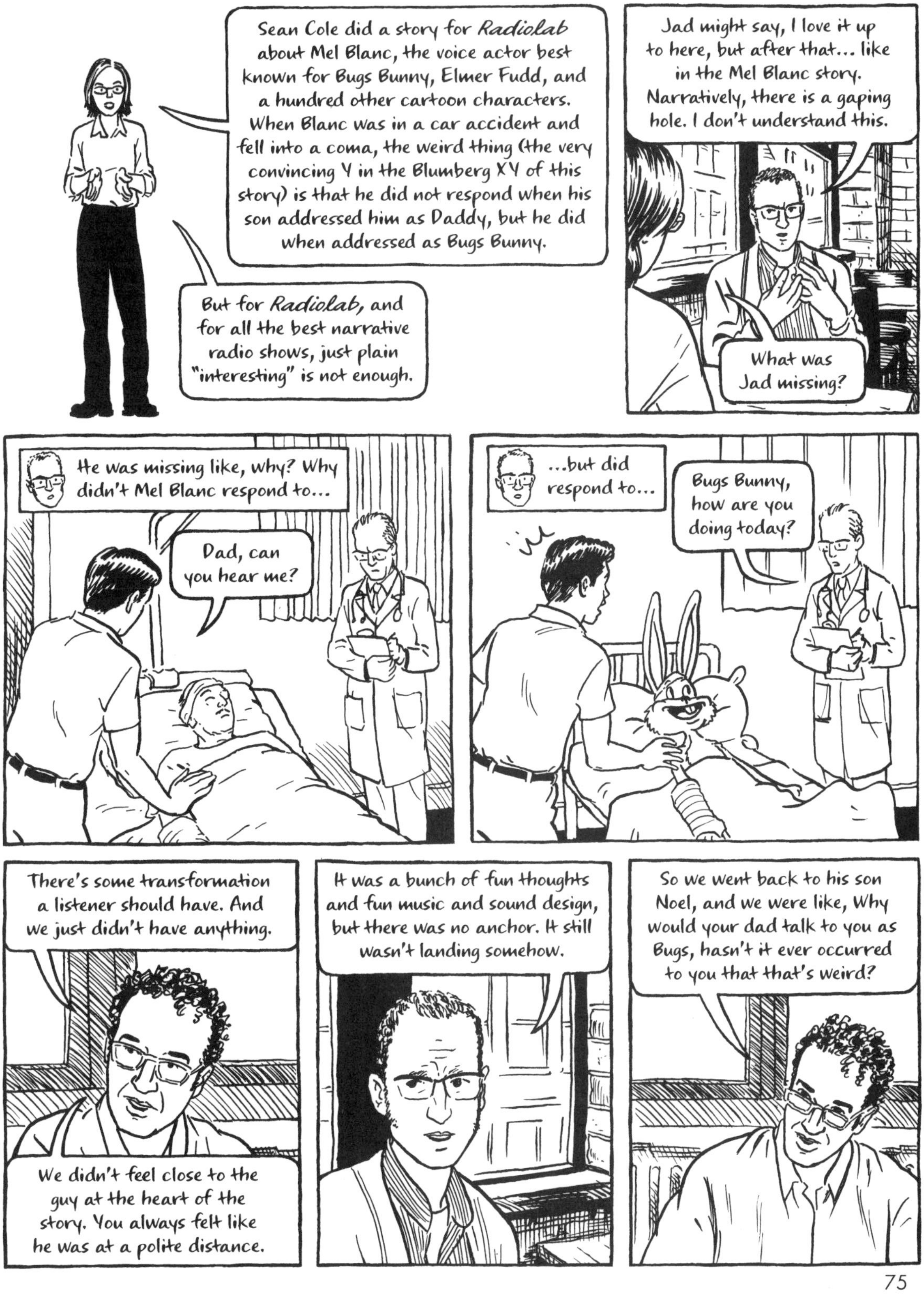
Sean Cole did a story for *Radiolab* about Mel Blanc, the voice actor best known for Bugs Bunny, Elmer Fudd, and a hundred other cartoon characters. When Blanc was in a car accident and fell into a coma, the weird thing (the very convincing Y in the Blumberg XY of this story) is that he did not respond when his son addressed him as Daddy, but he did when addressed as Bugs Bunny.
But for *Radiolab*, and for all the best narrative radio shows, just plain "interesting" is not enough.
Jad might say, I love it up to here, but after that... like in the Mel Blanc story. Narratively, there is a gaping hole. I don't understand this.
What was Jad missing?
He was missing like, why? Why didn't Mel Blanc respond to...
Dad, can you hear me?
...but did respond to...
Bugs Bunny, how are you doing today?
There's some transformation a listener should have. And we just didn't have anything.
We didn't feel close to the guy at the heart of the story. You always felt like he was at a polite distance.
It was a bunch of fun thoughts and fun music and sound design, but there was no anchor. It still wasn't landing somehow.
So we went back to his son Noel, and we were like, Why would your dad talk to you as Bugs, hasn't it ever occurred to you that that's weird?

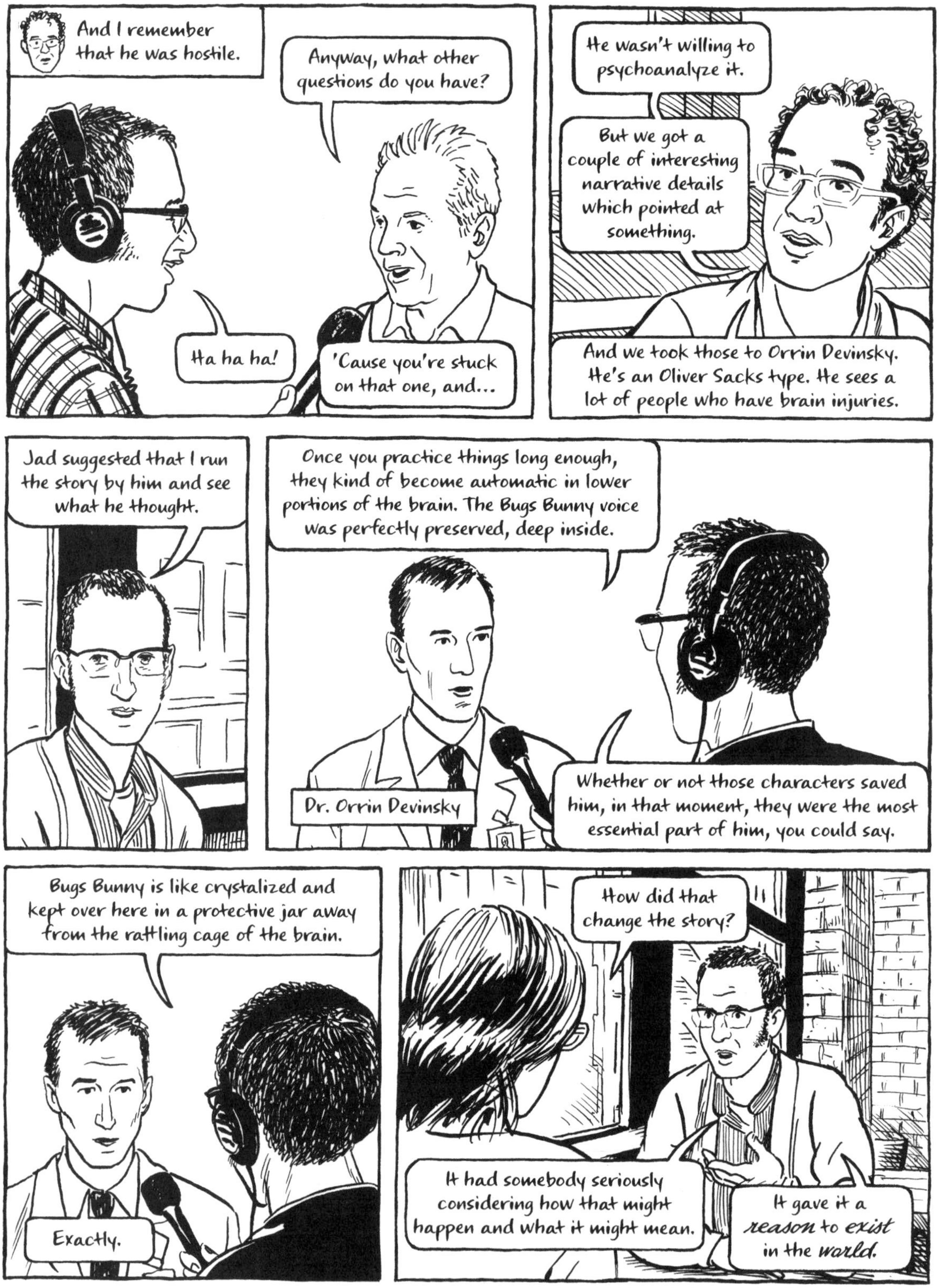

And I remember that he was hostile.
Anyway, what other questions do you have?
Ha ha ha!
'Cause you're stuck on that one, and...
He wasn't willing to psychoanalyze it.
But we got a couple of interesting narrative details which pointed at something.
And we took those to Orrin Devinsky. He's an Oliver Sacks type. He sees a lot of people who have brain injuries.
Jad suggested that I run the story by him and see what he thought.
Once you practice things long enough, they kind of become automatic in lower portions of the brain. The Bugs Bunny voice was perfectly preserved, deep inside.
Dr. Orrin Devinsky
Whether or not those characters saved him, in that moment, they were the most essential part of him, you could say.
Bugs Bunny is like crystalized and kept over here in a protective jar away from the rattling cage of the brain.
Exactly.
How did that change the story?
It had somebody seriously considering how that might happen and what it might mean.
It gave it a *reason* to *exist* in the *world*.

THE HEAT OF THEIR BREATH:
Character and Voice

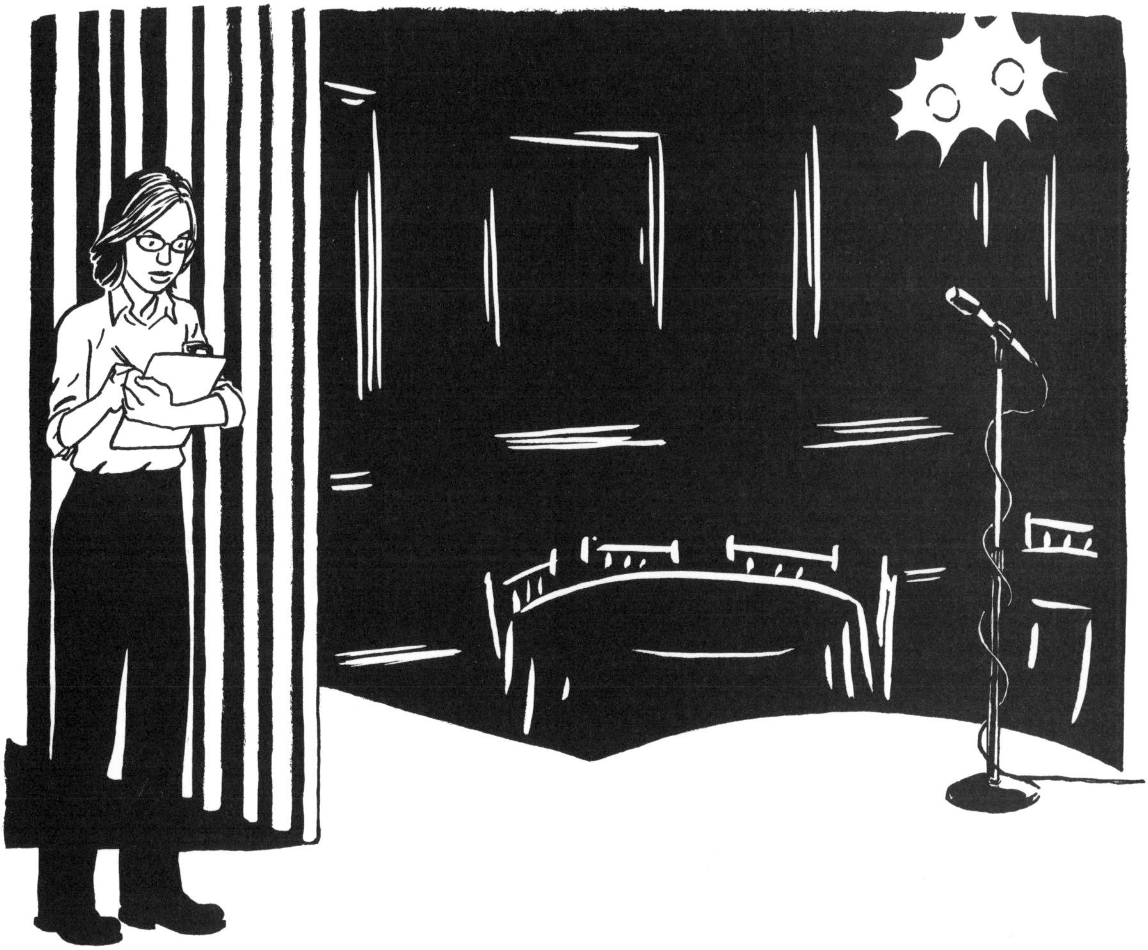

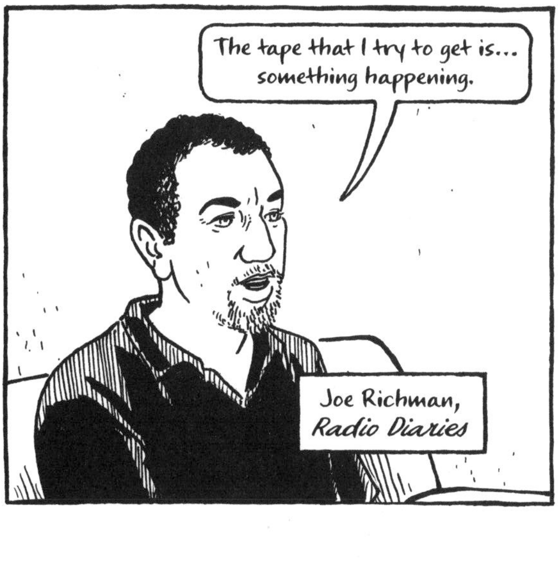
The tape that I try to get is... something happening.
Joe Richman,
Radio Diaries

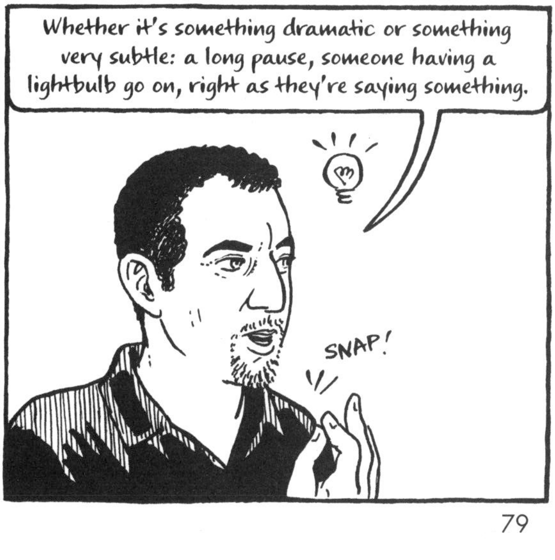
Whether it's something dramatic or something very subtle: a long pause, someone having a lightbulb go on, right as they're saying something.
SNAP!

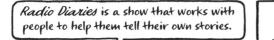 *Radio Diaries* is a show that works with people to help them tell their own stories.

Producer Joe Richman hands a person a recorder, and works with him or her for up to a year to self-record. Then Joe edits a story from that material.

Joe uses a style often known as "non-narrated," meaning he uses only the diarists' recordings of themselves and their friends and family to construct his story.

"Non-narrated" is kind of a misnomer in this case. The stories *are* narrated—by the diarist. There is no reporter and there is no script.

This means the tape-gathering Joe needs to do is that much more demanding. If the person doesn't say what he needs, in the way that he needs it, well, he's gotta come up with some other way to tell the story.

The advantage to this way of working is that the way people speak becomes much more a part of the story, and that can make characters come alive in a way that no other style can.

I just know it's happening right there. I think the listener knows. And you want to experience something as the listener, not just be told.

And perhaps the most important, most magic ingredient of the kind of stories that make you just stop, and pay attention, is a character experiencing a change in his or her life, right there, as you listen.

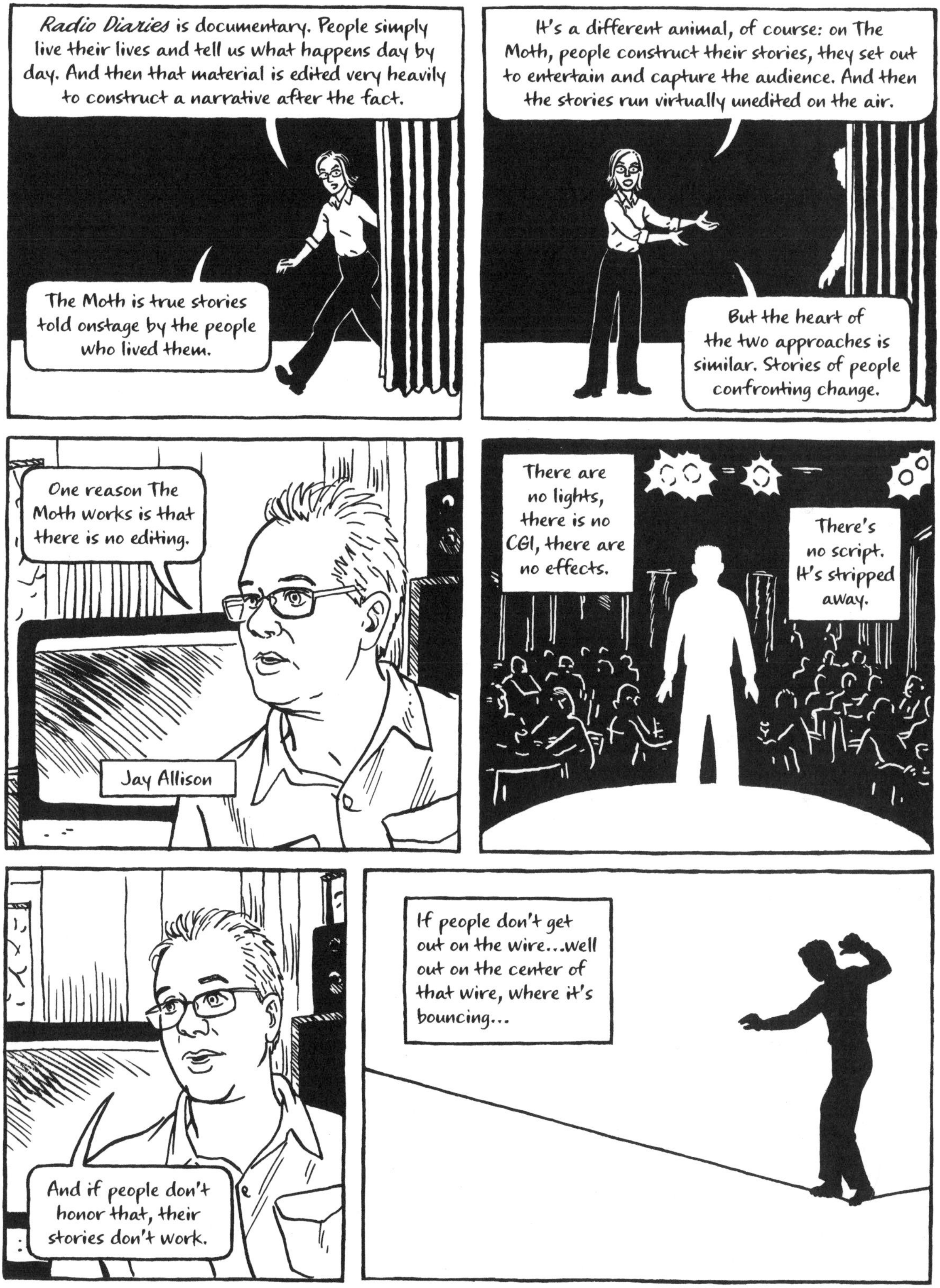
Radio Diaries is documentary. People simply live their lives and tell us what happens day by day. And then that material is edited very heavily to construct a narrative after the fact.
The Moth is true stories told onstage by the people who lived them.
It's a different animal, of course: on The Moth, people construct their stories, they set out to entertain and capture the audience. And then the stories run virtually unedited on the air.
But the heart of the two approaches is similar. Stories of people confronting change.
One reason The Moth works is that there is no editing.
Jay Allison
There are no lights, there is no CGI, there are no effects.
There's no script. It's stripped away.
And if people don't honor that, their stories don't work.
If people don't get out on the wire...well out on the center of that wire, where it's bouncing...

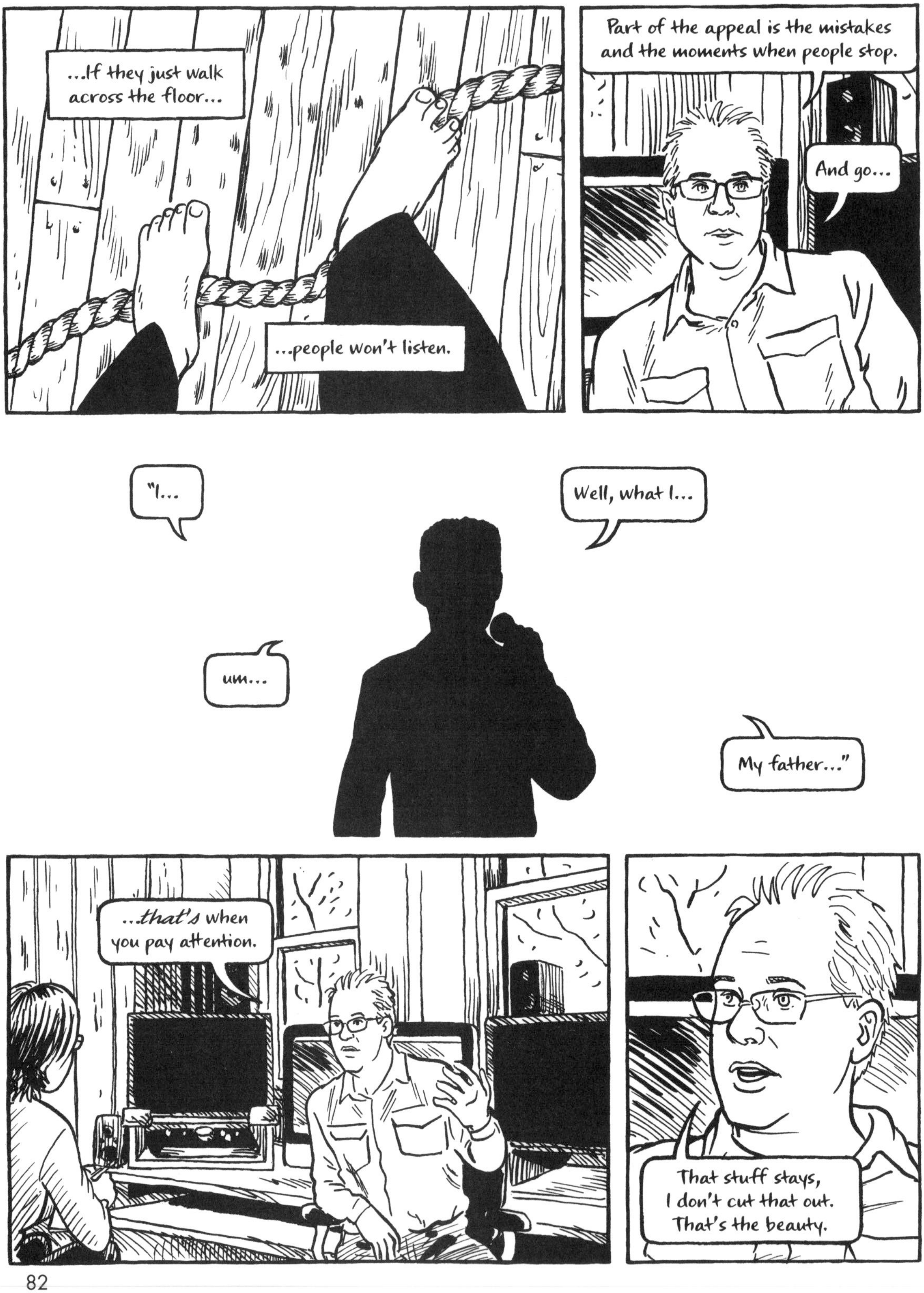
...If they just walk across the floor...
...people won't listen.
Part of the appeal is the mistakes and the moments when people stop.
And go...
"I...
Well, what I...
um...
My father..."
...*that's* when you pay attention.
That stuff stays, I don't cut that out. That's the beauty.

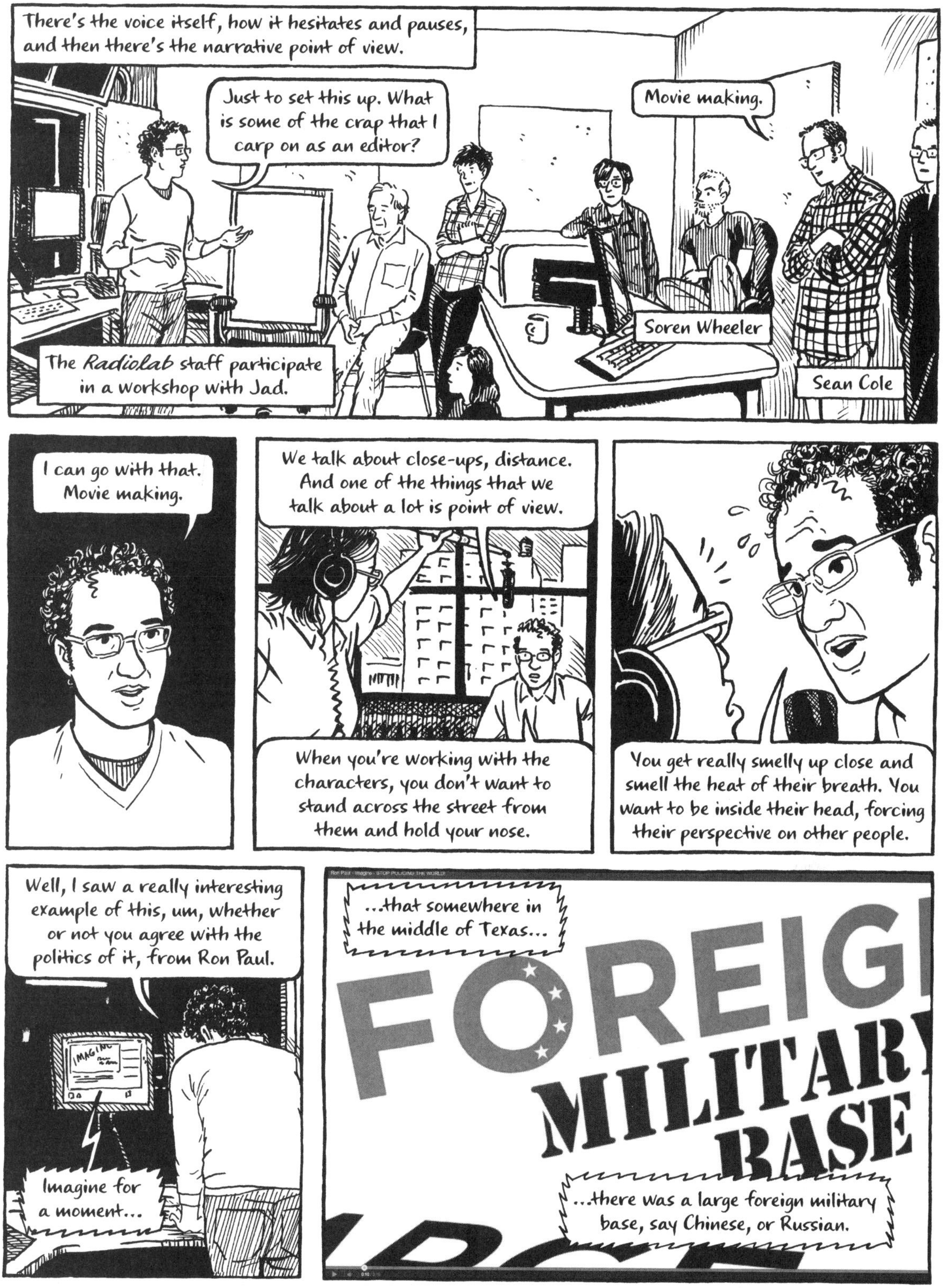

There's the voice itself, how it hesitates and pauses, and then there's the narrative point of view.
Just to set this up. What is some of the crap that I carp on as an editor?
Movie making.
The *Radiolab* staff participate in a workshop with Jad.
Soren Wheeler
Sean Cole
I can go with that. Movie making.
We talk about close-ups, distance. And one of the things that we talk about a lot is point of view.
When you're working with the characters, you don't want to stand across the street from them and hold your nose.
You get really smelly up close and smell the heat of their breath. You want to be inside their head, forcing their perspective on other people.
Well, I saw a really interesting example of this, um, whether or not you agree with the politics of it, from Ron Paul.
Imagine for a moment...
...that somewhere in the middle of Texas...
FOREIG
MILITARY
BASE
...there was a large foreign military base, say Chinese, or Russian.

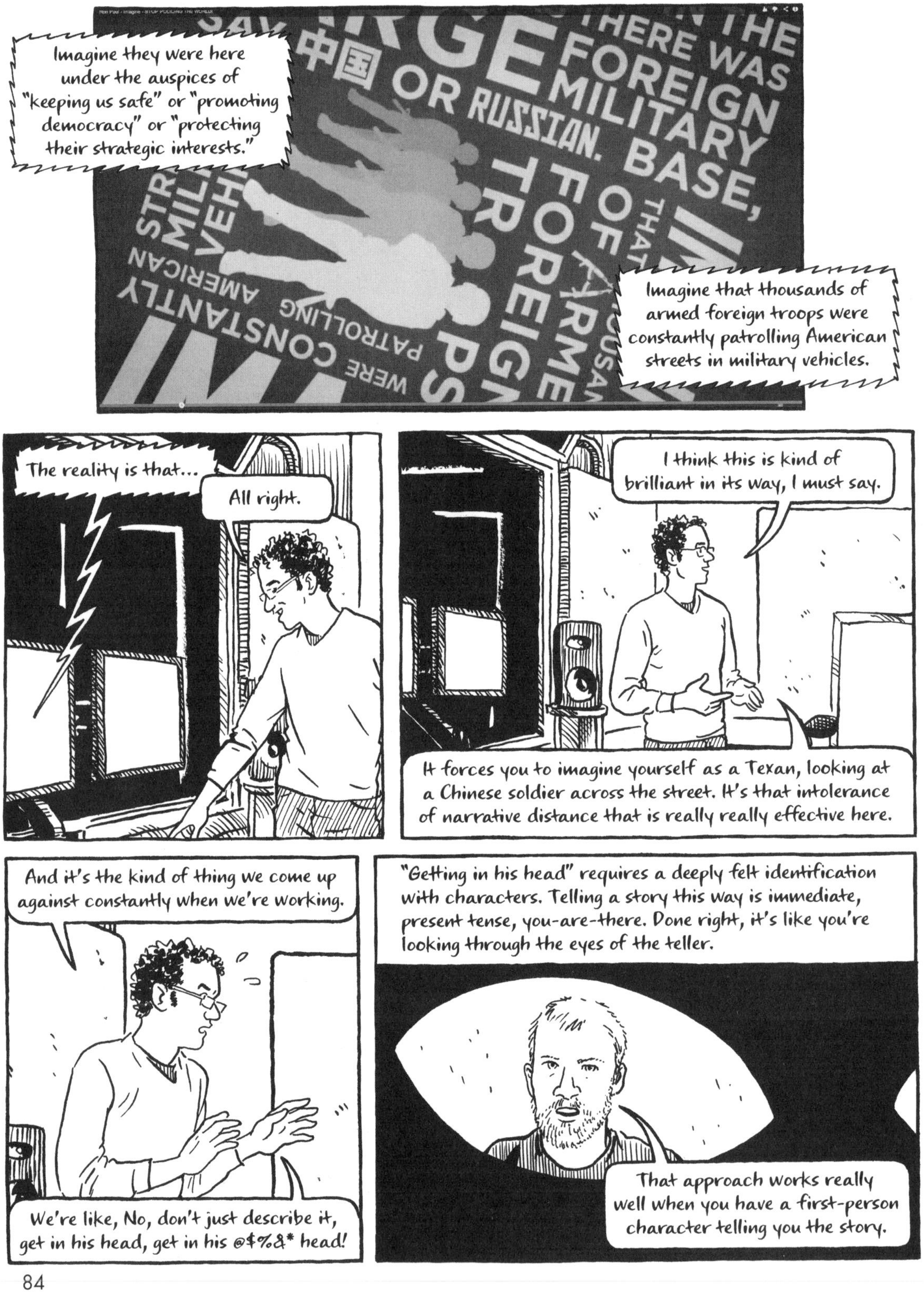
Imagine they were here under the auspices of "keeping us safe" or "promoting democracy" or "protecting their strategic interests."
Imagine that thousands of armed foreign troops were constantly patrolling American streets in military vehicles.
The reality is that...
All right.
I think this is kind of brilliant in its way, I must say.
It forces you to imagine yourself as a Texan, looking at a Chinese soldier across the street. It's that intolerance of narrative distance that is really really effective here.
And it's the kind of thing we come up against constantly when we're working.
We're like, No, don't just describe it, get in his head, get in his @$%&* head!
"Getting in his head" requires a deeply felt identification with characters. Telling a story this way is immediate, present tense, you-are-there. Done right, it's like you're looking through the eyes of the teller.
That approach works really well when you have a first-person character telling you the story.

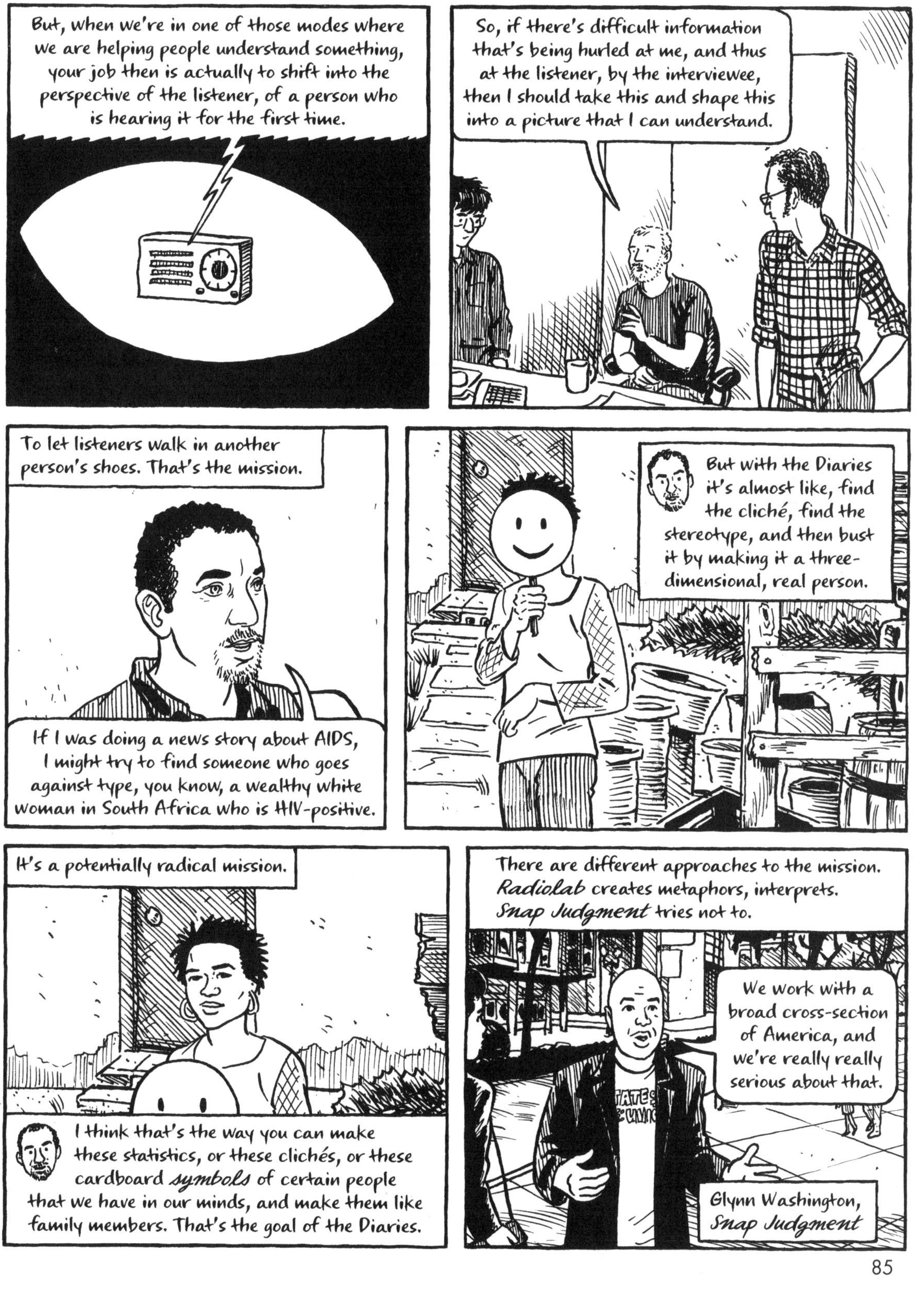
But, when we're in one of those modes where we are helping people understand something, your job then is actually to shift into the perspective of the listener, of a person who is hearing it for the first time.
So, if there's difficult information that's being hurled at me, and thus at the listener, by the interviewee, then I should take this and shape this into a picture that I can understand.
To let listeners walk in another person's shoes. That's the mission.
If I was doing a news story about AIDS, I might try to find someone who goes against type, you know, a wealthy white woman in South Africa who is HIV-positive.
But with the Diaries it's almost like, find the cliché, find the stereotype, and then bust it by making it a three-dimensional, real person.
It's a potentially radical mission.
I think that's the way you can make these statistics, or these clichés, or these cardboard *symbols* of certain people that we have in our minds, and make them like family members. That's the goal of the Diaries.
There are different approaches to the mission. *Radiolab* creates metaphors, interprets. *Snap Judgment* tries not to.
We work with a broad cross-section of America, and we're really really serious about that.
Glynn Washington, *Snap Judgment*

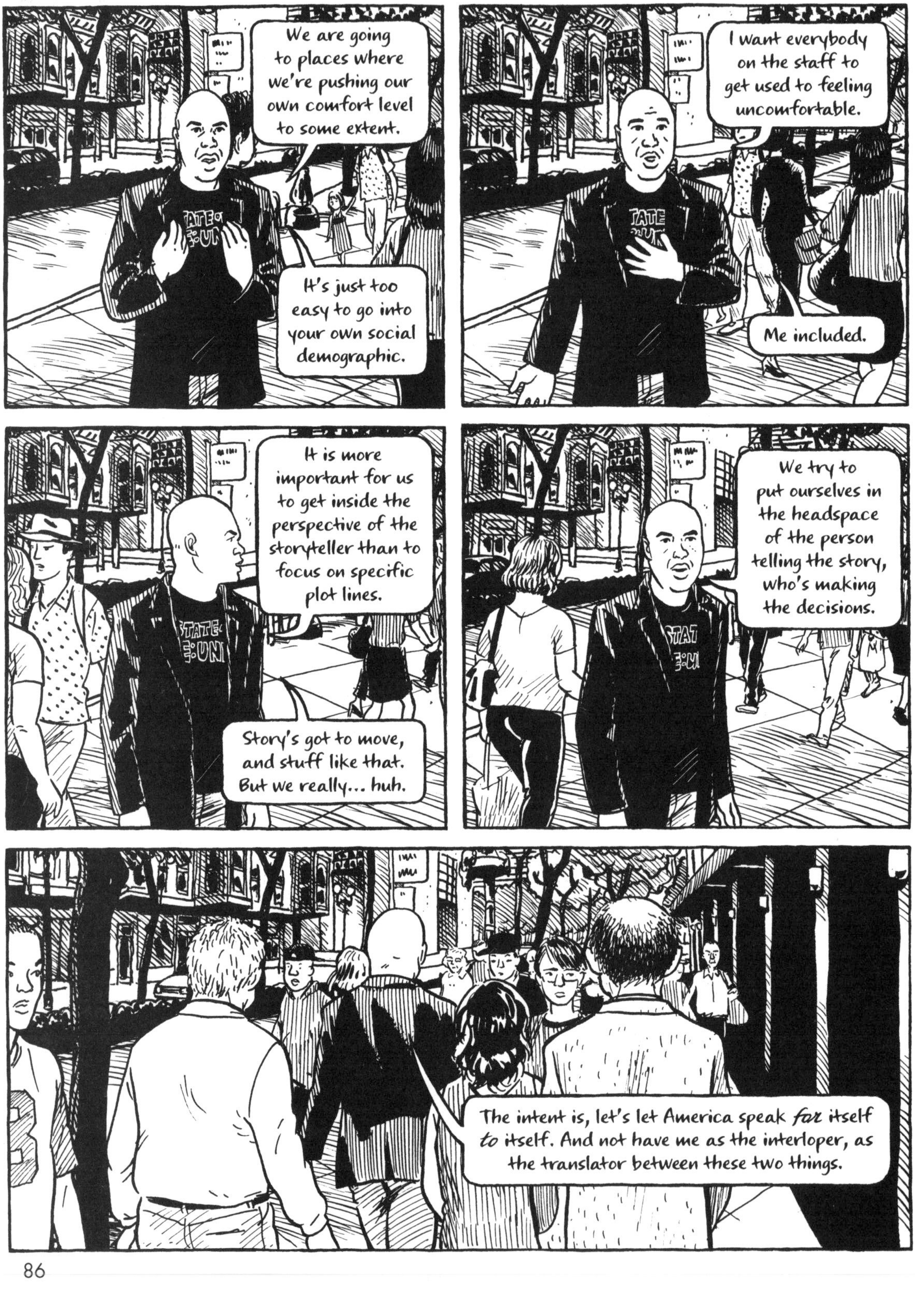
We are going to places where we're pushing our own comfort level to some extent.
It's just too easy to go into your own social demographic.
I want everybody on the staff to get used to feeling uncomfortable.
Me included.
It is more important for us to get inside the perspective of the storyteller than to focus on specific plot lines.
Story's got to move, and stuff like that. But we really... huh.
We try to put ourselves in the headspace of the person telling the story, who's making the decisions.
The intent is, let's let America speak *for* itself *to* itself. And not have me as the interloper, as the translator between these two things.

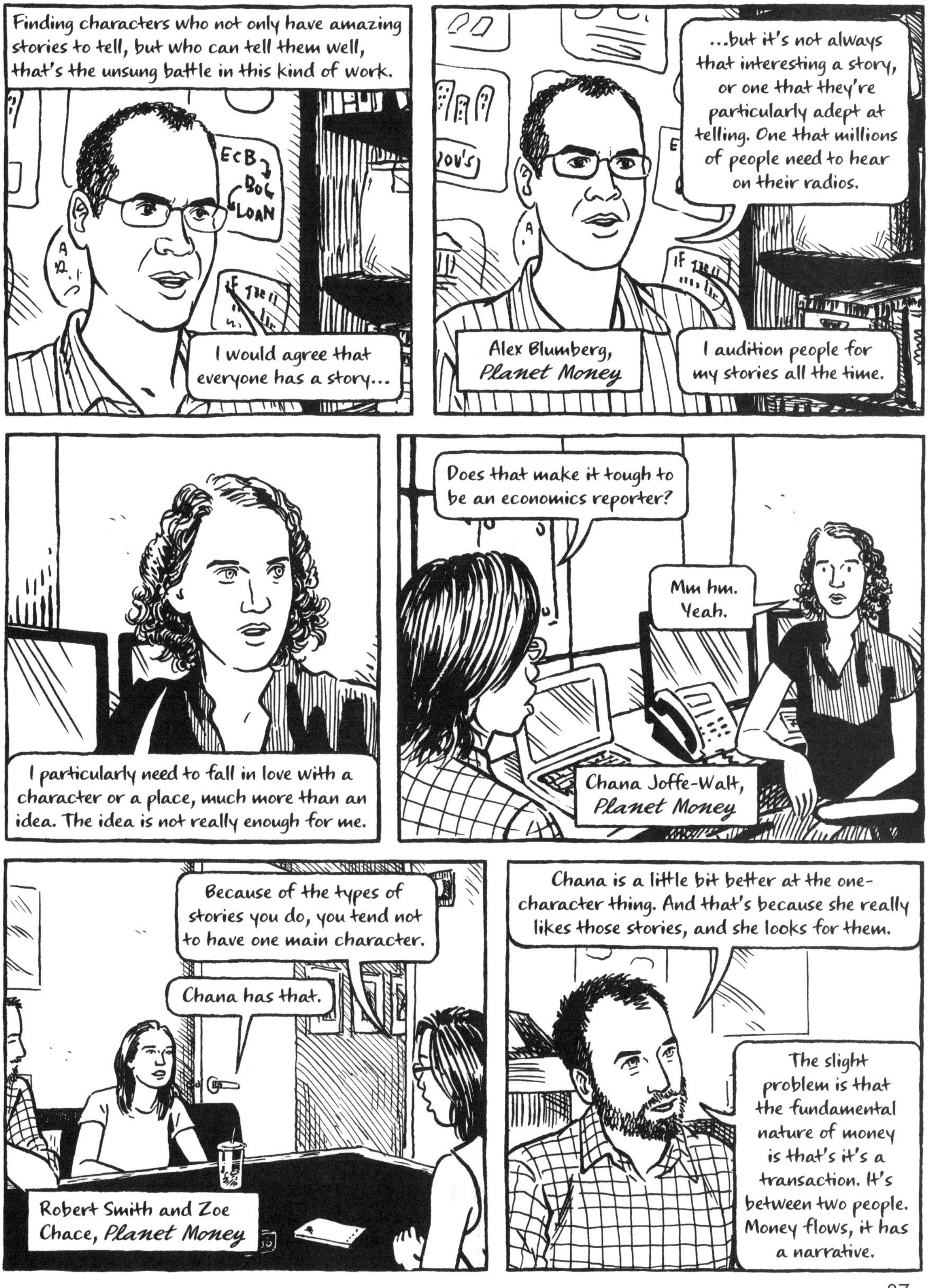
Finding characters who not only have amazing stories to tell, but who can tell them well, that's the unsung battle in this kind of work.
I would agree that everyone has a story...
Alex Blumberg, *Planet Money*
...but it's not always that interesting a story, or one that they're particularly adept at telling. One that millions of people need to hear on their radios.
I audition people for my stories all the time.
I particularly need to fall in love with a character or a place, much more than an idea. The idea is not really enough for me.
Does that make it tough to be an economics reporter?
Mm hm. Yeah.
Chana Joffe-Walt, *Planet Money*
Because of the types of stories you do, you tend not to have one main character.
Chana has that.
Robert Smith and Zoe Chace, *Planet Money*
Chana is a little bit better at the one-character thing. And that's because she really likes those stories, and she looks for them.
The slight problem is that the fundamental nature of money is that's it's a transaction. It's between two people. Money flows, it has a narrative.

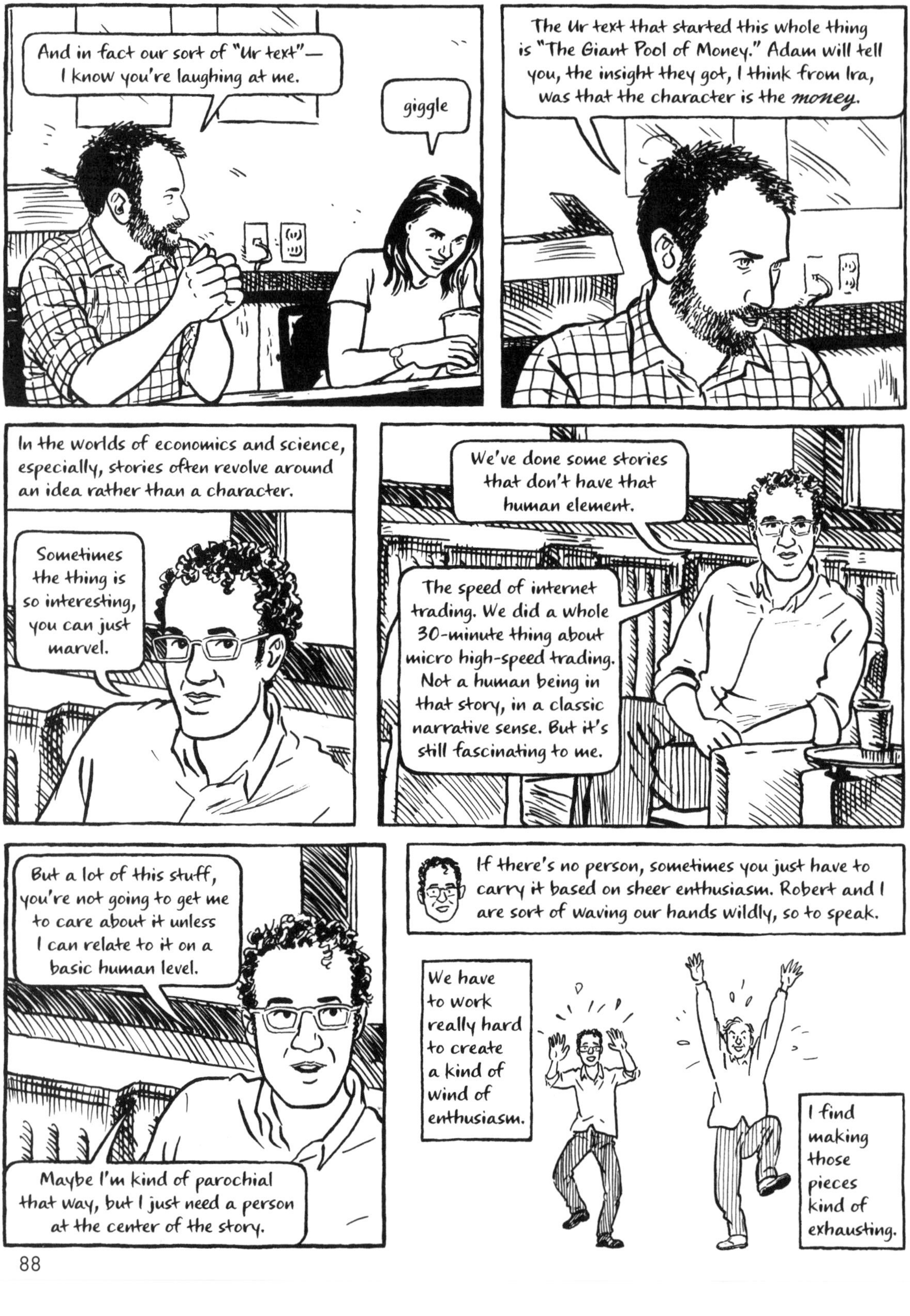
And in fact our sort of "Ur text"— I know you're laughing at me.
giggle
The Ur text that started this whole thing is "The Giant Pool of Money." Adam will tell you, the insight they got, I think from Ira, was that the character is the *money*.
In the worlds of economics and science, especially, stories often revolve around an idea rather than a character.
Sometimes the thing is so interesting, you can just marvel.
We've done some stories that don't have that human element.
The speed of internet trading. We did a whole 30-minute thing about micro high-speed trading. Not a human being in that story, in a classic narrative sense. But it's still fascinating to me.
But a lot of this stuff, you're not going to get me to care about it unless I can relate to it on a basic human level.
Maybe I'm kind of parochial that way, but I just need a person at the center of the story.
If there's no person, sometimes you just have to carry it based on sheer enthusiasm. Robert and I are sort of waving our hands wildly, so to speak.
We have to work really hard to create a kind of wind of enthusiasm.
I find making those pieces kind of exhausting.

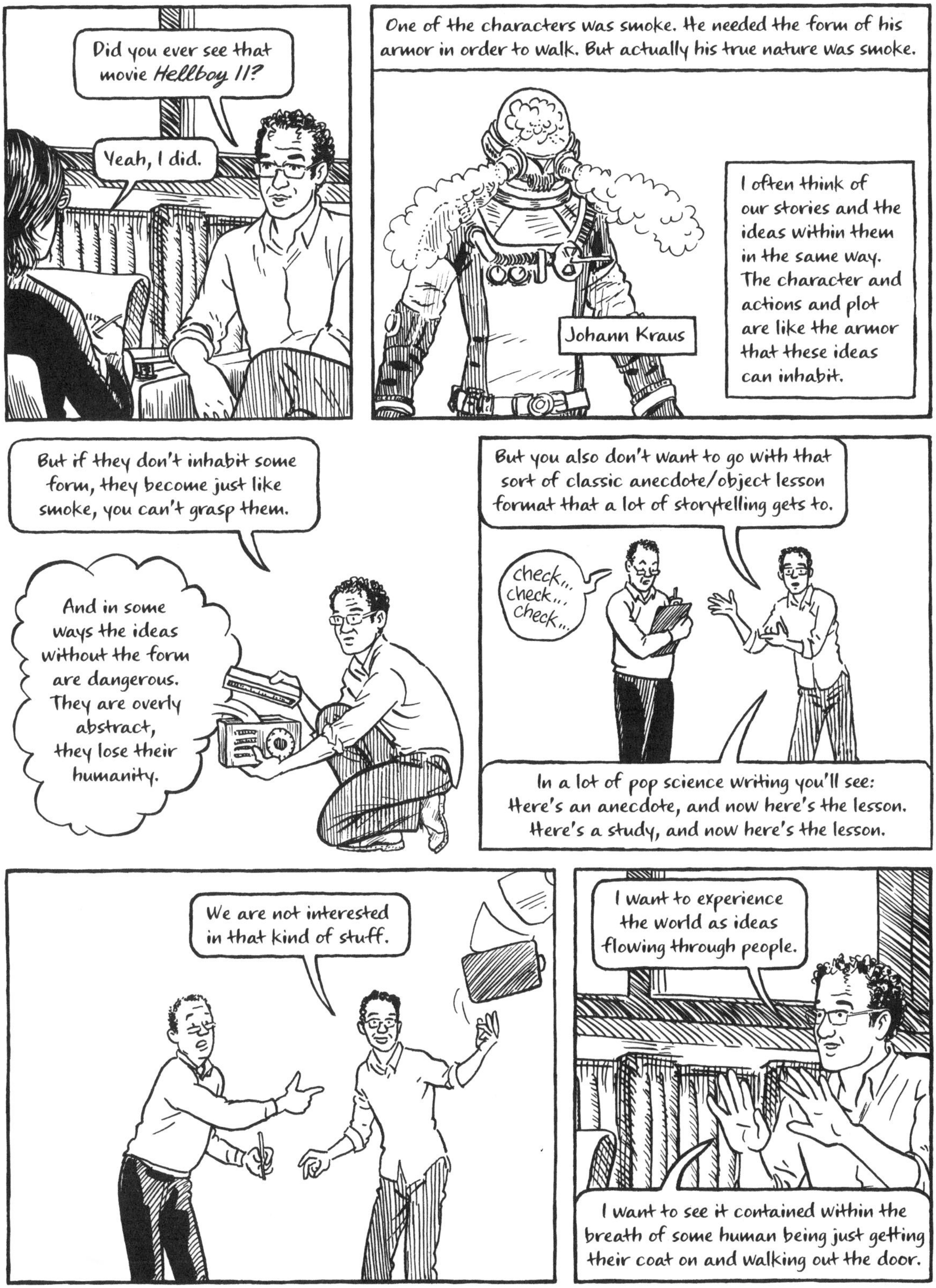
Did you ever see that movie *Hellboy II*?
Yeah, I did.
One of the characters was smoke. He needed the form of his armor in order to walk. But actually his true nature was smoke.
Johann Kraus
I often think of our stories and the ideas within them in the same way. The character and actions and plot are like the armor that these ideas can inhabit.
But if they don't inhabit some form, they become just like smoke, you can't grasp them.
And in some ways the ideas without the form are dangerous. They are overly abstract, they lose their humanity.
But you also don't want to go with that sort of classic anecdote/object lesson format that a lot of storytelling gets to.
check... check... check...
In a lot of pop science writing you'll see: Here's an anecdote, and now here's the lesson. Here's a study, and now here's the lesson.
We are not interested in that kind of stuff.
I want to experience the world as ideas flowing through people.
I want to see it contained within the breath of some human being just getting their coat on and walking out the door.

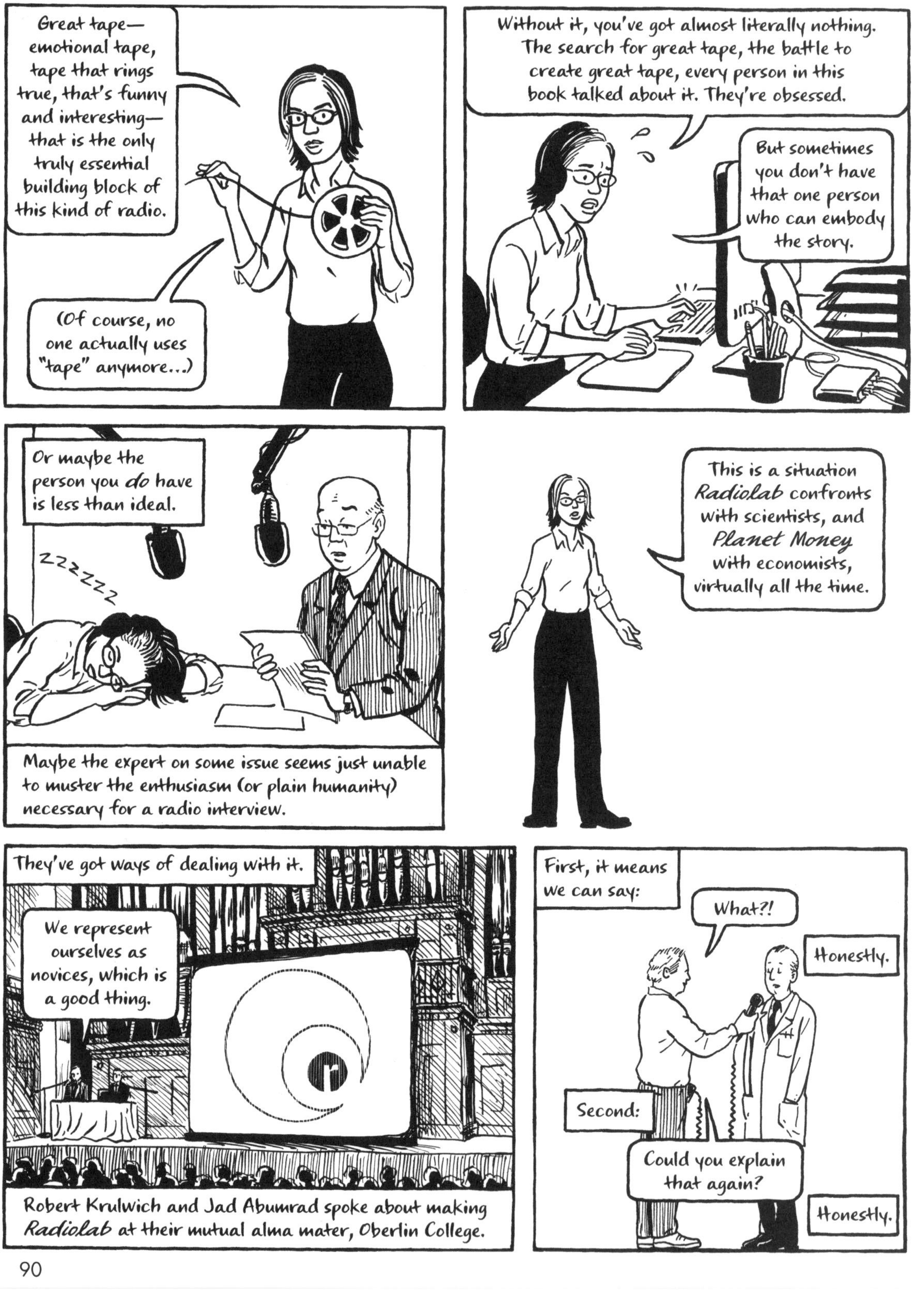
Great tape—emotional tape, tape that rings true, that's funny and interesting—that is the only truly essential building block of this kind of radio.
(Of course, no one actually uses "tape" anymore...)
Without it, you've got almost literally nothing. The search for great tape, the battle to create great tape, every person in this book talked about it. They're obsessed.
But sometimes you don't have that one person who can embody the story.
Or maybe the person you *do* have is less than ideal.
ZZZZZZ
Maybe the expert on some issue seems just unable to muster the enthusiasm (or plain humanity) necessary for a radio interview.
This is a situation *Radiolab* confronts with scientists, and *Planet Money* with economists, virtually all the time.
They've got ways of dealing with it.
We represent ourselves as novices, which is a good thing.
Robert Krulwich and Jad Abumrad spoke about making *Radiolab* at their mutual alma mater, Oberlin College.
First, it means we can say:
What?!
Honestly.
Second:
Could you explain that again?
Honestly.

And third, it allows us to challenge these people as though we were ordinary curious folks. We argue with them, and they give right back.

We are trying to model a kind of conversation with important people, powerful people, and particularly with knowledgable people.

 Including experts in stories can cause problems: Cutting to a professor or pundit to support someone's position can end up looking like you don't trust your storyteller. It undercuts them. It's often best to just let the character tell the story.

I'm the child of two scientists. My whole life, at the dinner table, my mom would say—she studies intake of fat into cells, that's her thing—

 But sometimes you've got to talk to an expert, and the job then is to find the ordinary human inside. That means clear language, but it also means helping the interviewees to find their true voices.

She'd say...

Here's how I think it works, Jad...

And she grabs a napkin and kind of curves it into a circle like a cell, and then she says...

This salt shaker is a fat molecule trying to get into the cell, and it's coming coming coming but it needs something to ferry it through the cell wall! So here's the fork, the fork is a protein...

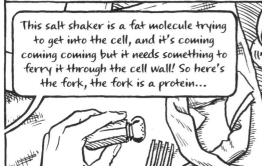

...and I don't know what the hell she's talking about. But what I get from her is excitement, a passion, a sense of mystery, of figuring something out about the universe.

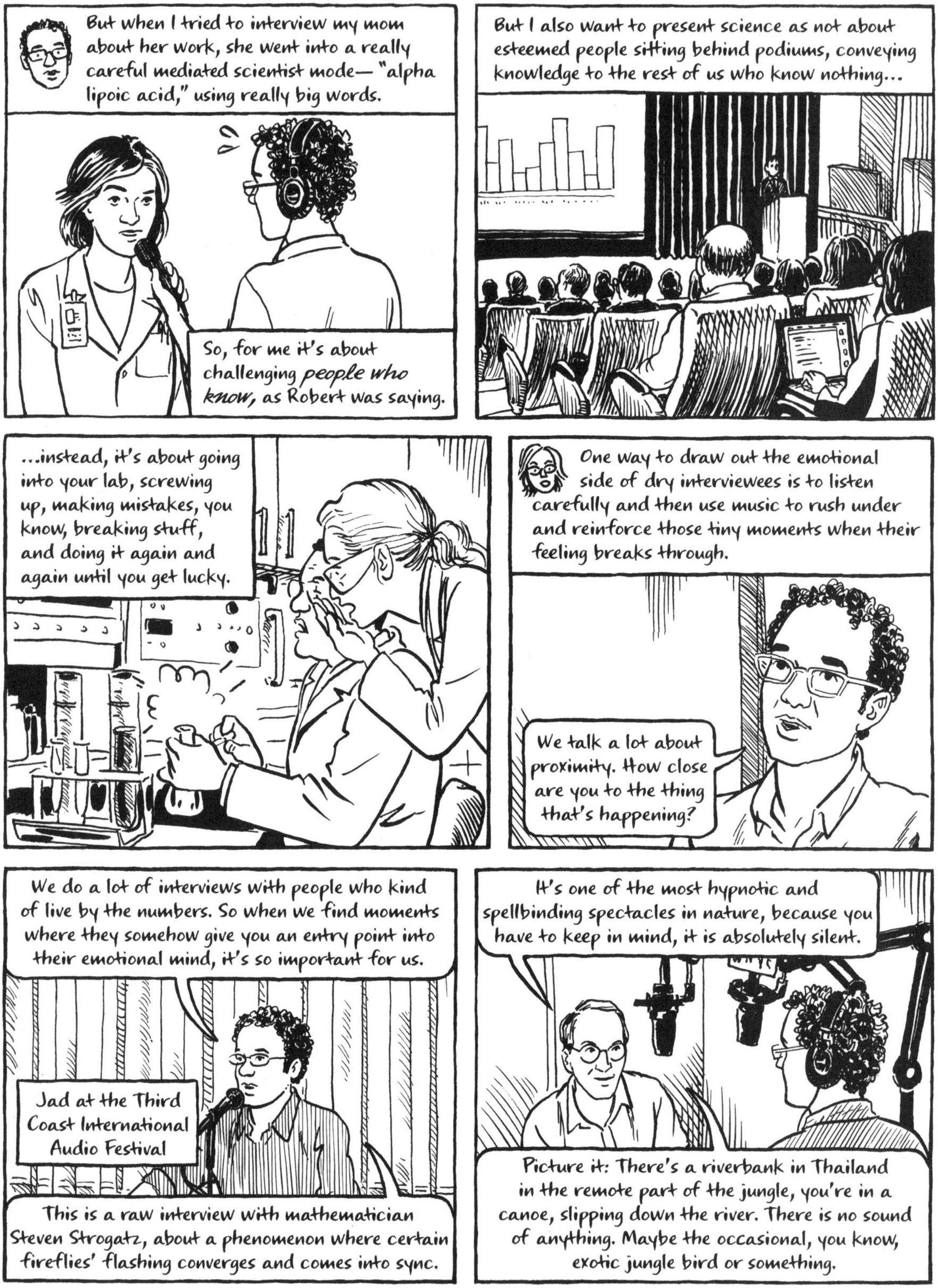

But when I tried to interview my mom about her work, she went into a really careful mediated scientist mode— "alpha lipoic acid," using really big words.
So, for me it's about challenging *people who know*, as Robert was saying.
But I also want to present science as not about esteemed people sitting behind podiums, conveying knowledge to the rest of us who know nothing...
...instead, it's about going into your lab, screwing up, making mistakes, you know, breaking stuff, and doing it again and again until you get lucky.
One way to draw out the emotional side of dry interviewees is to listen carefully and then use music to rush under and reinforce those tiny moments when their feeling breaks through.
We talk a lot about proximity. How close are you to the thing that's happening?
We do a lot of interviews with people who kind of live by the numbers. So when we find moments where they somehow give you an entry point into their emotional mind, it's so important for us.
Jad at the Third Coast International Audio Festival
This is a raw interview with mathematician Steven Strogatz, about a phenomenon where certain fireflies' flashing converges and comes into sync.
It's one of the most hypnotic and spellbinding spectacles in nature, because you have to keep in mind, it is absolutely silent.
Picture it: There's a riverbank in Thailand in the remote part of the jungle, you're in a canoe, slipping down the river. There is no sound of anything. Maybe the occasional, you know, exotic jungle bird or something.

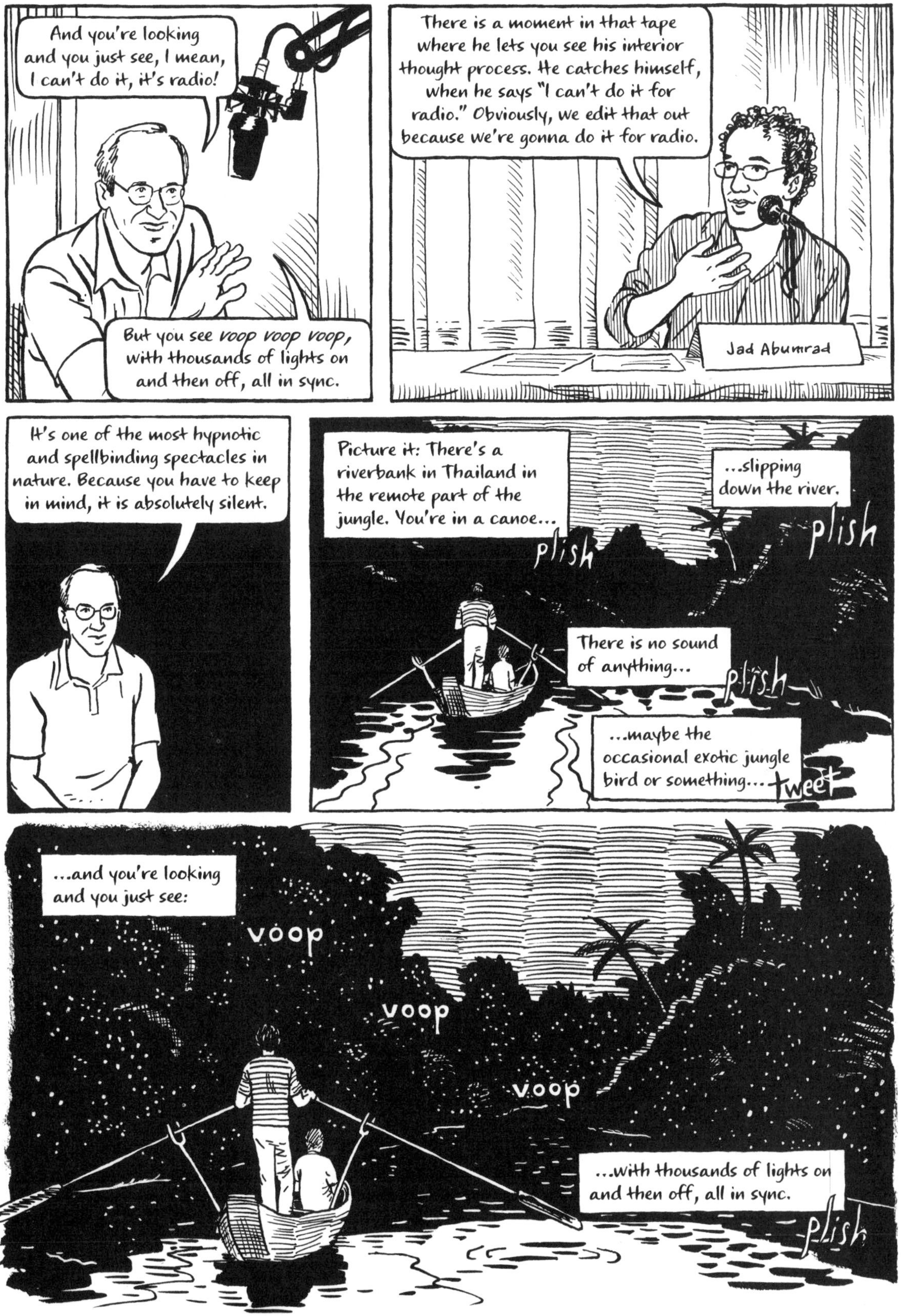
And you're looking and you just see, I mean, I can't do it, it's radio!
But you see *voop voop voop*, with thousands of lights on and then off, all in sync.
There is a moment in that tape where he lets you see his interior thought process. He catches himself, when he says "I can't do it for radio." Obviously, we edit that out because we're gonna do it for radio.
Jad Abumrad
It's one of the most hypnotic and spellbinding spectacles in nature. Because you have to keep in mind, it is absolutely silent.
Picture it: There's a riverbank in Thailand in the remote part of the jungle. You're in a canoe...
...slipping down the river.
plish
plish
There is no sound of anything...
plish
...maybe the occasional exotic jungle bird or something...
tweet
...and you're looking and you just see:
voop
voop
voop
...with thousands of lights on and then off, all in sync.
plish

Steve starts to see things, he sees flashing lights, and he has this wonderful rhythmic sound that he makes; he's almost hearing things.

He was feeling a sort of awe. We're always chasing the moment of awe, where the scientist goes out of the empirical mode of thinking and becomes like a child, looking at fireflies.

That moment of tape of Steve was a moment when you were in his head, you were in his emotional mind. You were: Oh yeah, he's feeling it...

I'm feeling it because he's feeling it. And you are in there, and the distance has been obliterated.

That's always the moment that you want.

And you develop this very very keen sense in an interview for, whoa, there it is. I feel that vibration, which is the vibration of being close.

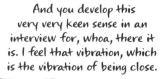

I'm close now, I'm close. Go in. I don't know what I'm curious about, but stay here, don't move on.

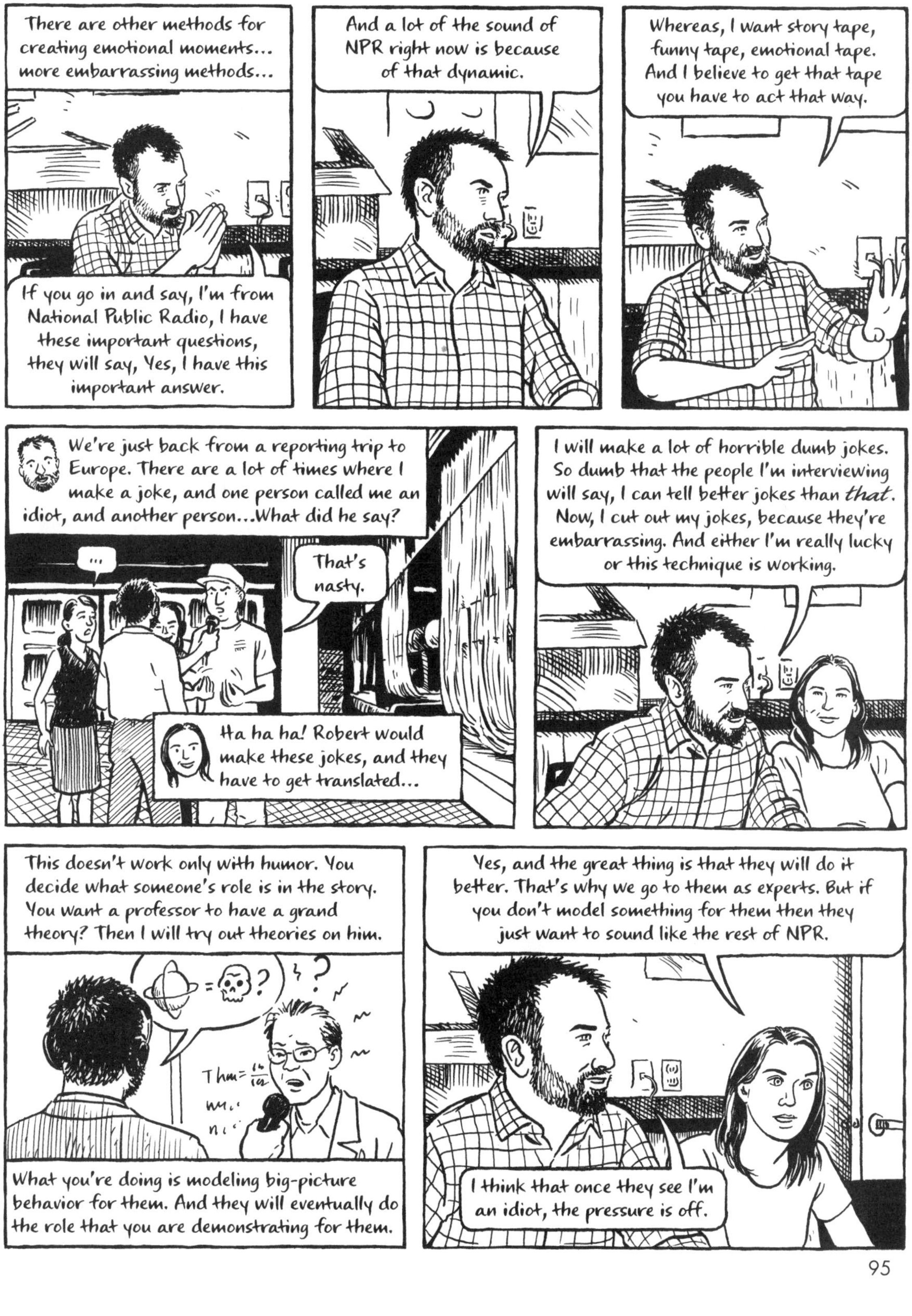

There are other methods for creating emotional moments... more embarrassing methods...
If you go in and say, I'm from National Public Radio, I have these important questions, they will say, Yes, I have this important answer.
And a lot of the sound of NPR right now is because of that dynamic.
Whereas, I want story tape, funny tape, emotional tape. And I believe to get that tape you have to act that way.
We're just back from a reporting trip to Europe. There are a lot of times where I make a joke, and one person called me an idiot, and another person...What did he say?
...
That's nasty.
Ha ha ha! Robert would make these jokes, and they have to get translated...
I will make a lot of horrible dumb jokes. So dumb that the people I'm interviewing will say, I can tell better jokes than *that*. Now, I cut out my jokes, because they're embarrassing. And either I'm really lucky or this technique is working.
This doesn't work only with humor. You decide what someone's role is in the story. You want a professor to have a grand theory? Then I will try out theories on him.
What you're doing is modeling big-picture behavior for them. And they will eventually do the role that you are demonstrating for them.
Yes, and the great thing is that they will do it better. That's why we go to them as experts. But if you don't model something for them then they just want to sound like the rest of NPR.
I think that once they see I'm an idiot, the pressure is off.

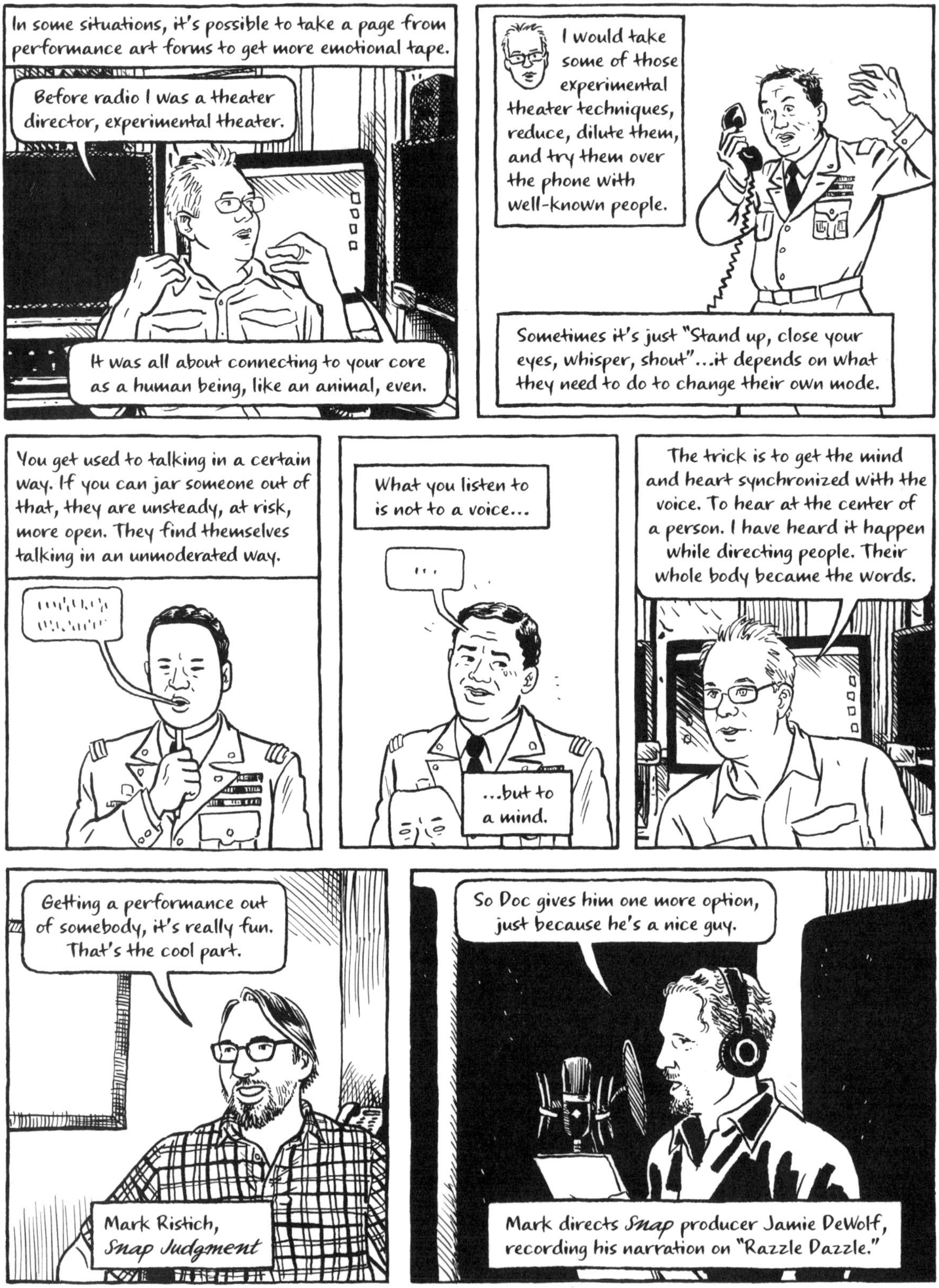

In some situations, it's possible to take a page from performance art forms to get more emotional tape.
Before radio I was a theater director, experimental theater.
It was all about connecting to your core as a human being, like an animal, even.
I would take some of those experimental theater techniques, reduce, dilute them, and try them over the phone with well-known people.
Sometimes it's just "Stand up, close your eyes, whisper, shout"...it depends on what they need to do to change their own mode.
You get used to talking in a certain way. If you can jar someone out of that, they are unsteady, at risk, more open. They find themselves talking in an unmoderated way.
What you listen to is not to a voice...
...
...but to a mind.
The trick is to get the mind and heart synchronized with the voice. To hear at the center of a person. I have heard it happen while directing people. Their whole body became the words.
Getting a performance out of somebody, it's really fun. That's the cool part.
Mark Ristich, *Snap Judgment*
So Doc gives him one more option, just because he's a nice guy.
Mark directs *Snap* producer Jamie DeWolf, recording his narration on "Razzle Dazzle."

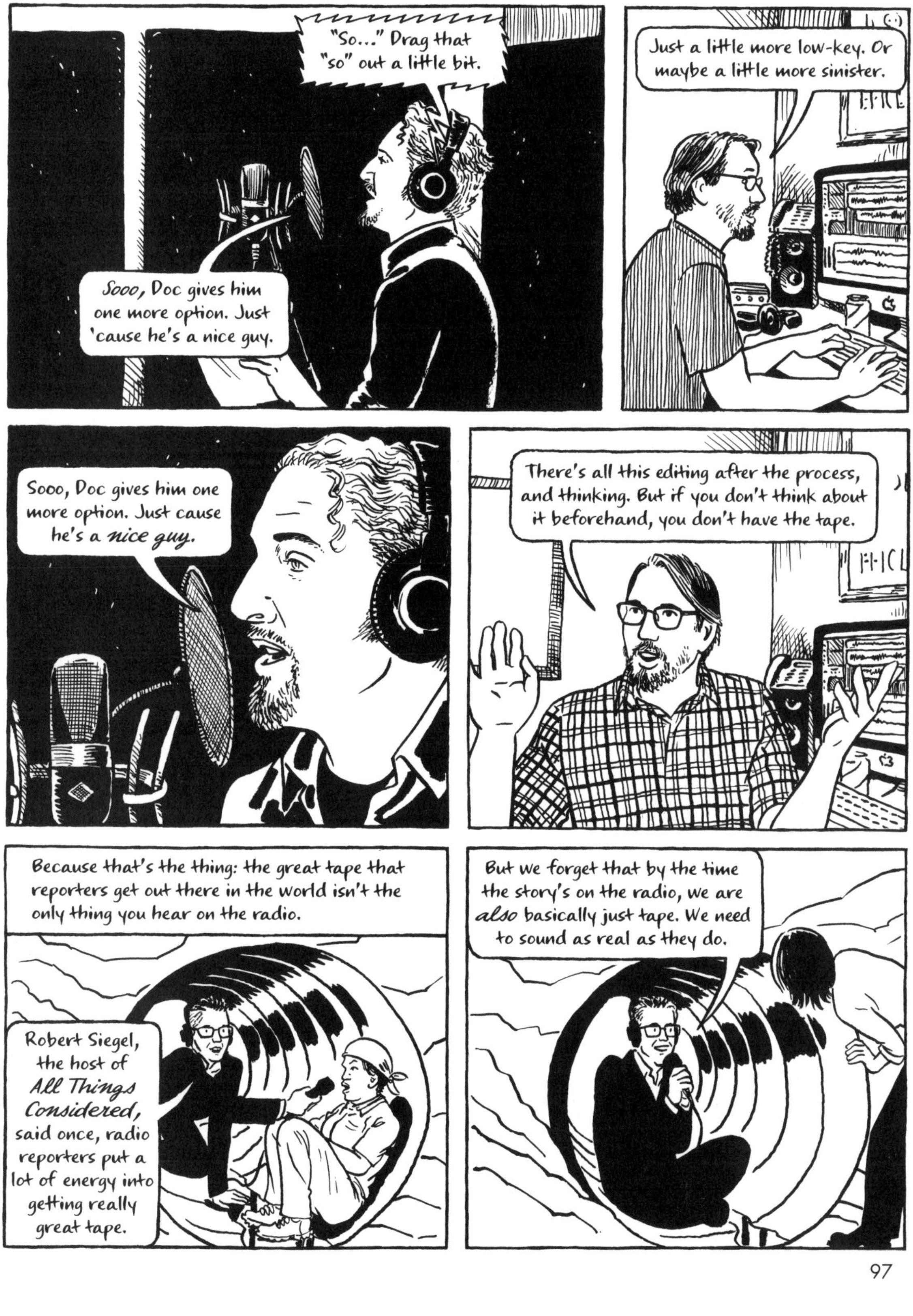
"So..." Drag that "so" out a little bit.
Sooo, Doc gives him one more option. Just 'cause he's a nice guy.
Just a little more low-key. Or maybe a little more sinister.
Sooo, Doc gives him one more option. Just cause he's a *nice guy*.
There's all this editing after the process, and thinking. But if you don't think about it beforehand, you don't have the tape.
Because that's the thing: the great tape that reporters get out there in the world isn't the only thing you hear on the radio.
Robert Siegel, the host of *All Things Considered*, said once, radio reporters put a lot of energy into getting really great tape.
But we forget that by the time the story's on the radio, we are *also* basically just tape. We need to sound as real as they do.

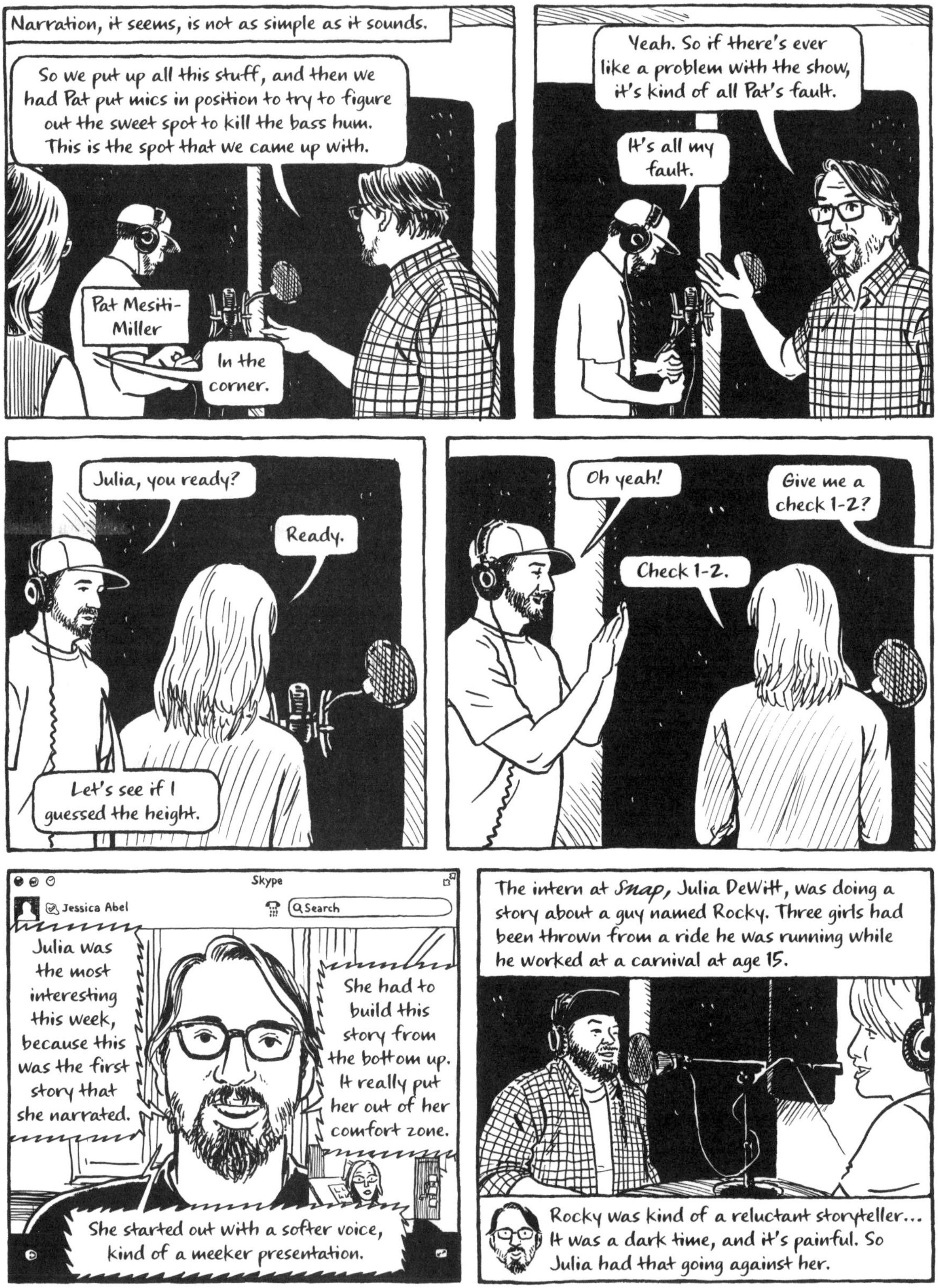
Narration, it seems, is not as simple as it sounds.
So we put up all this stuff, and then we had Pat put mics in position to try to figure out the sweet spot to kill the bass hum. This is the spot that we came up with.
Pat Mesiti-Miller
In the corner.
Yeah. So if there's ever like a problem with the show, it's kind of all Pat's fault.
It's all my fault.
Julia, you ready?
Ready.
Let's see if I guessed the height.
Oh yeah!
Give me a check 1-2?
Check 1-2.
Skype
Jessica Abel
Search
Julia was the most interesting this week, because this was the first story that she narrated.
She had to build this story from the bottom up. It really put her out of her comfort zone.
She started out with a softer voice, kind of a meeker presentation.
The intern at *Snap*, Julia DeWitt, was doing a story about a guy named Rocky. Three girls had been thrown from a ride he was running while he worked at a carnival at age 15.
Rocky was kind of a reluctant storyteller... It was a dark time, and it's painful. So Julia had that going against her.

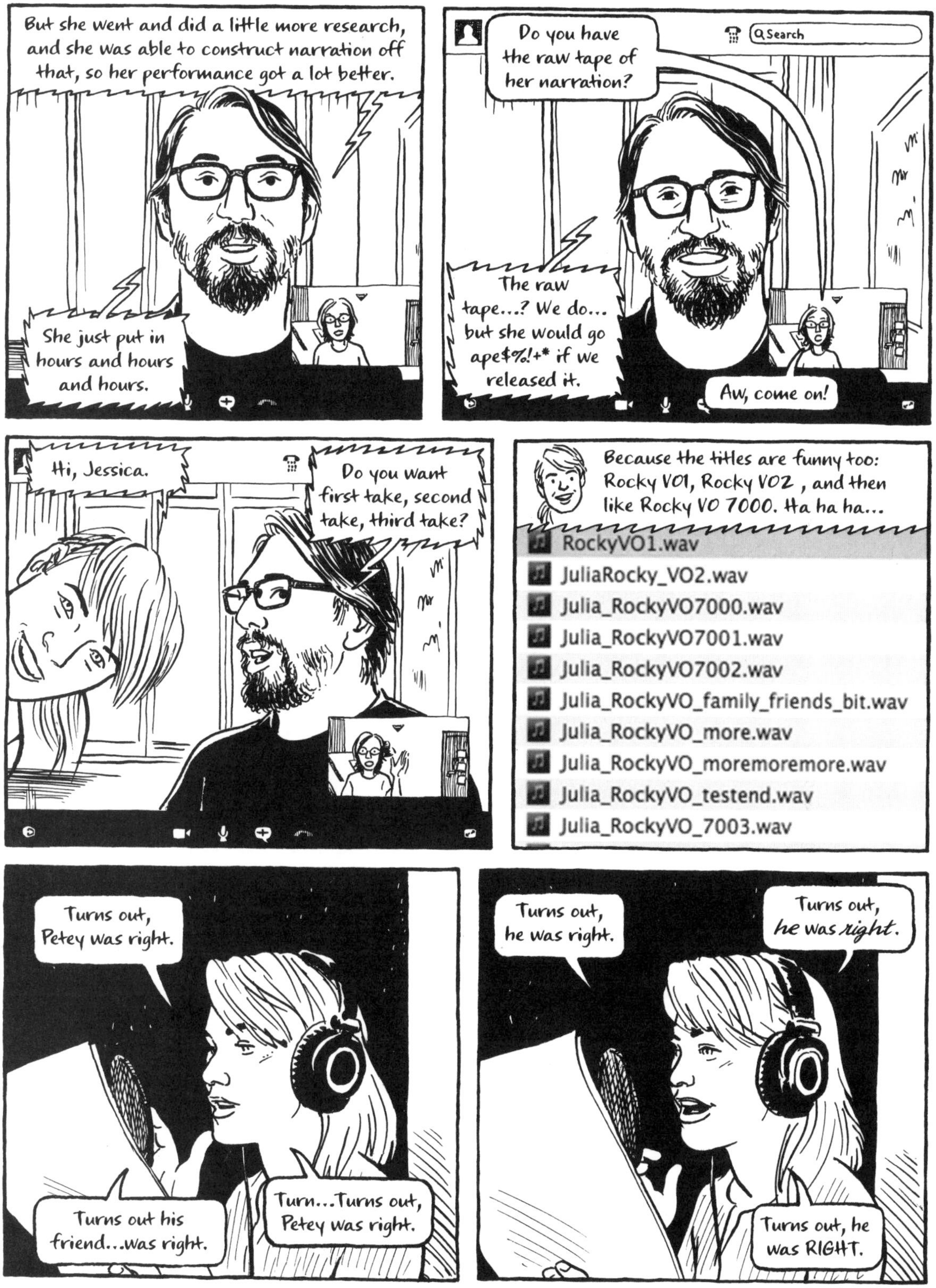
But she went and did a little more research, and she was able to construct narration off that, so her performance got a lot better.
She just put in hours and hours and hours.
Do you have the raw tape of her narration?
Search
The raw tape...? We do... but she would go ape$%!+* if we released it.
Aw, come on!
Hi, Jessica.
Do you want first take, second take, third take?
Because the titles are funny too: Rocky VO1, Rocky VO2 , and then like Rocky VO 7000. Ha ha ha...
RockyVO1.wav
JuliaRocky_VO2.wav
Julia_RockyVO7000.wav
Julia_RockyVO7001.wav
Julia_RockyVO7002.wav
Julia_RockyVO_family_friends_bit.wav
Julia_RockyVO_more.wav
Julia_RockyVO_moremoremore.wav
Julia_RockyVO_testend.wav
Julia_RockyVO_7003.wav
Turns out, Petey was right.
Turns out his friend...was right.
Turn...Turns out, Petey was right.
Turns out, he was right.
Turns out, *he* was *right*.
Turns out, he was RIGHT.

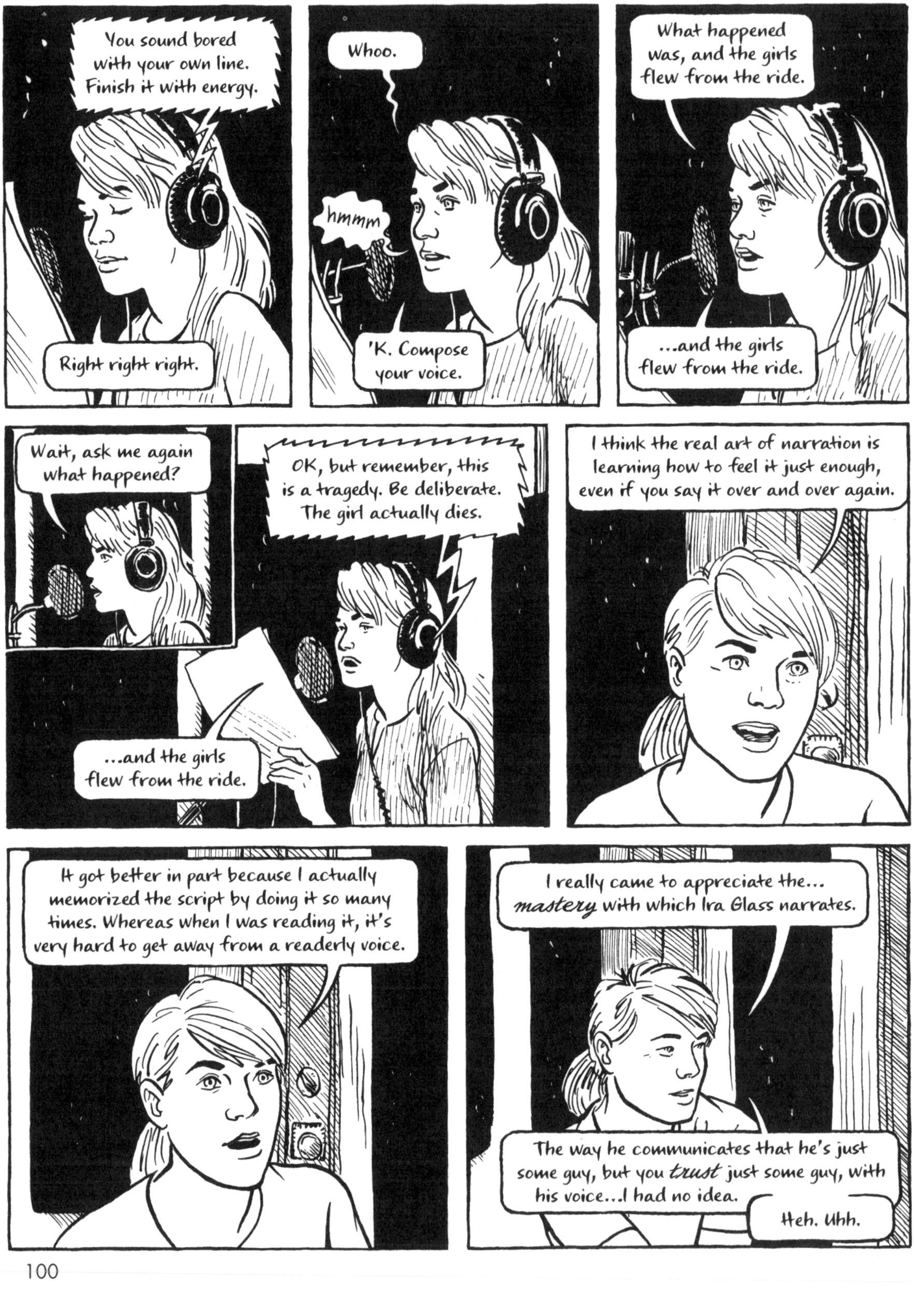
You sound bored with your own line. Finish it with energy.
Right right right.
Whoo.
hmmm
'K. Compose your voice.
What happened was, and the girls flew from the ride.
...and the girls flew from the ride.
Wait, ask me again what happened?
OK, but remember, this is a tragedy. Be deliberate. The girl actually dies.
...and the girls flew from the ride.
I think the real art of narration is learning how to feel it just enough, even if you say it over and over again.
It got better in part because I actually memorized the script by doing it so many times. Whereas when I was reading it, it's very hard to get away from a readerly voice.
I really came to appreciate the... *mastery* with which Ira Glass narrates.
The way he communicates that he's just some guy, but you *trust* just some guy, with his voice...I had no idea.
Heh. Uhh.

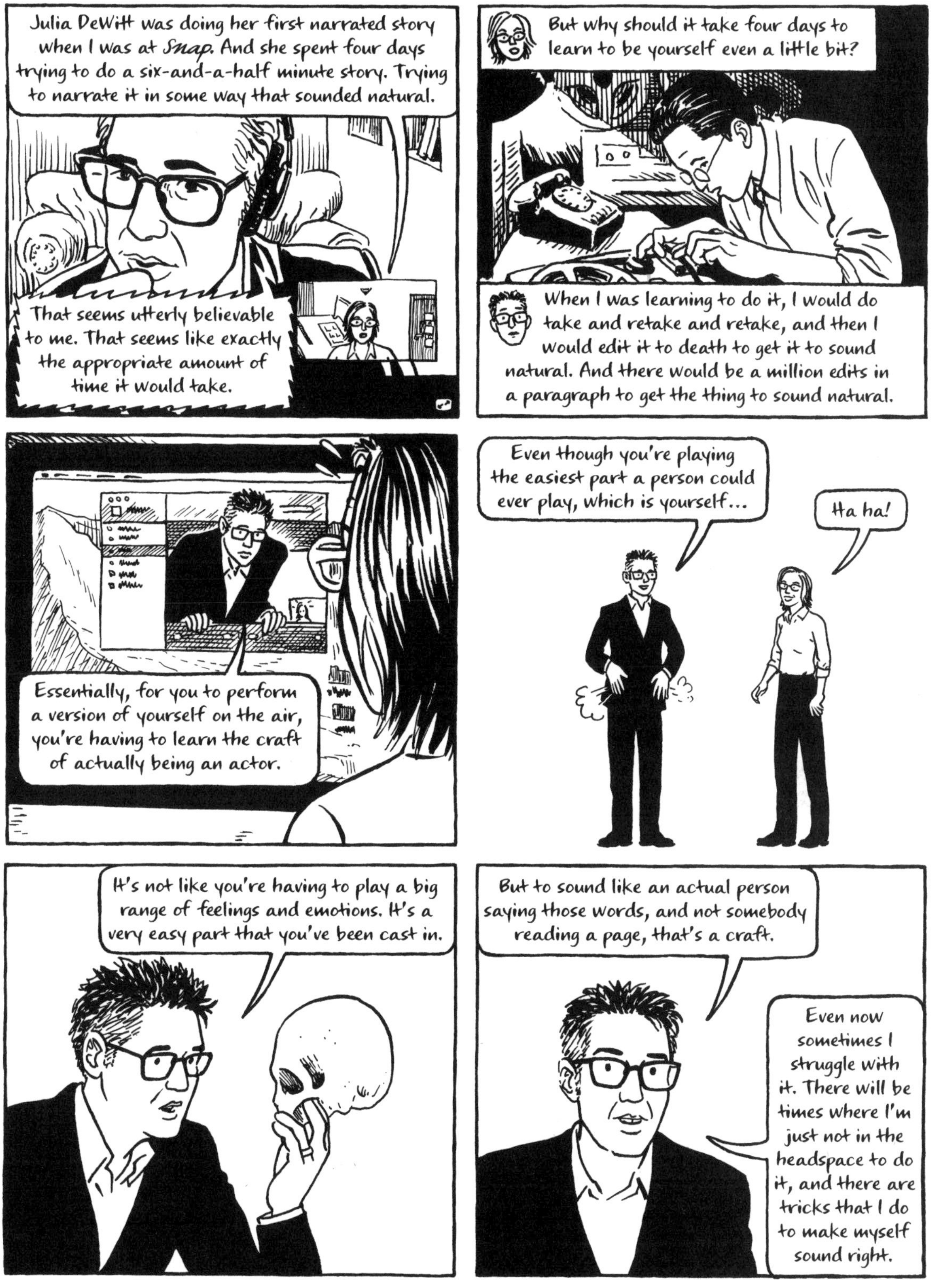

Julia DeWitt was doing her first narrated story when I was at *Snap.* And she spent four days trying to do a six-and-a-half minute story. Trying to narrate it in some way that sounded natural.
That seems utterly believable to me. That seems like exactly the appropriate amount of time it would take.
But why should it take four days to learn to be yourself even a little bit?
When I was learning to do it, I would do take and retake and retake, and then I would edit it to death to get it to sound natural. And there would be a million edits in a paragraph to get the thing to sound natural.
Essentially, for you to perform a version of yourself on the air, you're having to learn the craft of actually being an actor.
Even though you're playing the easiest part a person could ever play, which is yourself...
Ha ha!
It's not like you're having to play a big range of feelings and emotions. It's a very easy part that you've been cast in.
But to sound like an actual person saying those words, and not somebody reading a page, that's a craft.
Even now sometimes I struggle with it. There will be times where I'm just not in the headspace to do it, and there are tricks that I do to make myself sound right.

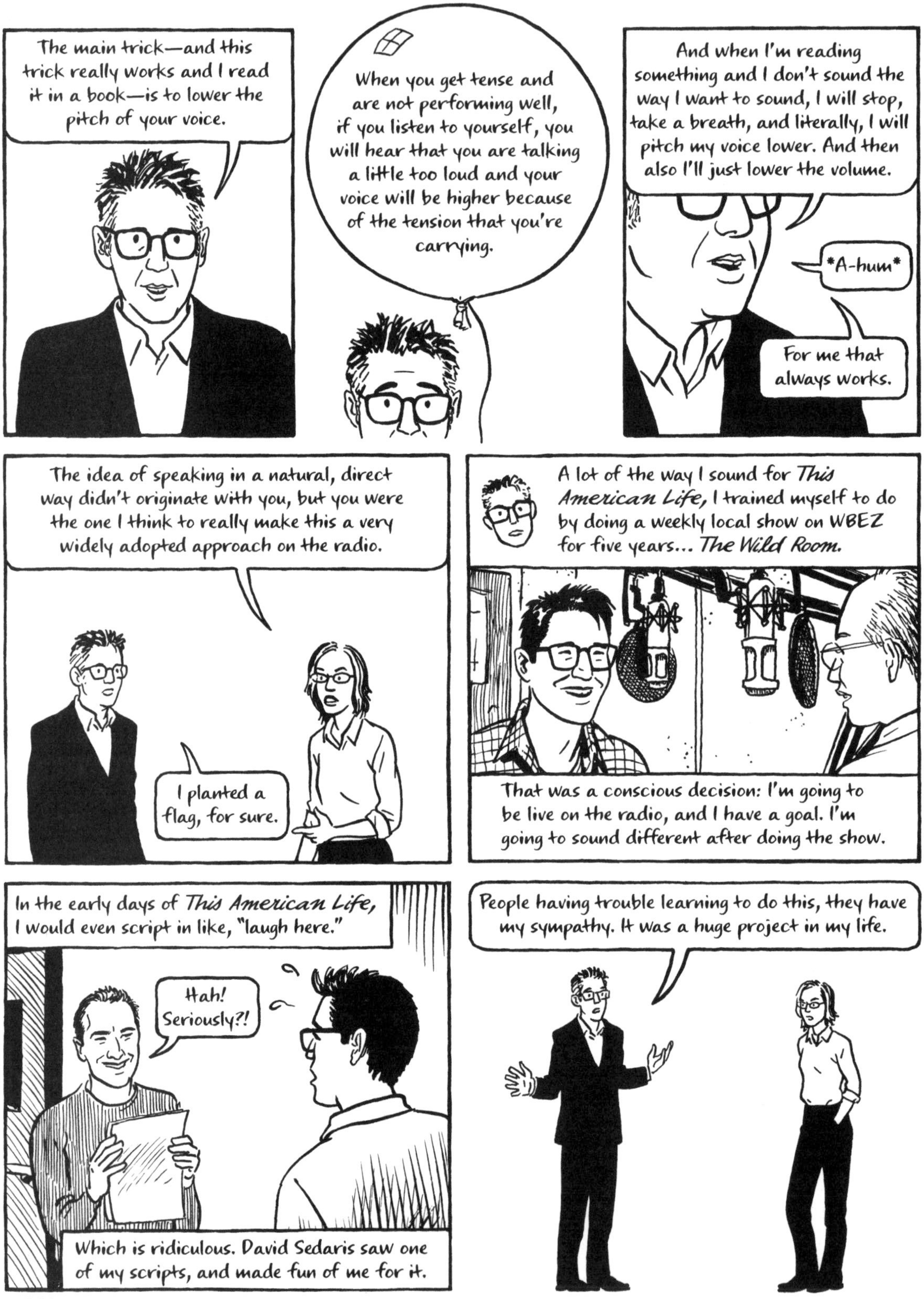
The main trick—and this trick really works and I read it in a book—is to lower the pitch of your voice.
When you get tense and are not performing well, if you listen to yourself, you will hear that you are talking a little too loud and your voice will be higher because of the tension that you're carrying.
And when I'm reading something and I don't sound the way I want to sound, I will stop, take a breath, and literally, I will pitch my voice lower. And then also I'll just lower the volume.
A-hum
For me that always works.
The idea of speaking in a natural, direct way didn't originate with you, but you were the one I think to really make this a very widely adopted approach on the radio.
I planted a flag, for sure.
A lot of the way I sound for *This American Life,* I trained myself to do by doing a weekly local show on WBEZ for five years... *The Wild Room.*
That was a conscious decision: I'm going to be live on the radio, and I have a goal. I'm going to sound different after doing the show.
In the early days of *This American Life,* I would even script in like, "laugh here."
Hah! Seriously?!
Which is ridiculous. David Sedaris saw one of my scripts, and made fun of me for it.
People having trouble learning to do this, they have my sympathy. It was a huge project in my life.

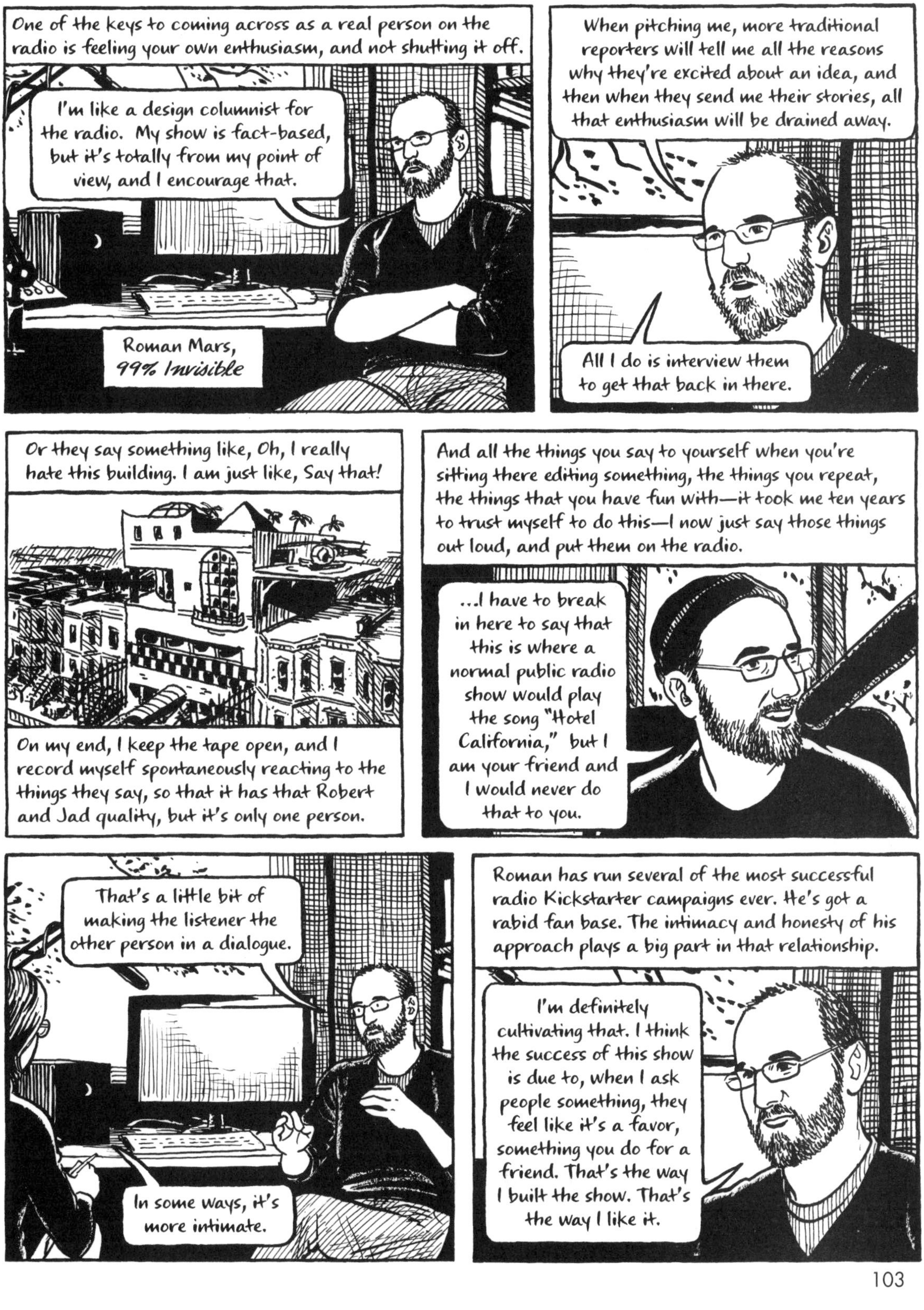
One of the keys to coming across as a real person on the radio is feeling your own enthusiasm, and not shutting it off.
I'm like a design columnist for the radio. My show is fact-based, but it's totally from my point of view, and I encourage that.
Roman Mars, 99% Invisible
When pitching me, more traditional reporters will tell me all the reasons why they're excited about an idea, and then when they send me their stories, all that enthusiasm will be drained away.
All I do is interview them to get that back in there.
Or they say something like, Oh, I really hate this building. I am just like, Say that!
On my end, I keep the tape open, and I record myself spontaneously reacting to the things they say, so that it has that Robert and Jad quality, but it's only one person.
And all the things you say to yourself when you're sitting there editing something, the things you repeat, the things that you have fun with—it took me ten years to trust myself to do this—I now just say those things out loud, and put them on the radio.
...I have to break in here to say that this is where a normal public radio show would play the song "Hotel California," but I am your friend and I would never do that to you.
That's a little bit of making the listener the other person in a dialogue.
In some ways, it's more intimate.
Roman has run several of the most successful radio Kickstarter campaigns ever. He's got a rabid fan base. The intimacy and honesty of his approach plays a big part in that relationship.
I'm definitely cultivating that. I think the success of this show is due to, when I ask people something, they feel like it's a favor, something you do for a friend. That's the way I built the show. That's the way I like it.

TAKE A DEEP BREATH

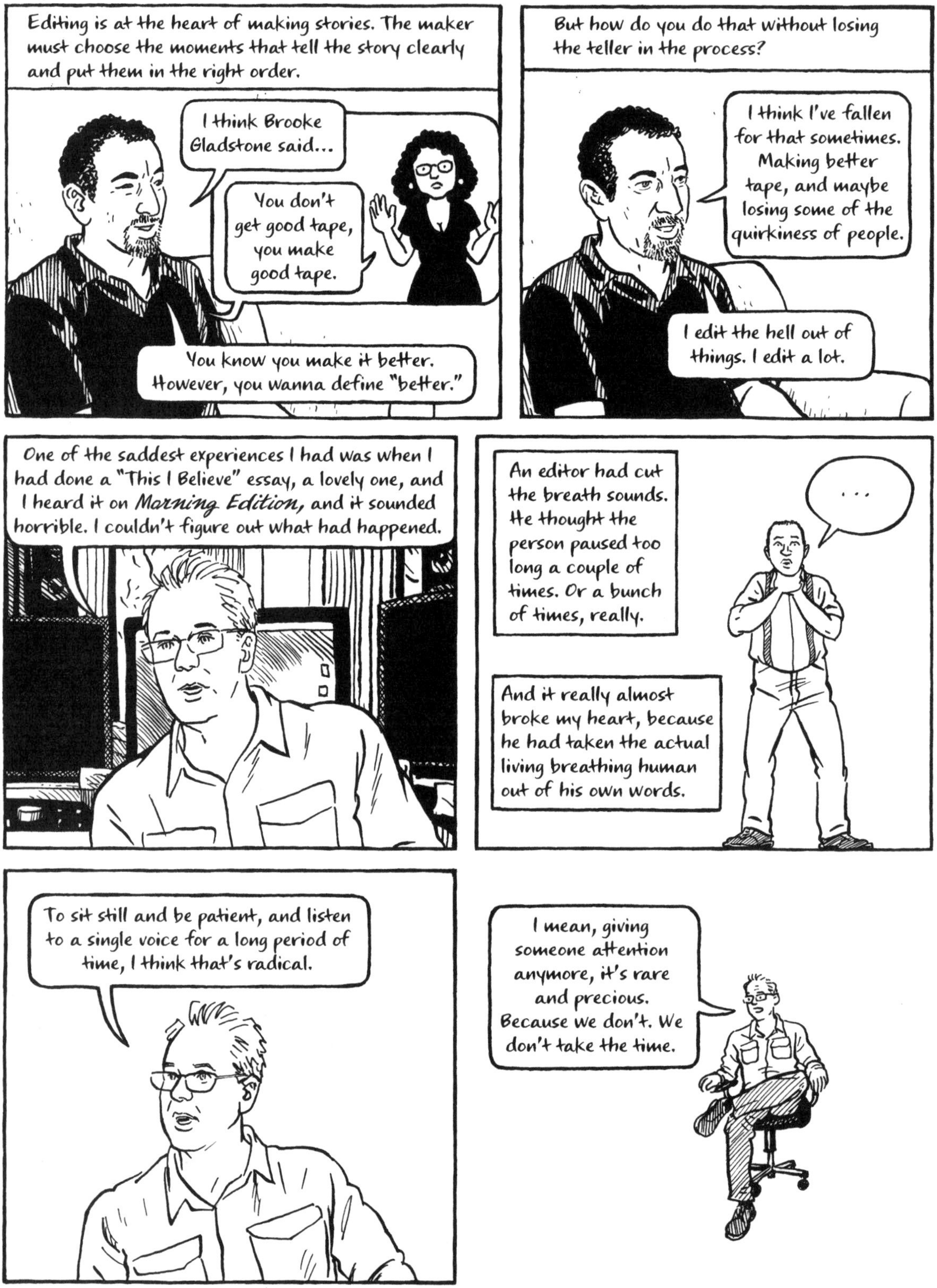
Editing is at the heart of making stories. The maker must choose the moments that tell the story clearly and put them in the right order.
I think Brooke Gladstone said...
You don't get good tape, you make good tape.
You know you make it better. However, you wanna define "better."
But how do you do that without losing the teller in the process?
I think I've fallen for that sometimes. Making better tape, and maybe losing some of the quirkiness of people.
I edit the hell out of things. I edit a lot.
One of the saddest experiences I had was when I had done a "This I Believe" essay, a lovely one, and I heard it on *Morning Edition,* and it sounded horrible. I couldn't figure out what had happened.
An editor had cut the breath sounds. He thought the person paused too long a couple of times. Or a bunch of times, really.
...
And it really almost broke my heart, because he had taken the actual living breathing human out of his own words.
To sit still and be patient, and listen to a single voice for a long period of time, I think that's radical.
I mean, giving someone attention anymore, it's rare and precious. Because we don't. We don't take the time.

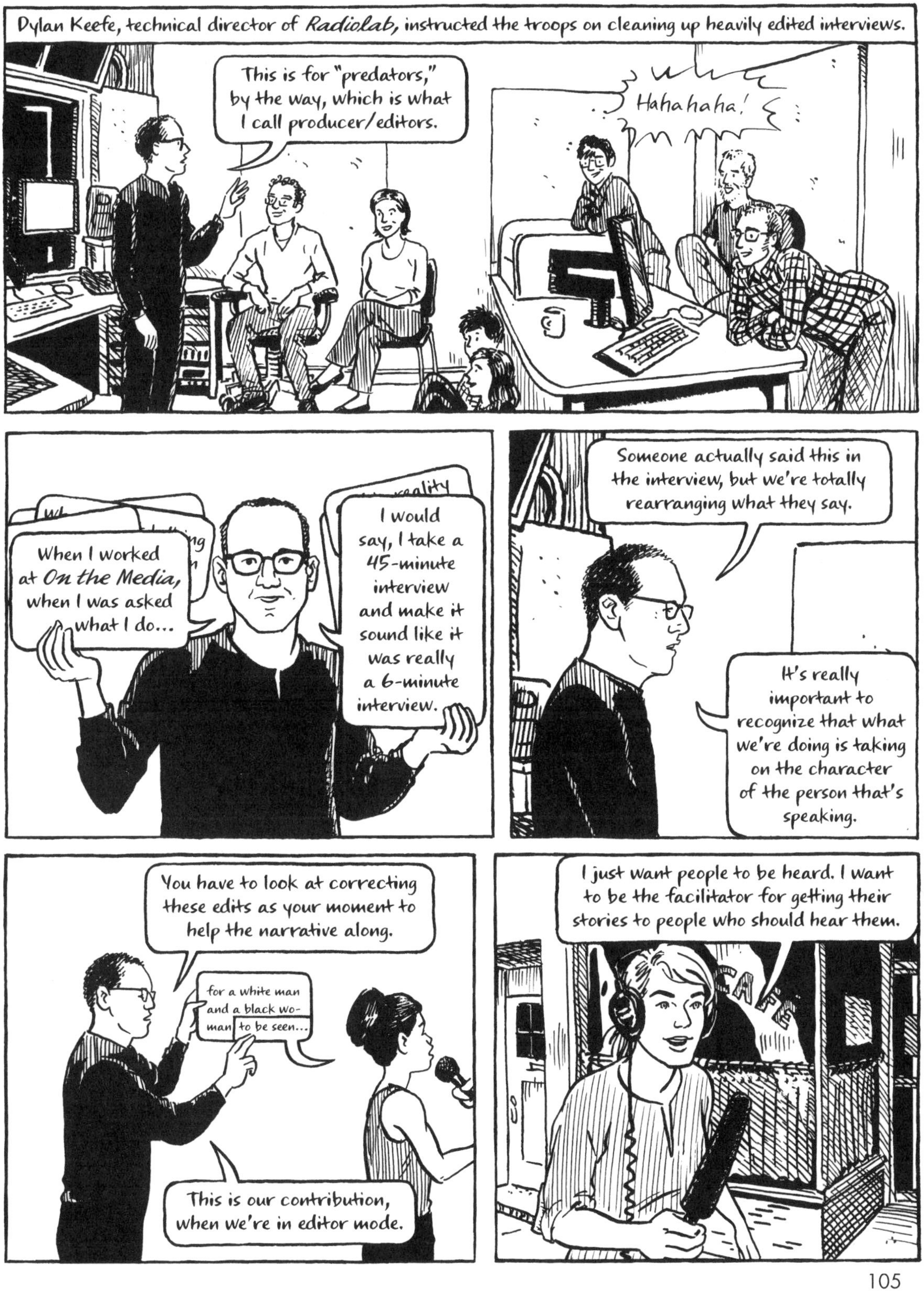

Dylan Keefe, technical director of *Radiolab,* instructed the troops on cleaning up heavily edited interviews.
This is for "predators," by the way, which is what I call producer/editors.
Hahahaha!
When I worked at *On the Media,* when I was asked what I do...
I would say, I take a 45-minute interview and make it sound like it was really a 6-minute interview.
Someone actually said this in the interview, but we're totally rearranging what they say.
It's really important to recognize that what we're doing is taking on the character of the person that's speaking.
You have to look at correcting these edits as your moment to help the narrative along.
for a white man and a black woman to be seen...
This is our contribution, when we're in editor mode.
I just want people to be heard. I want to be the facilitator for getting their stories to people who should hear them.

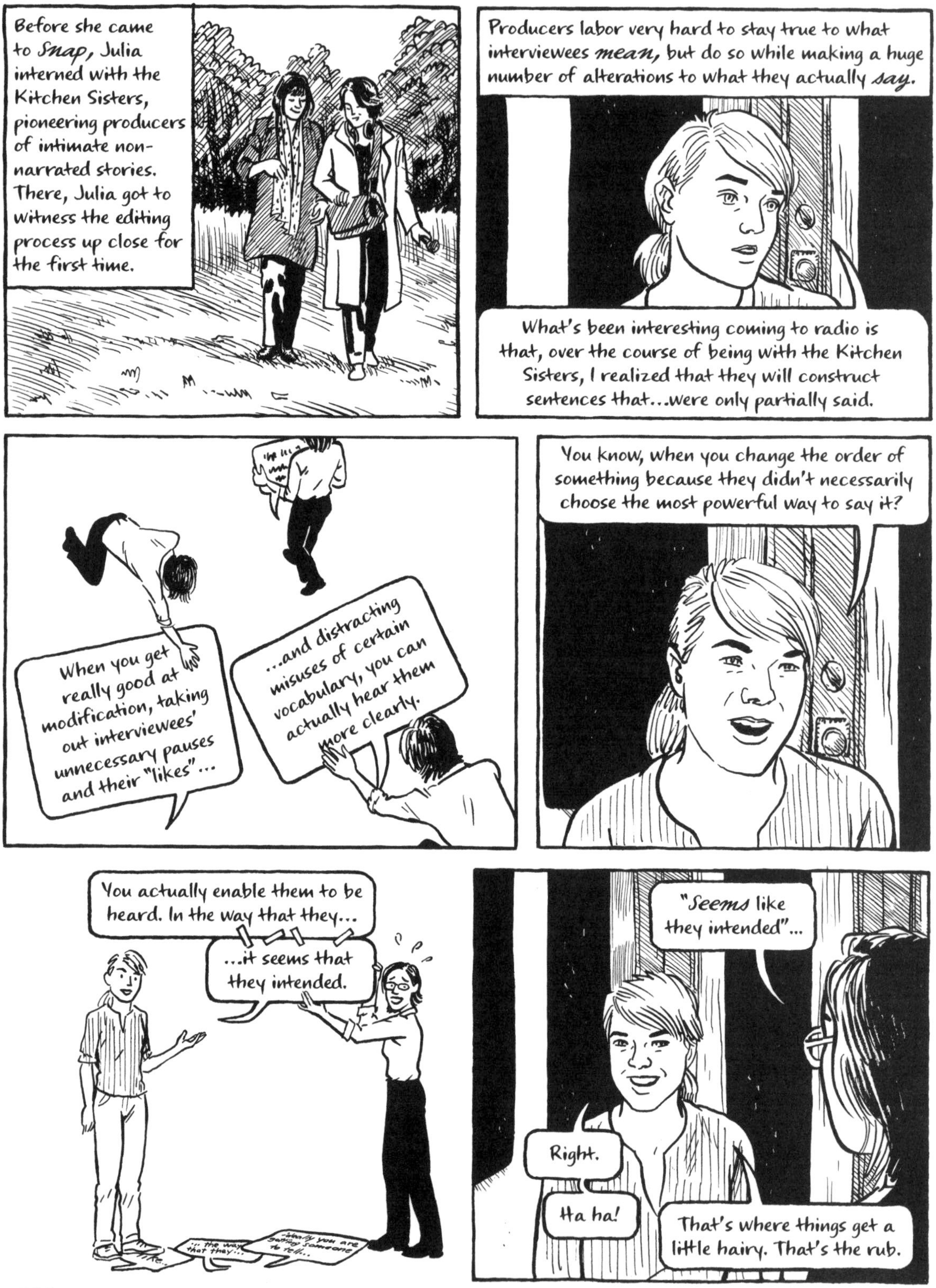

Before she came to *Snap,* Julia interned with the Kitchen Sisters, pioneering producers of intimate non-narrated stories. There, Julia got to witness the editing process up close for the first time.
Producers labor very hard to stay true to what interviewees *mean,* but do so while making a huge number of alterations to what they actually *say.*
What's been interesting coming to radio is that, over the course of being with the Kitchen Sisters, I realized that they will construct sentences that...were only partially said.
When you get really good at modification, taking out interviewees' unnecessary pauses and their "likes"...
...and distracting misuses of certain vocabulary, you can actually hear them more clearly.
You know, when you change the order of something because they didn't necessarily choose the most powerful way to say it?
You actually enable them to be heard. In the way that they...
...it seems that they intended.
"*Seems* like they intended"...
Right.
Ha ha!
That's where things get a little hairy. That's the rub.

KEEP OR KILL:

Story Structure

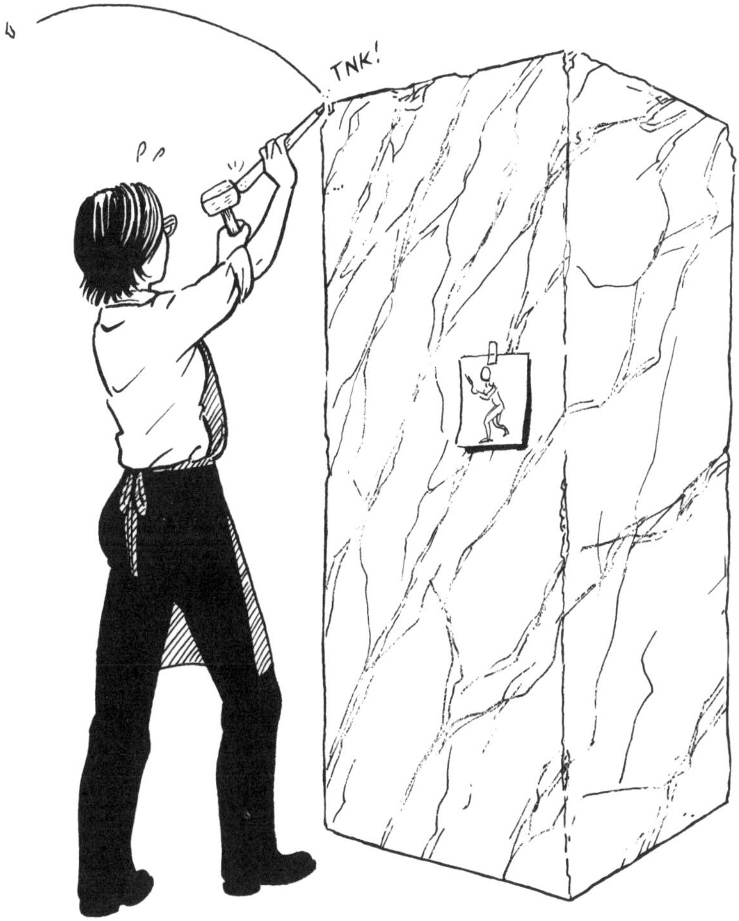
TNK!

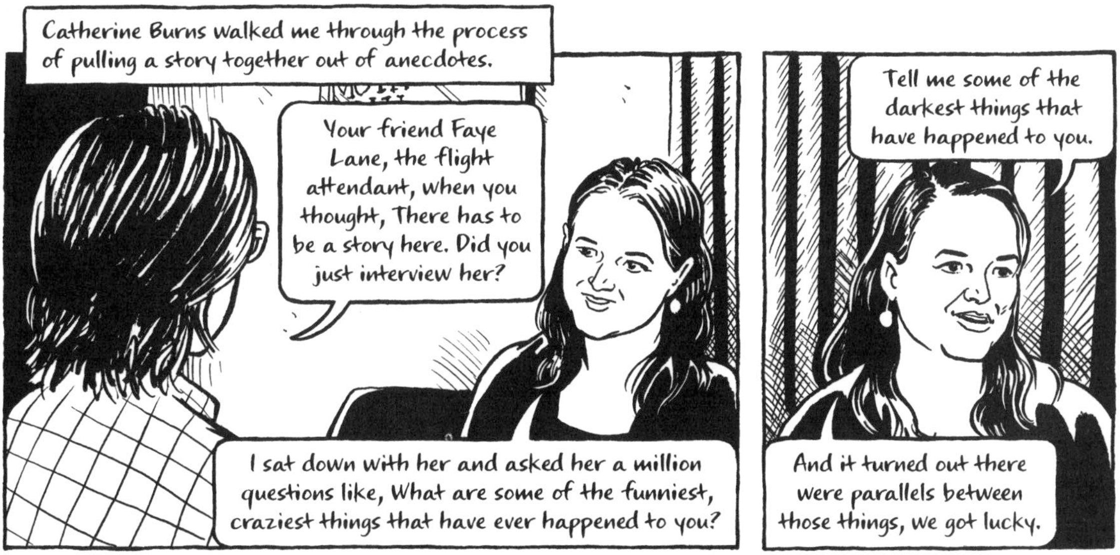
Catherine Burns walked me through the process of pulling a story together out of anecdotes.
Your friend Faye Lane, the flight attendant, when you thought, There has to be a story here. Did you just interview her?
I sat down with her and asked her a million questions like, What are some of the funniest, craziest things that have ever happened to you?
Tell me some of the darkest things that have happened to you.
And it turned out there were parallels between those things, we got lucky.

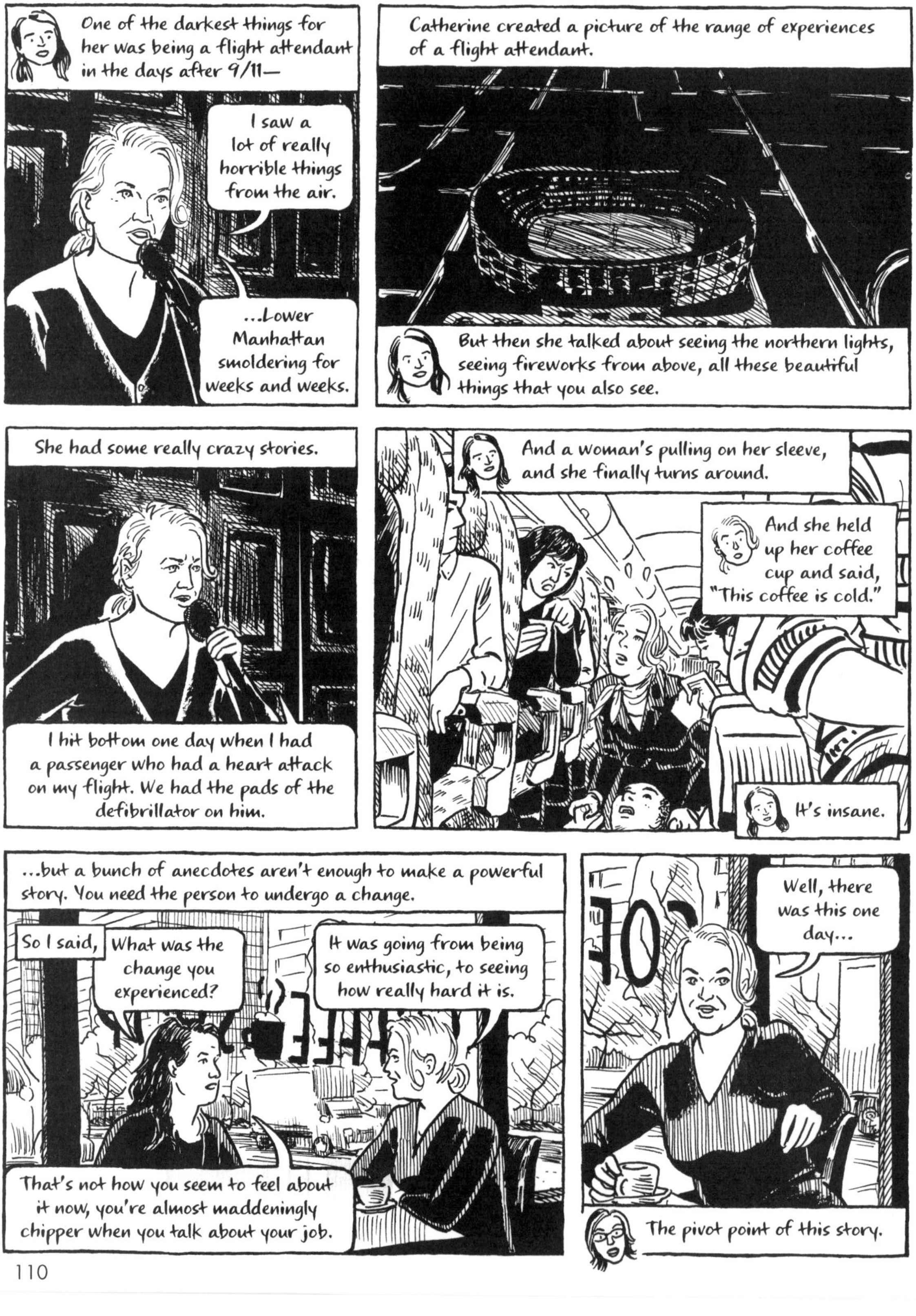
One of the darkest things for her was being a flight attendant in the days after 9/11—
I saw a lot of really horrible things from the air.
...Lower Manhattan smoldering for weeks and weeks.
Catherine created a picture of the range of experiences of a flight attendant.
But then she talked about seeing the northern lights, seeing fireworks from above, all these beautiful things that you also see.
She had some really crazy stories.
I hit bottom one day when I had a passenger who had a heart attack on my flight. We had the pads of the defibrillator on him.
And a woman's pulling on her sleeve, and she finally turns around.
And she held up her coffee cup and said, "This coffee is cold."
It's insane.
...but a bunch of anecdotes aren't enough to make a powerful story. You need the person to undergo a change.
So I said,
What was the change you experienced?
It was going from being so enthusiastic, to seeing how really hard it is.
That's not how you seem to feel about it now, you're almost maddeningly chipper when you talk about your job.
Well, there was this one day...
The pivot point of this story.

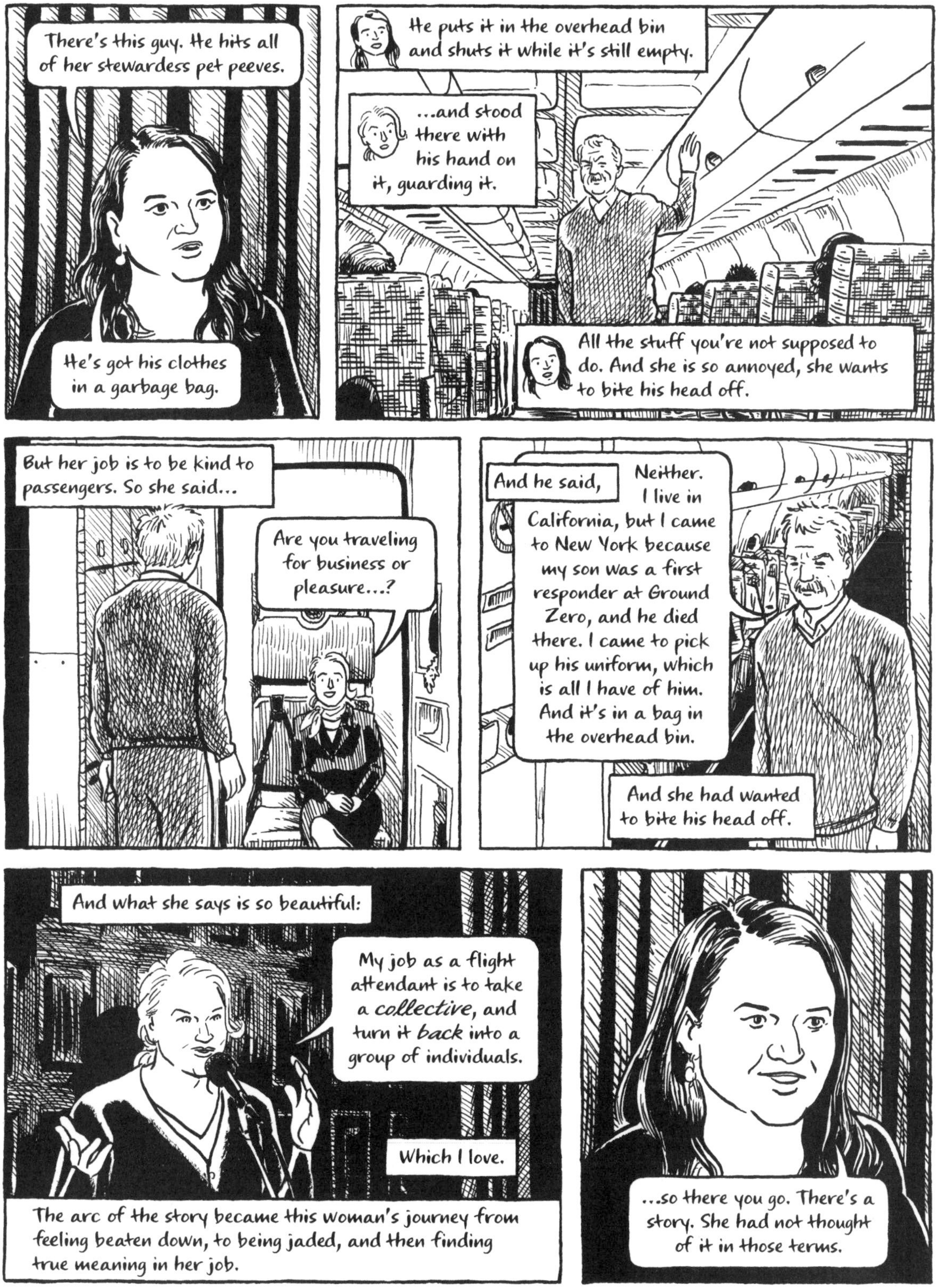
There's this guy. He hits all of her stewardess pet peeves.
He's got his clothes in a garbage bag.
He puts it in the overhead bin and shuts it while it's still empty.
...and stood there with his hand on it, guarding it.
All the stuff you're not supposed to do. And she is so annoyed, she wants to bite his head off.
But her job is to be kind to passengers. So she said...
Are you traveling for business or pleasure...?
And he said,
Neither. I live in California, but I came to New York because my son was a first responder at Ground Zero, and he died there. I came to pick up his uniform, which is all I have of him. And it's in a bag in the overhead bin.
And she had wanted to bite his head off.
And what she says is so beautiful:
My job as a flight attendant is to take a *collective*, and turn it *back* into a group of individuals.
Which I love.
The arc of the story became this woman's journey from feeling beaten down, to being jaded, and then finding true meaning in her job.
...so there you go. There's a story. She had not thought of it in those terms.

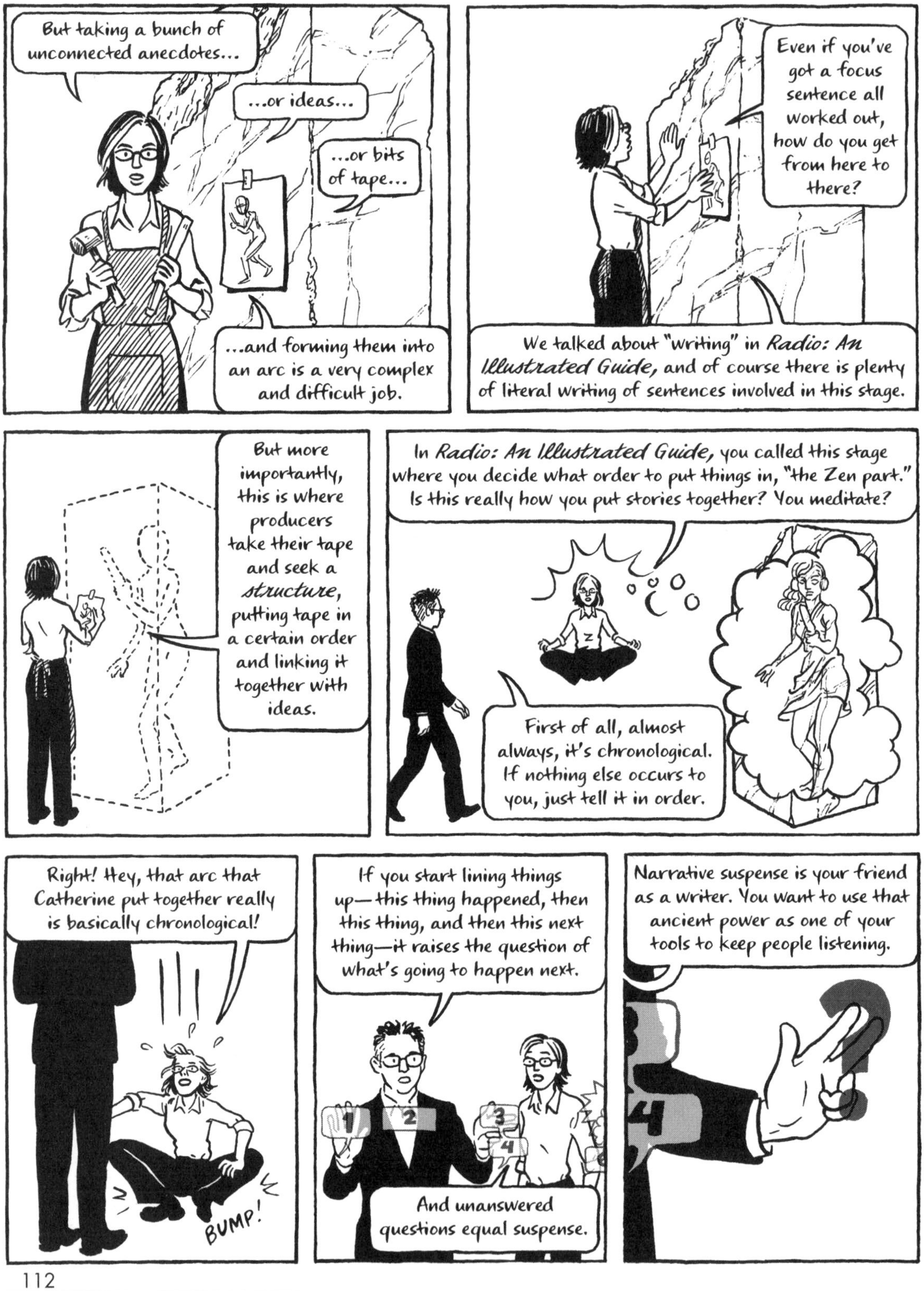
But taking a bunch of unconnected anecdotes...
...or ideas...
...or bits of tape...
...and forming them into an arc is a very complex and difficult job.
Even if you've got a focus sentence all worked out, how do you get from here to there?
We talked about "writing" in *Radio: An Illustrated Guide,* and of course there is plenty of literal writing of sentences involved in this stage.
But more importantly, this is where producers take their tape and seek a *structure,* putting tape in a certain order and linking it together with ideas.
In *Radio: An Illustrated Guide,* you called this stage where you decide what order to put things in, "the Zen part." Is this really how you put stories together? You meditate?
First of all, almost always, it's chronological. If nothing else occurs to you, just tell it in order.
Right! Hey, that arc that Catherine put together really is basically chronological!
BUMP!
If you start lining things up—this thing happened, then this thing, and then this next thing—it raises the question of what's going to happen next.
And unanswered questions equal suspense.
Narrative suspense is your friend as a writer. You want to use that ancient power as one of your tools to keep people listening.

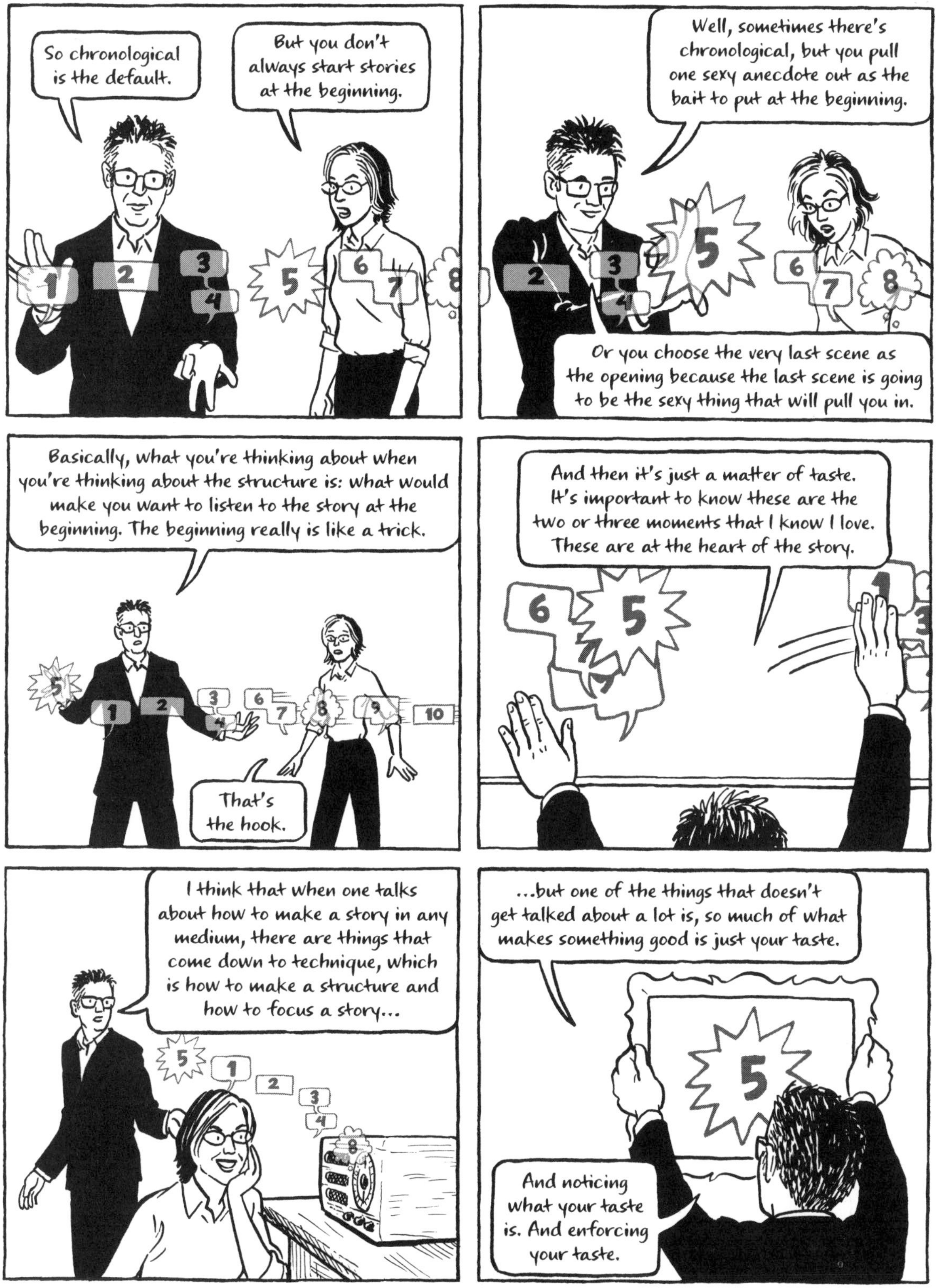
So chronological is the default.
But you don't always start stories at the beginning.
Well, sometimes there's chronological, but you pull one sexy anecdote out as the bait to put at the beginning.
Or you choose the very last scene as the opening because the last scene is going to be the sexy thing that will pull you in.
Basically, what you're thinking about when you're thinking about the structure is: what would make you want to listen to the story at the beginning. The beginning really is like a trick.
That's the hook.
And then it's just a matter of taste. It's important to know these are the two or three moments that I know I love. These are at the heart of the story.
I think that when one talks about how to make a story in any medium, there are things that come down to technique, which is how to make a structure and how to focus a story...
...but one of the things that doesn't get talked about a lot is, so much of what makes something good is just your taste.
And noticing what your taste is. And enforcing your taste.

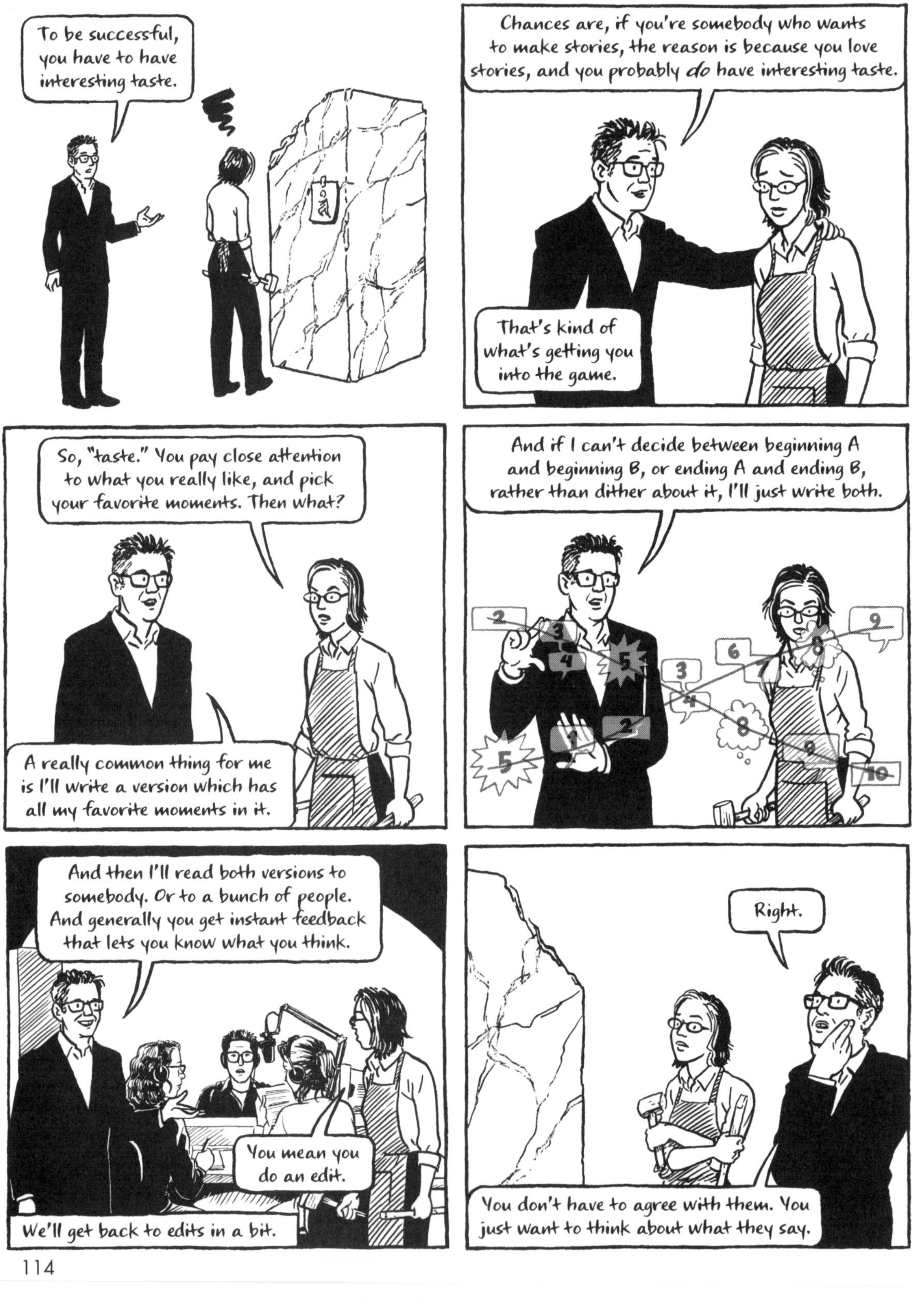

To be successful, you have to have interesting taste.
Chances are, if you're somebody who wants to make stories, the reason is because you love stories, and you probably *do* have interesting taste.
That's kind of what's getting you into the game.
So, "taste." You pay close attention to what you really like, and pick your favorite moments. Then what?
A really common thing for me is I'll write a version which has all my favorite moments in it.
And if I can't decide between beginning A and beginning B, or ending A and ending B, rather than dither about it, I'll just write both.
And then I'll read both versions to somebody. Or to a bunch of people. And generally you get instant feedback that lets you know what you think.
You mean you do an edit.
We'll get back to edits in a bit.
Right.
You don't have to agree with them. You just want to think about what they say.

BUILDING BLOCKS

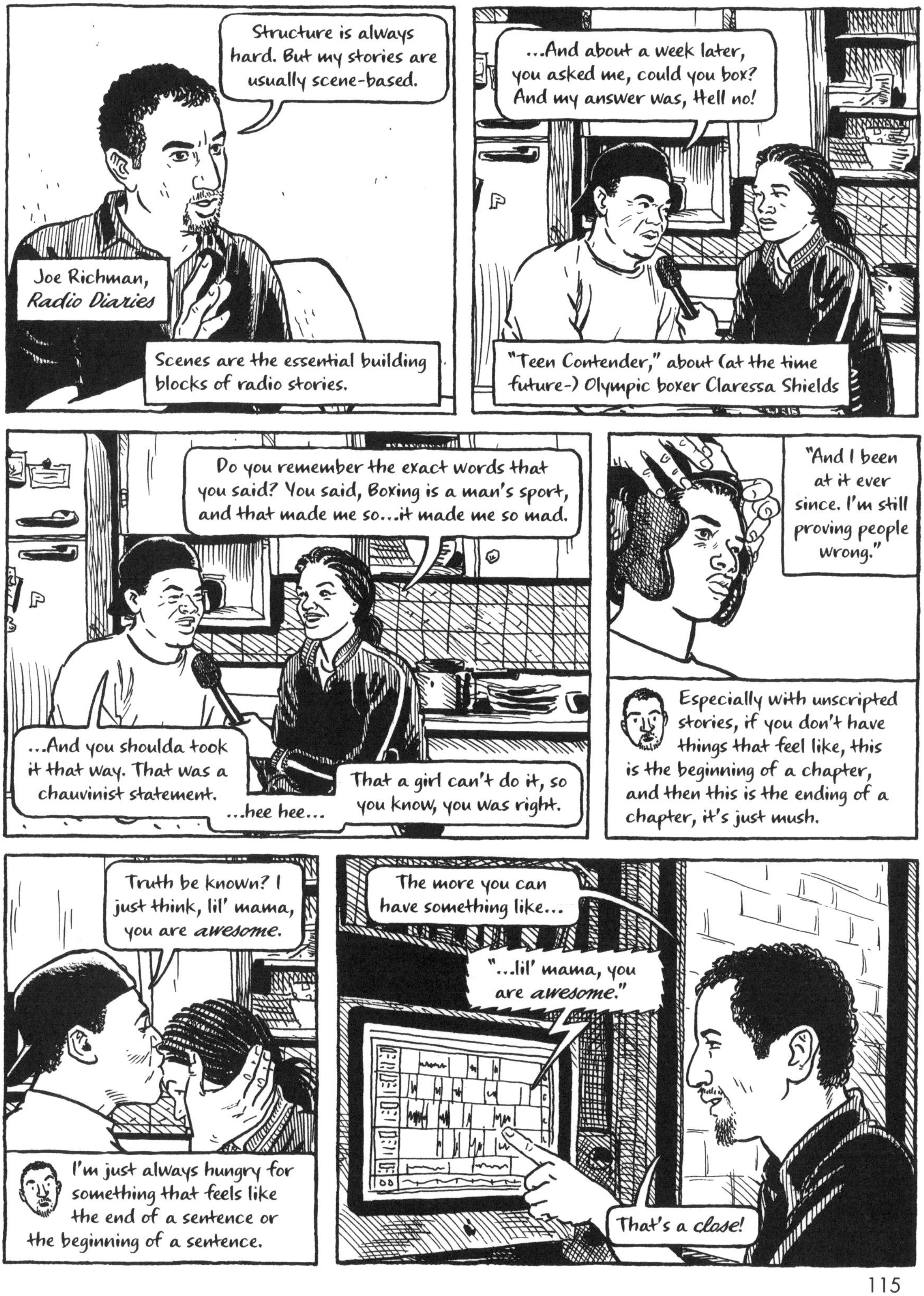
Structure is always hard. But my stories are usually scene-based.
Joe Richman, *Radio Diaries*
Scenes are the essential building blocks of radio stories.
...And about a week later, you asked me, could you box? And my answer was, Hell no!
"Teen Contender," about (at the time future-) Olympic boxer Claressa Shields
Do you remember the exact words that you said? You said, Boxing is a man's sport, and that made me so...it made me so mad.
...And you shoulda took it that way. That was a chauvinist statement.
...hee hee...
That a girl can't do it, so you know, you was right.
"And I been at it ever since. I'm still proving people wrong."
Especially with unscripted stories, if you don't have things that feel like, this is the beginning of a chapter, and then this is the ending of a chapter, it's just mush.
Truth be known? I just think, lil' mama, you are *awesome*.
I'm just always hungry for something that feels like the end of a sentence or the beginning of a sentence.
The more you can have something like...
"...lil' mama, you are *awesome*."
That's a *close*!

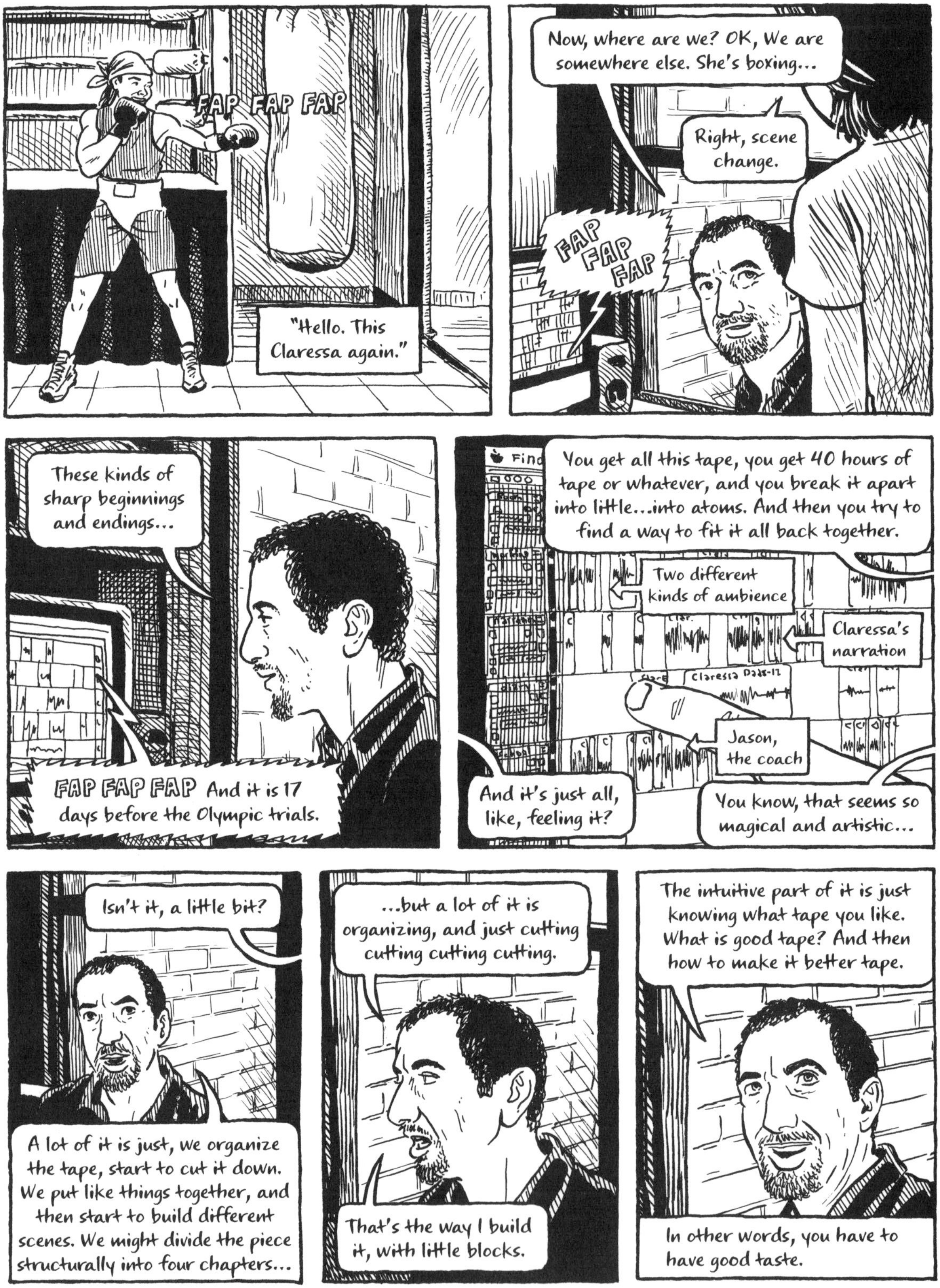

FAP FAP FAP
"Hello. This Claressa again."
Now, where are we? OK, We are somewhere else. She's boxing...
Right, scene change.
FAP FAP FAP
These kinds of sharp beginnings and endings...
FAP FAP FAP And it is 17 days before the Olympic trials.
You get all this tape, you get 40 hours of tape or whatever, and you break it apart into little...into atoms. And then you try to find a way to fit it all back together.
Two different kinds of ambience
Claressa's narration
Jason, the coach
And it's just all, like, feeling it?
You know, that seems so magical and artistic...
Isn't it, a little bit?
A lot of it is just, we organize the tape, start to cut it down. We put like things together, and then start to build different scenes. We might divide the piece structurally into four chapters...
...but a lot of it is organizing, and just cutting cutting cutting cutting.
That's the way I build it, with little blocks.
The intuitive part of it is just knowing what tape you like. What is good tape? And then how to make it better tape.
In other words, you have to have good taste.

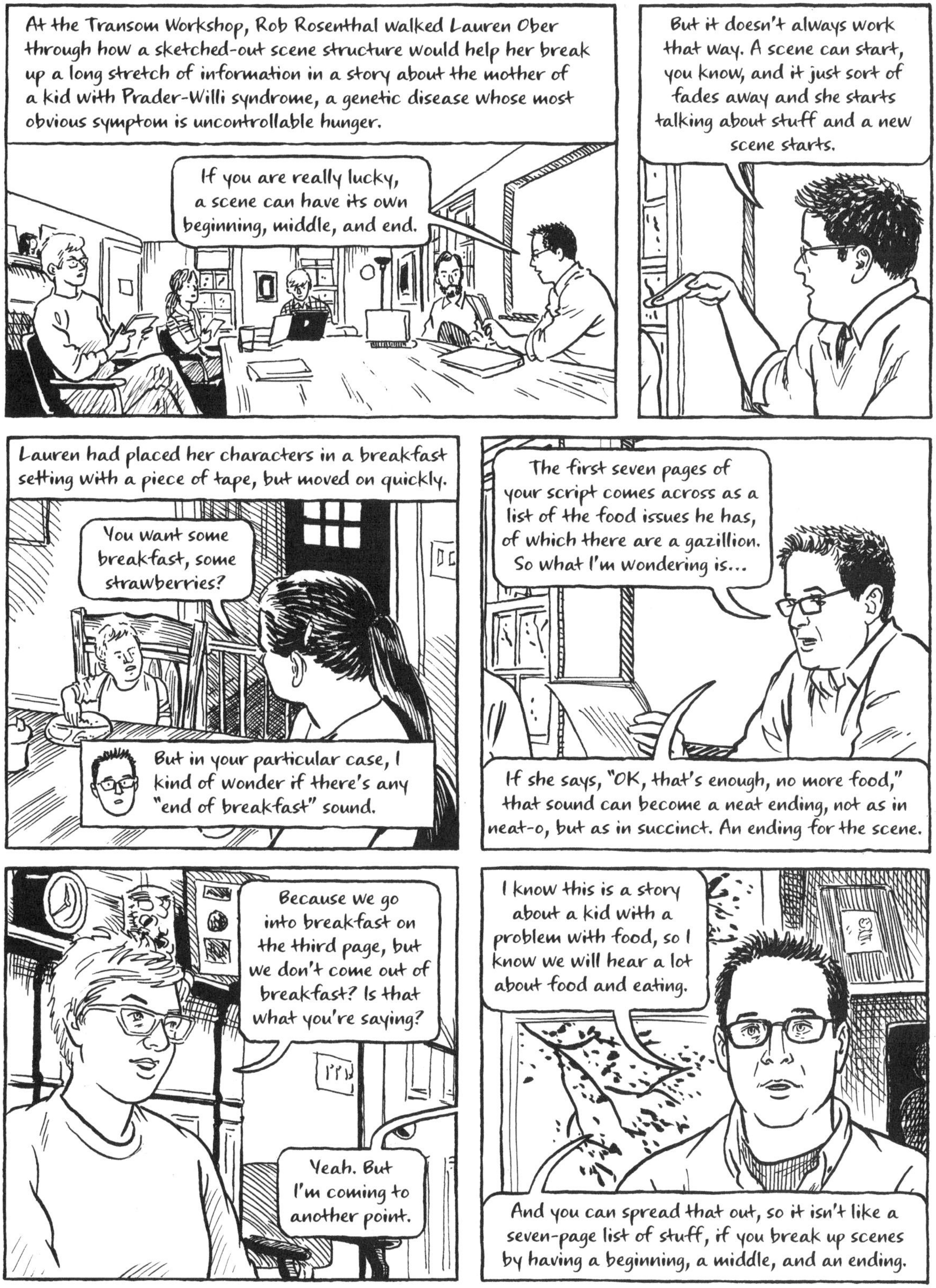
At the Transom Workshop, Rob Rosenthal walked Lauren Ober through how a sketched-out scene structure would help her break up a long stretch of information in a story about the mother of a kid with Prader-Willi syndrome, a genetic disease whose most obvious symptom is uncontrollable hunger.
If you are really lucky, a scene can have its own beginning, middle, and end.
But it doesn't always work that way. A scene can start, you know, and it just sort of fades away and she starts talking about stuff and a new scene starts.
Lauren had placed her characters in a breakfast setting with a piece of tape, but moved on quickly.
You want some breakfast, some strawberries?
But in your particular case, I kind of wonder if there's any "end of breakfast" sound.
The first seven pages of your script comes across as a list of the food issues he has, of which there are a gazillion. So what I'm wondering is...
If she says, "OK, that's enough, no more food," that sound can become a neat ending, not as in neat-o, but as in succinct. An ending for the scene.
Because we go into breakfast on the third page, but we don't come out of breakfast? Is that what you're saying?
Yeah. But I'm coming to another point.
I know this is a story about a kid with a problem with food, so I know we will hear a lot about food and eating.
And you can spread that out, so it isn't like a seven-page list of stuff, if you break up scenes by having a beginning, a middle, and an ending.

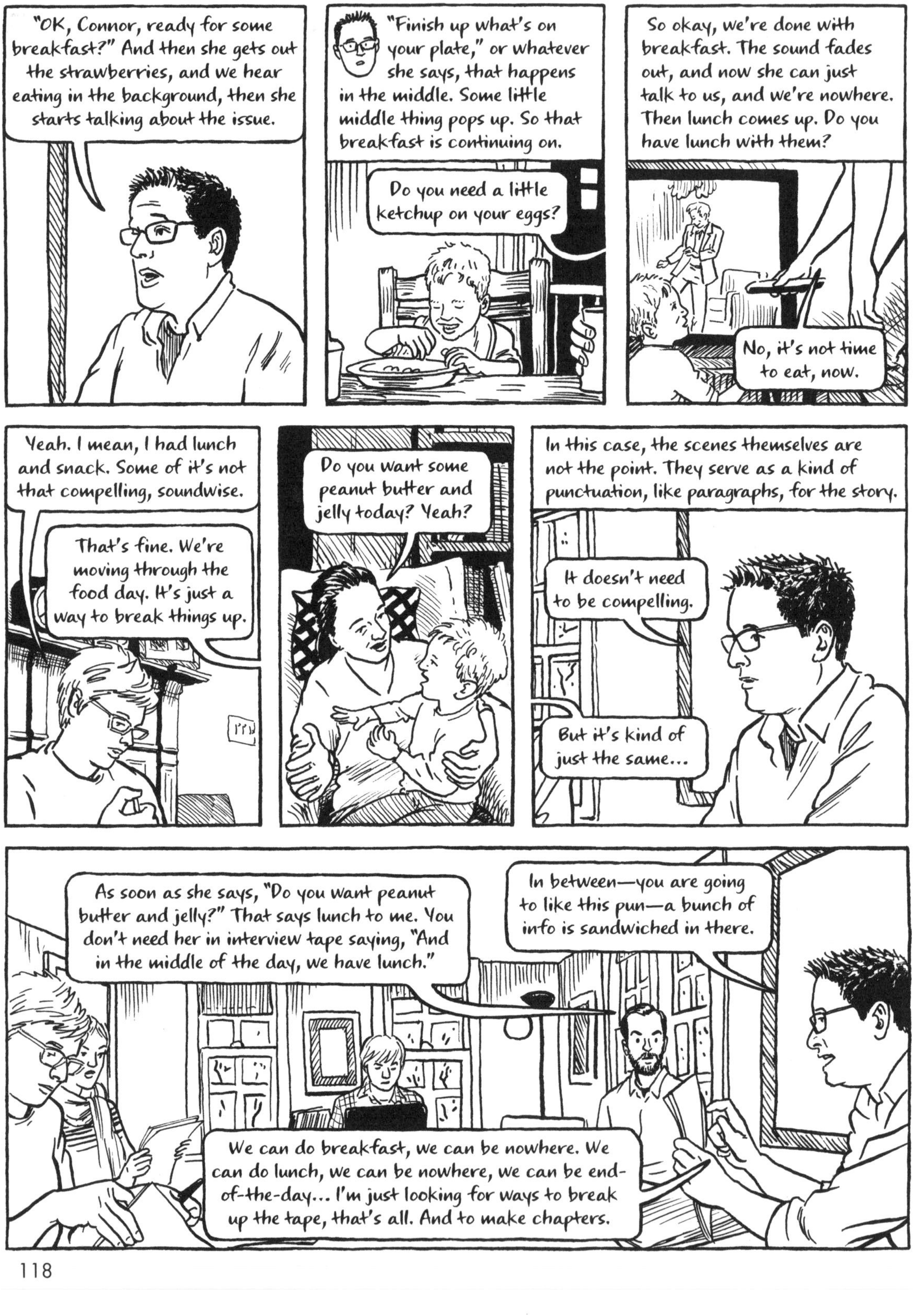
"OK, Connor, ready for some breakfast?" And then she gets out the strawberries, and we hear eating in the background, then she starts talking about the issue.
"Finish up what's on your plate," or whatever she says, that happens in the middle. Some little middle thing pops up. So that breakfast is continuing on.
Do you need a little ketchup on your eggs?
So okay, we're done with breakfast. The sound fades out, and now she can just talk to us, and we're nowhere. Then lunch comes up. Do you have lunch with them?
No, it's not time to eat, now.
Yeah. I mean, I had lunch and snack. Some of it's not that compelling, soundwise.
That's fine. We're moving through the food day. It's just a way to break things up.
Do you want some peanut butter and jelly today? Yeah?
In this case, the scenes themselves are not the point. They serve as a kind of punctuation, like paragraphs, for the story.
It doesn't need to be compelling.
But it's kind of just the same...
As soon as she says, "Do you want peanut butter and jelly?" That says lunch to me. You don't need her in interview tape saying, "And in the middle of the day, we have lunch."
In between—you are going to like this pun—a bunch of info is sandwiched in there.
We can do breakfast, we can be nowhere. We can do lunch, we can be nowhere, we can be end-of-the-day... I'm just looking for ways to break up the tape, that's all. And to make chapters.

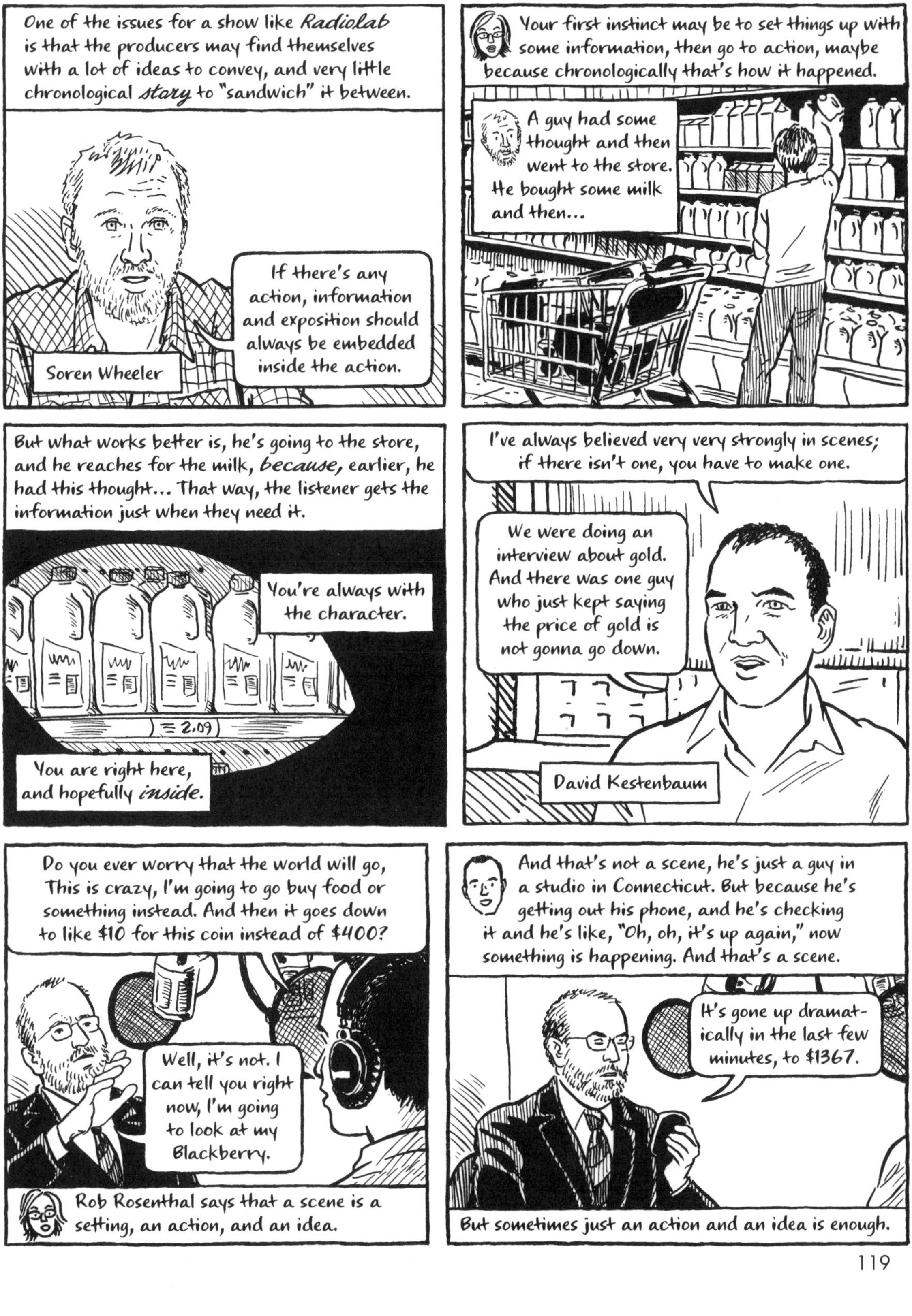
One of the issues for a show like *Radiolab* is that the producers may find themselves with a lot of ideas to convey, and very little chronological *story* to "sandwich" it between.
If there's any action, information and exposition should always be embedded inside the action.
Soren Wheeler
Your first instinct may be to set things up with some information, then go to action, maybe because chronologically that's how it happened.
A guy had some thought and then went to the store. He bought some milk and then...
But what works better is, he's going to the store, and he reaches for the milk, *because,* earlier, he had this thought... That way, the listener gets the information just when they need it.
You're always with the character.
2.09
You are right here, and hopefully *inside.*
I've always believed very very strongly in scenes; if there isn't one, you have to make one.
We were doing an interview about gold. And there was one guy who just kept saying the price of gold is not gonna go down.
David Kestenbaum
Do you ever worry that the world will go, This is crazy, I'm going to go buy food or something instead. And then it goes down to like $10 for this coin instead of $400?
Well, it's not. I can tell you right now, I'm going to look at my Blackberry.
Rob Rosenthal says that a scene is a setting, an action, and an idea.
And that's not a scene, he's just a guy in a studio in Connecticut. But because he's getting out his phone, and he's checking it and he's like, "Oh, oh, it's up again," now something is happening. And that's a scene.
It's gone up dramatically in the last few minutes, to $1367.
But sometimes just an action and an idea is enough.

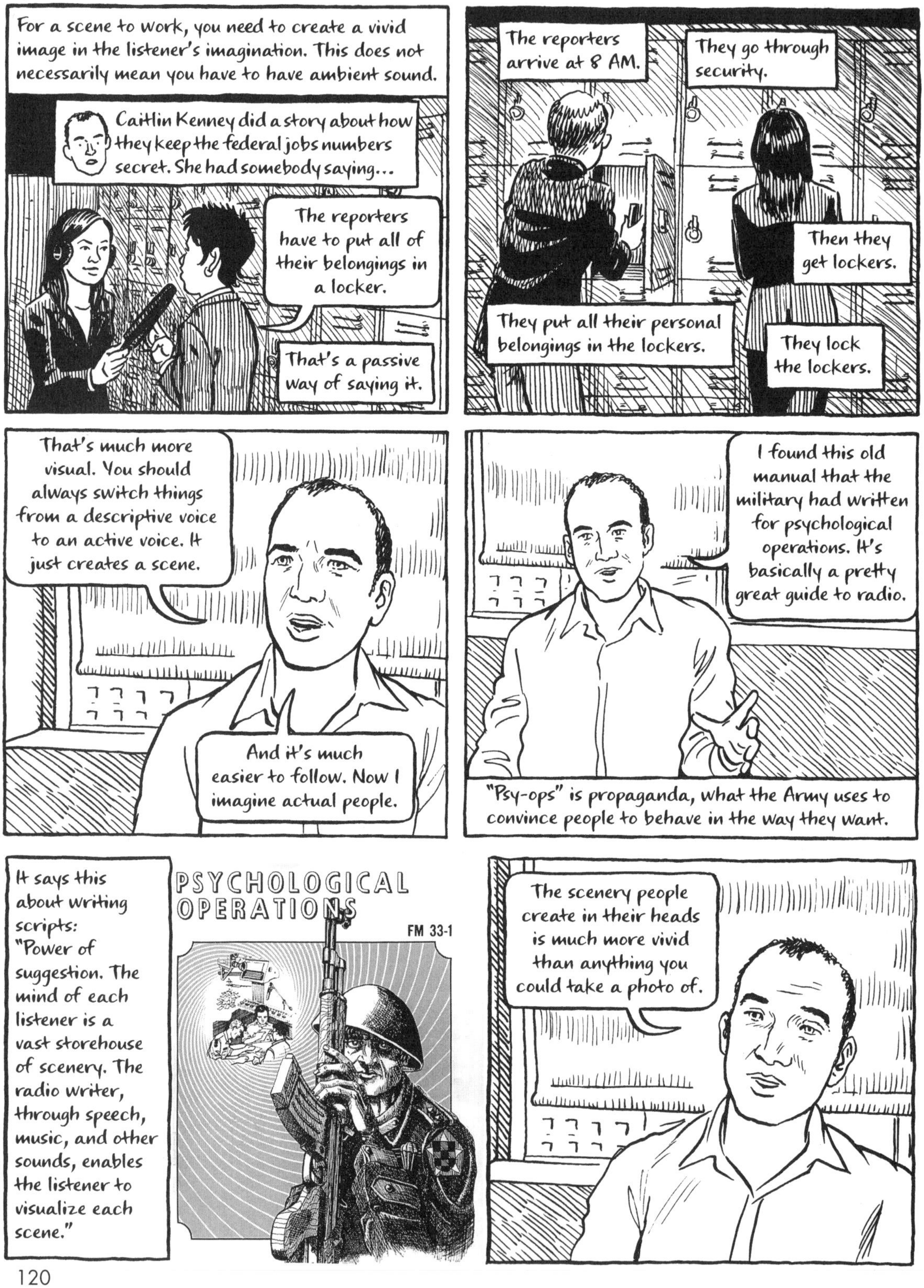
For a scene to work, you need to create a vivid image in the listener's imagination. This does not necessarily mean you have to have ambient sound.
Caitlin Kenney did a story about how they keep the federal jobs numbers secret. She had somebody saying...
The reporters have to put all of their belongings in a locker.
That's a passive way of saying it.
The reporters arrive at 8 AM.
They go through security.
Then they get lockers.
They put all their personal belongings in the lockers.
They lock the lockers.
That's much more visual. You should always switch things from a descriptive voice to an active voice. It just creates a scene.
And it's much easier to follow. Now I imagine actual people.
I found this old manual that the military had written for psychological operations. It's basically a pretty great guide to radio.
"Psy-ops" is propaganda, what the Army uses to convince people to behave in the way they want.
It says this about writing scripts: "Power of suggestion. The mind of each listener is a vast storehouse of scenery. The radio writer, through speech, music, and other sounds, enables the listener to visualize each scene."
PSYCHOLOGICAL OPERATIONS
FM 33-1
The scenery people create in their heads is much more vivid than anything you could take a photo of.

WRITING IN THE SPACE BETWEEN TWO PEOPLE

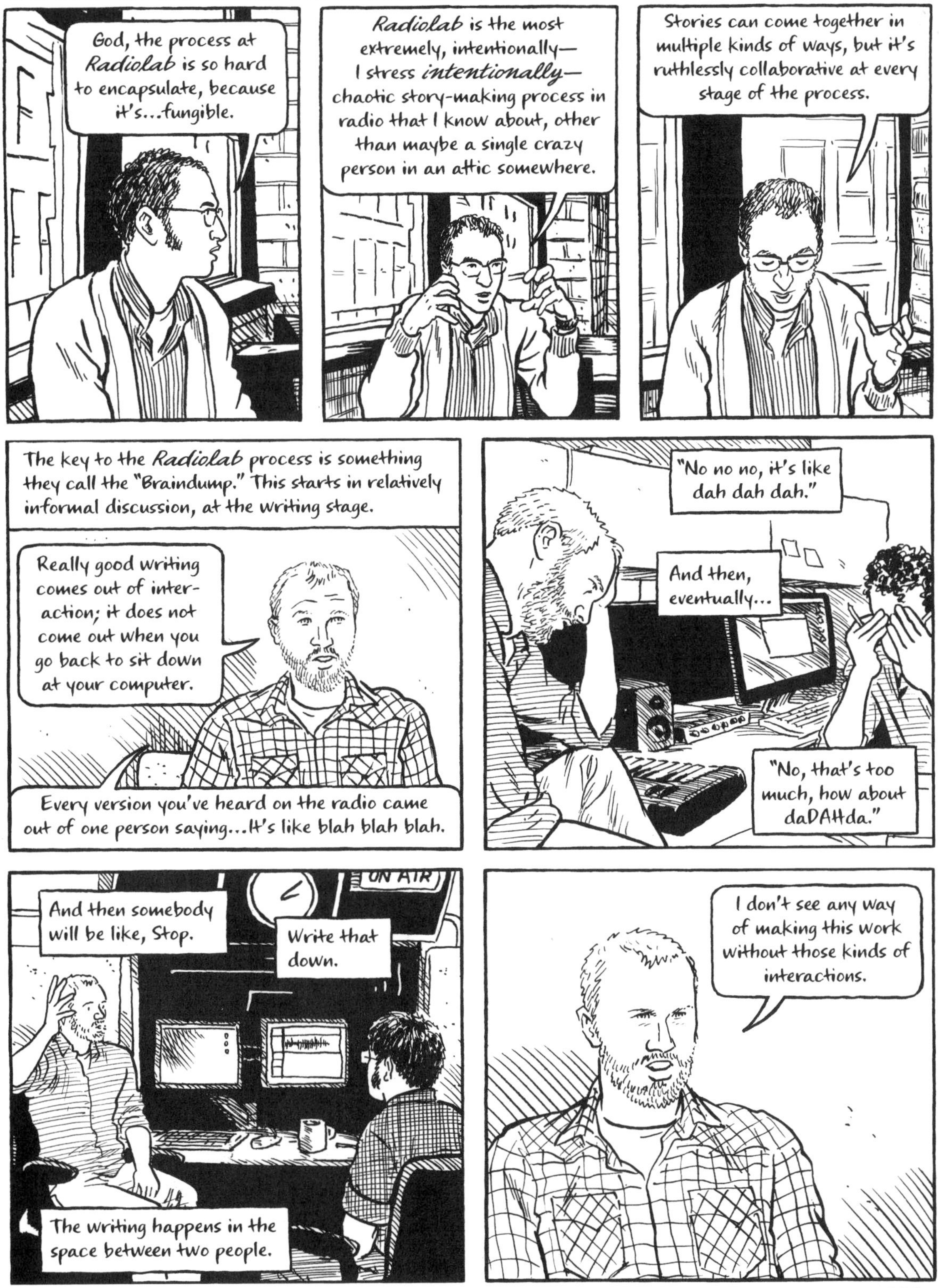
God, the process at *Radiolab* is so hard to encapsulate, because it's...fungible.
Radiolab is the most extremely, intentionally—I stress *intentionally*—chaotic story-making process in radio that I know about, other than maybe a single crazy person in an attic somewhere.
Stories can come together in multiple kinds of ways, but it's ruthlessly collaborative at every stage of the process.
The key to the *Radiolab* process is something they call the "Braindump." This starts in relatively informal discussion, at the writing stage.
Really good writing comes out of inter-action; it does not come out when you go back to sit down at your computer.
Every version you've heard on the radio came out of one person saying...It's like blah blah blah.
"No no no, it's like dah dah dah."
And then, eventually...
"No, that's too much, how about daDAHda."
And then somebody will be like, Stop.
Write that down.
ON AIR
The writing happens in the space between two people.
I don't see any way of making this work without those kinds of interactions.

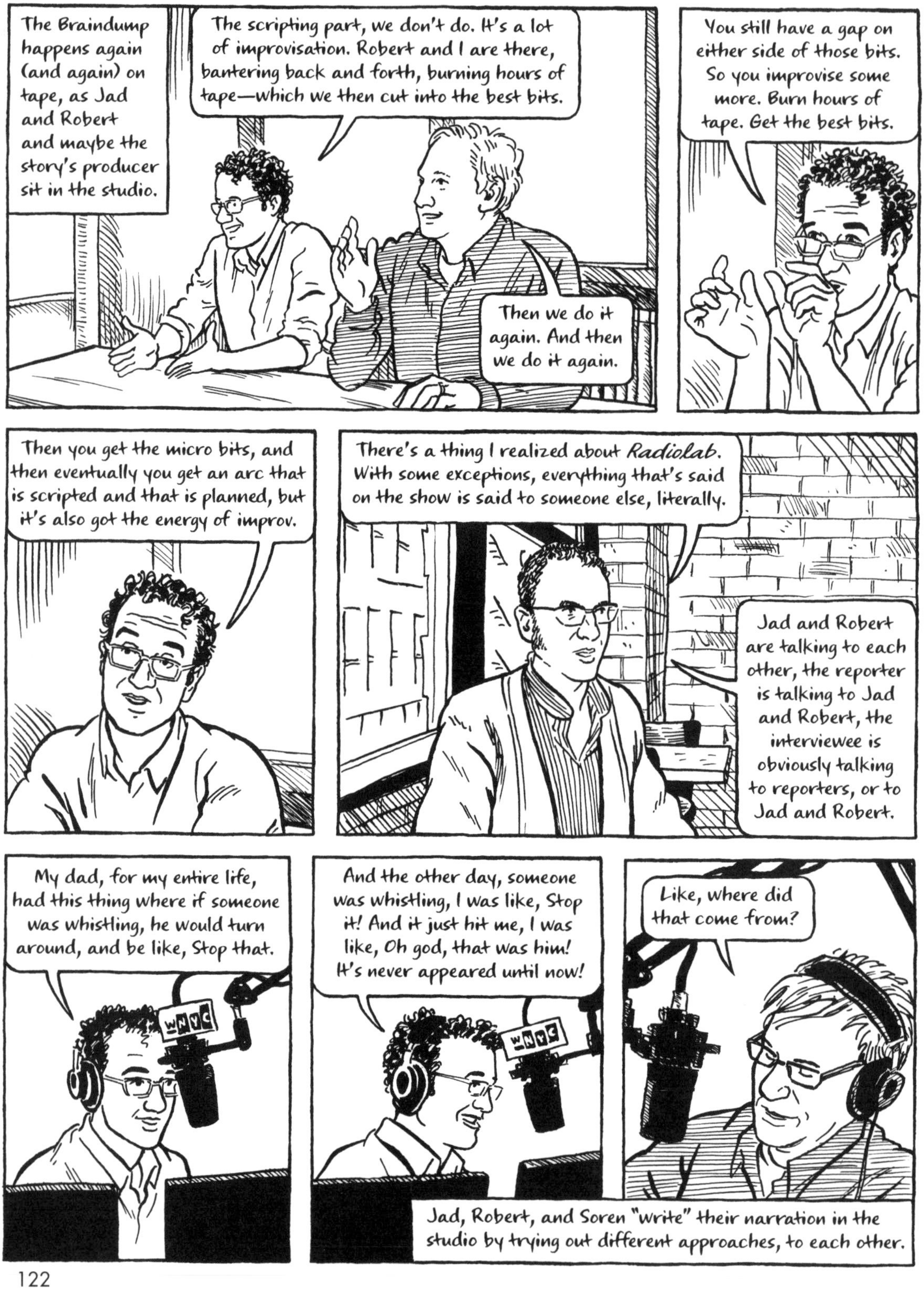
The Braindump happens again (and again) on tape, as Jad and Robert and maybe the story's producer sit in the studio.
The scripting part, we don't do. It's a lot of improvisation. Robert and I are there, bantering back and forth, burning hours of tape—which we then cut into the best bits.
Then we do it again. And then we do it again.
You still have a gap on either side of those bits. So you improvise some more. Burn hours of tape. Get the best bits.
Then you get the micro bits, and then eventually you get an arc that is scripted and that is planned, but it's also got the energy of improv.
There's a thing I realized about *Radiolab*. With some exceptions, everything that's said on the show is said to someone else, literally.
Jad and Robert are talking to each other, the reporter is talking to Jad and Robert, the interviewee is obviously talking to reporters, or to Jad and Robert.
My dad, for my entire life, had this thing where if someone was whistling, he would turn around, and be like, Stop that.
WNYC
And the other day, someone was whistling, I was like, Stop it! And it just hit me, I was like, Oh god, that was him! It's never appeared until now!
WNYC
Like, where did that come from?
Jad, Robert, and Soren "write" their narration in the studio by trying out different approaches, to each other.

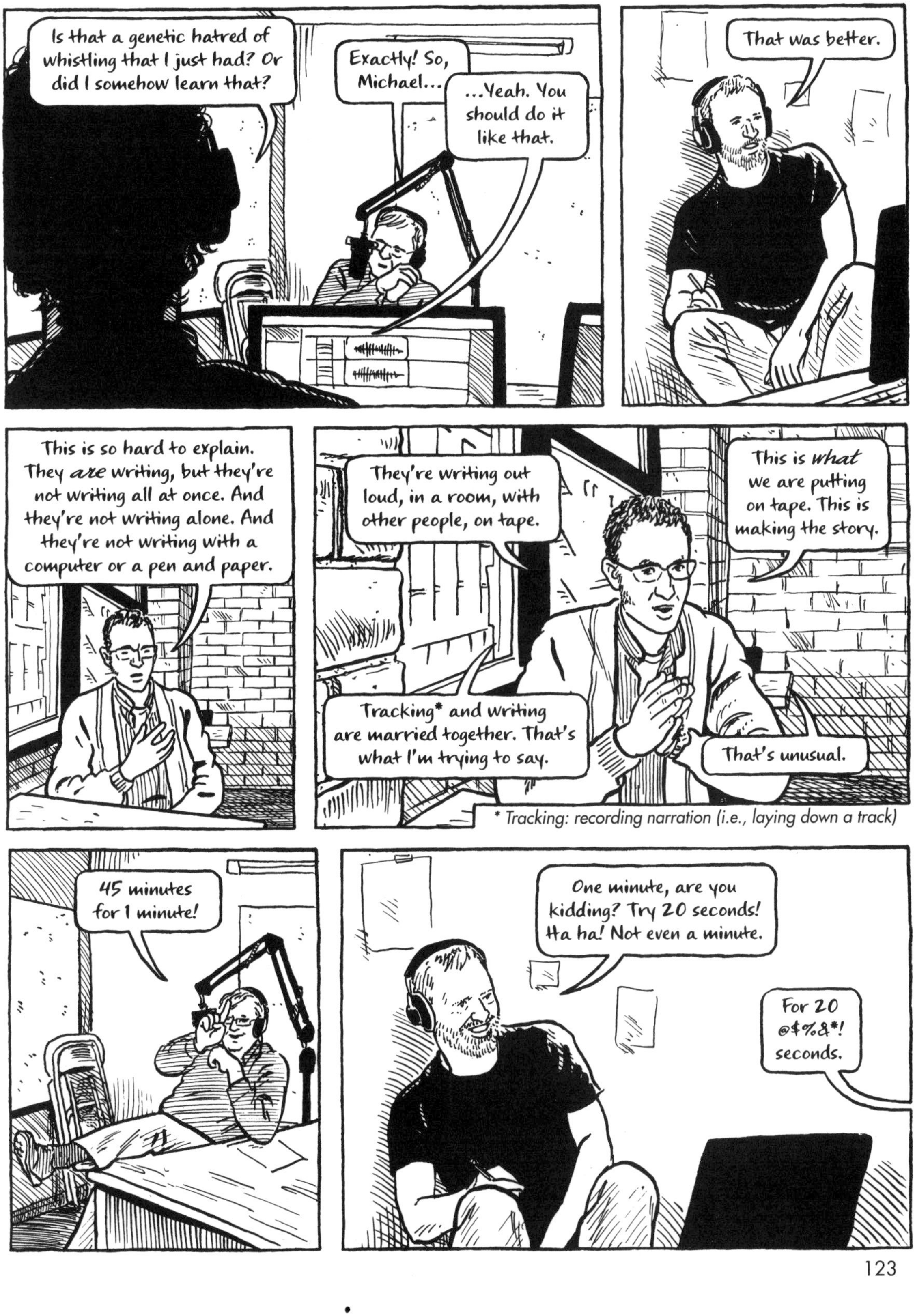
Is that a genetic hatred of whistling that I just had? Or did I somehow learn that?
Exactly! So, Michael...
...Yeah. You should do it like that.
That was better.
This is so hard to explain. They *are* writing, but they're not writing all at once. And they're not writing alone. And they're not writing with a computer or a pen and paper.
They're writing out loud, in a room, with other people, on tape.
This is *what* we are putting on tape. This is making the story.
Tracking* and writing are married together. That's what I'm trying to say.
That's unusual.
45 minutes for 1 minute!
One minute, are you kidding? Try 20 seconds! Ha ha! Not even a minute.
For 20 @$%&*! seconds.

* *Tracking: recording narration (i.e., laying down a track)*

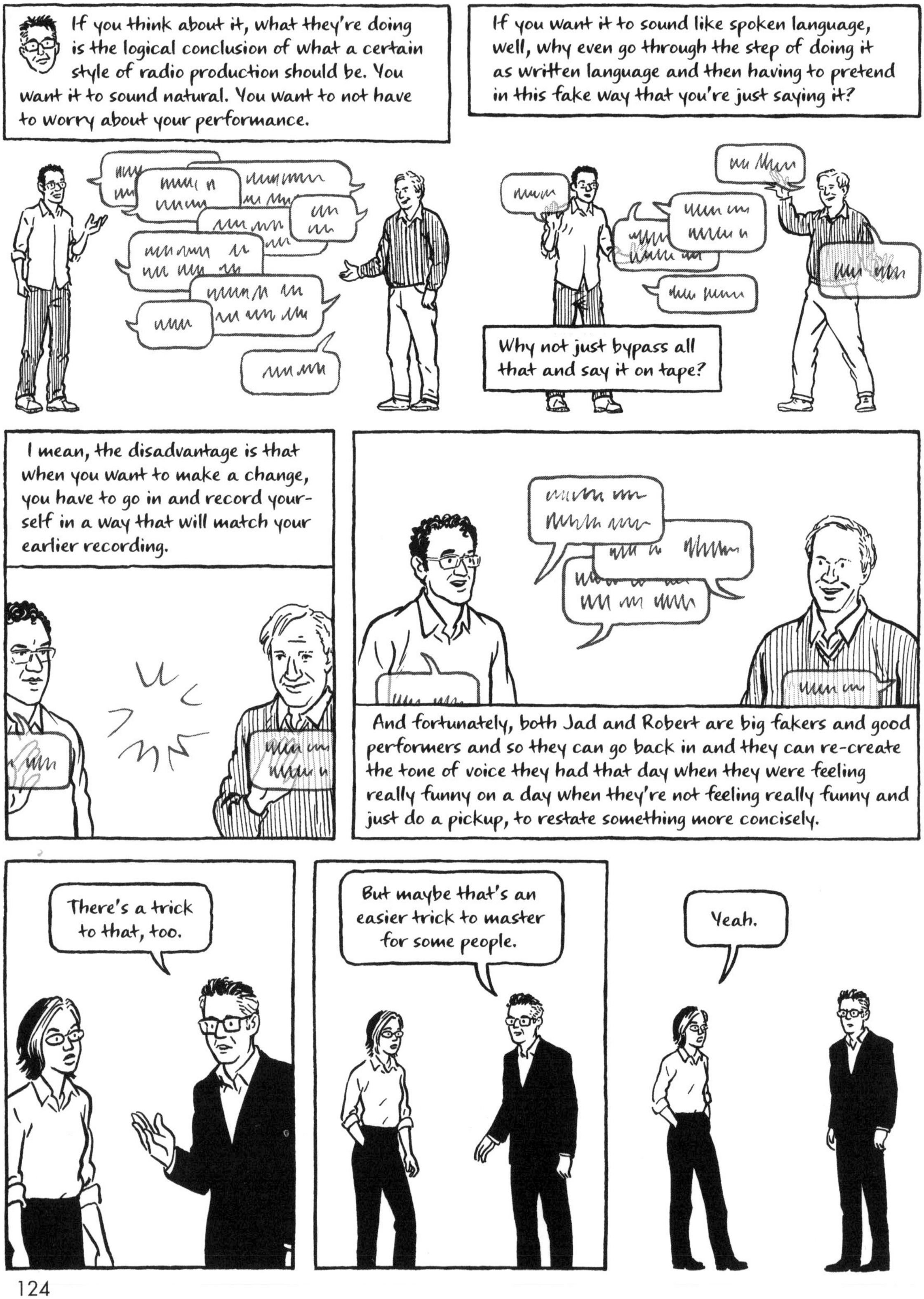
If you think about it, what they're doing is the logical conclusion of what a certain style of radio production should be. You want it to sound natural. You want to not have to worry about your performance.
If you want it to sound like spoken language, well, why even go through the step of doing it as written language and then having to pretend in this fake way that you're just saying it?
Why not just bypass all that and say it on tape?
I mean, the disadvantage is that when you want to make a change, you have to go in and record yourself in a way that will match your earlier recording.
And fortunately, both Jad and Robert are big fakers and good performers and so they can go back in and they can re-create the tone of voice they had that day when they were feeling really funny on a day when they're not feeling really funny and just do a pickup, to restate something more concisely.
There's a trick to that, too.
But maybe that's an easier trick to master for some people.
Yeah.

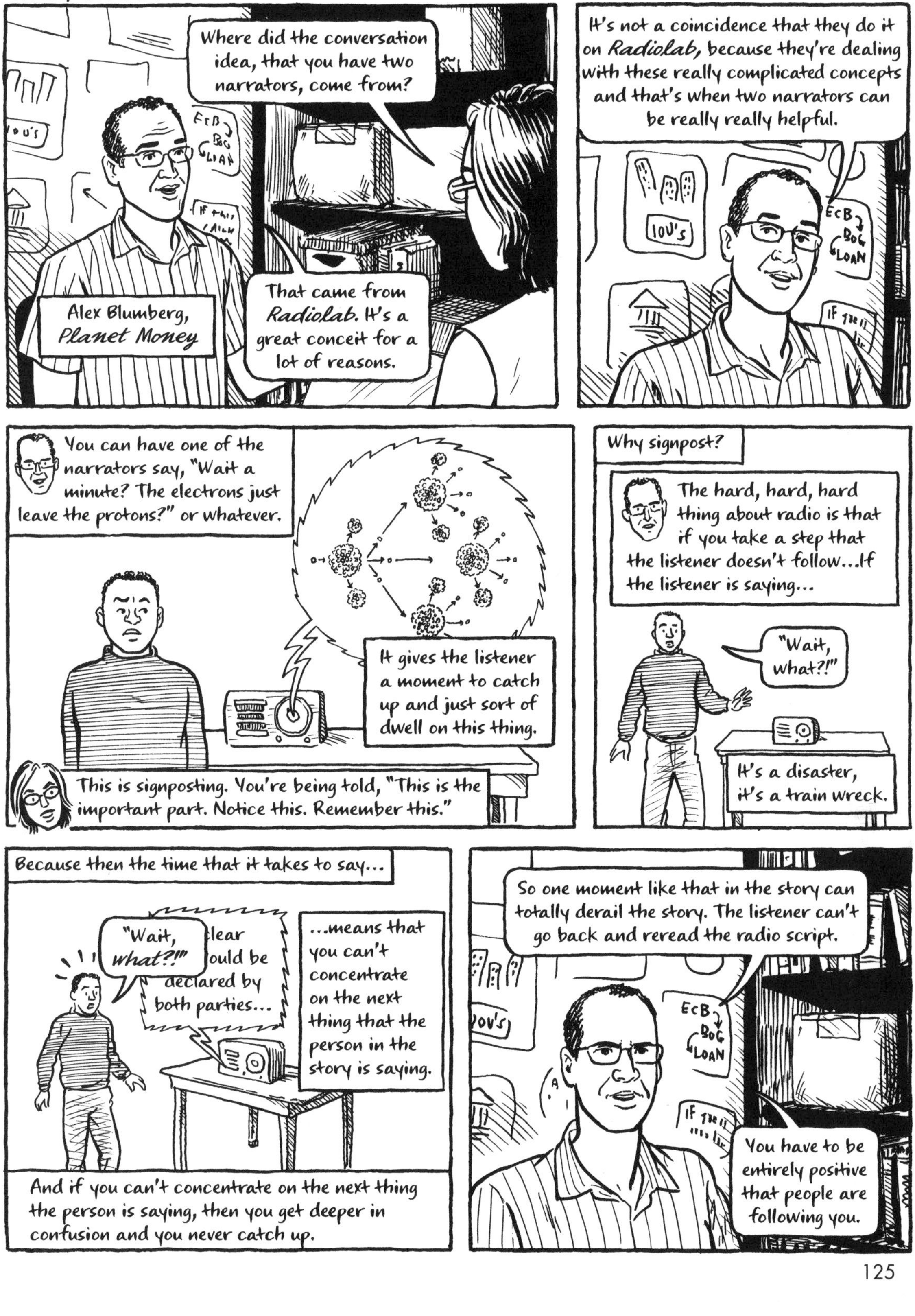
Where did the conversation idea, that you have two narrators, come from?
Alex Blumberg, *Planet Money*
That came from *Radiolab*. It's a great conceit for a lot of reasons.
It's not a coincidence that they do it on *Radiolab*, because they're dealing with these really complicated concepts and that's when two narrators can be really really helpful.
You can have one of the narrators say, "Wait a minute? The electrons just leave the protons?" or whatever.
It gives the listener a moment to catch up and just sort of dwell on this thing.
This is signposting. You're being told, "This is the important part. Notice this. Remember this."
Why signpost?
The hard, hard, hard thing about radio is that if you take a step that the listener doesn't follow…If the listener is saying…
"Wait, what?!"
It's a disaster, it's a train wreck.
Because then the time that it takes to say…
"Wait, *what?!*"
declared by both parties…
…means that you can't concentrate on the next thing that the person in the story is saying.
And if you can't concentrate on the next thing the person is saying, then you get deeper in confusion and you never catch up.
So one moment like that in the story can totally derail the story. The listener can't go back and reread the radio script.
You have to be entirely positive that people are following you.

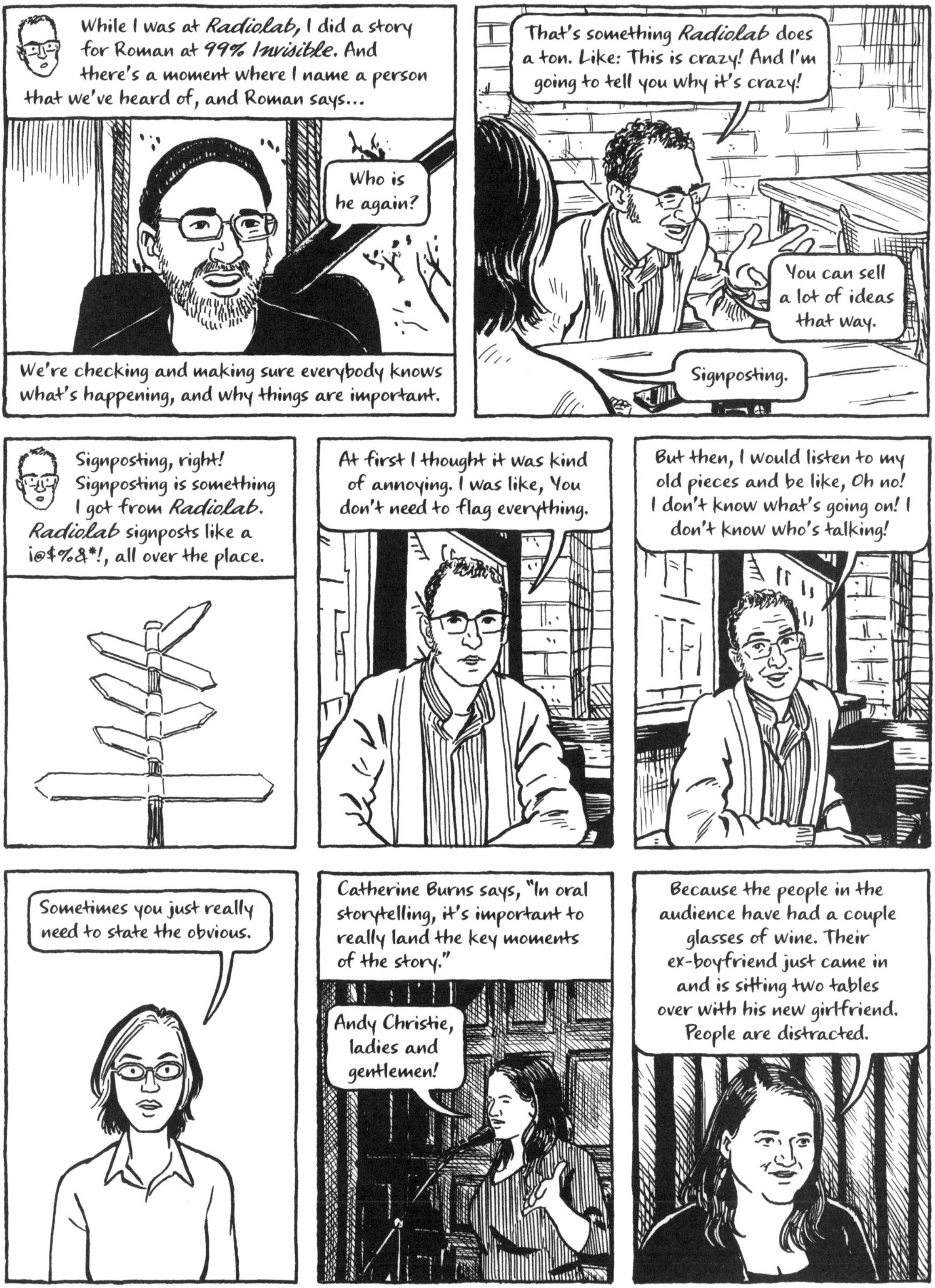
While I was at Radiolab, I did a story for Roman at 99% Invisible. And there's a moment where I name a person that we've heard of, and Roman says...
Who is he again?
We're checking and making sure everybody knows what's happening, and why things are important.
That's something Radiolab does a ton. Like: This is crazy! And I'm going to tell you why it's crazy!
You can sell a lot of ideas that way.
Signposting.
Signposting, right! Signposting is something I got from Radiolab. Radiolab signposts like a i@$%&*!, all over the place.
At first I thought it was kind of annoying. I was like, You don't need to flag everything.
But then, I would listen to my old pieces and be like, Oh no! I don't know what's going on! I don't know who's talking!
Sometimes you just really need to state the obvious.
Catherine Burns says, "In oral storytelling, it's important to really land the key moments of the story."
Andy Christie, ladies and gentlemen!
Because the people in the audience have had a couple glasses of wine. Their ex-boyfriend just came in and is sitting two tables over with his new girlfriend. People are distracted.

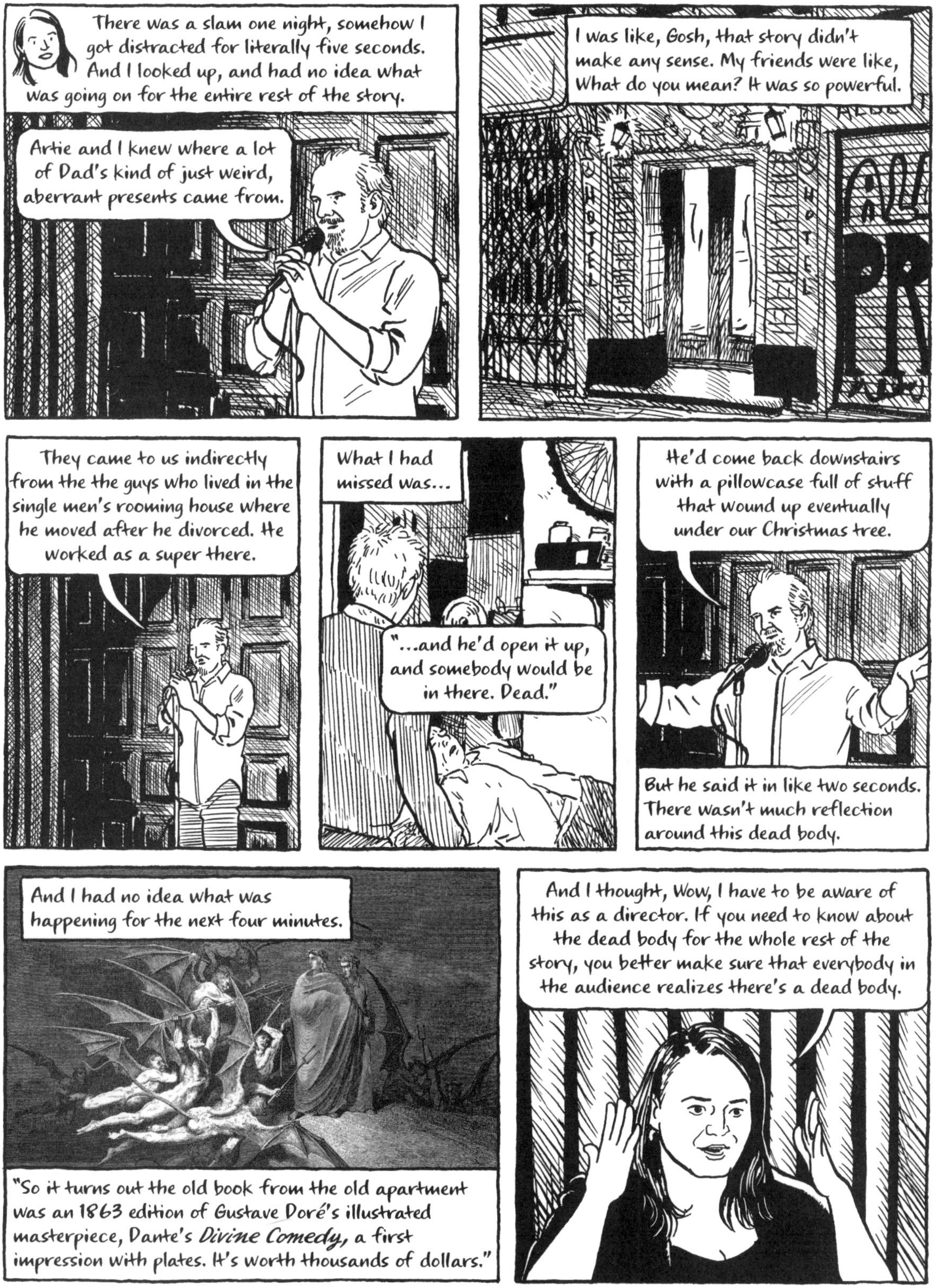
There was a slam one night, somehow I got distracted for literally five seconds. And I looked up, and had no idea what was going on for the entire rest of the story.
Artie and I knew where a lot of Dad's kind of just weird, aberrant presents came from.
I was like, Gosh, that story didn't make any sense. My friends were like, What do you mean? It was so powerful.
HOTEL
HOTEL
They came to us indirectly from the the guys who lived in the single men's rooming house where he moved after he divorced. He worked as a super there.
What I had missed was...
"...and he'd open it up, and somebody would be in there. Dead."
He'd come back downstairs with a pillowcase full of stuff that wound up eventually under our Christmas tree.
But he said it in like two seconds. There wasn't much reflection around this dead body.
And I had no idea what was happening for the next four minutes.
"So it turns out the old book from the old apartment was an 1863 edition of Gustave Doré's illustrated masterpiece, Dante's *Divine Comedy*, a first impression with plates. It's worth thousands of dollars."
And I thought, Wow, I have to be aware of this as a director. If you need to know about the dead body for the whole rest of the story, you better make sure that everybody in the audience realizes there's a dead body.

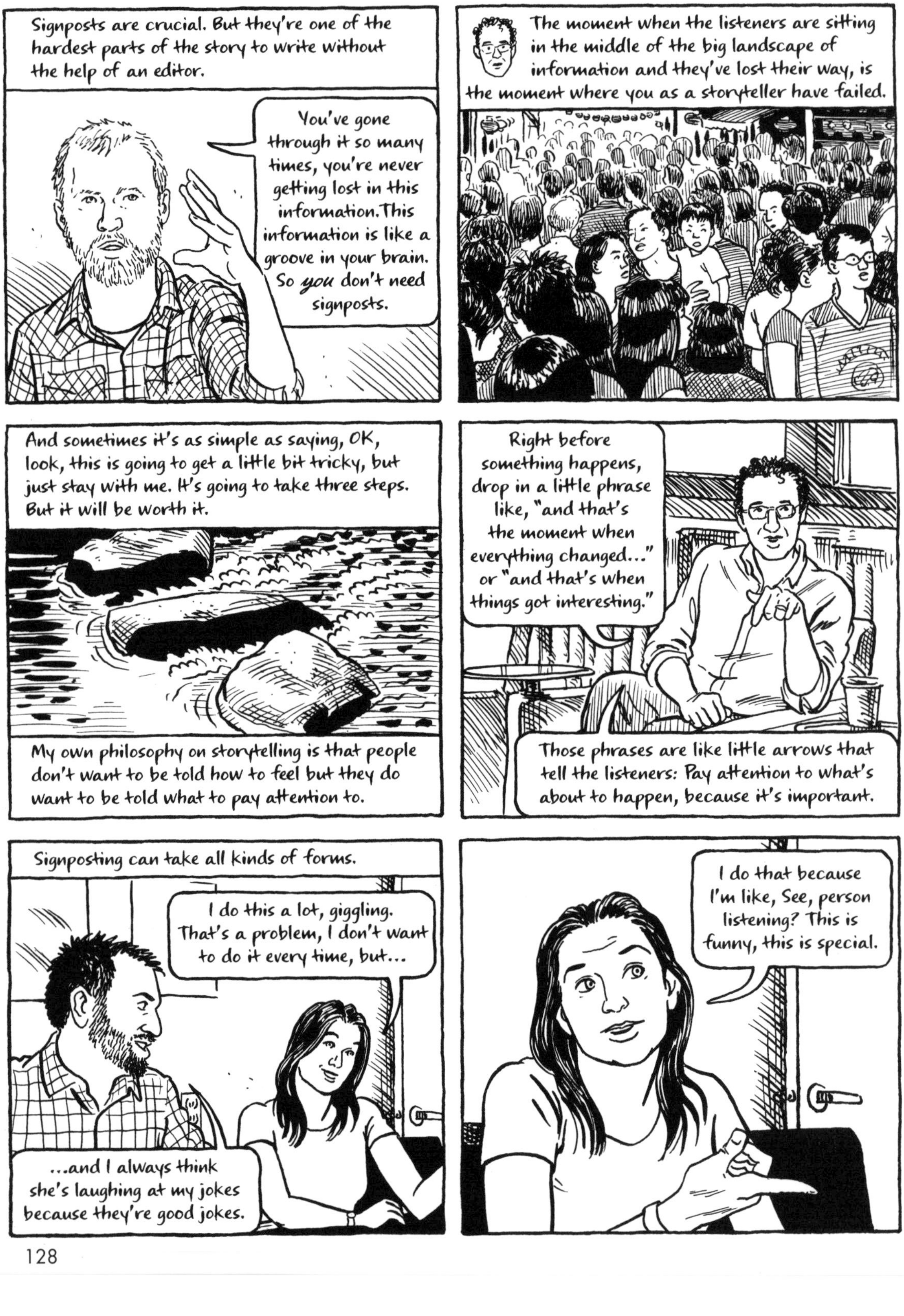
Signposts are crucial. But they're one of the hardest parts of the story to write without the help of an editor.
You've gone through it so many times, you're never getting lost in this information. This information is like a groove in your brain. So *you* don't need signposts.
The moment when the listeners are sitting in the middle of the big landscape of information and they've lost their way, is the moment where you as a storyteller have failed.
And sometimes it's as simple as saying, OK, look, this is going to get a little bit tricky, but just stay with me. It's going to take three steps. But it will be worth it.
My own philosophy on storytelling is that people don't want to be told how to feel but they do want to be told what to pay attention to.
Right before something happens, drop in a little phrase like, "and that's the moment when everything changed..." or "and that's when things got interesting."
Those phrases are like little arrows that tell the listeners: Pay attention to what's about to happen, because it's important.
Signposting can take all kinds of forms.
I do this a lot, giggling. That's a problem, I don't want to do it every time, but...
...and I always think she's laughing at my jokes because they're good jokes.
I do that because I'm like, See, person listening? This is funny, this is special.

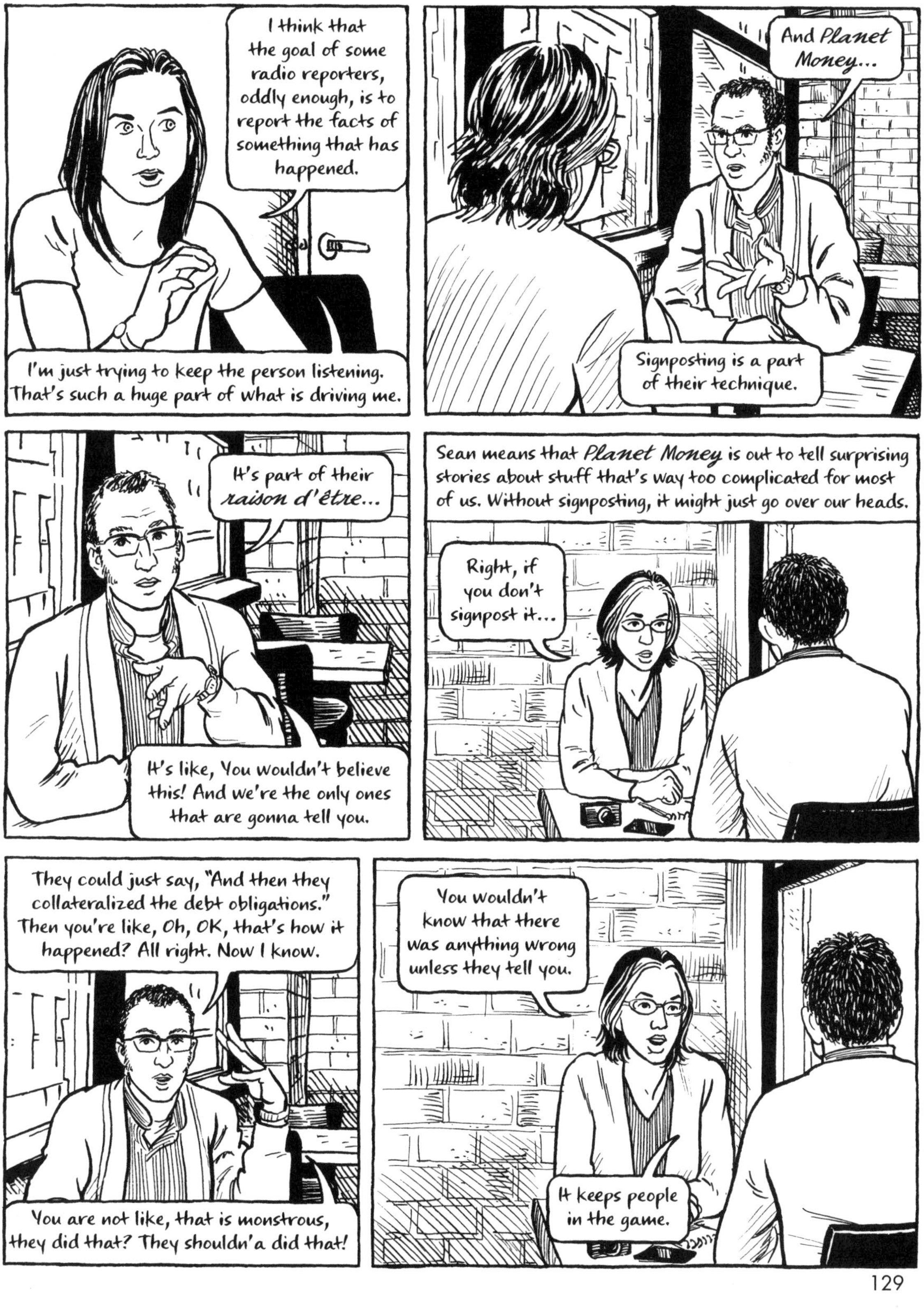
I think that the goal of some radio reporters, oddly enough, is to report the facts of something that has happened.
I'm just trying to keep the person listening. That's such a huge part of what is driving me.
And *Planet Money*...
Signposting is a part of their technique.
It's part of their *raison d'être*...
It's like, You wouldn't believe this! And we're the only ones that are gonna tell you.
Sean means that *Planet Money* is out to tell surprising stories about stuff that's way too complicated for most of us. Without signposting, it might just go over our heads.
Right, if you don't signpost it...
They could just say, "And then they collateralized the debt obligations." Then you're like, Oh, OK, that's how it happened? All right. Now I know.
You are not like, that is monstrous, they did that? They shouldn'a did that!
You wouldn't know that there was anything wrong unless they tell you.
It keeps people in the game.

REFLECTING

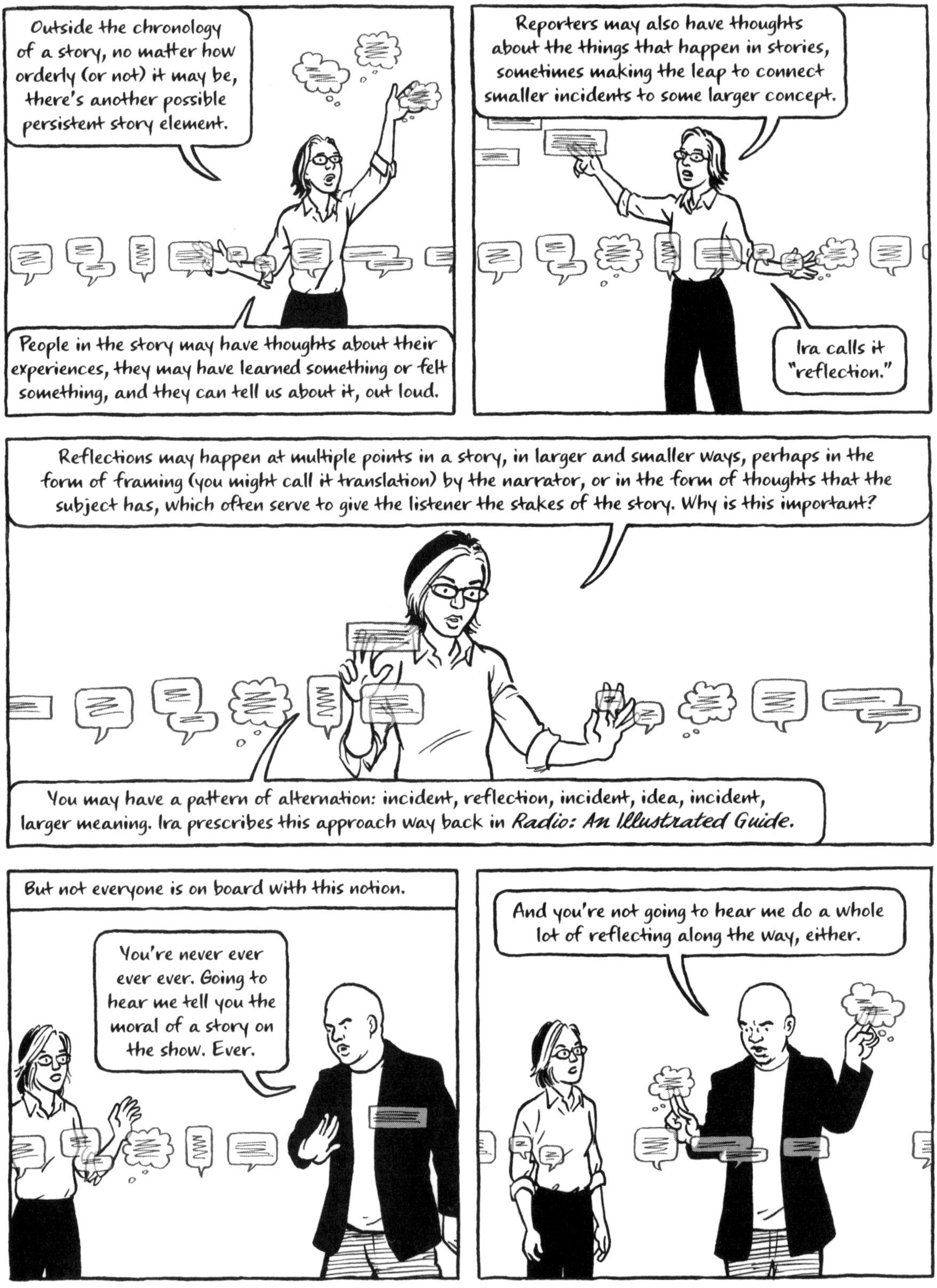

Outside the chronology of a story, no matter how orderly (or not) it may be, there's another possible persistent story element.
People in the story may have thoughts about their experiences, they may have learned something or felt something, and they can tell us about it, out loud.
Reporters may also have thoughts about the things that happen in stories, sometimes making the leap to connect smaller incidents to some larger concept.
Ira calls it "reflection."
Reflections may happen at multiple points in a story, in larger and smaller ways, perhaps in the form of framing (you might call it translation) by the narrator, or in the form of thoughts that the subject has, which often serve to give the listener the stakes of the story. Why is this important?
You may have a pattern of alternation: incident, reflection, incident, idea, incident, larger meaning. Ira prescribes this approach way back in *Radio: An Illustrated Guide*.
But not everyone is on board with this notion.
You're never ever ever ever. Going to hear me tell you the moral of a story on the show. Ever.
And you're not going to hear me do a whole lot of reflecting along the way, either.

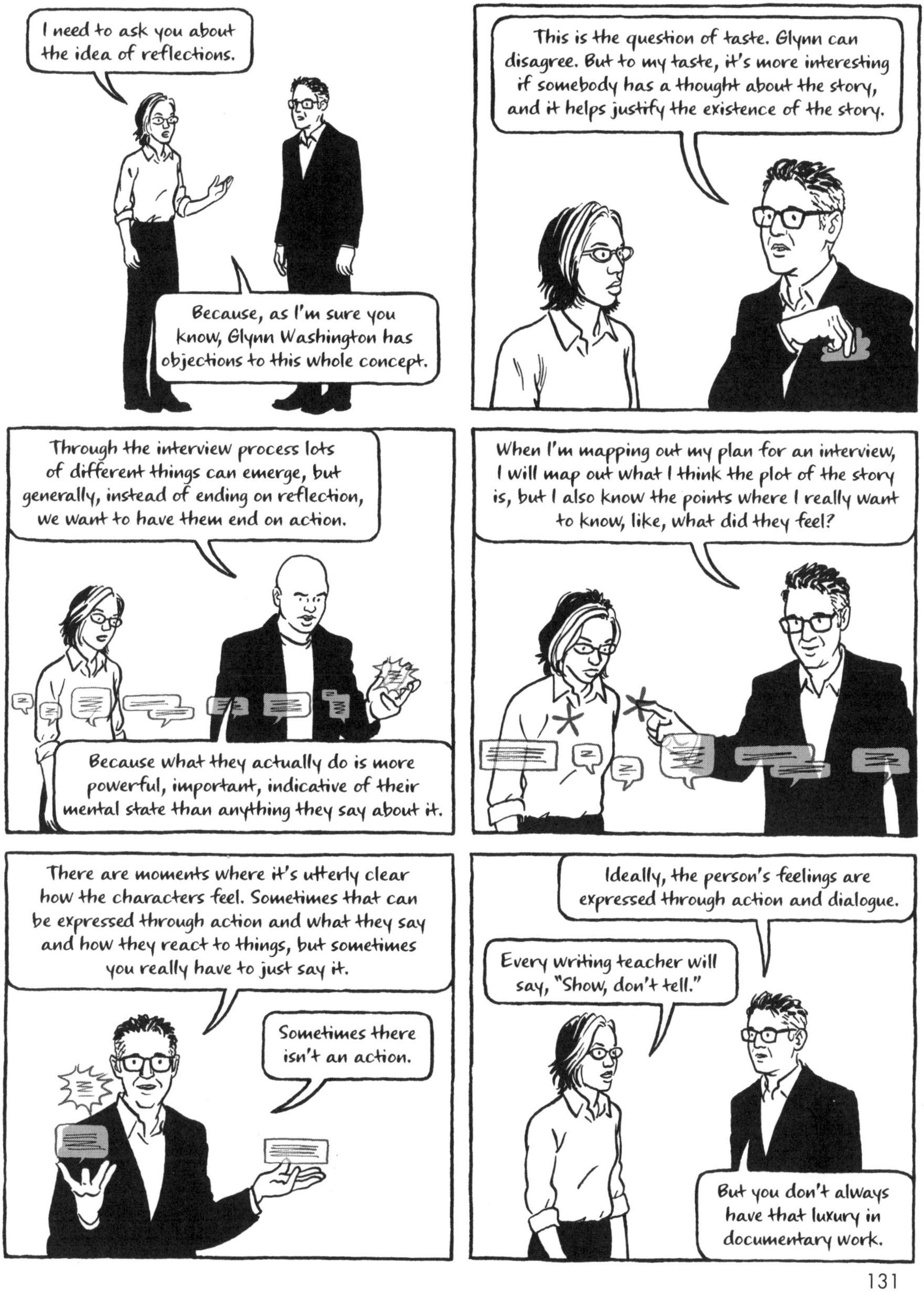
I need to ask you about the idea of reflections.
Because, as I'm sure you know, Glynn Washington has objections to this whole concept.
This is the question of taste. Glynn can disagree. But to my taste, it's more interesting if somebody has a thought about the story, and it helps justify the existence of the story.
Through the interview process lots of different things can emerge, but generally, instead of ending on reflection, we want to have them end on action.
Because what they actually do is more powerful, important, indicative of their mental state than anything they say about it.
When I'm mapping out my plan for an interview, I will map out what I think the plot of the story is, but I also know the points where I really want to know, like, what did they feel?
There are moments where it's utterly clear how the characters feel. Sometimes that can be expressed through action and what they say and how they react to things, but sometimes you really have to just say it.
Sometimes there isn't an action.
Ideally, the person's feelings are expressed through action and dialogue.
Every writing teacher will say, "Show, don't tell."
But you don't always have that luxury in documentary work.

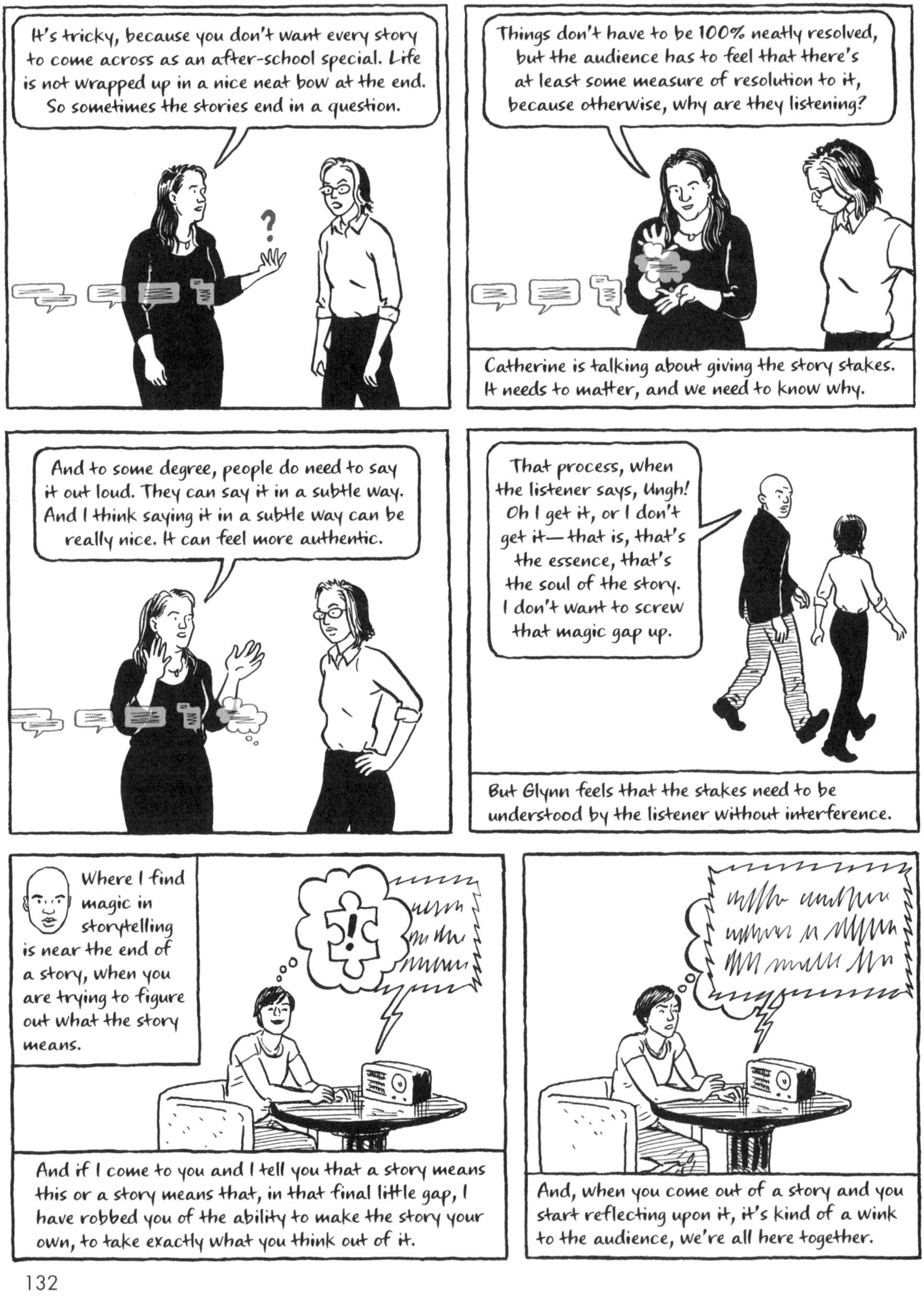
It's tricky, because you don't want every story to come across as an after-school special. Life is not wrapped up in a nice neat bow at the end. So sometimes the stories end in a question.
Things don't have to be 100% neatly resolved, but the audience has to feel that there's at least some measure of resolution to it, because otherwise, why are they listening?
Catherine is talking about giving the story stakes. It needs to matter, and we need to know why.
And to some degree, people do need to say it out loud. They can say it in a subtle way. And I think saying it in a subtle way can be really nice. It can feel more authentic.
That process, when the listener says, Ungh! Oh I get it, or I don't get it— that is, that's the essence, that's the soul of the story. I don't want to screw that magic gap up.
But Glynn feels that the stakes need to be understood by the listener without interference.
Where I find magic in storytelling is near the end of a story, when you are trying to figure out what the story means.
And if I come to you and I tell you that a story means this or a story means that, in that final little gap, I have robbed you of the ability to make the story your own, to take exactly what you think out of it.
And, when you come out of a story and you start reflecting upon it, it's kind of a wink to the audience, we're all here together.

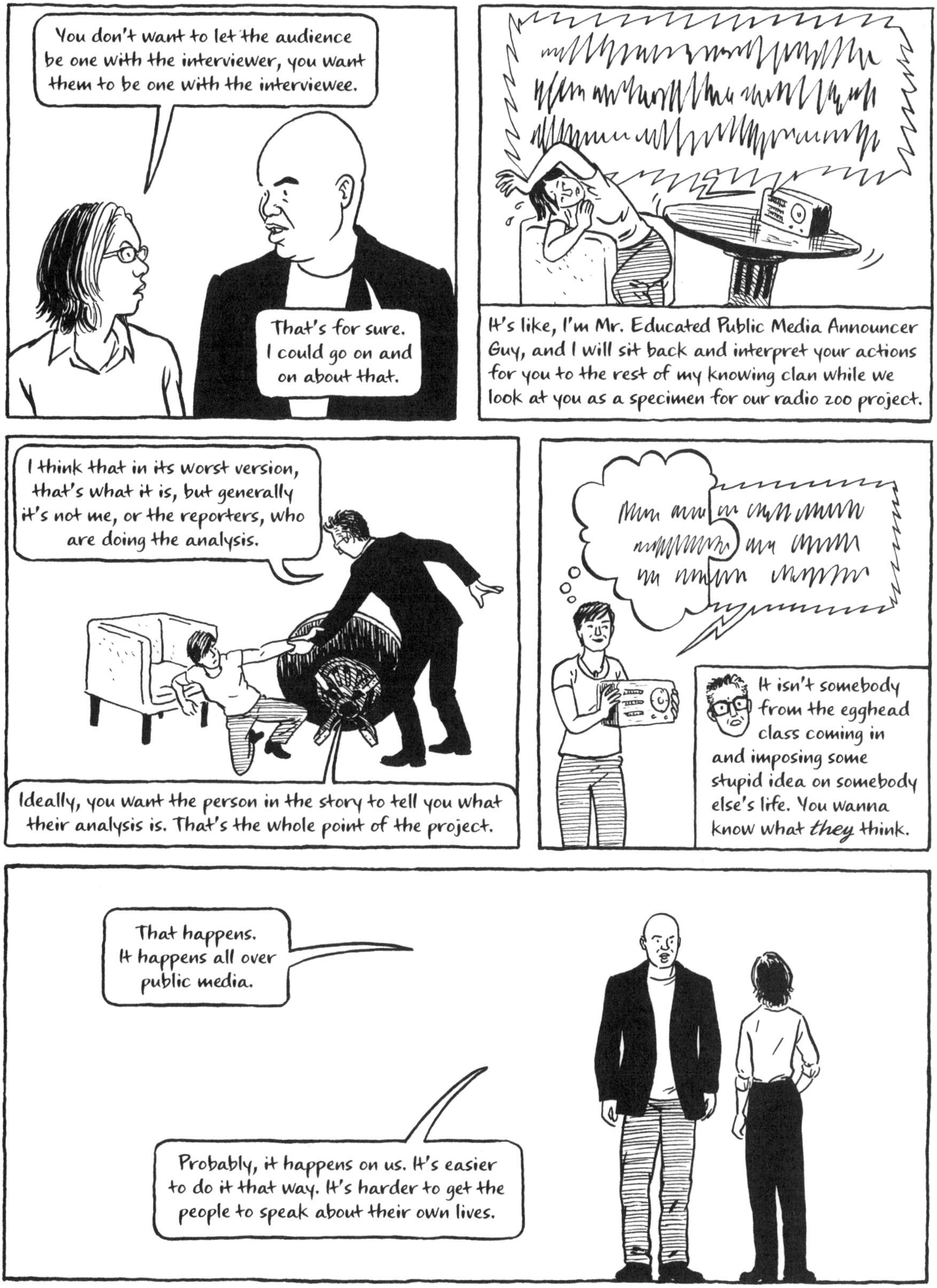
You don't want to let the audience be one with the interviewer, you want them to be one with the interviewee.
That's for sure. I could go on and on about that.
It's like, I'm Mr. Educated Public Media Announcer Guy, and I will sit back and interpret your actions for you to the rest of my knowing clan while we look at you as a specimen for our radio zoo project.
I think that in its worst version, that's what it is, but generally it's not me, or the reporters, who are doing the analysis.
Ideally, you want the person in the story to tell you what their analysis is. That's the whole point of the project.
It isn't somebody from the egghead class coming in and imposing some stupid idea on somebody else's life. You wanna know what *they* think.
That happens. It happens all over public media.
Probably, it happens on us. It's easier to do it that way. It's harder to get the people to speak about their own lives.

RULES? THERE ARE NO STINKIN' RULES.

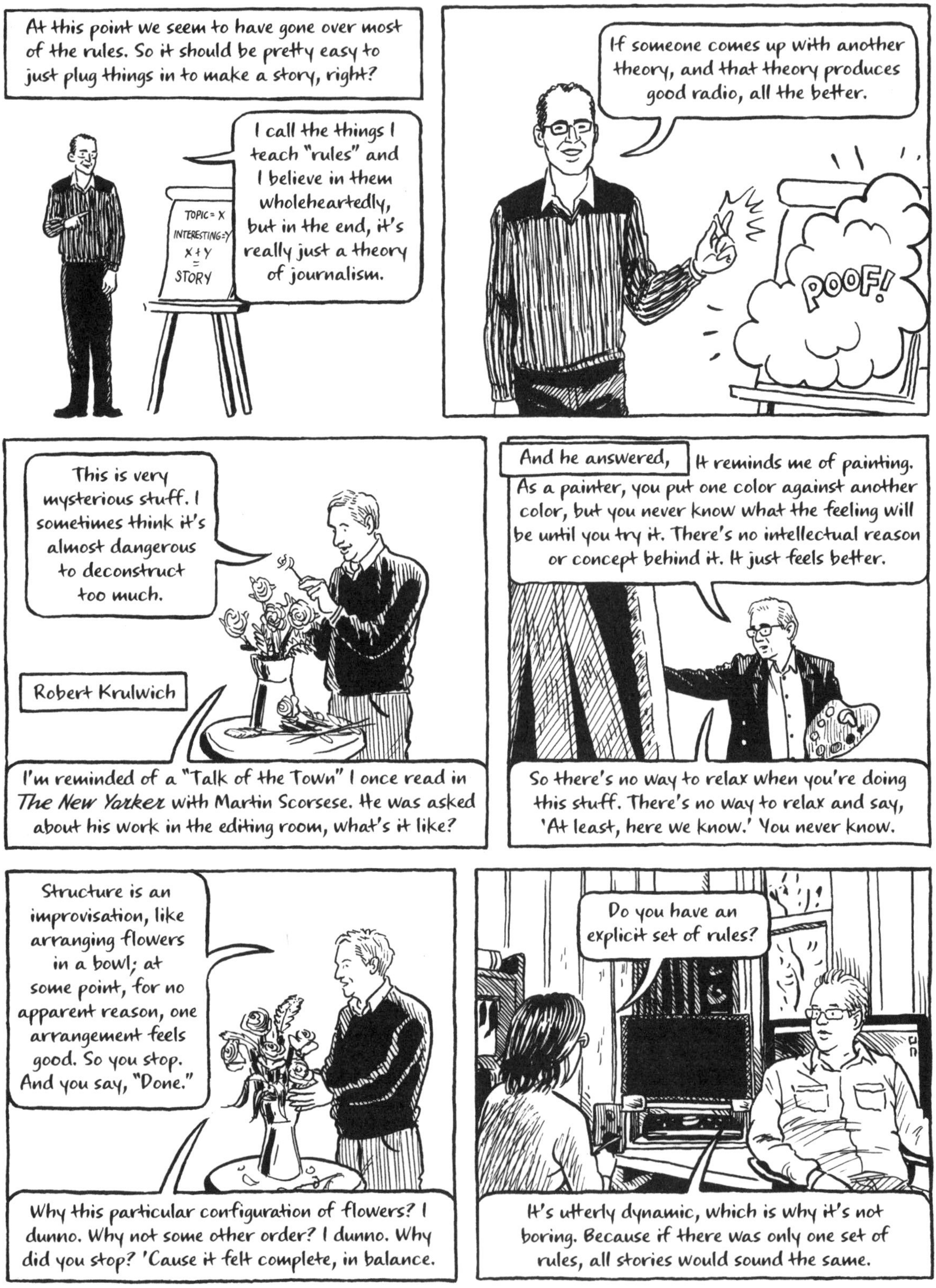

At this point we seem to have gone over most of the rules. So it should be pretty easy to just plug things in to make a story, right?
TOPIC = X
INTERESTING = Y
X + Y
=
STORY
I call the things I teach "rules" and I believe in them wholeheartedly, but in the end, it's really just a theory of journalism.
If someone comes up with another theory, and that theory produces good radio, all the better.
POOF!
This is very mysterious stuff. I sometimes think it's almost dangerous to deconstruct too much.
Robert Krulwich
I'm reminded of a "Talk of the Town" I once read in *The New Yorker* with Martin Scorsese. He was asked about his work in the editing room, what's it like?
And he answered,
It reminds me of painting. As a painter, you put one color against another color, but you never know what the feeling will be until you try it. There's no intellectual reason or concept behind it. It just feels better.
So there's no way to relax when you're doing this stuff. There's no way to relax and say, 'At least, here we know.' You never know.
Structure is an improvisation, like arranging flowers in a bowl; at some point, for no apparent reason, one arrangement feels good. So you stop. And you say, "Done."
Why this particular configuration of flowers? I dunno. Why not some other order? I dunno. Why did you stop? 'Cause it felt complete, in balance.
Do you have an explicit set of rules?
It's utterly dynamic, which is why it's not boring. Because if there was only one set of rules, all stories would sound the same.

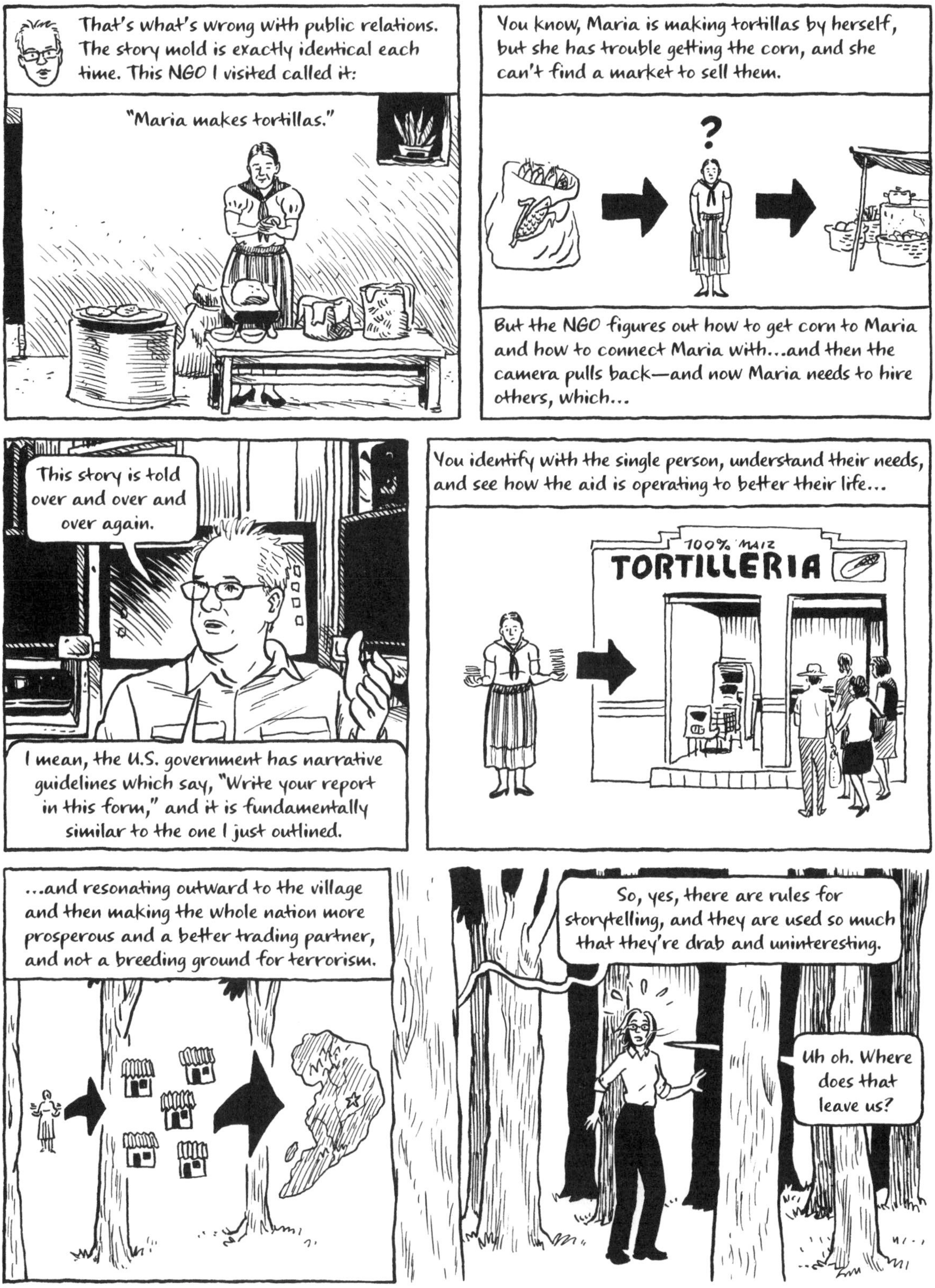
That's what's wrong with public relations. The story mold is exactly identical each time. This NGO I visited called it:
"Maria makes tortillas."
You know, Maria is making tortillas by herself, but she has trouble getting the corn, and she can't find a market to sell them.
?
But the NGO figures out how to get corn to Maria and how to connect Maria with...and then the camera pulls back—and now Maria needs to hire others, which...
This story is told over and over and over again.
I mean, the U.S. government has narrative guidelines which say, "Write your report in this form," and it is fundamentally similar to the one I just outlined.
You identify with the single person, understand their needs, and see how the aid is operating to better their life...
100% MAIZ
TORTILLERIA
...and resonating outward to the village and then making the whole nation more prosperous and a better trading partner, and not a breeding ground for terrorism.
So, yes, there are rules for storytelling, and they are used so much that they're drab and uninteresting.
Uh oh. Where does that leave us?

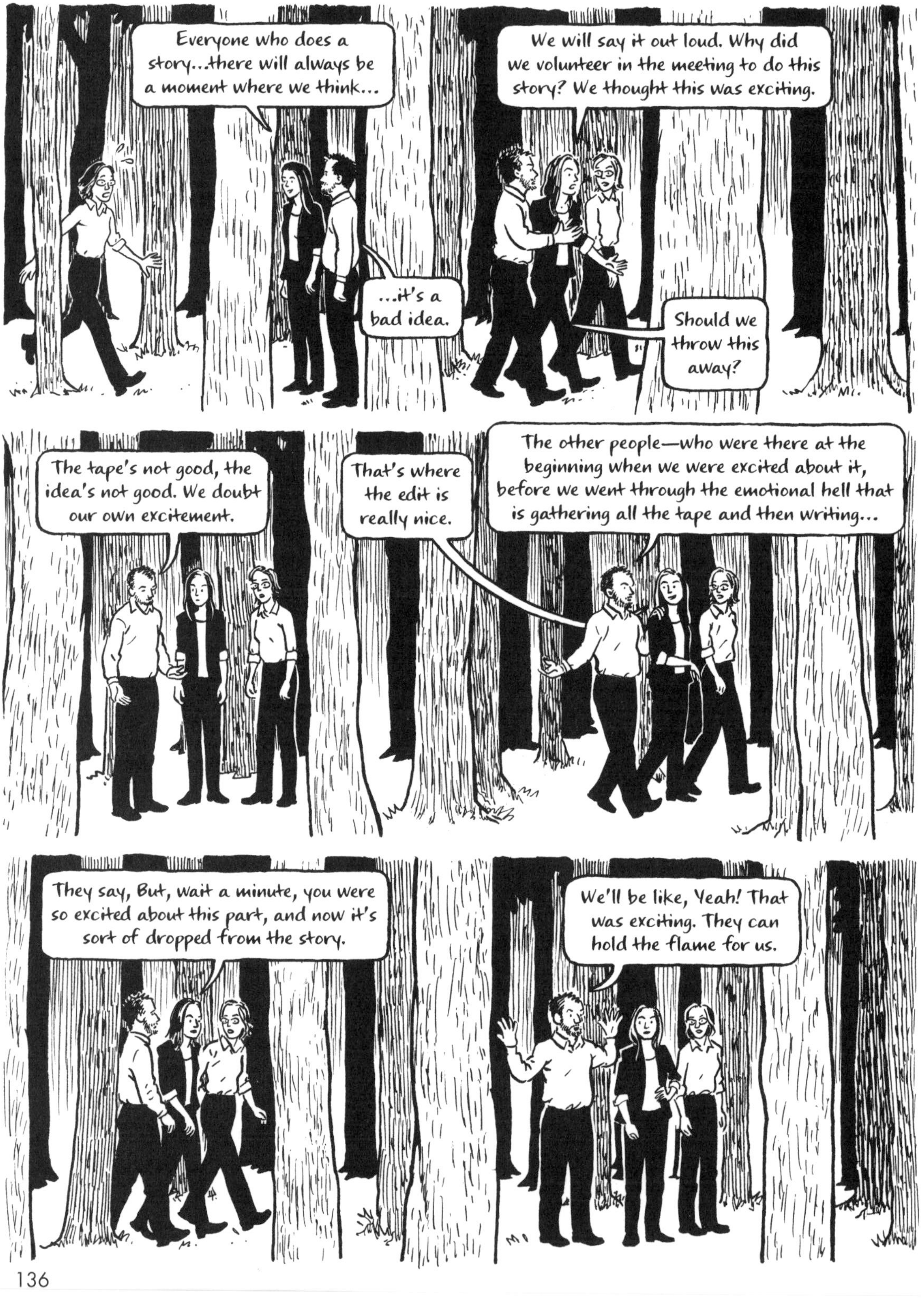
Everyone who does a story...there will always be a moment where we think...
...it's a bad idea.
We will say it out loud. Why did we volunteer in the meeting to do this story? We thought this was exciting.
Should we throw this away?
The tape's not good, the idea's not good. We doubt our own excitement.
That's where the edit is really nice.
The other people—who were there at the beginning when we were excited about it, before we went through the emotional hell that is gathering all the tape and then writing...
They say, But, wait a minute, you were so excited about this part, and now it's sort of dropped from the story.
We'll be like, Yeah! That was exciting. They can hold the flame for us.

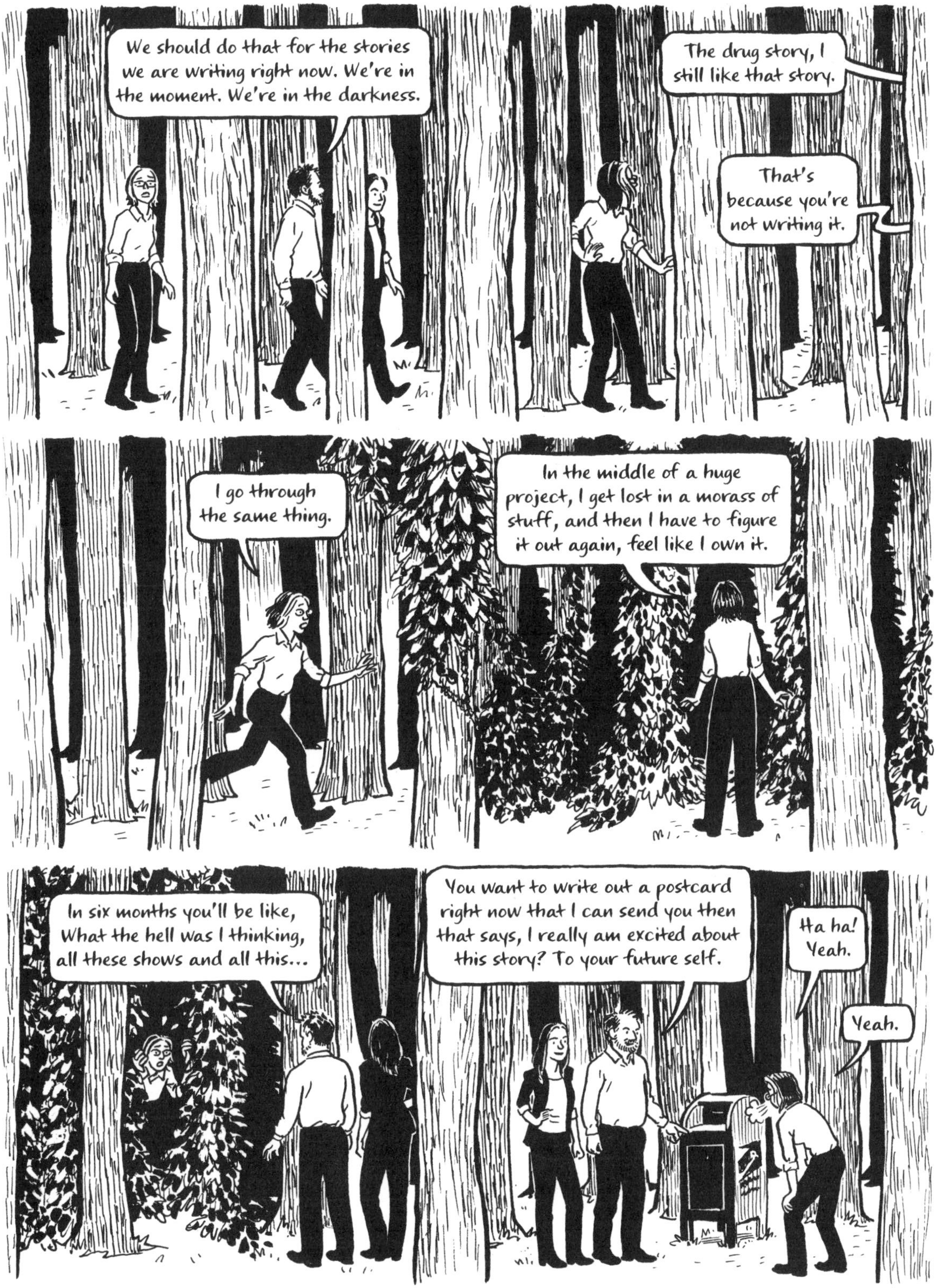

We should do that for the stories we are writing right now. We're in the moment. We're in the darkness.
The drug story, I still like that story.
That's because you're not writing it.
I go through the same thing.
In the middle of a huge project, I get lost in a morass of stuff, and then I have to figure it out again, feel like I own it.
In six months you'll be like, What the hell was I thinking, all these shows and all this...
You want to write out a postcard right now that I can send you then that says, I really am excited about this story? To your future self.
Ha ha! Yeah.
Yeah.

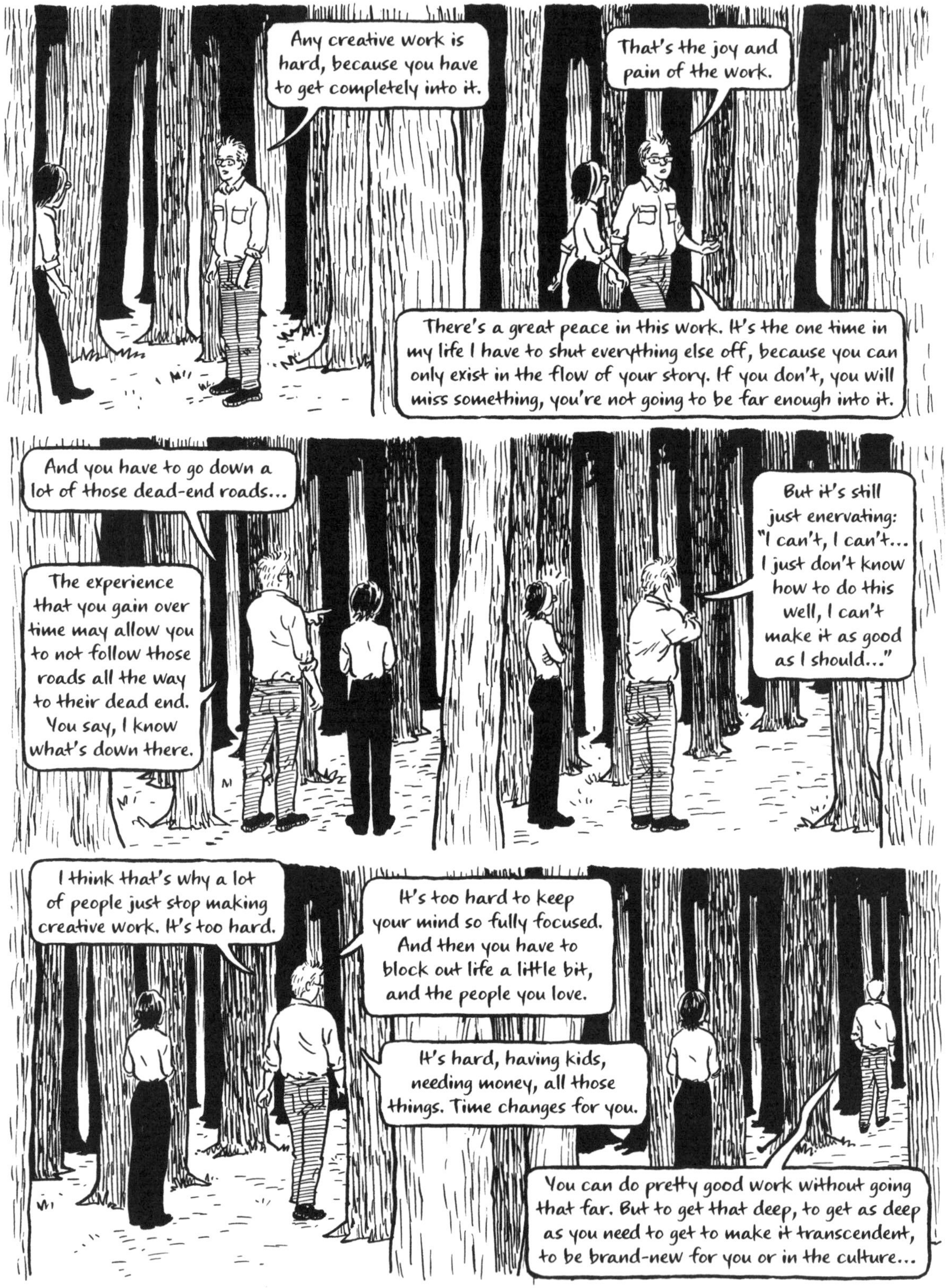

Any creative work is hard, because you have to get completely into it.
That's the joy and pain of the work.
There's a great peace in this work. It's the one time in my life I have to shut everything else off, because you can only exist in the flow of your story. If you don't, you will miss something, you're not going to be far enough into it.
And you have to go down a lot of those dead-end roads...
The experience that you gain over time may allow you to not follow those roads all the way to their dead end. You say, I know what's down there.
But it's still just enervating: "I can't, I can't... I just don't know how to do this well, I can't make it as good as I should..."
I think that's why a lot of people just stop making creative work. It's too hard.
It's too hard to keep your mind so fully focused. And then you have to block out life a little bit, and the people you love.
It's hard, having kids, needing money, all those things. Time changes for you.
You can do pretty good work without going that far. But to get that deep, to get as deep as you need to get to make it transcendent, to be brand-new for you or in the culture...

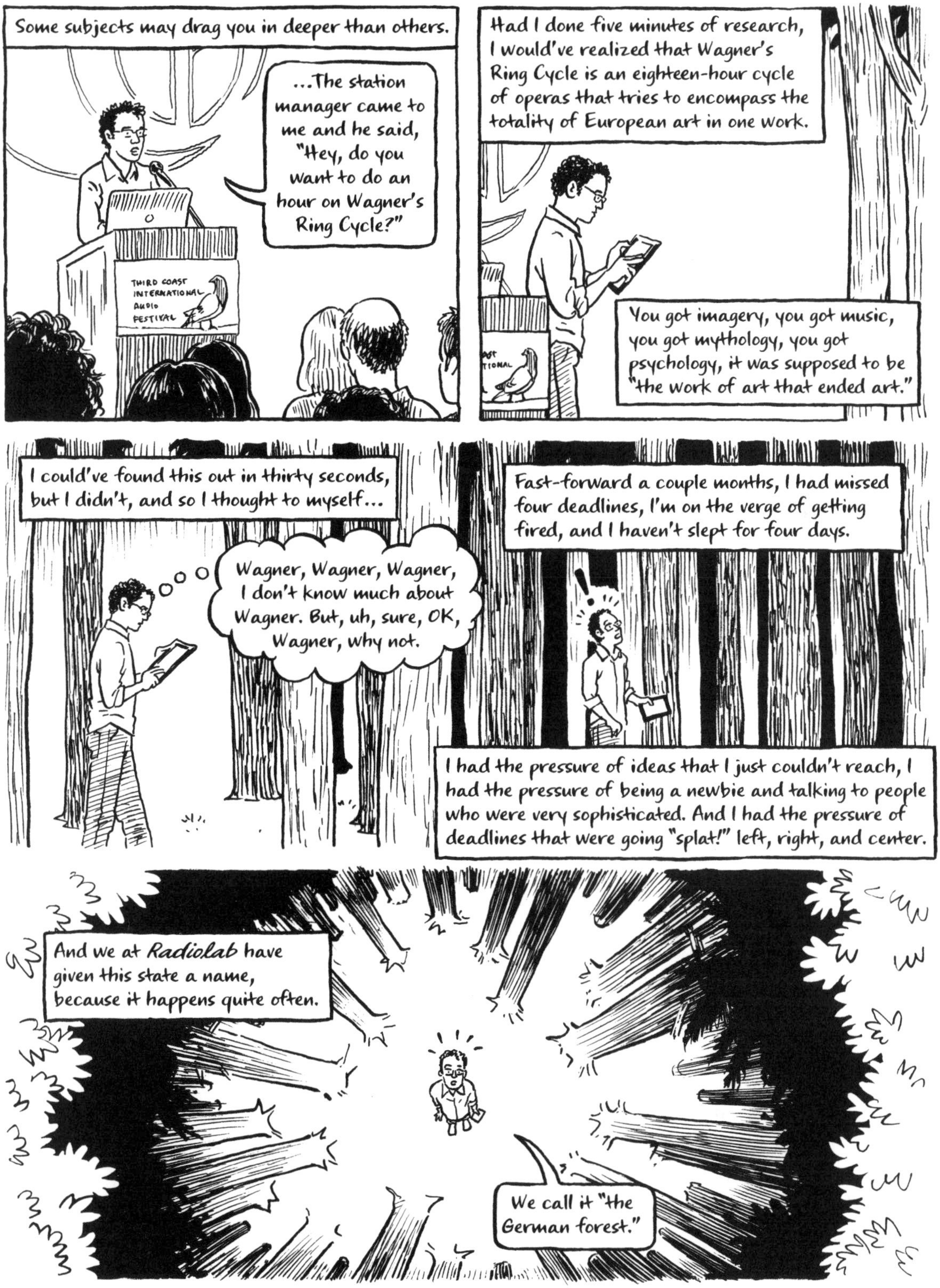
Some subjects may drag you in deeper than others.
...The station manager came to me and he said, "Hey, do you want to do an hour on Wagner's Ring Cycle?"
THIRD COAST INTERNATIONAL AUDIO FESTIVAL
Had I done five minutes of research, I would've realized that Wagner's Ring Cycle is an eighteen-hour cycle of operas that tries to encompass the totality of European art in one work.
You got imagery, you got music, you got mythology, you got psychology, it was supposed to be "the work of art that ended art."
I could've found this out in thirty seconds, but I didn't, and so I thought to myself...
Wagner, Wagner, Wagner, I don't know much about Wagner. But, uh, sure, OK, Wagner, why not.
Fast-forward a couple months, I had missed four deadlines, I'm on the verge of getting fired, and I haven't slept for four days.
!
I had the pressure of ideas that I just couldn't reach, I had the pressure of being a newbie and talking to people who were very sophisticated. And I had the pressure of deadlines that were going "splat!" left, right, and center.
And we at *Radiolab* have given this state a name, because it happens quite often.
We call it "the German forest."

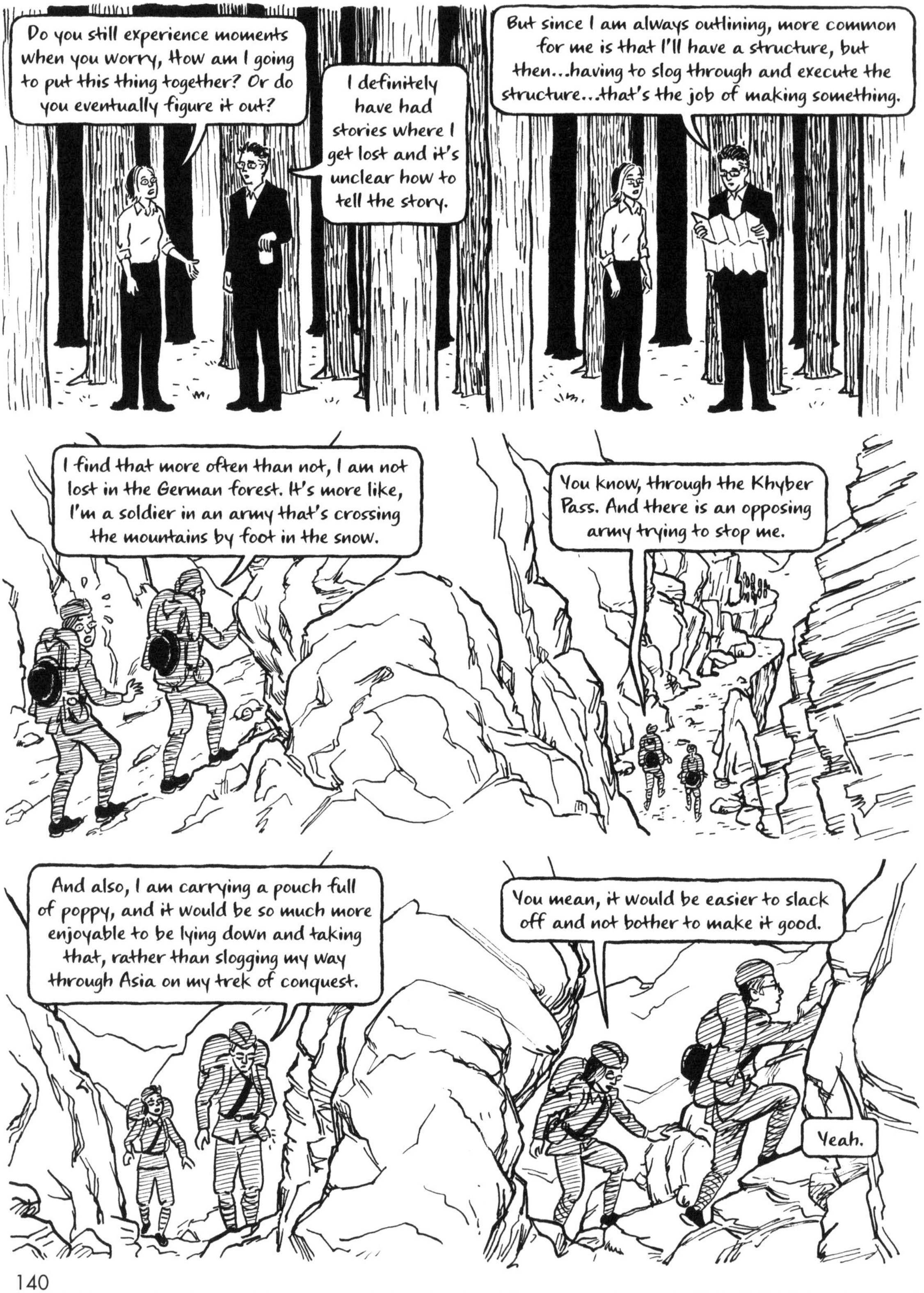

Do you still experience moments when you worry, How am I going to put this thing together? Or do you eventually figure it out?
I definitely have had stories where I get lost and it's unclear how to tell the story.
But since I am always outlining, more common for me is that I'll have a structure, but then...having to slog through and execute the structure...that's the job of making something.
I find that more often than not, I am not lost in the German forest. It's more like, I'm a soldier in an army that's crossing the mountains by foot in the snow.
You know, through the Khyber Pass. And there is an opposing army trying to stop me.
And also, I am carrying a pouch full of poppy, and it would be so much more enjoyable to be lying down and taking that, rather than slogging my way through Asia on my trek of conquest.
You mean, it would be easier to slack off and not bother to make it good.
Yeah.

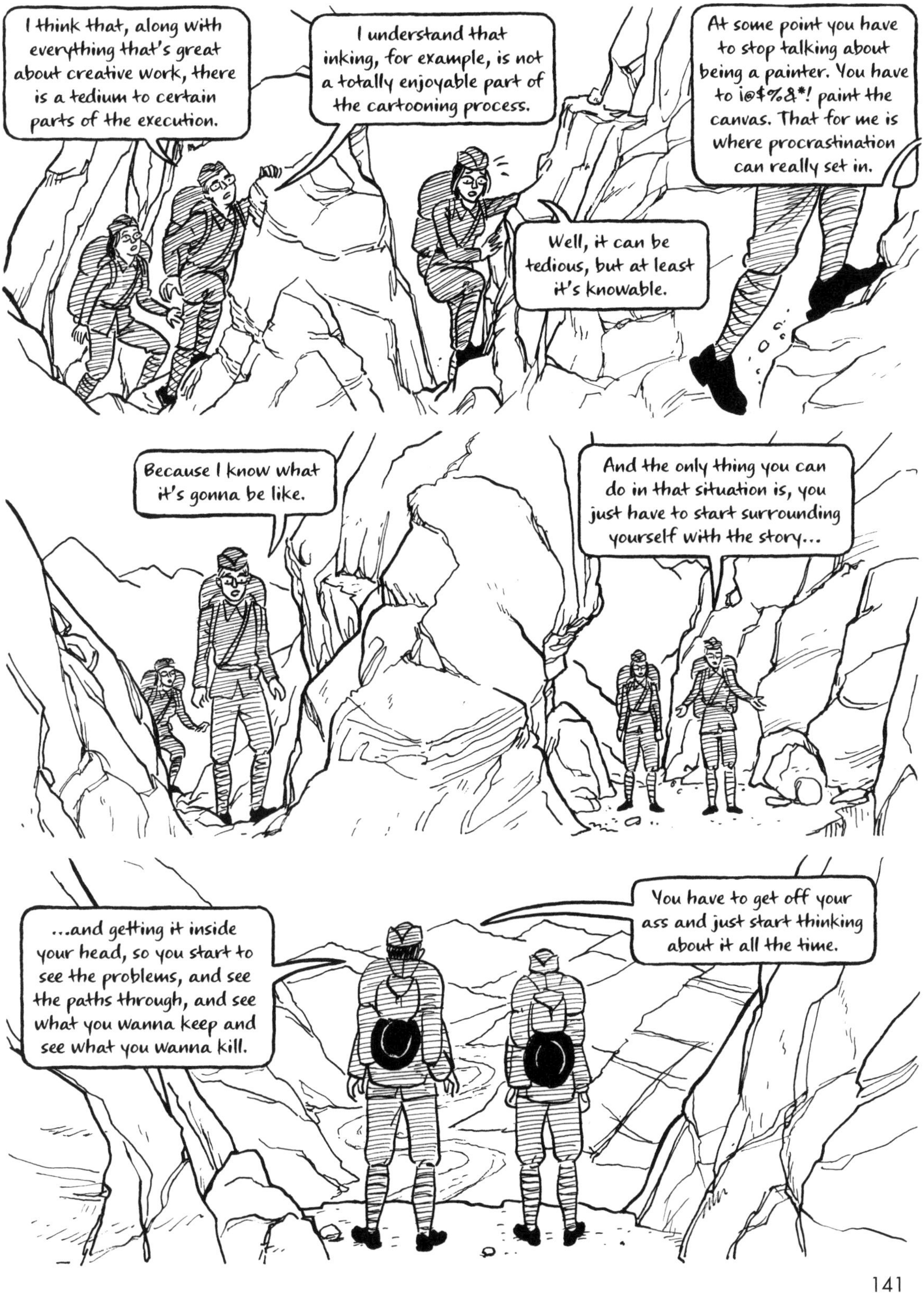
I think that, along with everything that's great about creative work, there is a tedium to certain parts of the execution.
I understand that inking, for example, is not a totally enjoyable part of the cartooning process.
Well, it can be tedious, but at least it's knowable.
At some point you have to stop talking about being a painter. You have to i@$%&*! paint the canvas. That for me is where procrastination can really set in.
Because I know what it's gonna be like.
And the only thing you can do in that situation is, you just have to start surrounding yourself with the story...
...and getting it inside your head, so you start to see the problems, and see the paths through, and see what you wanna keep and see what you wanna kill.
You have to get off your ass and just start thinking about it all the time.

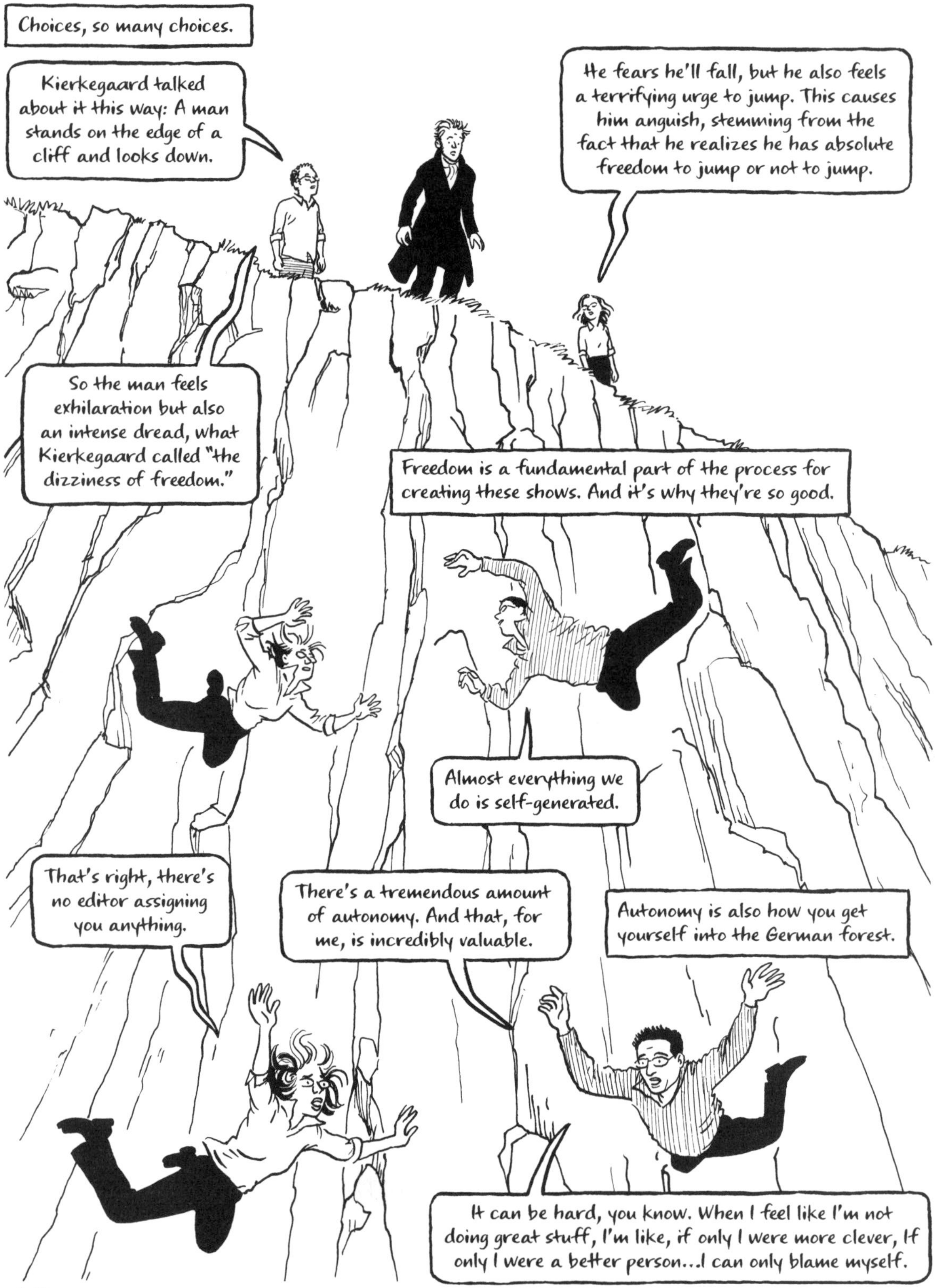
Choices, so many choices.
Kierkegaard talked about it this way: A man stands on the edge of a cliff and looks down.
He fears he'll fall, but he also feels a terrifying urge to jump. This causes him anguish, stemming from the fact that he realizes he has absolute freedom to jump or not to jump.
So the man feels exhilaration but also an intense dread, what Kierkegaard called "the dizziness of freedom."
Freedom is a fundamental part of the process for creating these shows. And it's why they're so good.
Almost everything we do is self-generated.
That's right, there's no editor assigning you anything.
There's a tremendous amount of autonomy. And that, for me, is incredibly valuable.
Autonomy is also how you get yourself into the German forest.
It can be hard, you know. When I feel like I'm not doing great stuff, I'm like, if only I were more clever, If only I were a better person...I can only blame myself.

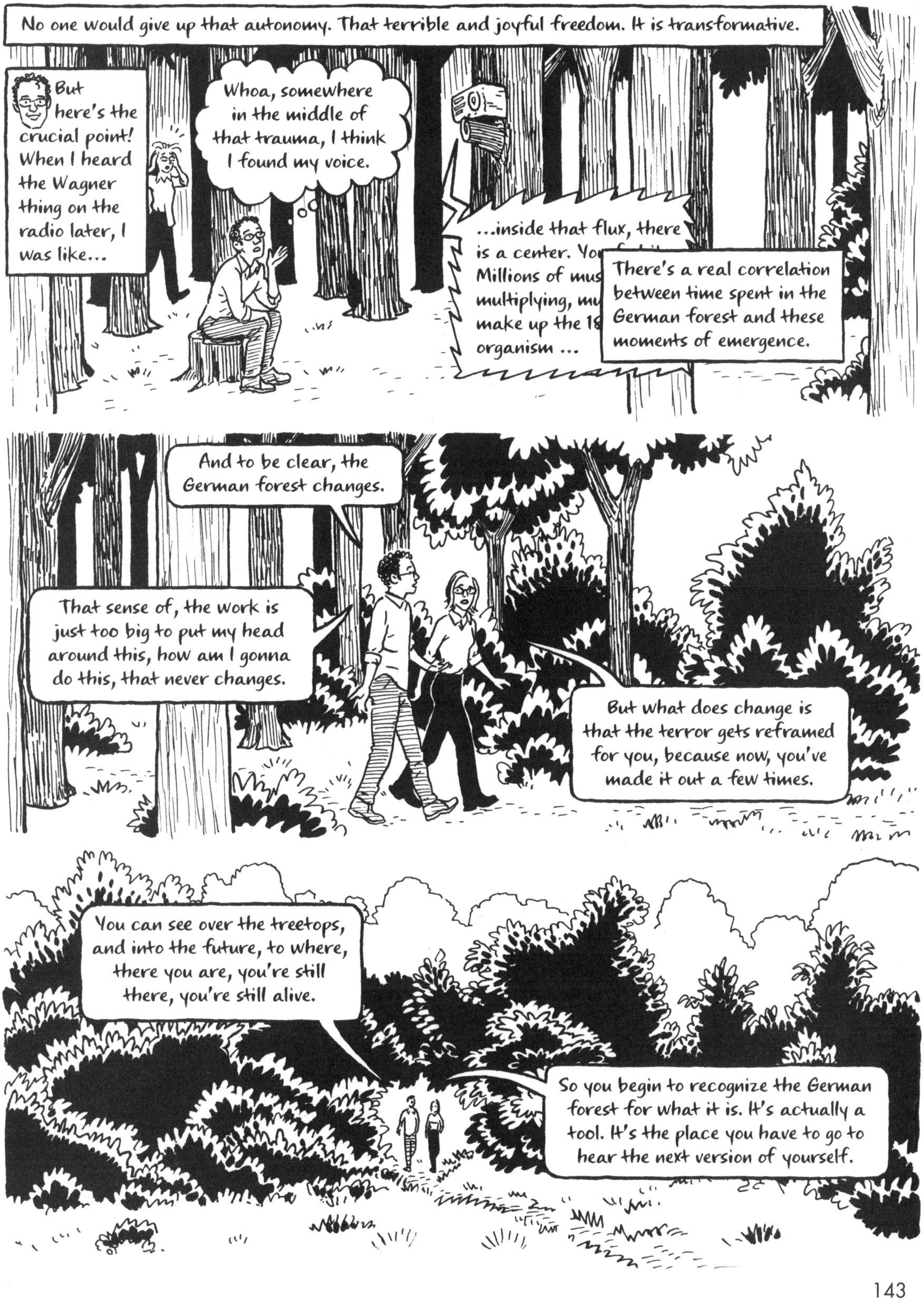

No one would give up that autonomy. That terrible and joyful freedom. It is transformative.
But here's the crucial point! When I heard the Wagner thing on the radio later, I was like...
Whoa, somewhere in the middle of that trauma, I think I found my voice.
...inside that flux, there is a center.
Millions of
multiplying,
make up the
organism ...
There's a real correlation between time spent in the German forest and these moments of emergence.
And to be clear, the German forest changes.
That sense of, the work is just too big to put my head around this, how am I gonna do this, that never changes.
But what does change is that the terror gets reframed for you, because now, you've made it out a few times.
You can see over the treetops, and into the future, to where, there you are, you're still there, you're still alive.
So you begin to recognize the German forest for what it is. It's actually a tool. It's the place you have to go to hear the next version of yourself.

THE DEEP SEA:
Sound

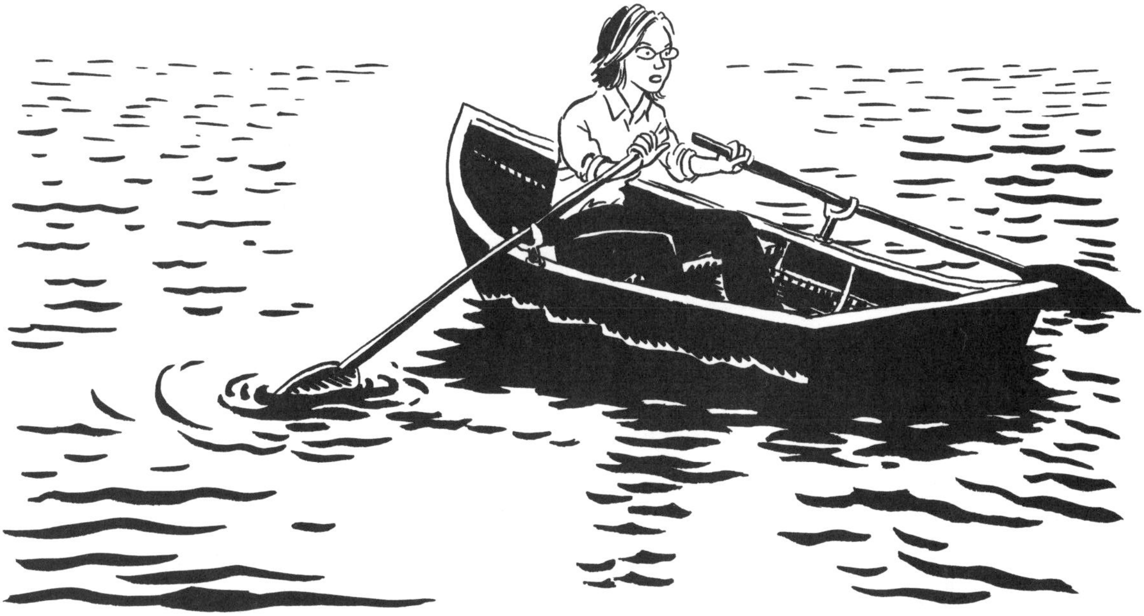

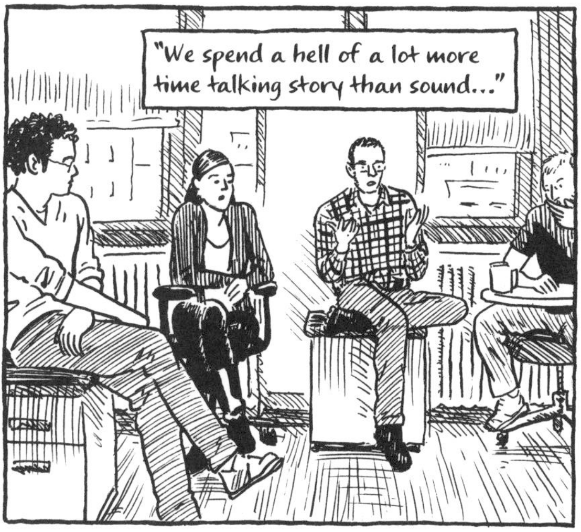
"We spend a hell of a lot more time talking story than sound..."

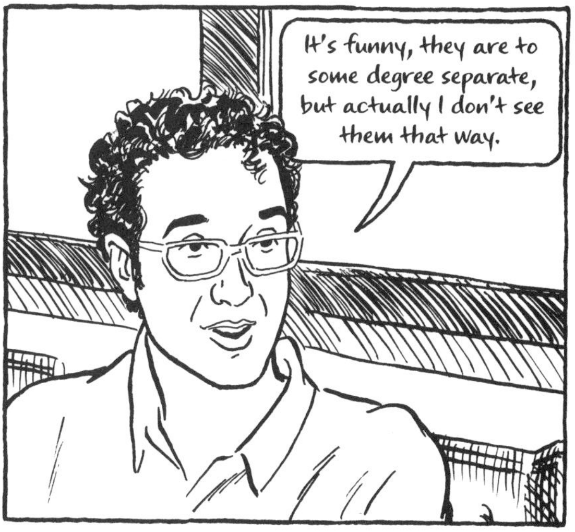
It's funny, they are to some degree separate, but actually I don't see them that way.

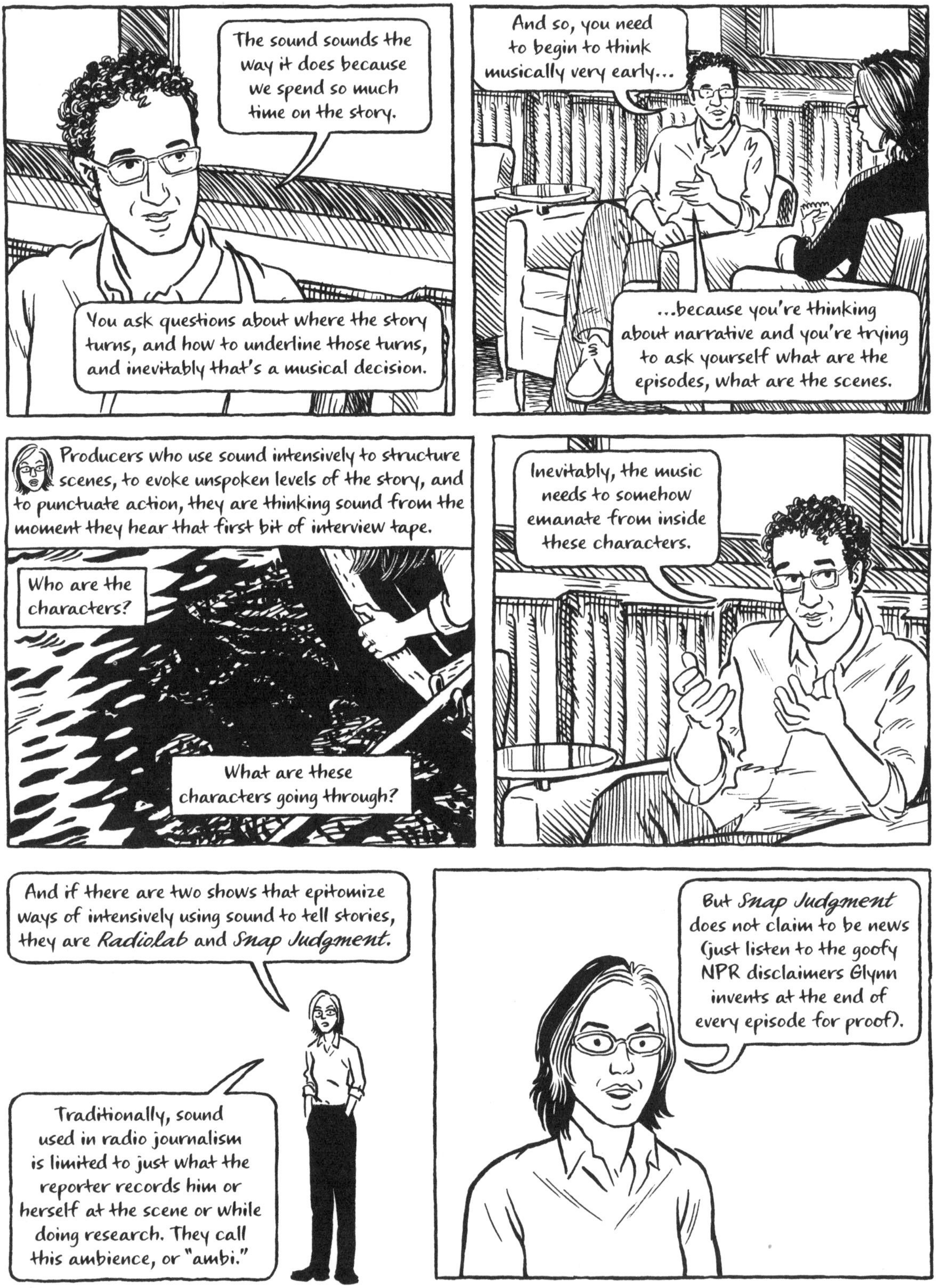

The sound sounds the way it does because we spend so much time on the story.
You ask questions about where the story turns, and how to underline those turns, and inevitably that's a musical decision.
And so, you need to begin to think musically very early...
...because you're thinking about narrative and you're trying to ask yourself what are the episodes, what are the scenes.
Producers who use sound intensively to structure scenes, to evoke unspoken levels of the story, and to punctuate action, they are thinking sound from the moment they hear that first bit of interview tape.
Who are the characters?
What are these characters going through?
Inevitably, the music needs to somehow emanate from inside these characters.
And if there are two shows that epitomize ways of intensively using sound to tell stories, they are *Radiolab* and *Snap Judgment*.
Traditionally, sound used in radio journalism is limited to just what the reporter records him or herself at the scene or while doing research. They call this ambience, or "ambi."
But *Snap Judgment* does not claim to be news (just listen to the goofy NPR disclaimers Glynn invents at the end of every episode for proof).

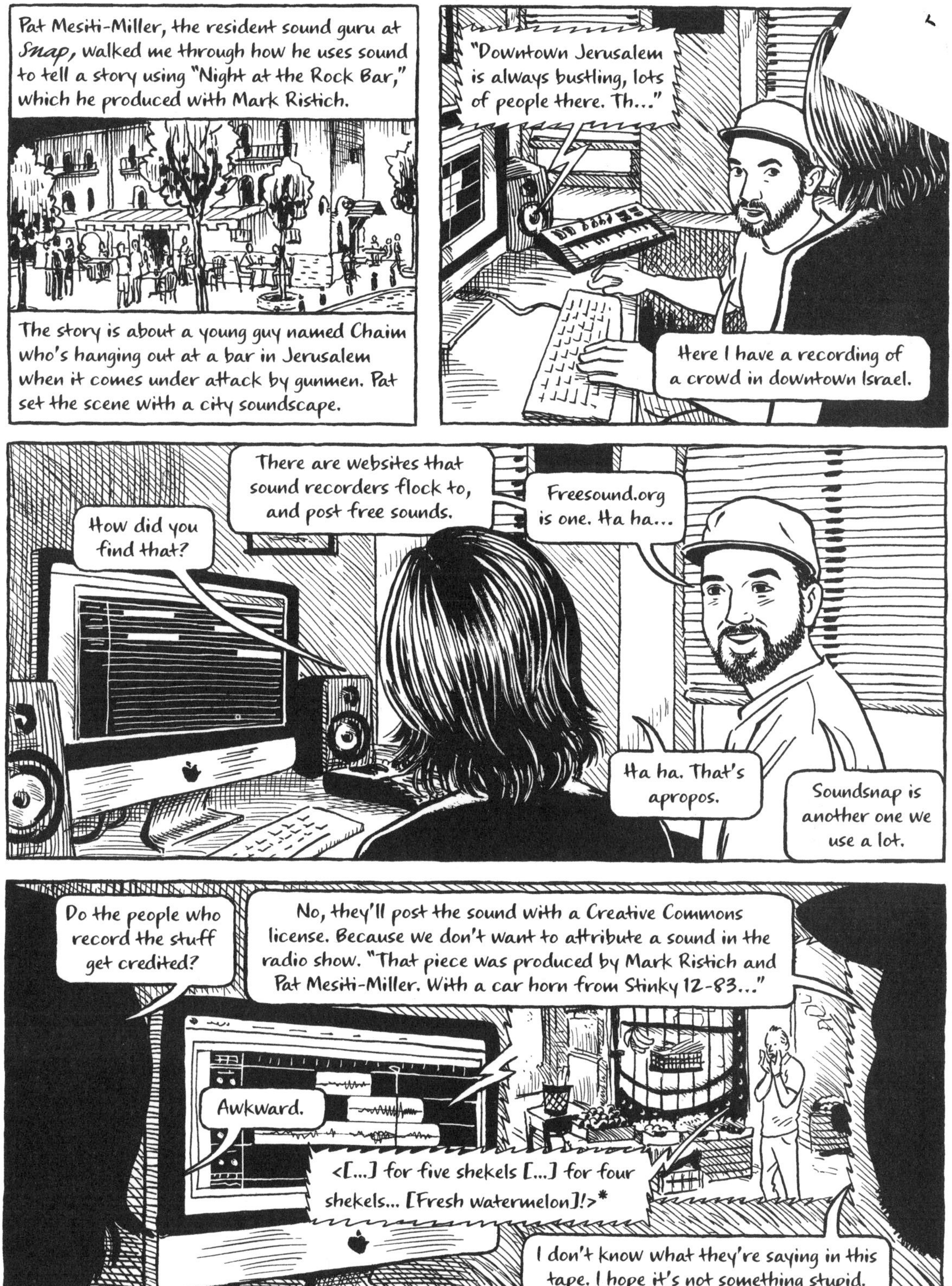
Pat Mesiti-Miller, the resident sound guru at *Snap*, walked me through how he uses sound to tell a story using "Night at the Rock Bar," which he produced with Mark Ristich.
The story is about a young guy named Chaim who's hanging out at a bar in Jerusalem when it comes under attack by gunmen. Pat set the scene with a city soundscape.
"Downtown Jerusalem is always bustling, lots of people there. Th..."
Here I have a recording of a crowd in downtown Israel.
How did you find that?
There are websites that sound recorders flock to, and post free sounds.
Freesound.org is one. Ha ha...
Ha ha. That's apropos.
Soundsnap is another one we use a lot.
Do the people who record the stuff get credited?
No, they'll post the sound with a Creative Commons license. Because we don't want to attribute a sound in the radio show. "That piece was produced by Mark Ristich and Pat Mesiti-Miller. With a car horn from Stinky 12-83..."
Awkward.
<[...] for five shekels [...] for four shekels... [Fresh watermelon]!>*
I don't know what they're saying in this tape. I hope it's not something stupid.

Pat does not know that this is what they're saying.

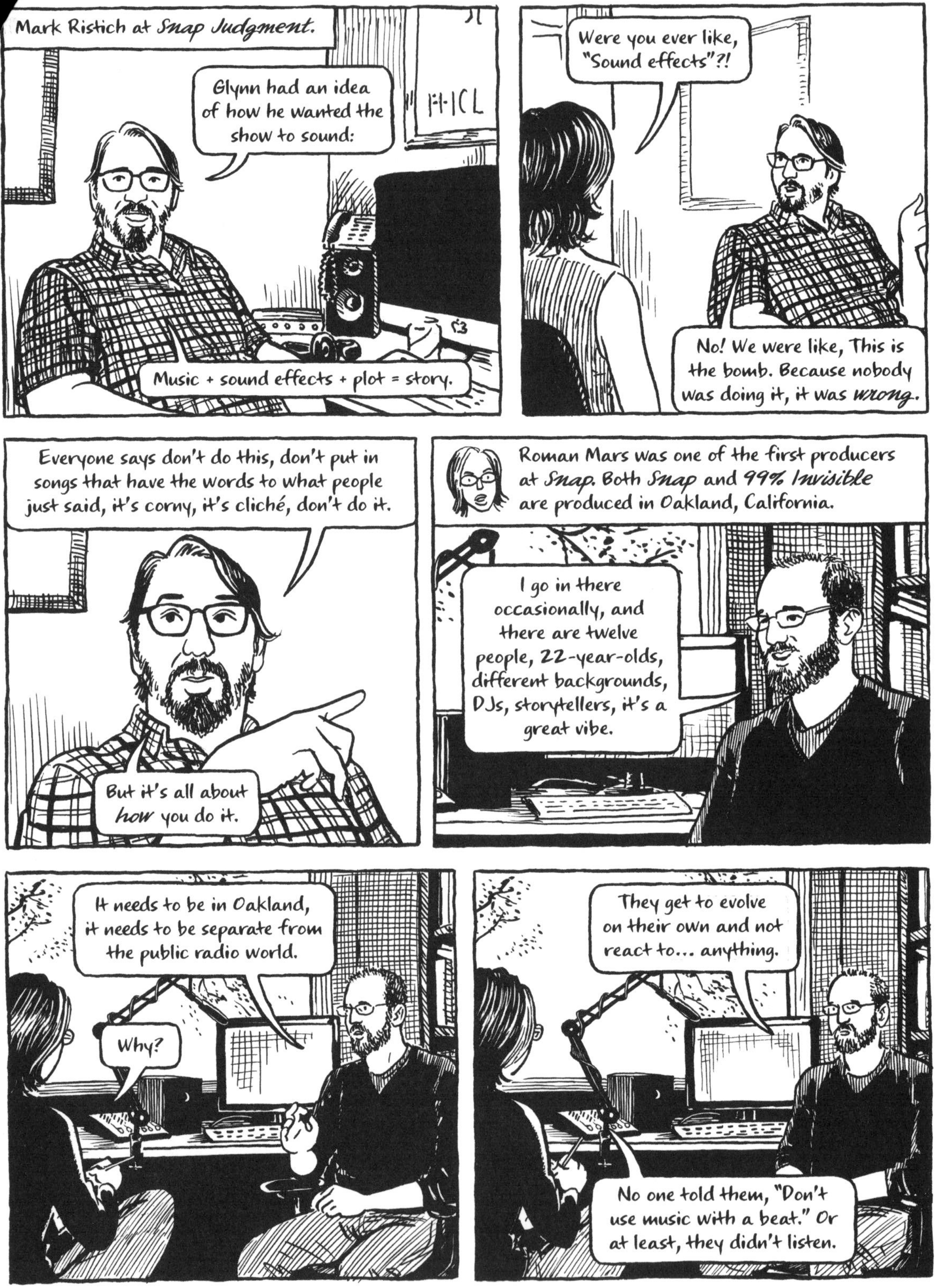
Mark Ristich at *Snap Judgment*.
Glynn had an idea of how he wanted the show to sound:
Music + sound effects + plot = story.
Were you ever like, "Sound effects"?!
No! We were like, This is the bomb. Because nobody was doing it, it was *wrong*.
Everyone says don't do this, don't put in songs that have the words to what people just said, it's corny, it's cliché, don't do it.
But it's all about *how* you do it.
Roman Mars was one of the first producers at *Snap*. Both *Snap* and *99% Invisible* are produced in Oakland, California.
I go in there occasionally, and there are twelve people, 22-year-olds, different backgrounds, DJs, storytellers, it's a great vibe.
It needs to be in Oakland, it needs to be separate from the public radio world.
Why?
They get to evolve on their own and not react to... anything.
No one told them, "Don't use music with a beat." Or at least, they didn't listen.

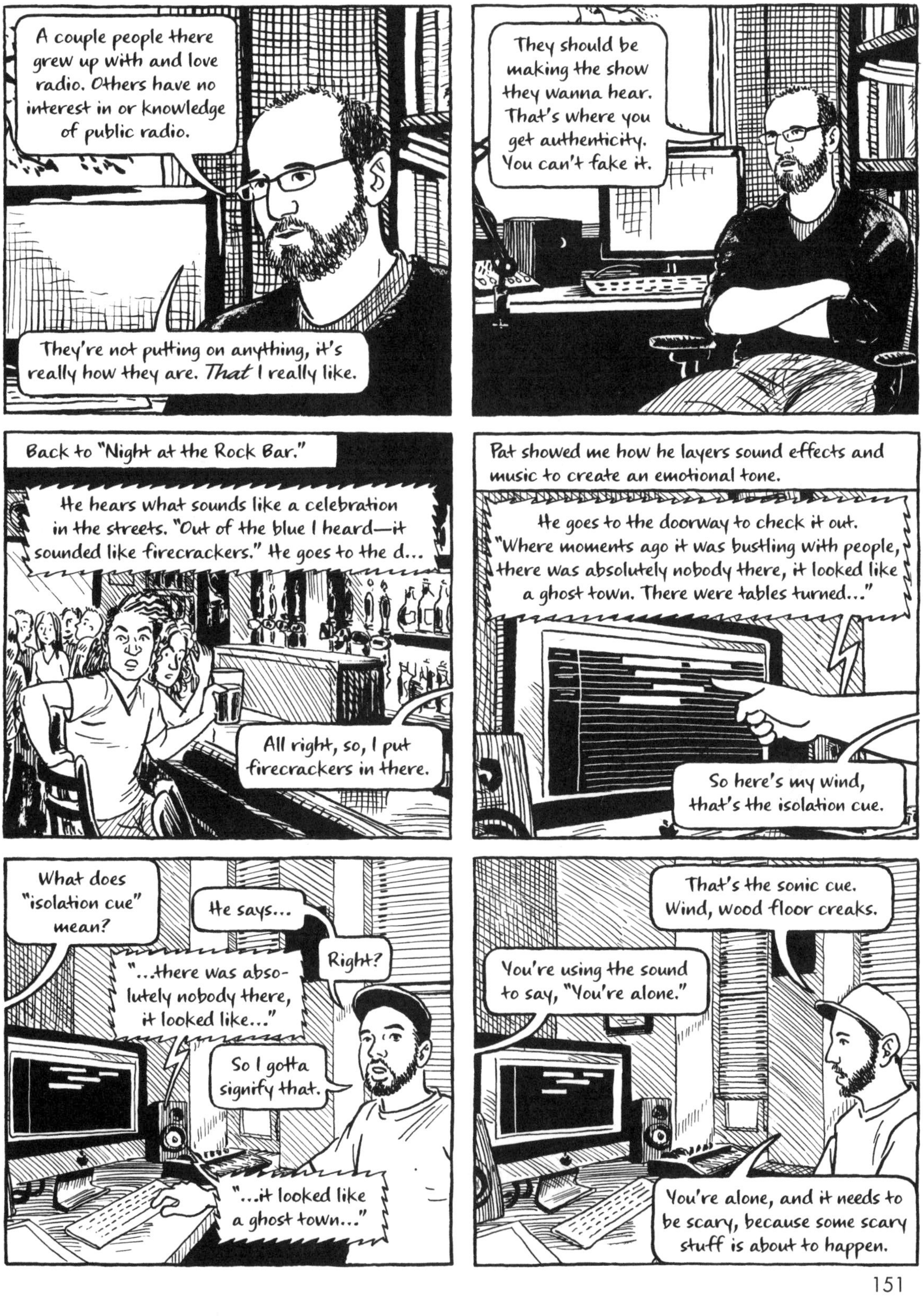
A couple people there grew up with and love radio. Others have no interest in or knowledge of public radio.
They're not putting on anything, it's really how they are. *That* I really like.
They should be making the show they wanna hear. That's where you get authenticity. You can't fake it.
Back to "Night at the Rock Bar."
He hears what sounds like a celebration in the streets. "Out of the blue I heard—it sounded like firecrackers." He goes to the d...
All right, so, I put firecrackers in there.
Pat showed me how he layers sound effects and music to create an emotional tone.
He goes to the doorway to check it out. "Where moments ago it was bustling with people, there was absolutely nobody there, it looked like a ghost town. There were tables turned..."
So here's my wind, that's the isolation cue.
What does "isolation cue" mean?
He says...
Right?
"...there was absolutely nobody there, it looked like..."
So I gotta signify that.
"...it looked like a ghost town..."
That's the sonic cue. Wind, wood floor creaks.
You're using the sound to say, "You're alone."
You're alone, and it needs to be scary, because some scary stuff is about to happen.

The Rock Bar looks out on a plaza. And there, 10 feet away, is a lone figure with a machine gun.

"He had an AK-47, and he had a red bandanna."

This is not an Israeli soldier.

Across the plaza a civilian runs across the street to escape the gunfire.

"And the guy turned the gun and shot him."

TAPTAPTAPTAPTAP PANT PANT PANT PANT **PANNNNNNNN**NNNNNNNNnnnng

That was a cool effect on the gunshot, I wanted it to be that "scared" moment.

That long reverb is part of the...

Part of the effect that I added to it, to be like a frozen moment in time.

Sound can create an emotional tone. It can also simply create *room* for emotion to hit you.

With radio you have a peculiar problem. If somebody stops talking, you can't just go to silence for very long.

And so if you just want to pause, you need something there. Often the main thing that music is doing is just holding the space, and letting the moment live for another three or four seconds.

Which doesn't seem like it would have that much of an emotional impact, but turns out actually to mean all the difference in the world.

Often the kind of music that we're using on *This American Life* has forward motion and a melody, but doesn't have a strong feeling to it.

If it has a feeling at all, the feeling is just a big sort of yearniness. We tend to need a lot of music that has a vague sort of free-floating yearning.

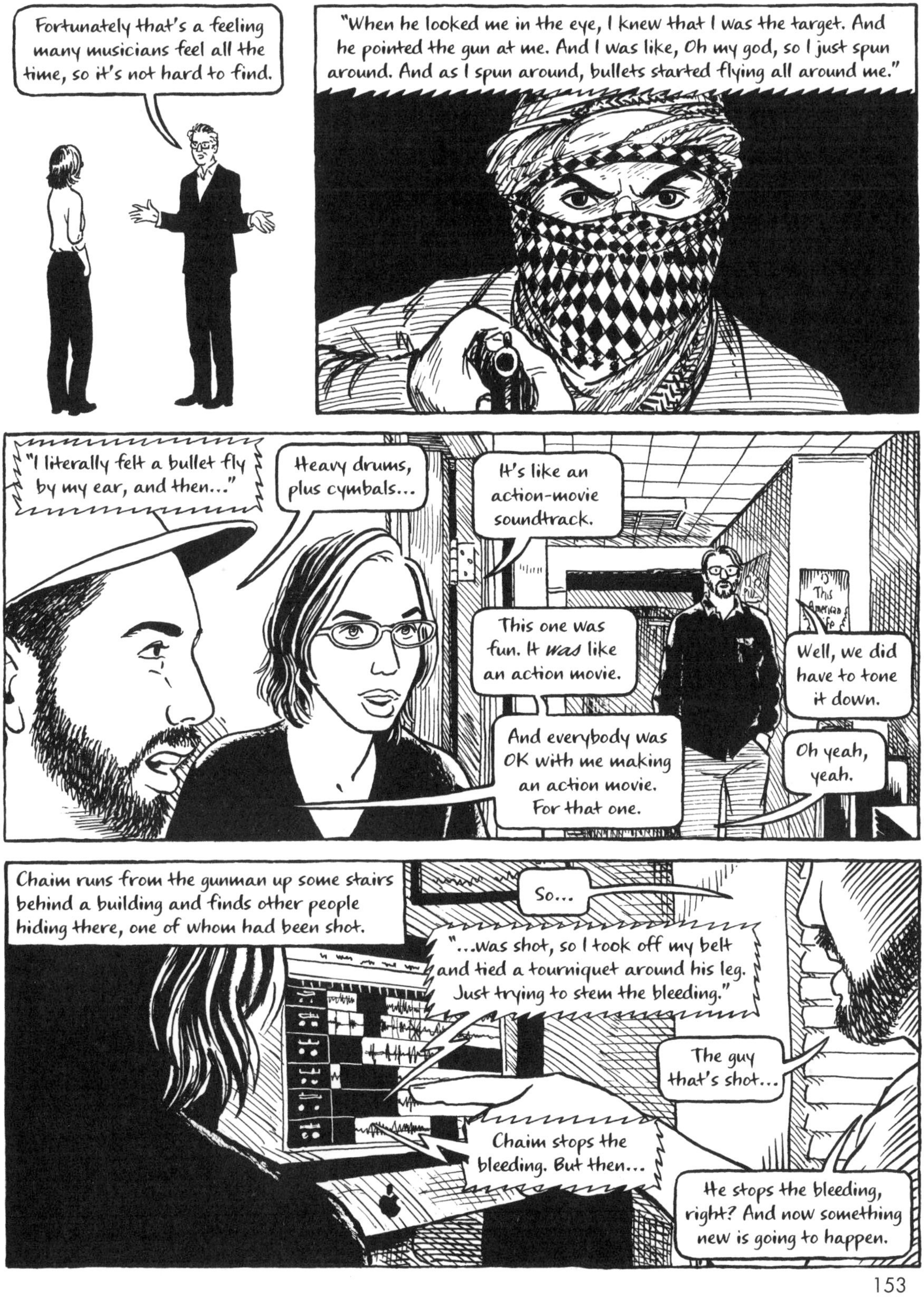
Fortunately that's a feeling many musicians feel all the time, so it's not hard to find.
"When he looked me in the eye, I knew that I was the target. And he pointed the gun at me. And I was like, Oh my god, so I just spun around. And as I spun around, bullets started flying all around me."
"I literally felt a bullet fly by my ear, and then..."
Heavy drums, plus cymbals...
It's like an action-movie soundtrack.
This one was fun. It *was* like an action movie.
And everybody was OK with me making an action movie. For that one.
Well, we did have to tone it down.
Oh yeah, yeah.
Chaim runs from the gunman up some stairs behind a building and finds other people hiding there, one of whom had been shot.
So...
"...was shot, so I took off my belt and tied a tourniquet around his leg. Just trying to stem the bleeding."
The guy that's shot...
Chaim stops the bleeding. But then...
He stops the bleeding, right? And now something new is going to happen.

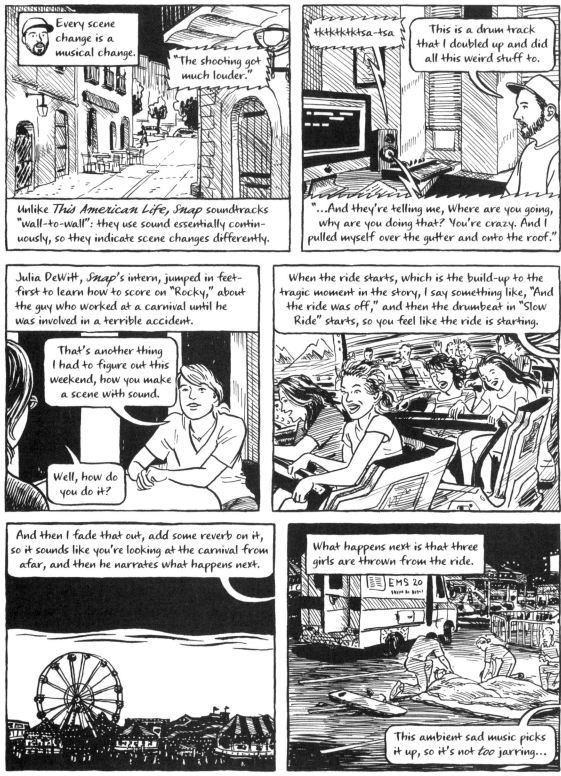

Every scene change is a musical change.

"The shooting got much louder."

Unlike *This American Life*, *Snap* soundtracks "wall-to-wall": they use sound essentially continuously, so they indicate scene changes differently.

tktktktktsa-tsa

This is a drum track that I doubled up and did all this weird stuff to.

"...And they're telling me, Where are you going, why are you doing that? You're crazy. And I pulled myself over the gutter and onto the roof."

Julia DeWitt, *Snap*'s intern, jumped in feet-first to learn how to score on "Rocky," about the guy who worked at a carnival until he was involved in a terrible accident.

That's another thing I had to figure out this weekend, how you make a scene with sound.

Well, how do you do it?

When the ride starts, which is the build-up to the tragic moment in the story, I say something like, "And the ride was off," and then the drumbeat in "Slow Ride" starts, so you feel like the ride is starting.

And then I fade that out, add some reverb on it, so it sounds like you're looking at the carnival from afar, and then he narrates what happens next.

What happens next is that three girls are thrown from the ride.

EMS 20

This ambient sad music picks it up, so it's not *too* jarring...

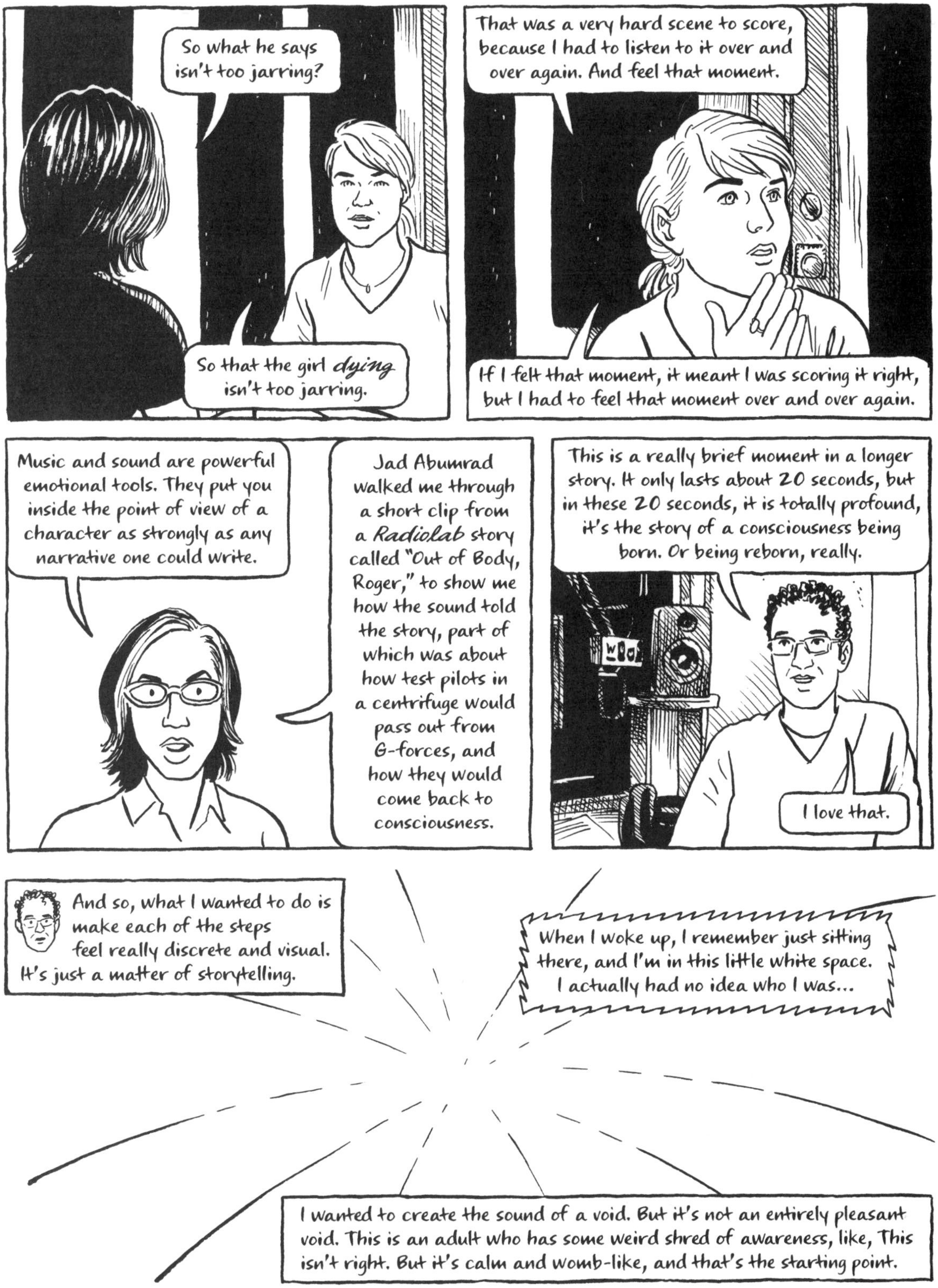
So what he says isn't too jarring?
So that the girl *dying* isn't too jarring.
That was a very hard scene to score, because I had to listen to it over and over again. And feel that moment.
If I felt that moment, it meant I was scoring it right, but I had to feel that moment over and over again.
Music and sound are powerful emotional tools. They put you inside the point of view of a character as strongly as any narrative one could write.
Jad Abumrad walked me through a short clip from a *Radiolab* story called "Out of Body, Roger," to show me how the sound told the story, part of which was about how test pilots in a centrifuge would pass out from G-forces, and how they would come back to consciousness.
This is a really brief moment in a longer story. It only lasts about 20 seconds, but in these 20 seconds, it is totally profound, it's the story of a consciousness being born. Or being reborn, really.
I love that.
And so, what I wanted to do is make each of the steps feel really discrete and visual. It's just a matter of storytelling.
When I woke up, I remember just sitting there, and I'm in this little white space. I actually had no idea who I was...
I wanted to create the sound of a void. But it's not an entirely pleasant void. This is an adult who has some weird shred of awareness, like, This isn't right. But it's calm and womb-like, and that's the starting point.

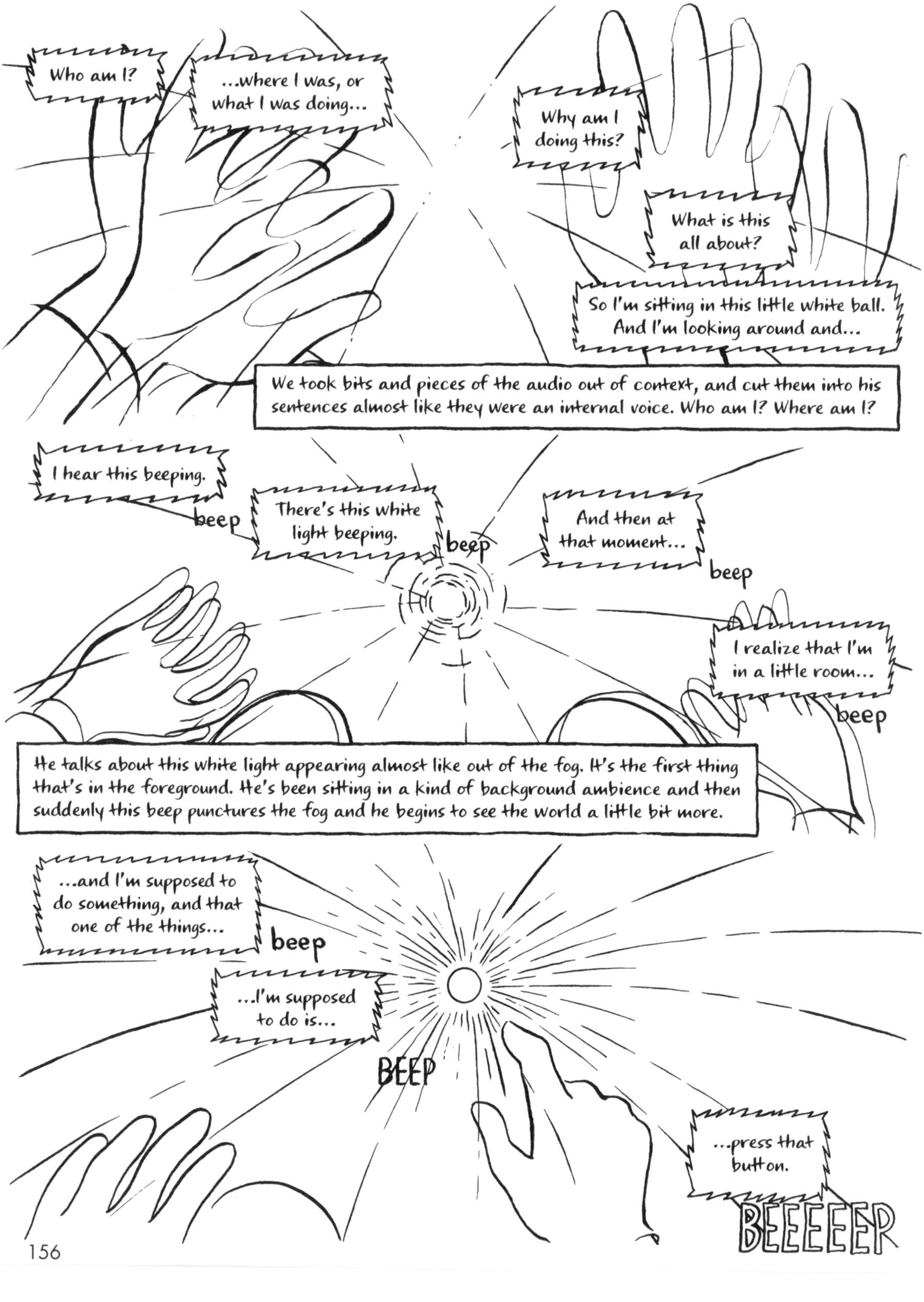

Who am I?
...where I was, or what I was doing...
Why am I doing this?
What is this all about?
So I'm sitting in this little white ball. And I'm looking around and...
We took bits and pieces of the audio out of context, and cut them into his sentences almost like they were an internal voice. Who am I? Where am I?
I hear this beeping.
beep
There's this white light beeping.
beep
And then at that moment...
beep
I realize that I'm in a little room...
beep
He talks about this white light appearing almost like out of the fog. It's the first thing that's in the foreground. He's been sitting in a kind of background ambience and then suddenly this beep punctures the fog and he begins to see the world a little bit more.
...and I'm supposed to do something, and that one of the things...
beep
...I'm supposed to do is...
BEEP
...press that button.
BEEEEEP

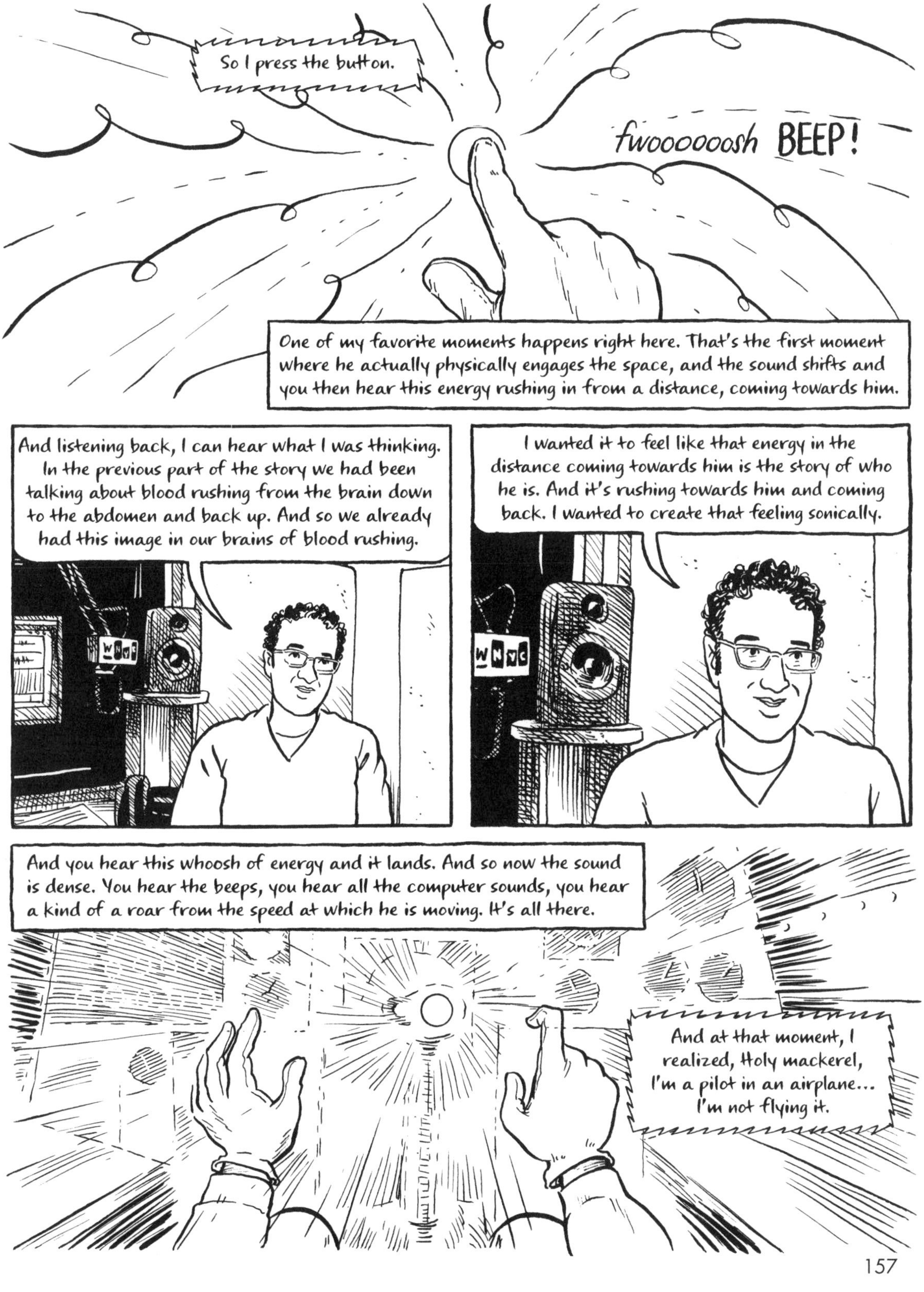
So I press the button.
fwoooooosh BEEP!
One of my favorite moments happens right here. That's the first moment where he actually physically engages the space, and the sound shifts and you then hear this energy rushing in from a distance, coming towards him.
And listening back, I can hear what I was thinking. In the previous part of the story we had been talking about blood rushing from the brain down to the abdomen and back up. And so we already had this image in our brains of blood rushing.
WNYC
I wanted it to feel like that energy in the distance coming towards him is the story of who he is. And it's rushing towards him and coming back. I wanted to create that feeling sonically.
WNYC
And you hear this whoosh of energy and it lands. And so now the sound is dense. You hear the beeps, you hear all the computer sounds, you hear a kind of a roar from the speed at which he is moving. It's all there.
And at that moment, I realized, Holy mackerel, I'm a pilot in an airplane... I'm not flying it.

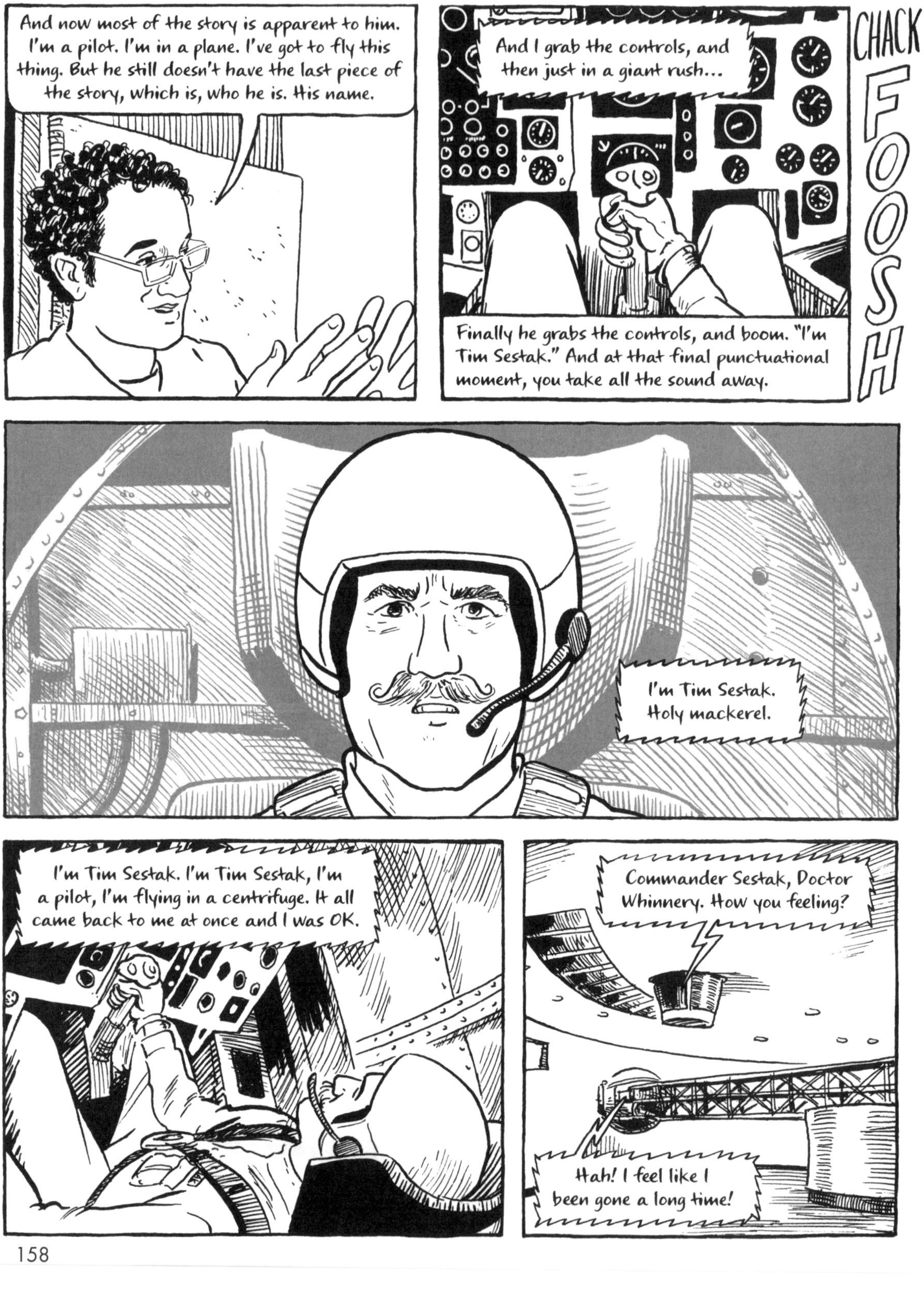
And now most of the story is apparent to him. I'm a pilot. I'm in a plane. I've got to fly this thing. But he still doesn't have the last piece of the story, which is, who he is. His name.
And I grab the controls, and then just in a giant rush...
Finally he grabs the controls, and boom. "I'm Tim Sestak." And at that final punctuational moment, you take all the sound away.
CHACK
FOOSH
I'm Tim Sestak. Holy mackerel.
I'm Tim Sestak. I'm Tim Sestak, I'm a pilot, I'm flying in a centrifuge. It all came back to me at once and I was OK.
Commander Sestak, Doctor Whinnery. How you feeling?
Hah! I feel like I been gone a long time!

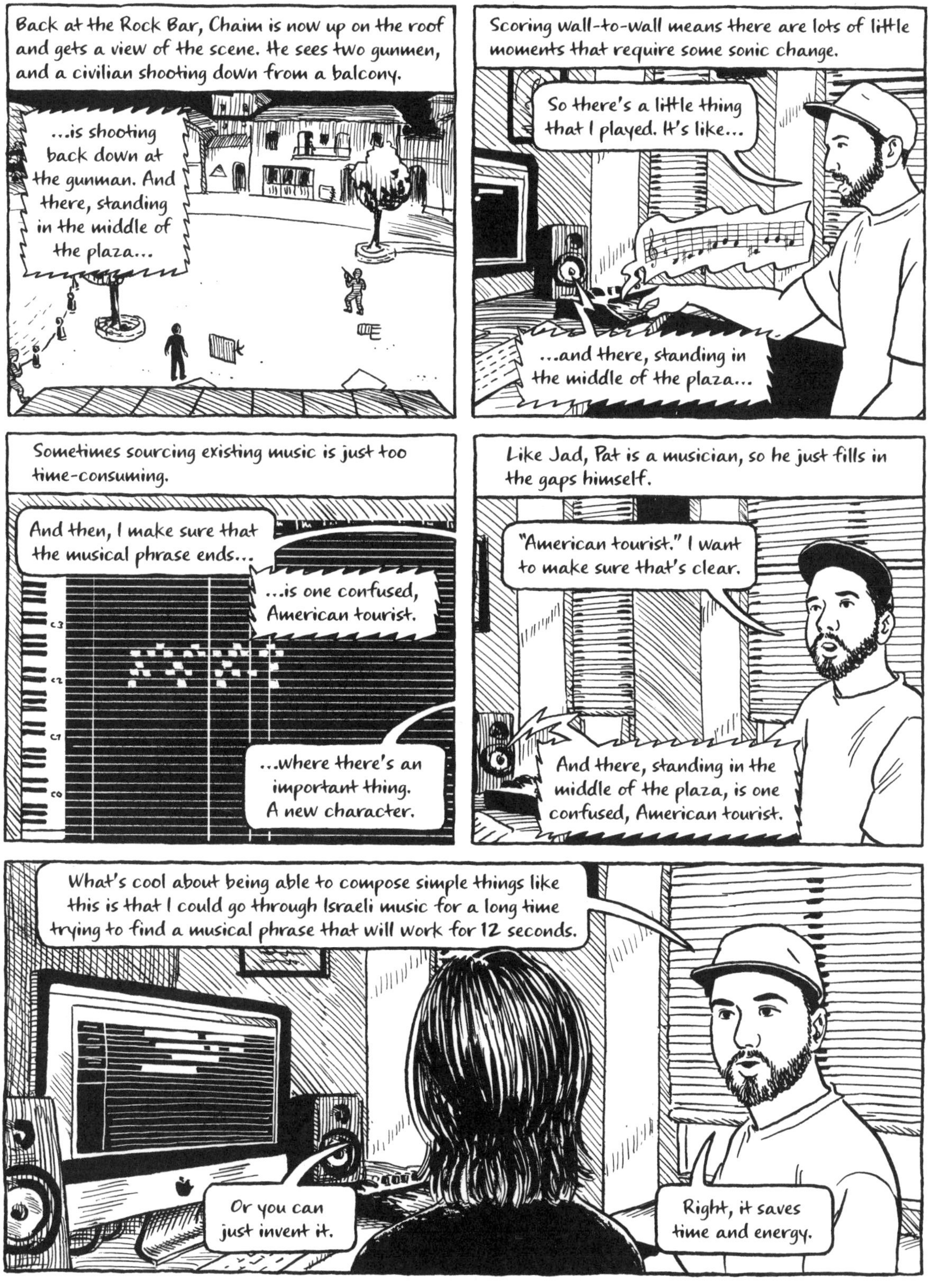
Back at the Rock Bar, Chaim is now up on the roof and gets a view of the scene. He sees two gunmen, and a civilian shooting down from a balcony.
...is shooting back down at the gunman. And there, standing in the middle of the plaza...
Scoring wall-to-wall means there are lots of little moments that require some sonic change.
So there's a little thing that I played. It's like...
...and there, standing in the middle of the plaza...
Sometimes sourcing existing music is just too time-consuming.
And then, I make sure that the musical phrase ends...
...is one confused, American tourist.
...where there's an important thing. A new character.
Like Jad, Pat is a musician, so he just fills in the gaps himself.
"American tourist." I want to make sure that's clear.
And there, standing in the middle of the plaza, is one confused, American tourist.
What's cool about being able to compose simple things like this is that I could go through Israeli music for a long time trying to find a musical phrase that will work for 12 seconds.
Or you can just invent it.
Right, it saves time and energy.

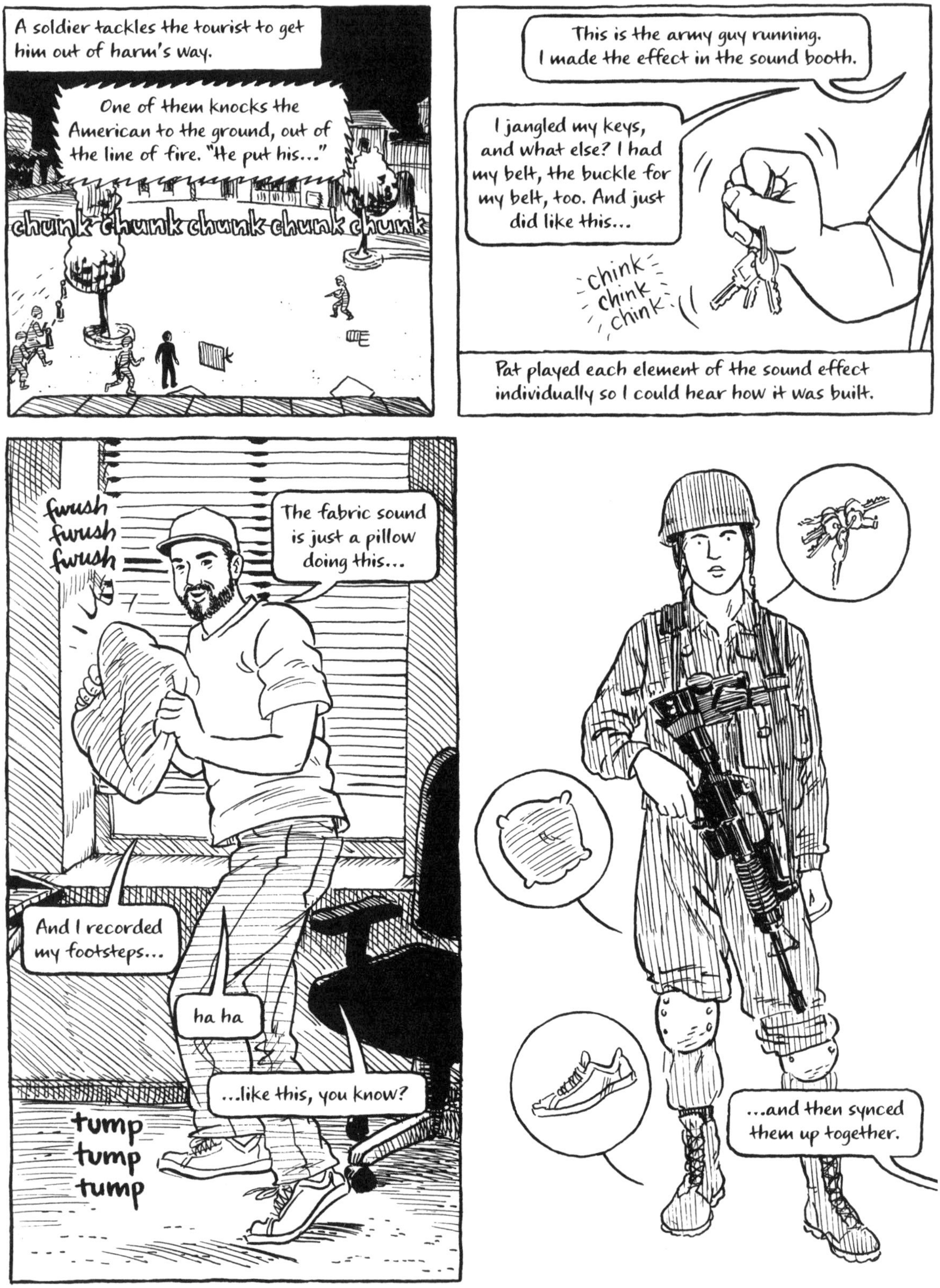
A soldier tackles the tourist to get him out of harm's way.
One of them knocks the American to the ground, out of the line of fire. "He put his..."
chunk chunk chunk chunk chunk
This is the army guy running. I made the effect in the sound booth.
I jangled my keys, and what else? I had my belt, the buckle for my belt, too. And just did like this...
chink chink chink
Pat played each element of the sound effect individually so I could hear how it was built.
fwush fwush fwush
The fabric sound is just a pillow doing this...
And I recorded my footsteps...
ha ha
...like this, you know?
tump tump tump
...and then synced them up together.

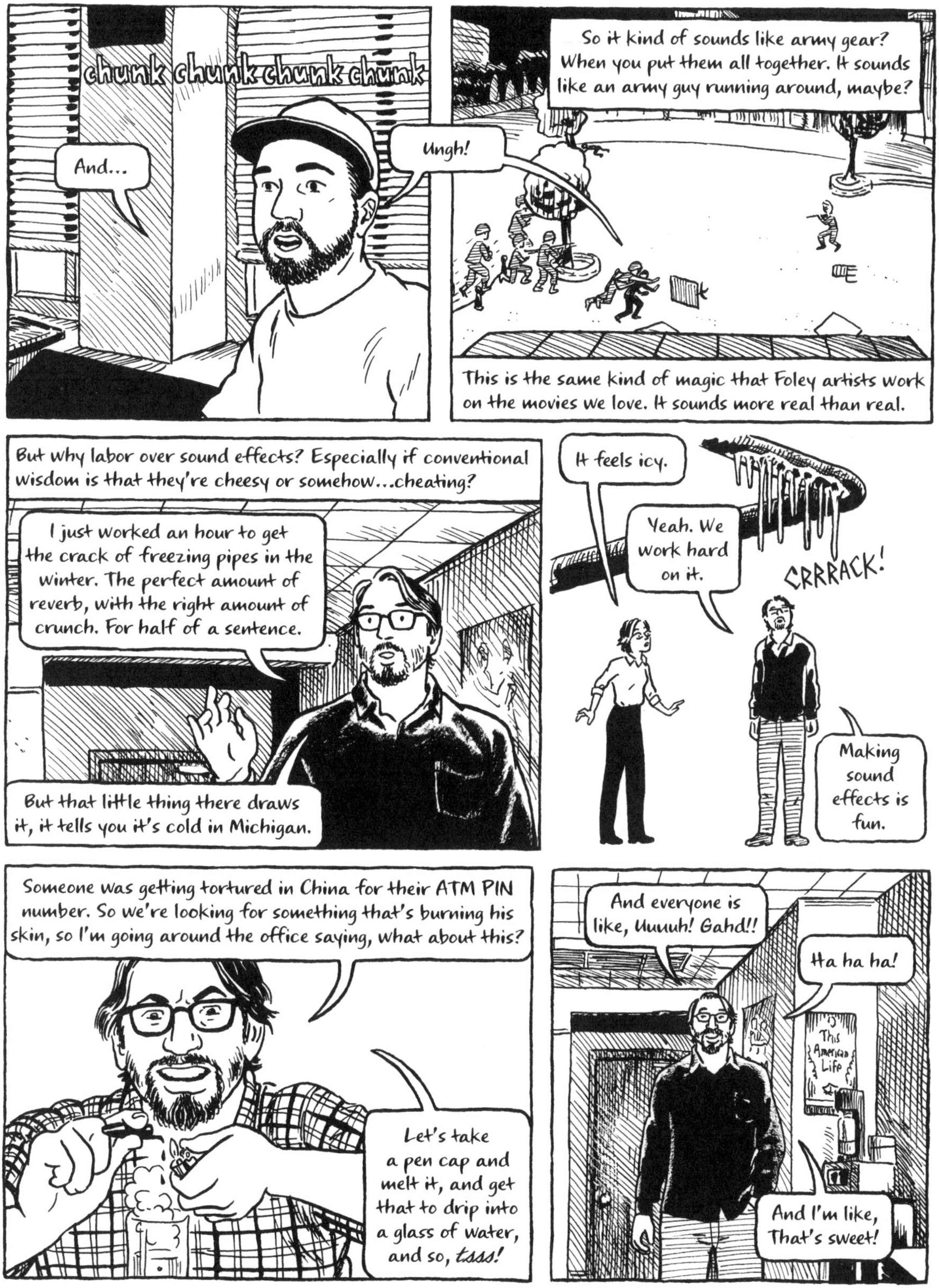
chunk chunk chunk chunk
And...
Ungh!
So it kind of sounds like army gear? When you put them all together. It sounds like an army guy running around, maybe?
This is the same kind of magic that Foley artists work on the movies we love. It sounds more real than real.
But why labor over sound effects? Especially if conventional wisdom is that they're cheesy or somehow...cheating?
I just worked an hour to get the crack of freezing pipes in the winter. The perfect amount of reverb, with the right amount of crunch. For half of a sentence.
But that little thing there draws it, it tells you it's cold in Michigan.
It feels icy.
Yeah. We work hard on it.
CRRRACK!
Making sound effects is fun.
Someone was getting tortured in China for their ATM PIN number. So we're looking for something that's burning his skin, so I'm going around the office saying, what about this?
Let's take a pen cap and melt it, and get that to drip into a glass of water, and so, *tsss!*
And everyone is like, Uuuuh! Gahd!!
Ha ha ha!
This American Life
And I'm like, That's sweet!

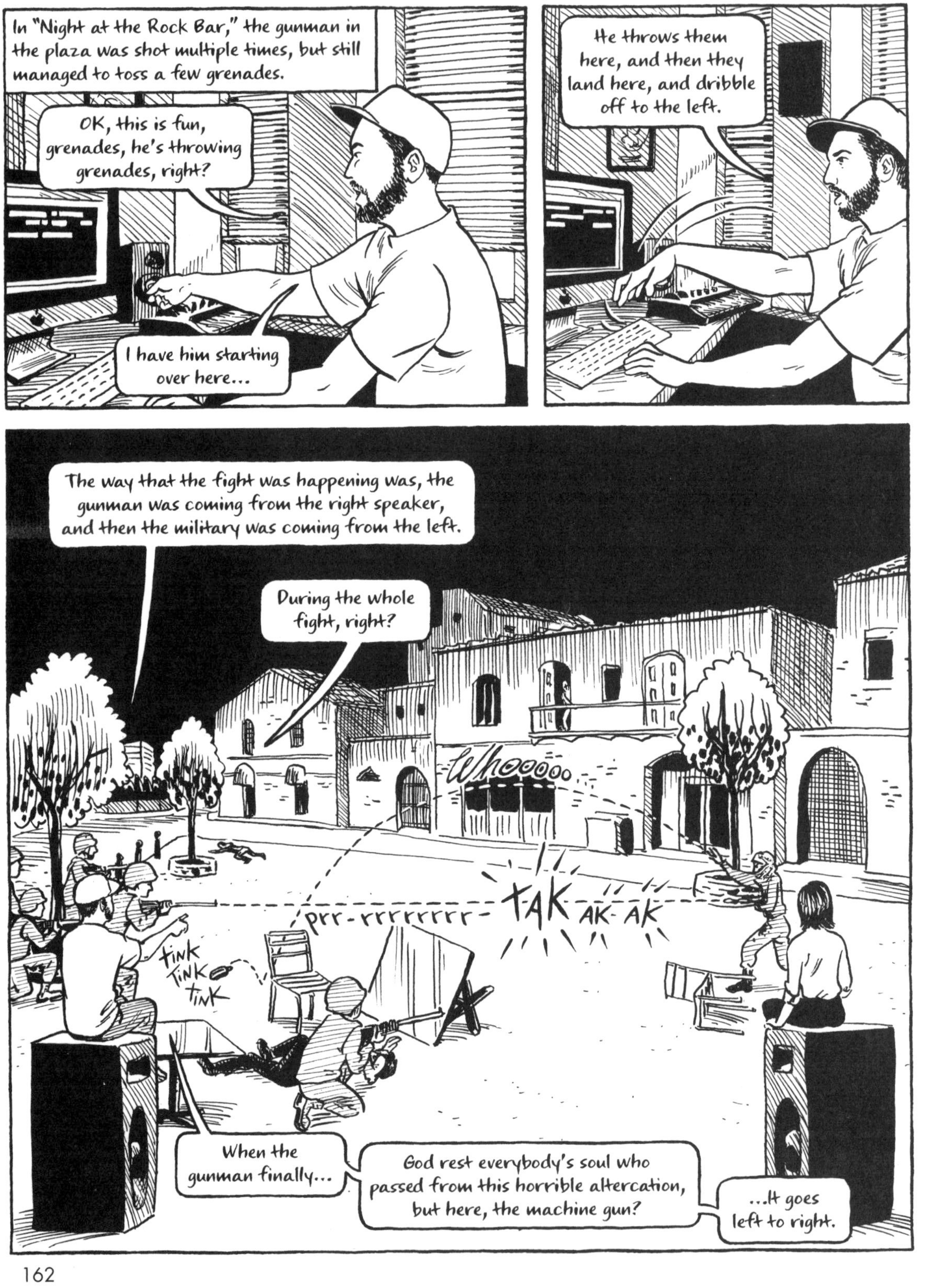
In "Night at the Rock Bar," the gunman in the plaza was shot multiple times, but still managed to toss a few grenades.
OK, this is fun, grenades, he's throwing grenades, right?
I have him starting over here...
He throws them here, and then they land here, and dribble off to the left.
The way that the fight was happening was, the gunman was coming from the right speaker, and then the military was coming from the left.
During the whole fight, right?
Whooooo
prr-rrrrrrrr-
TAK AK AK
TINK TINK TINK
When the gunman finally...
God rest everybody's soul who passed from this horrible altercation, but here, the machine gun?
...It goes left to right.

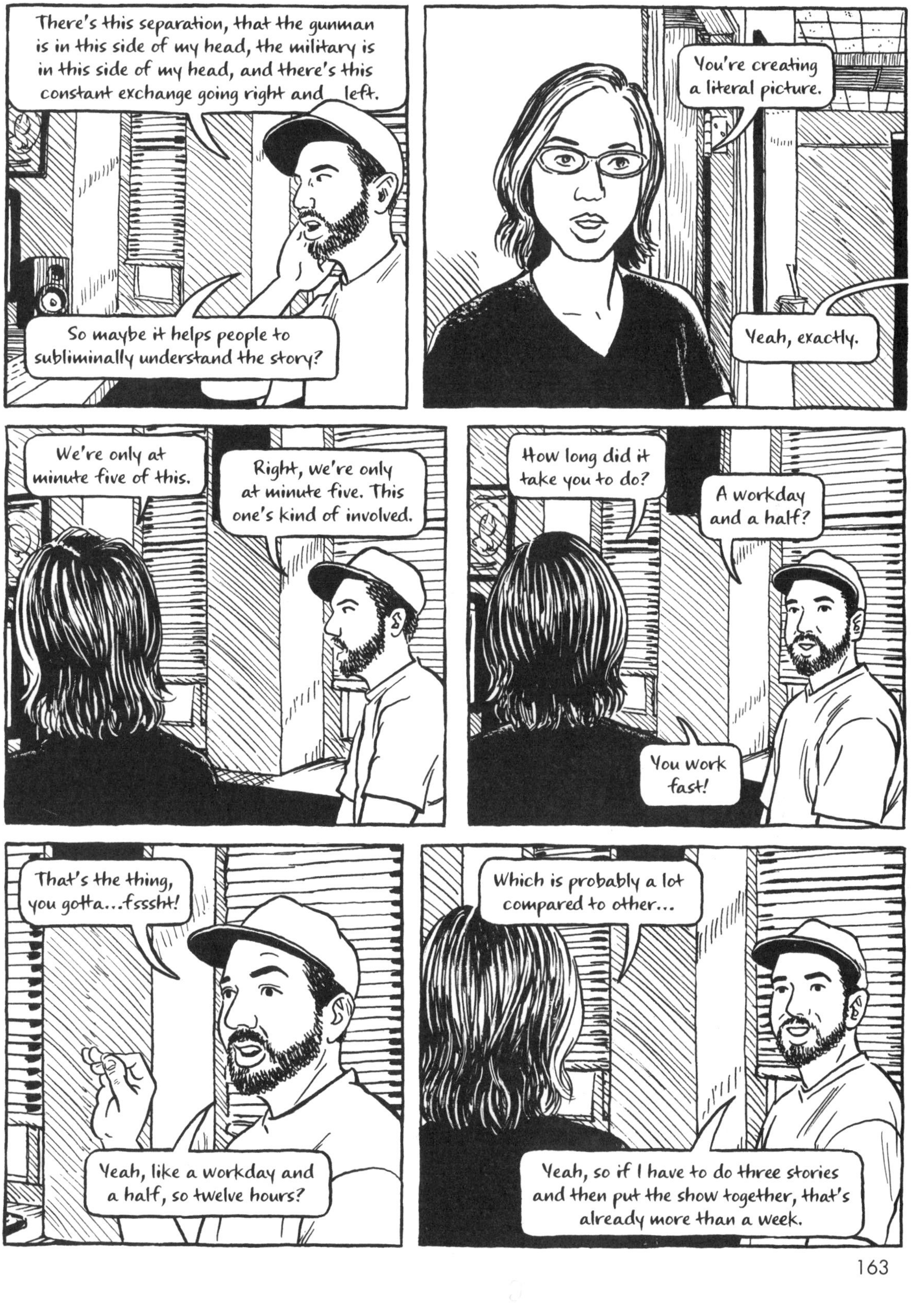
There's this separation, that the gunman is in this side of my head, the military is in this side of my head, and there's this constant exchange going right and left.
So maybe it helps people to subliminally understand the story?
You're creating a literal picture.
Yeah, exactly.
We're only at minute five of this.
Right, we're only at minute five. This one's kind of involved.
How long did it take you to do?
A workday and a half?
You work fast!
That's the thing, you gotta...fsssht!
Yeah, like a workday and a half, so twelve hours?
Which is probably a lot compared to other...
Yeah, so if I have to do three stories and then put the show together, that's already more than a week.

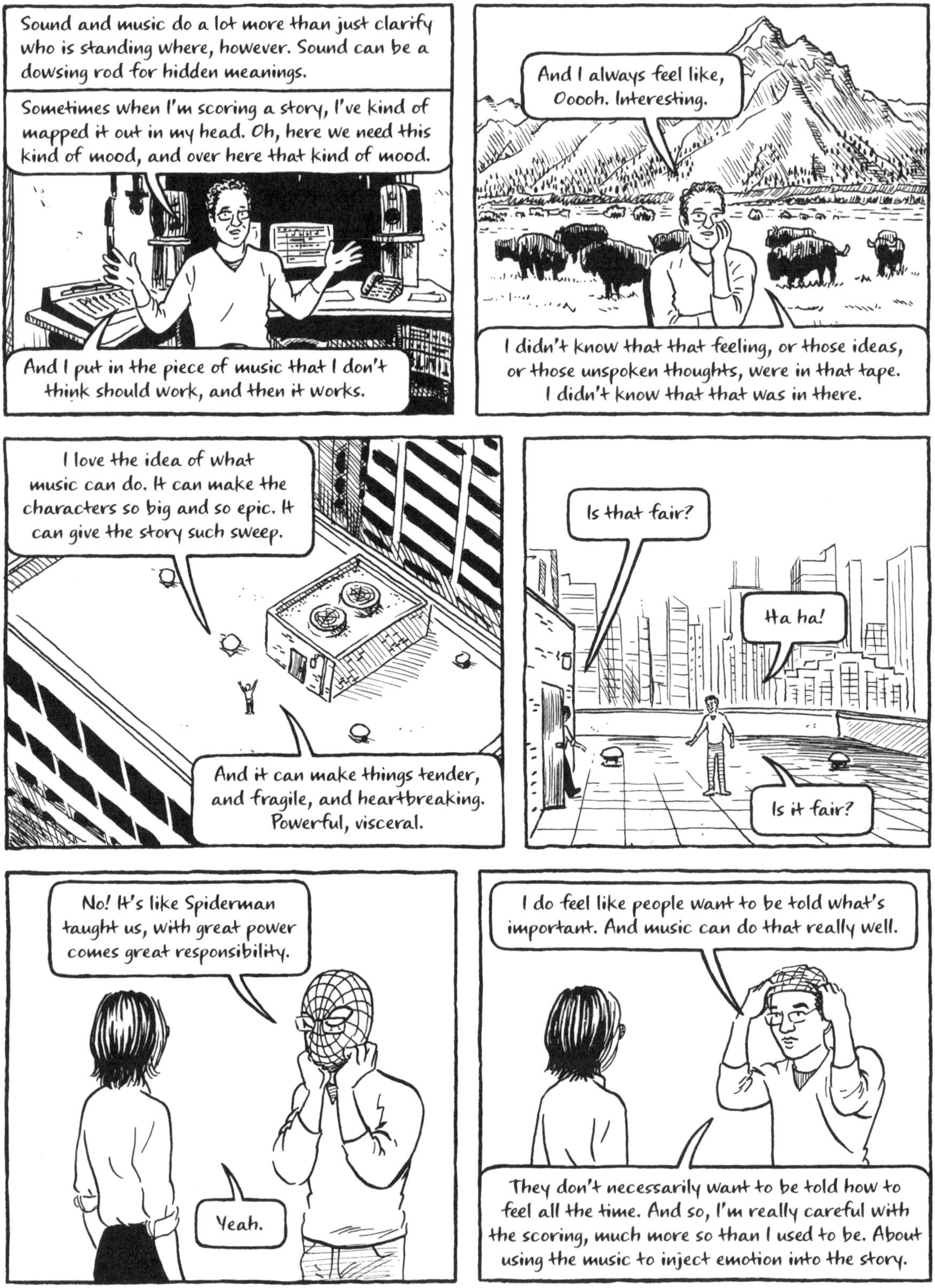
Sound and music do a lot more than just clarify who is standing where, however. Sound can be a dowsing rod for hidden meanings.
Sometimes when I'm scoring a story, I've kind of mapped it out in my head. Oh, here we need this kind of mood, and over here that kind of mood.
And I put in the piece of music that I don't think should work, and then it works.
And I always feel like, Ooooh. Interesting.
I didn't know that that feeling, or those ideas, or those unspoken thoughts, were in that tape. I didn't know that that was in there.
I love the idea of what music can do. It can make the characters so big and so epic. It can give the story such sweep.
And it can make things tender, and fragile, and heartbreaking. Powerful, visceral.
Is that fair?
Ha ha!
Is it fair?
No! It's like Spiderman taught us, with great power comes great responsibility.
Yeah.
I do feel like people want to be told what's important. And music can do that really well.
They don't necessarily want to be told how to feel all the time. And so, I'm really careful with the scoring, much more so than I used to be. About using the music to inject emotion into the story.

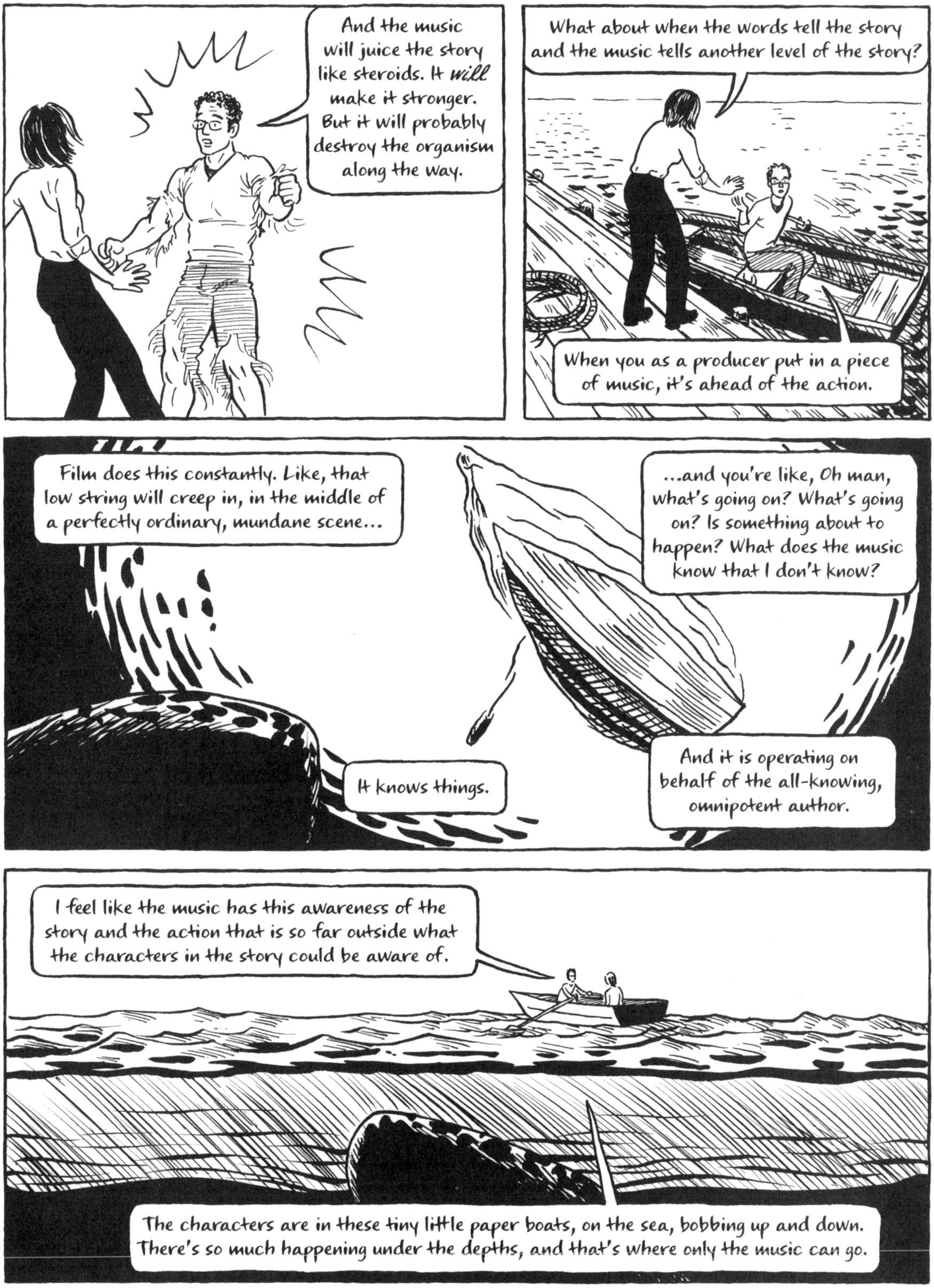
And the music will juice the story like steroids. It *will* make it stronger. But it will probably destroy the organism along the way.
What about when the words tell the story and the music tells another level of the story?
When you as a producer put in a piece of music, it's ahead of the action.
Film does this constantly. Like, that low string will creep in, in the middle of a perfectly ordinary, mundane scene...
...and you're like, Oh man, what's going on? What's going on? Is something about to happen? What does the music know that I don't know?
It knows things.
And it is operating on behalf of the all-knowing, omnipotent author.
I feel like the music has this awareness of the story and the action that is so far outside what the characters in the story could be aware of.
The characters are in these tiny little paper boats, on the sea, bobbing up and down. There's so much happening under the depths, and that's where only the music can go.

YOUR BABY'S UGLY:

The Edit

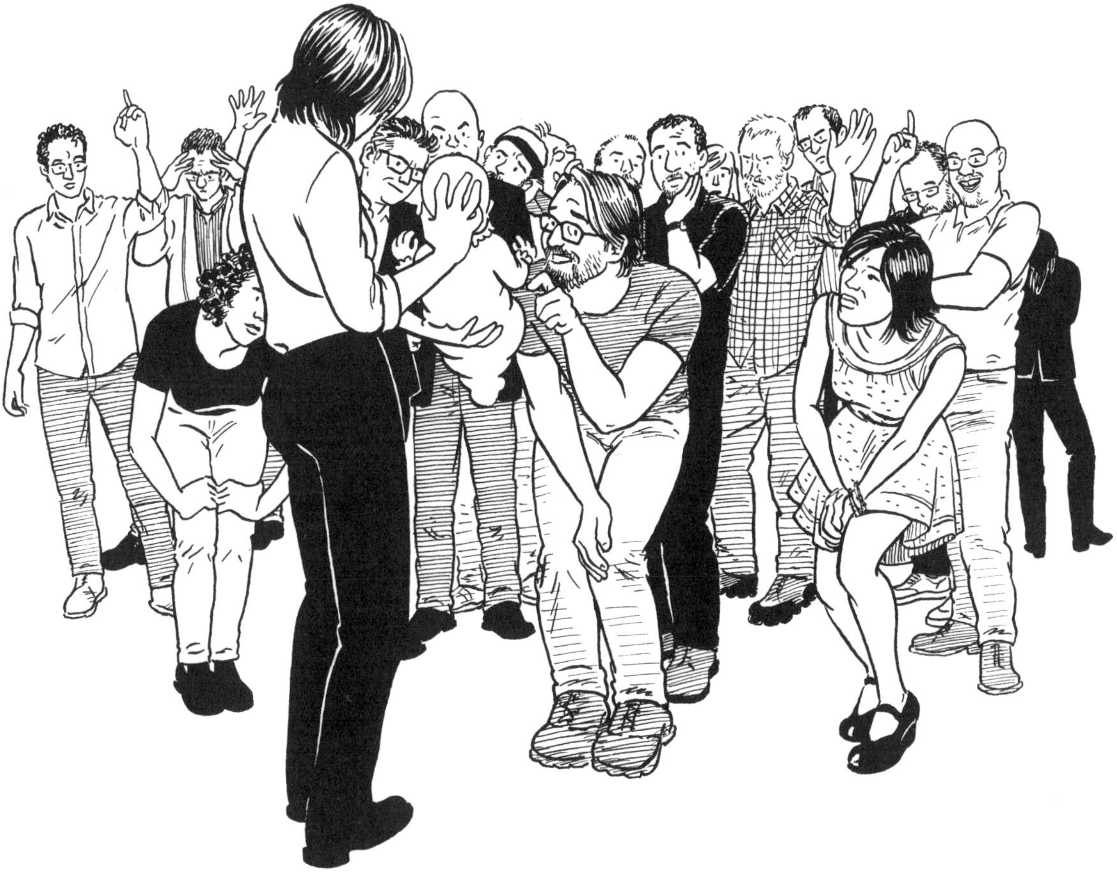

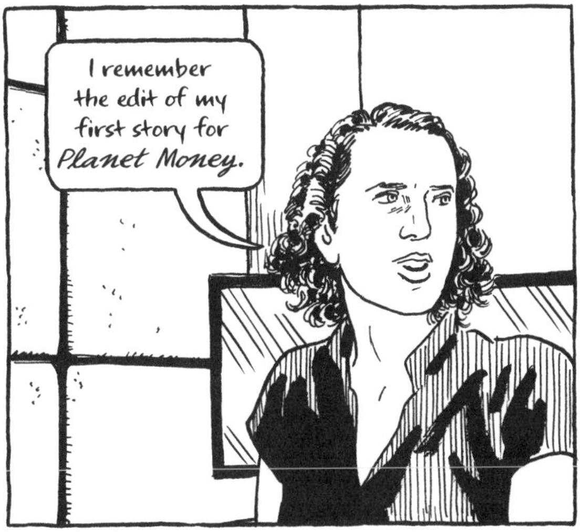
I remember the edit of my first story for *Planet Money.*

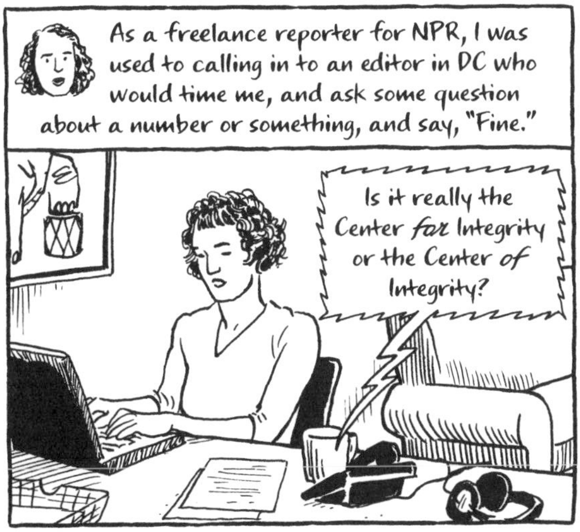
As a freelance reporter for NPR, I was used to calling in to an editor in DC who would time me, and ask some question about a number or something, and say, "Fine."
Is it really the Center *for* Integrity or the Center *of* Integrity?

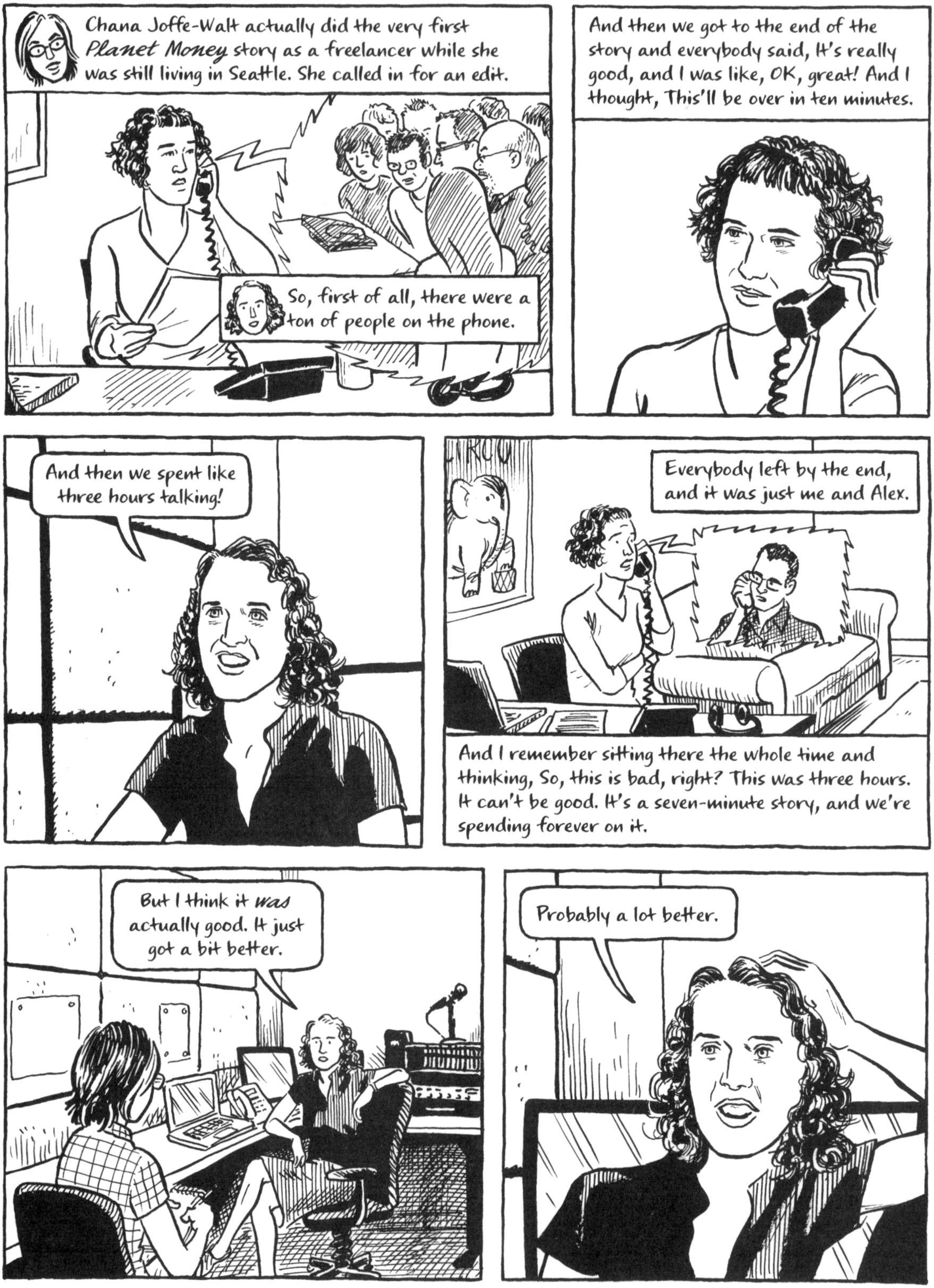
Chana Joffe-Walt actually did the very first *Planet Money* story as a freelancer while she was still living in Seattle. She called in for an edit.
So, first of all, there were a ton of people on the phone.
And then we got to the end of the story and everybody said, It's really good, and I was like, OK, great! And I thought, This'll be over in ten minutes.
And then we spent like three hours talking!
Everybody left by the end, and it was just me and Alex.
And I remember sitting there the whole time and thinking, So, this is bad, right? This was three hours. It can't be good. It's a seven-minute story, and we're spending forever on it.
But I think it *was* actually good. It just got a bit better.
Probably a lot better.

BACK AT THE SNAP...

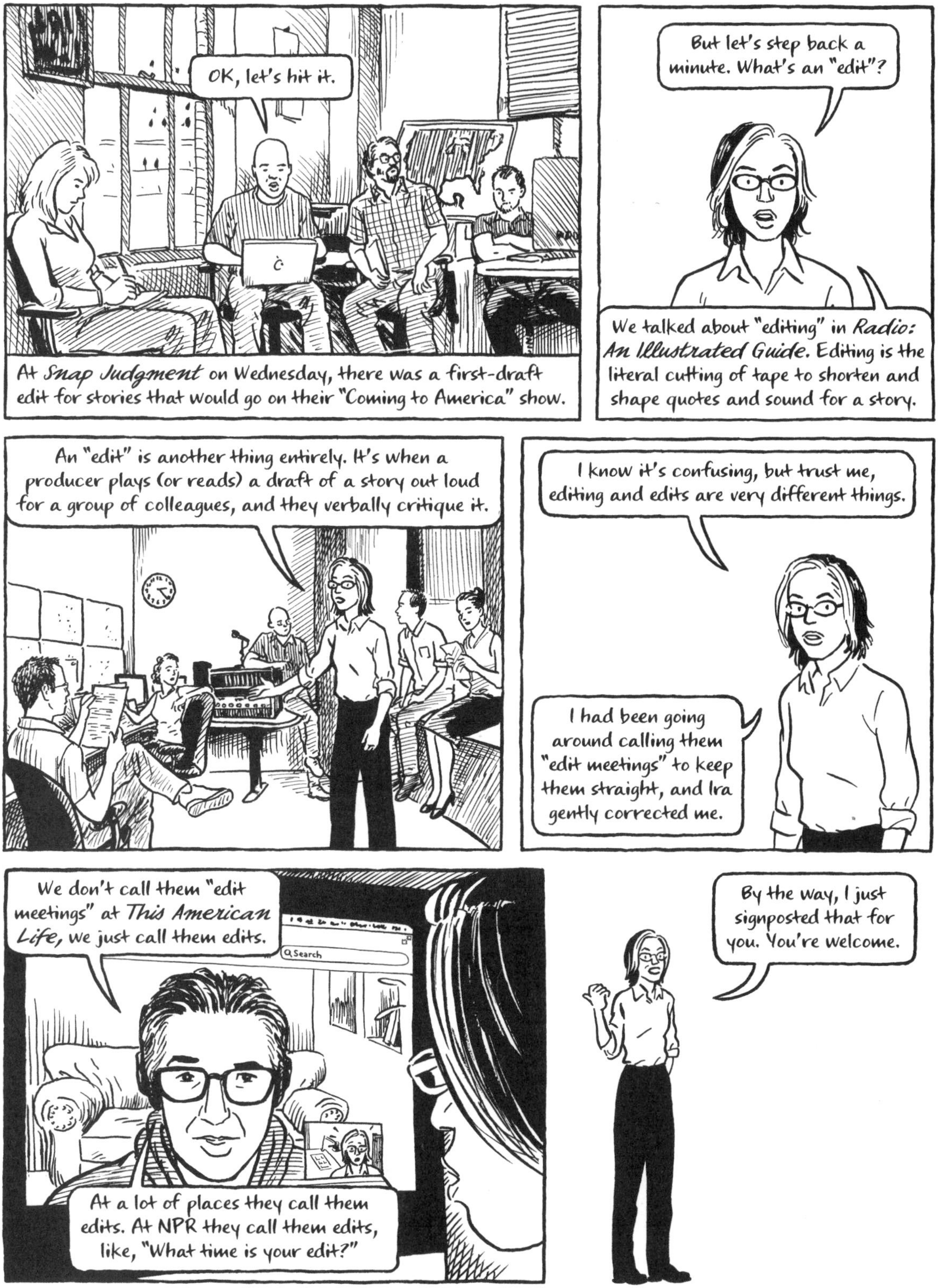

OK, let's hit it.
At *Snap Judgment* on Wednesday, there was a first-draft edit for stories that would go on their "Coming to America" show.
But let's step back a minute. What's an "edit"?
We talked about "editing" in *Radio: An Illustrated Guide*. Editing is the literal cutting of tape to shorten and shape quotes and sound for a story.
An "edit" is another thing entirely. It's when a producer plays (or reads) a draft of a story out loud for a group of colleagues, and they verbally critique it.
I know it's confusing, but trust me, editing and edits are very different things.
I had been going around calling them "edit meetings" to keep them straight, and Ira gently corrected me.
We don't call them "edit meetings" at *This American Life*, we just call them edits.
Search
At a lot of places they call them edits. At NPR they call them edits, like, "What time is your edit?"
By the way, I just signposted that for you. You're welcome.

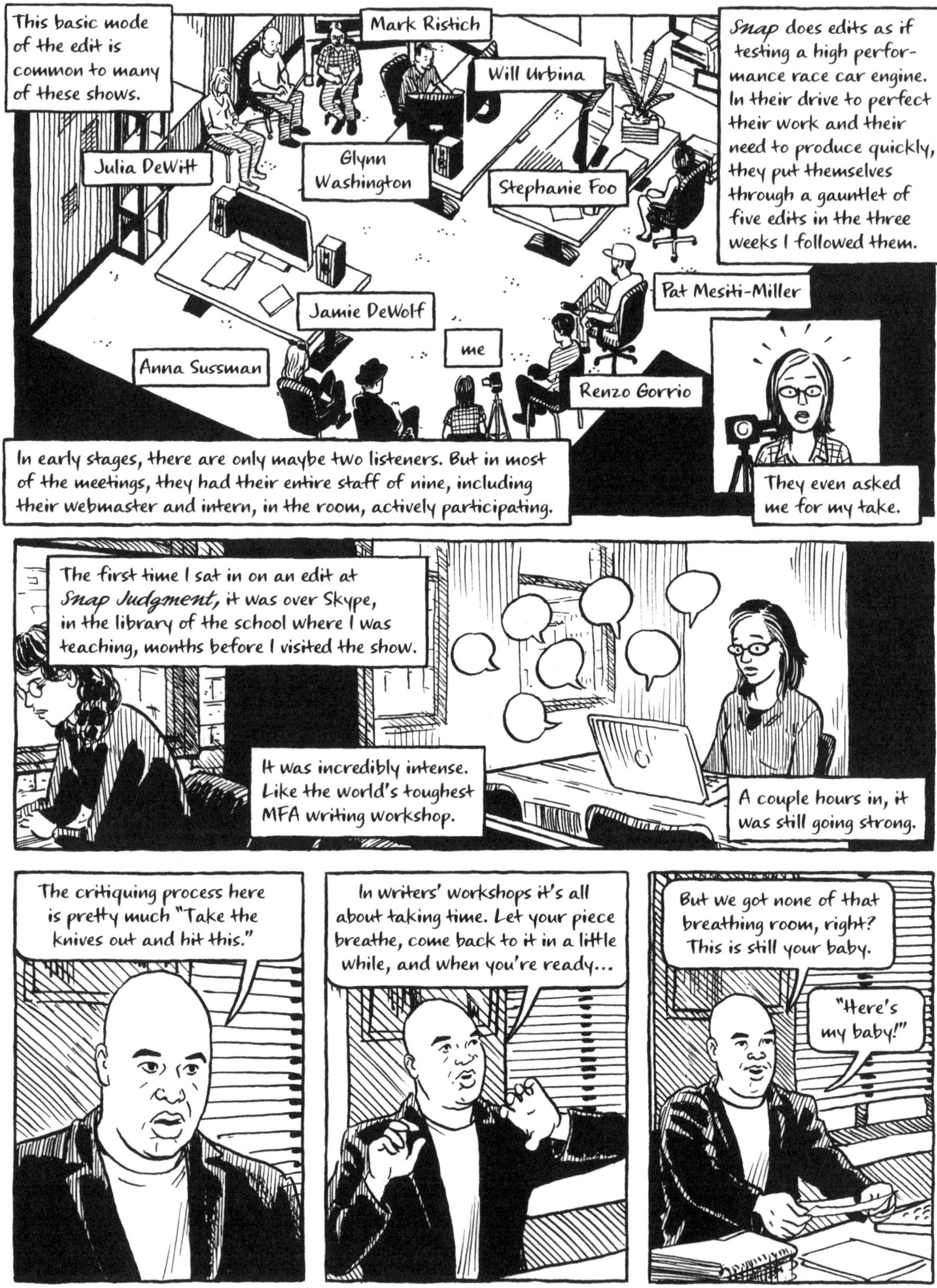
This basic mode of the edit is common to many of these shows.
Mark Ristich
Will Urbina
Snap does edits as if testing a high performance race car engine. In their drive to perfect their work and their need to produce quickly, they put themselves through a gauntlet of five edits in the three weeks I followed them.
Julia DeWitt
Glynn Washington
Stephanie Foo
Pat Mesiti-Miller
Jamie DeWolf
me
Anna Sussman
Renzo Gorrio
In early stages, there are only maybe two listeners. But in most of the meetings, they had their entire staff of nine, including their webmaster and intern, in the room, actively participating.
They even asked me for my take.
The first time I sat in on an edit at Snap Judgment, it was over Skype, in the library of the school where I was teaching, months before I visited the show.
It was incredibly intense. Like the world's toughest MFA writing workshop.
A couple hours in, it was still going strong.
The critiquing process here is pretty much "Take the knives out and hit this."
In writers' workshops it's all about taking time. Let your piece breathe, come back to it in a little while, and when you're ready...
But we got none of that breathing room, right? This is still your baby.
"Here's my baby!"

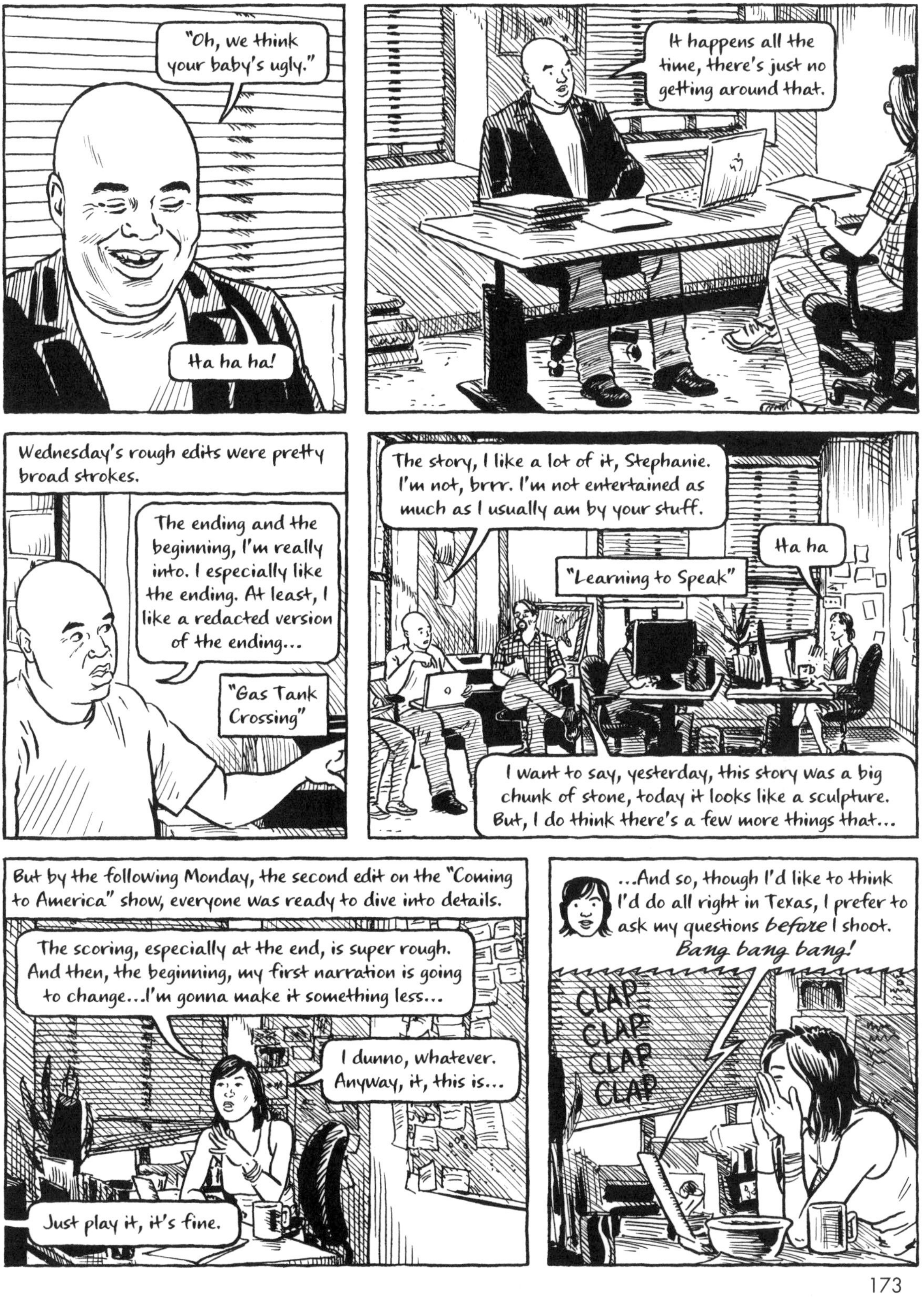
"Oh, we think your baby's ugly."
Ha ha ha!
It happens all the time, there's just no getting around that.
Wednesday's rough edits were pretty broad strokes.
The ending and the beginning, I'm really into. I especially like the ending. At least, I like a redacted version of the ending...
"Gas Tank Crossing"
The story, I like a lot of it, Stephanie. I'm not, brrr. I'm not entertained as much as I usually am by your stuff.
Ha ha
"Learning to Speak"
I want to say, yesterday, this story was a big chunk of stone, today it looks like a sculpture. But, I do think there's a few more things that...
But by the following Monday, the second edit on the "Coming to America" show, everyone was ready to dive into details.
The scoring, especially at the end, is super rough. And then, the beginning, my first narration is going to change...I'm gonna make it something less...
I dunno, whatever. Anyway, it, this is...
Just play it, it's fine.
...And so, though I'd like to think I'd do all right in Texas, I prefer to ask my questions *before* I shoot.
Bang bang bang!
CLAP
CLAP
CLAP
CLAP

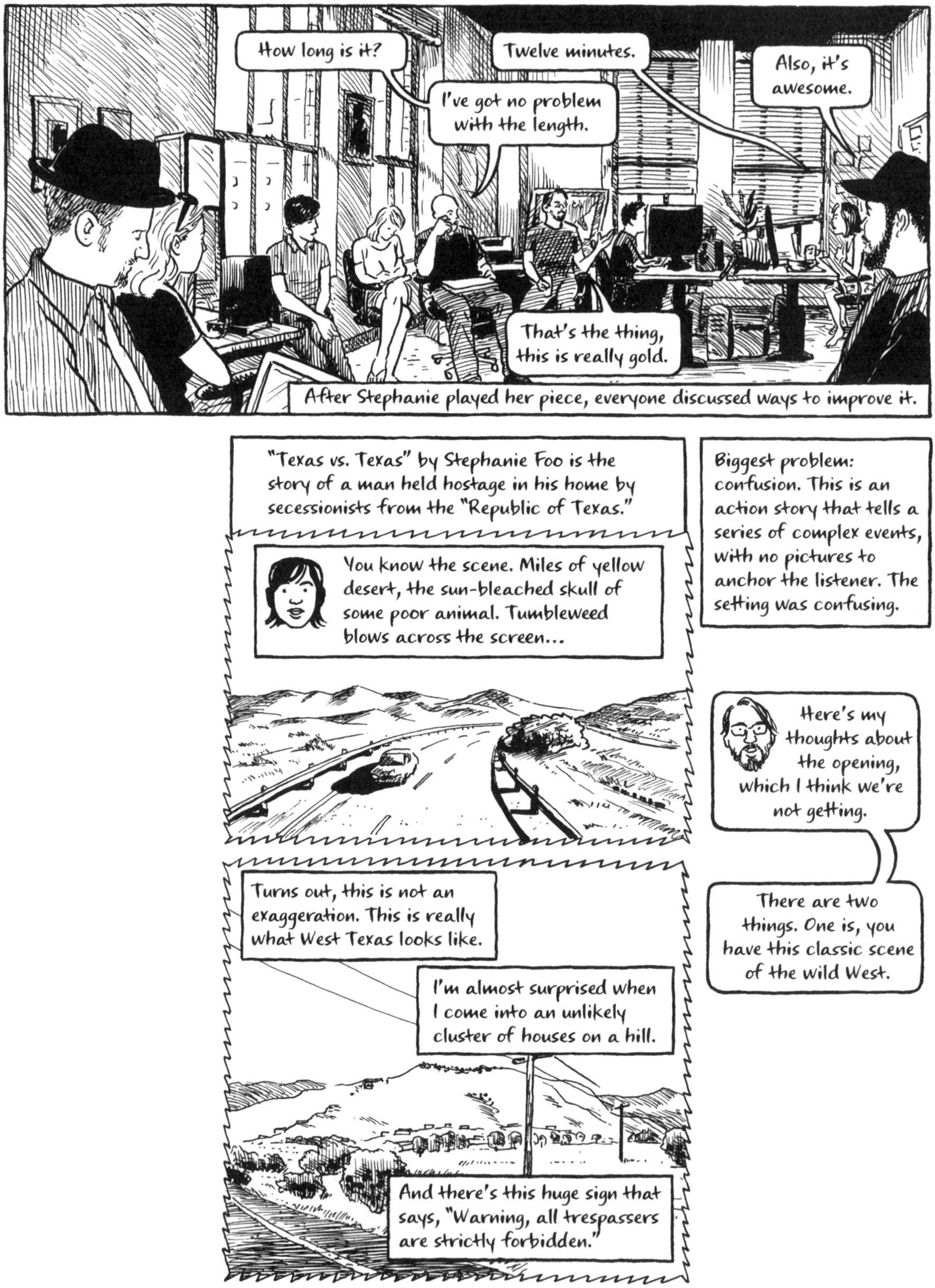
How long is it?
I've got no problem with the length.
Twelve minutes.
Also, it's awesome.
That's the thing, this is really gold.
After Stephanie played her piece, everyone discussed ways to improve it.
"Texas vs. Texas" by Stephanie Foo is the story of a man held hostage in his home by secessionists from the "Republic of Texas."
You know the scene. Miles of yellow desert, the sun-bleached skull of some poor animal. Tumbleweed blows across the screen...
Biggest problem: confusion. This is an action story that tells a series of complex events, with no pictures to anchor the listener. The setting was confusing.
Here's my thoughts about the opening, which I think we're not getting.
Turns out, this is not an exaggeration. This is really what West Texas looks like.
I'm almost surprised when I come into an unlikely cluster of houses on a hill.
And there's this huge sign that says, "Warning, all trespassers are strictly forbidden."
There are two things. One is, you have this classic scene of the wild West.

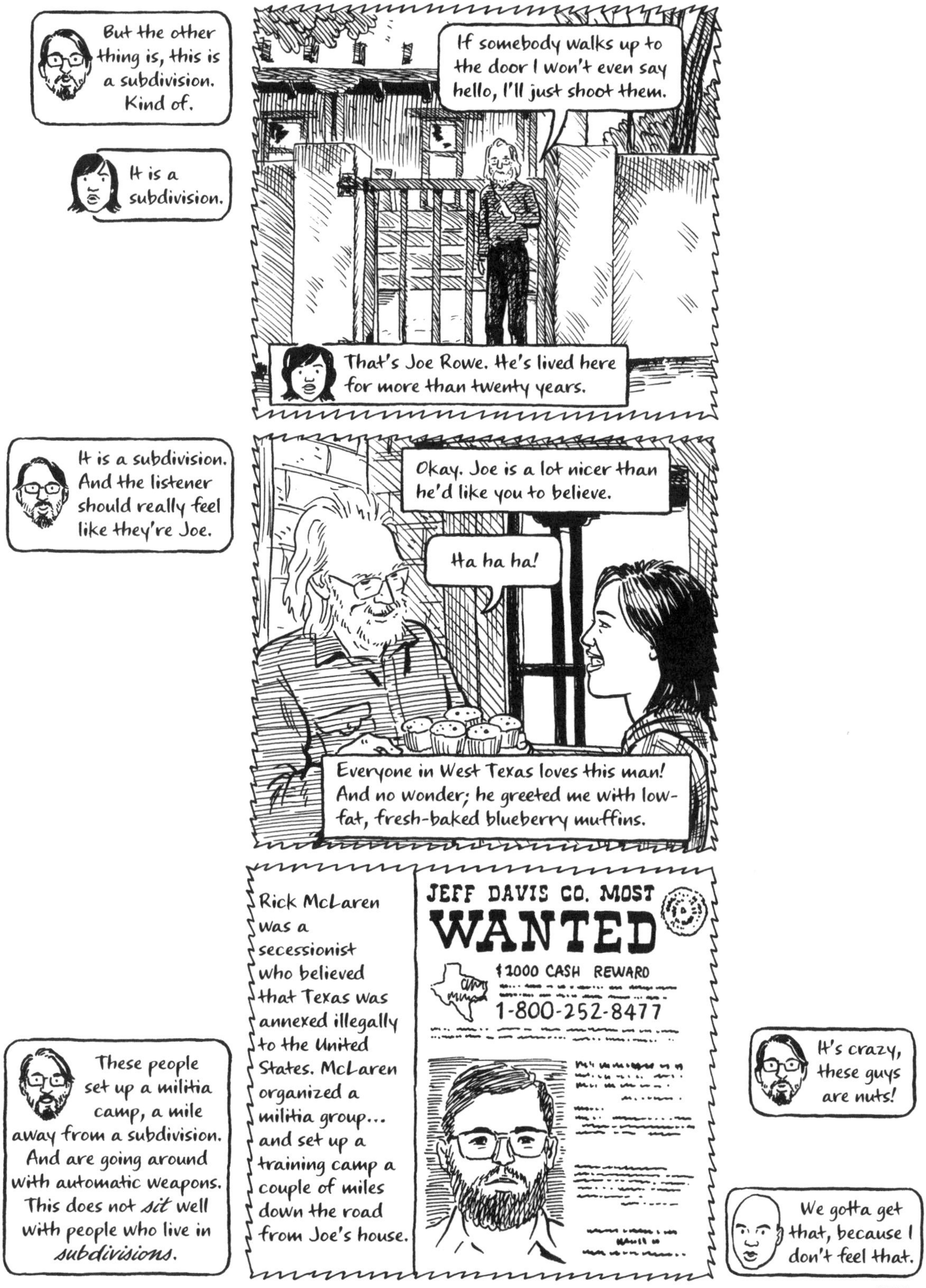
But the other thing is, this is a subdivision. Kind of.
It is a subdivision.
If somebody walks up to the door I won't even say hello, I'll just shoot them.
That's Joe Rowe. He's lived here for more than twenty years.
It is a subdivision. And the listener should really feel like they're Joe.
Okay. Joe is a lot nicer than he'd like you to believe.
Ha ha ha!
Everyone in West Texas loves this man! And no wonder; he greeted me with low-fat, fresh-baked blueberry muffins.
These people set up a militia camp, a mile away from a subdivision. And are going around with automatic weapons. This does not *sit* well with people who live in *subdivisions*.
Rick McLaren was a secessionist who believed that Texas was annexed illegally to the United States. McLaren organized a militia group... and set up a training camp a couple of miles down the road from Joe's house.
JEFF DAVIS CO. MOST
WANTED
$1000 CASH REWARD
1-800-252-8477
It's crazy, these guys are nuts!
We gotta get that, because I don't feel that.

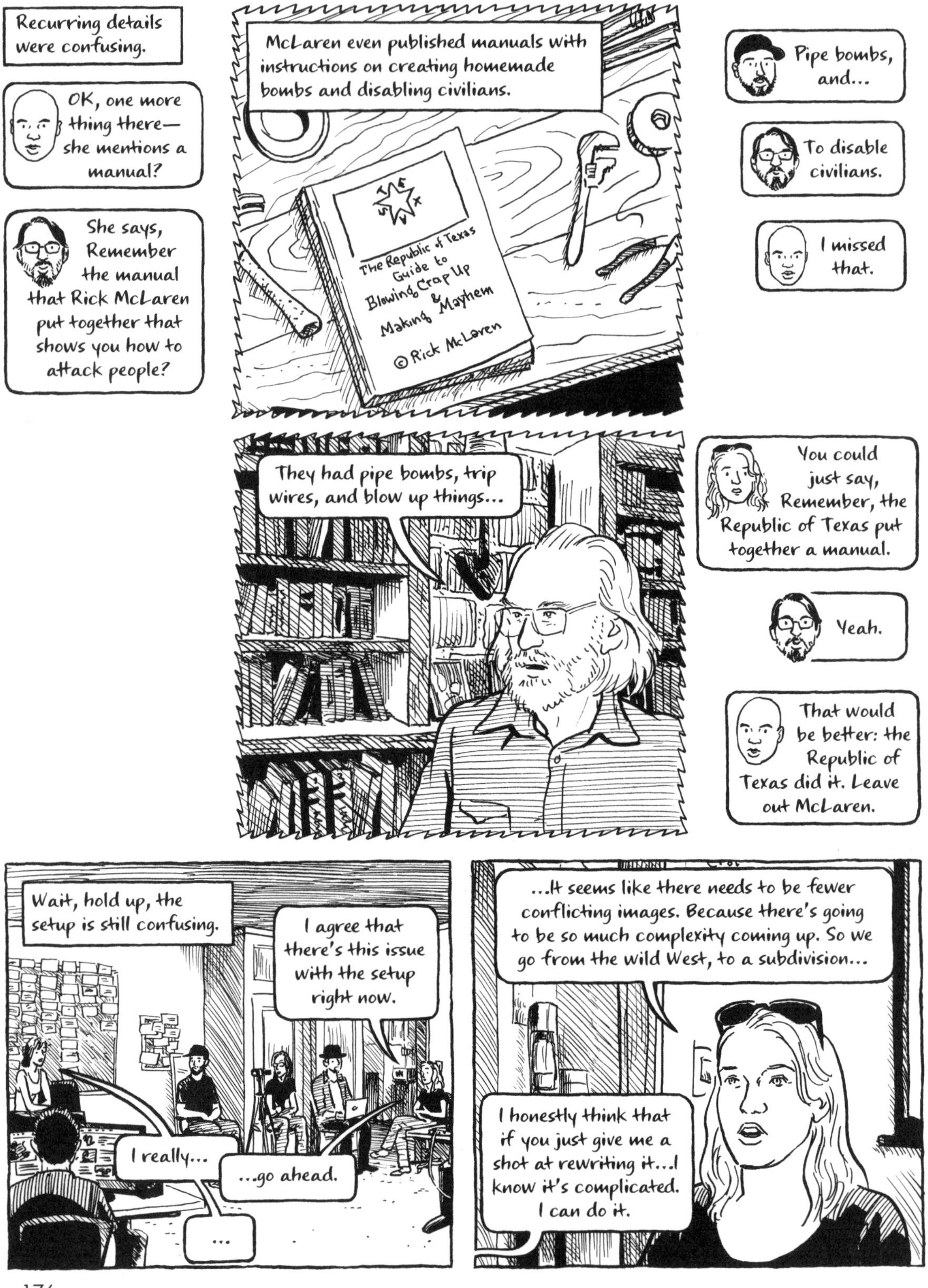
Recurring details were confusing.
OK, one more thing there—she mentions a manual?
She says, Remember the manual that Rick McLaren put together that shows you how to attack people?
McLaren even published manuals with instructions on creating homemade bombs and disabling civilians.
The Republic of Texas Guide to Blowing Crap Up & Making Mayhem
© Rick McLaren
Pipe bombs, and...
To disable civilians.
I missed that.
They had pipe bombs, trip wires, and blow up things...
You could just say, Remember, the Republic of Texas put together a manual.
Yeah.
That would be better: the Republic of Texas did it. Leave out McLaren.
Wait, hold up, the setup is still confusing.
I agree that there's this issue with the setup right now.
I really...
...go ahead.
...
...It seems like there needs to be fewer conflicting images. Because there's going to be so much complexity coming up. So we go from the wild West, to a subdivision...
I honestly think that if you just give me a shot at rewriting it...I know it's complicated. I can do it.

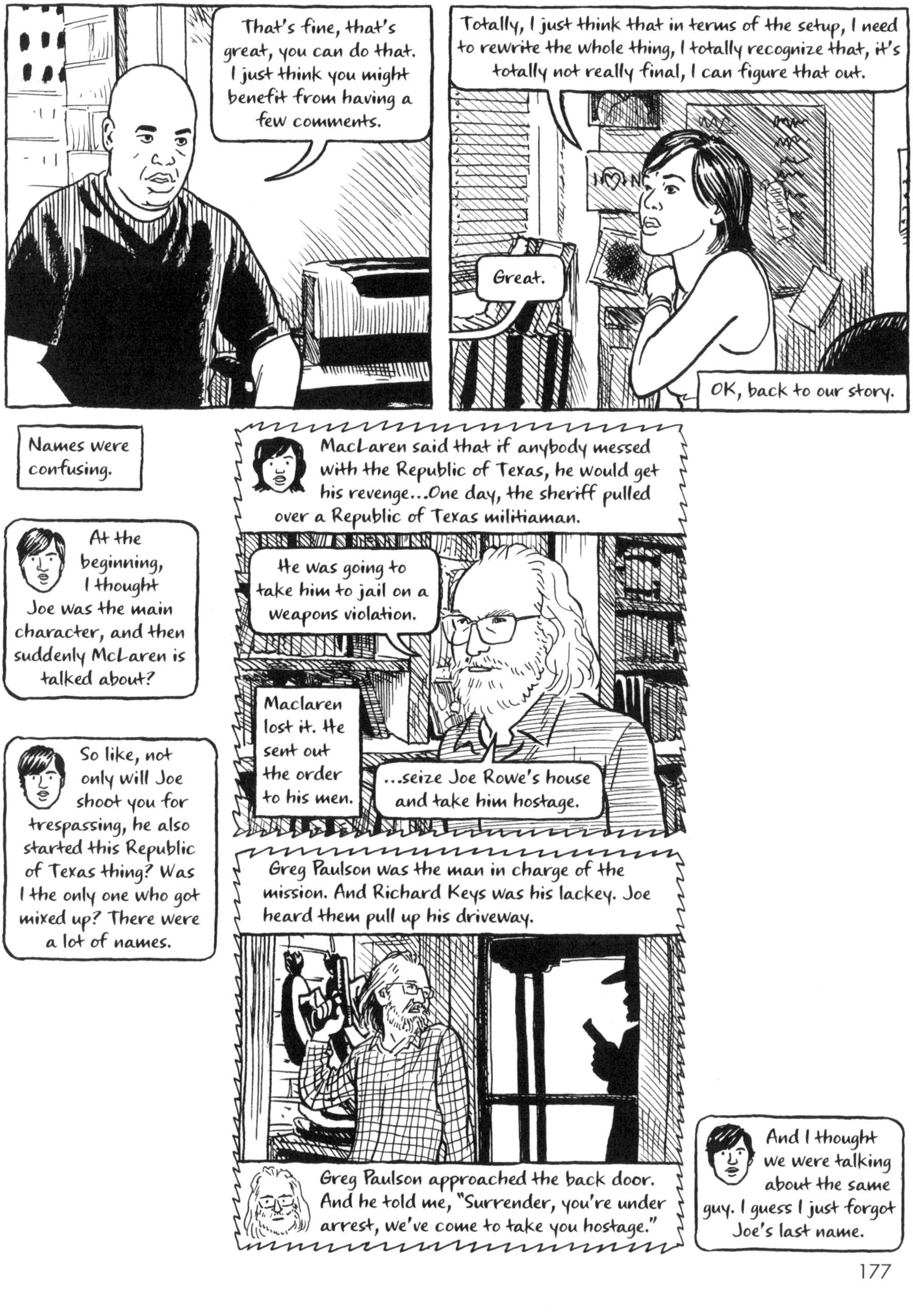
That's fine, that's great, you can do that. I just think you might benefit from having a few comments.
Totally, I just think that in terms of the setup, I need to rewrite the whole thing, I totally recognize that, it's totally not really final, I can figure that out.
Great.
OK, back to our story.
Names were confusing.
At the beginning, I thought Joe was the main character, and then suddenly McLaren is talked about?
So like, not only will Joe shoot you for trespassing, he also started this Republic of Texas thing? Was I the only one who got mixed up? There were a lot of names.
MacLaren said that if anybody messed with the Republic of Texas, he would get his revenge...One day, the sheriff pulled over a Republic of Texas militiaman.
He was going to take him to jail on a weapons violation.
Maclaren lost it. He sent out the order to his men.
...seize Joe Rowe's house and take him hostage.
Greg Paulson was the man in charge of the mission. And Richard Keys was his lackey. Joe heard them pull up his driveway.
Greg Paulson approached the back door. And he told me, "Surrender, you're under arrest, we've come to take you hostage."
And I thought we were talking about the same guy. I guess I just forgot Joe's last name.

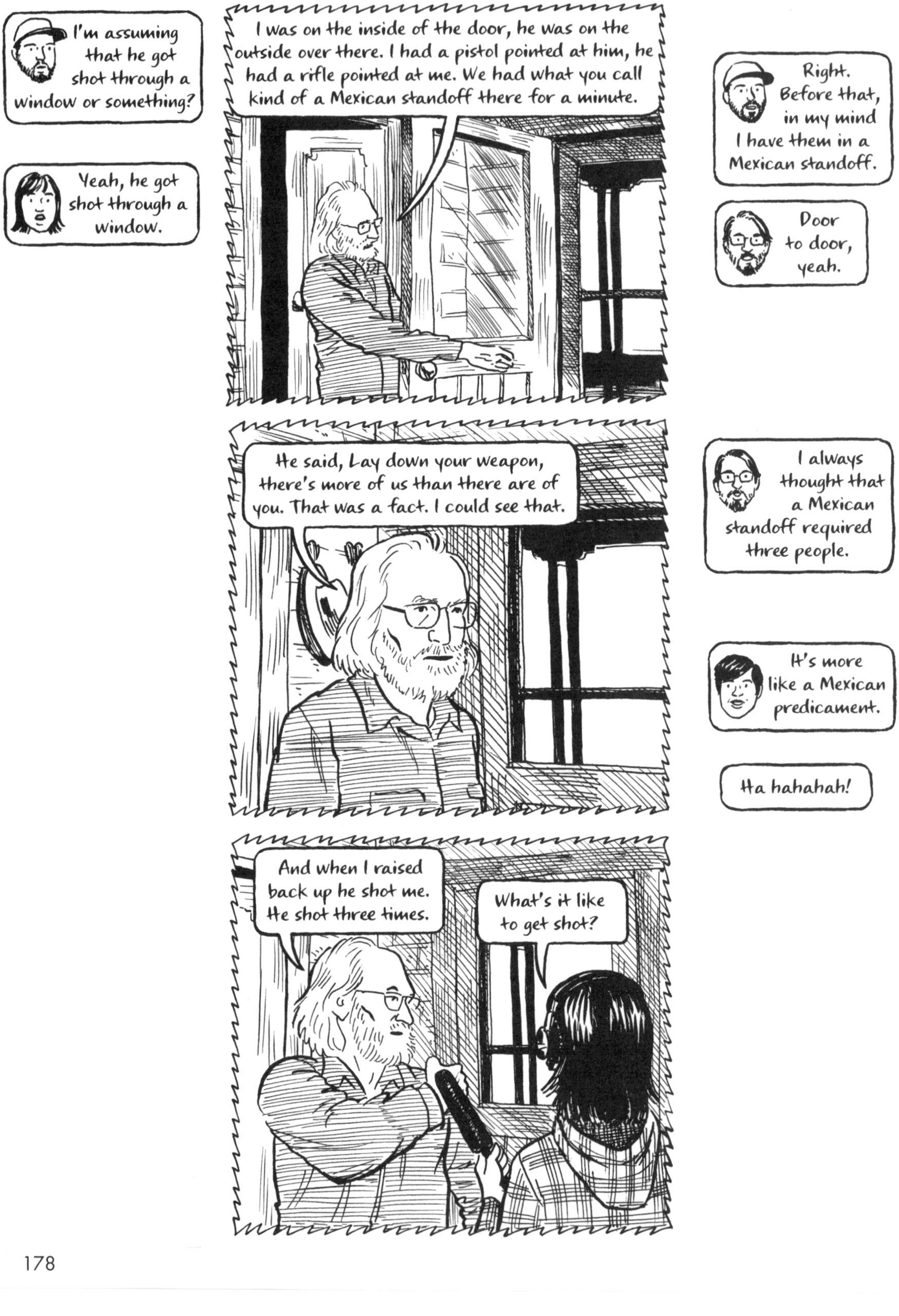
I'm assuming that he got shot through a window or something?
Yeah, he got shot through a window.
I was on the inside of the door, he was on the outside over there. I had a pistol pointed at him, he had a rifle pointed at me. We had what you call kind of a Mexican standoff there for a minute.
Right. Before that, in my mind I have them in a Mexican standoff.
Door to door, yeah.
He said, Lay down your weapon, there's more of us than there are of you. That was a fact. I could see that.
I always thought that a Mexican standoff required three people.
It's more like a Mexican predicament.
Ha hahahah!
And when I raised back up he shot me. He shot three times.
What's it like to get shot?

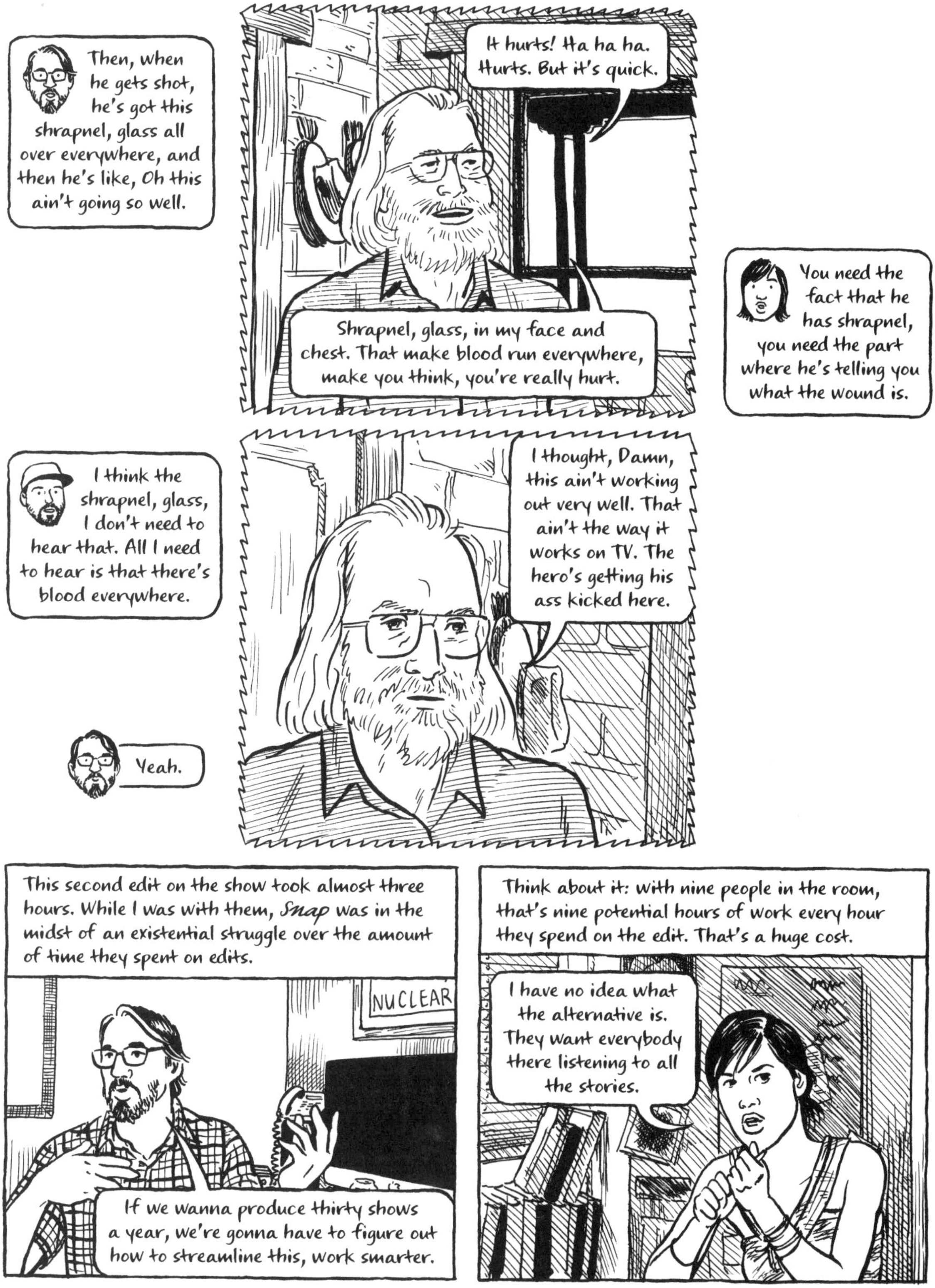
Then, when he gets shot, he's got this shrapnel, glass all over everywhere, and then he's like, Oh this ain't going so well.
It hurts! Ha ha ha. Hurts. But it's quick.
Shrapnel, glass, in my face and chest. That make blood run everywhere, make you think, you're really hurt.
You need the fact that he has shrapnel, you need the part where he's telling you what the wound is.
I think the shrapnel, glass, I don't need to hear that. All I need to hear is that there's blood everywhere.
I thought, Damn, this ain't working out very well. That ain't the way it works on TV. The hero's getting his ass kicked here.
Yeah.
This second edit on the show took almost three hours. While I was with them, *Snap* was in the midst of an existential struggle over the amount of time they spent on edits.
NUCLEAR
If we wanna produce thirty shows a year, we're gonna have to figure out how to streamline this, work smarter.
Think about it: with nine people in the room, that's nine potential hours of work every hour they spend on the edit. That's a huge cost.
I have no idea what the alternative is. They want everybody there listening to all the stories.

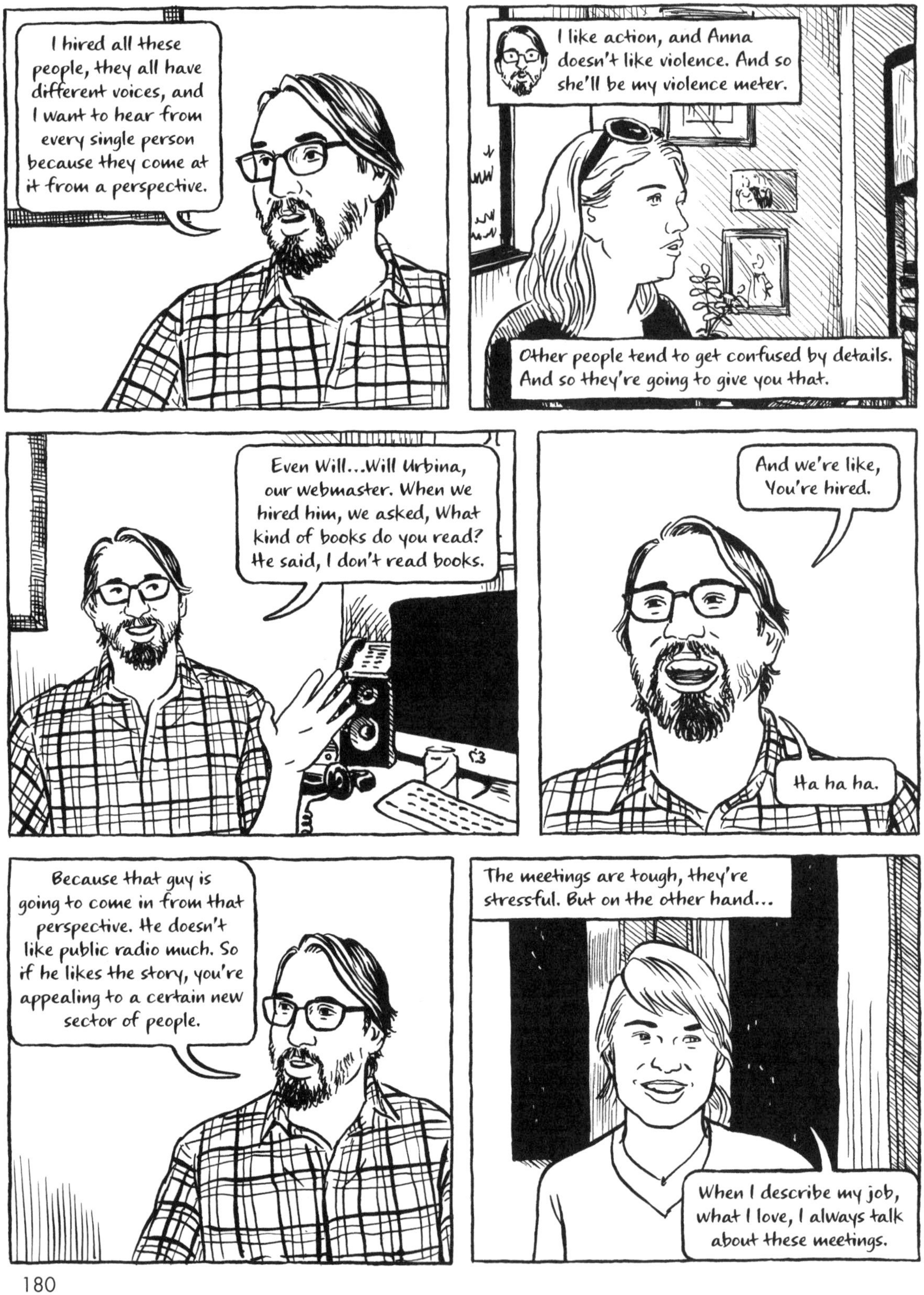
I hired all these people, they all have different voices, and I want to hear from every single person because they come at it from a perspective.
I like action, and Anna doesn't like violence. And so she'll be my violence meter.
Other people tend to get confused by details. And so they're going to give you that.
Even Will...Will Urbina, our webmaster. When we hired him, we asked, What kind of books do you read? He said, I don't read books.
And we're like, You're hired.
Ha ha ha.
Because that guy is going to come in from that perspective. He doesn't like public radio much. So if he likes the story, you're appealing to a certain new sector of people.
The meetings are tough, they're stressful. But on the other hand...
When I describe my job, what I love, I always talk about these meetings.

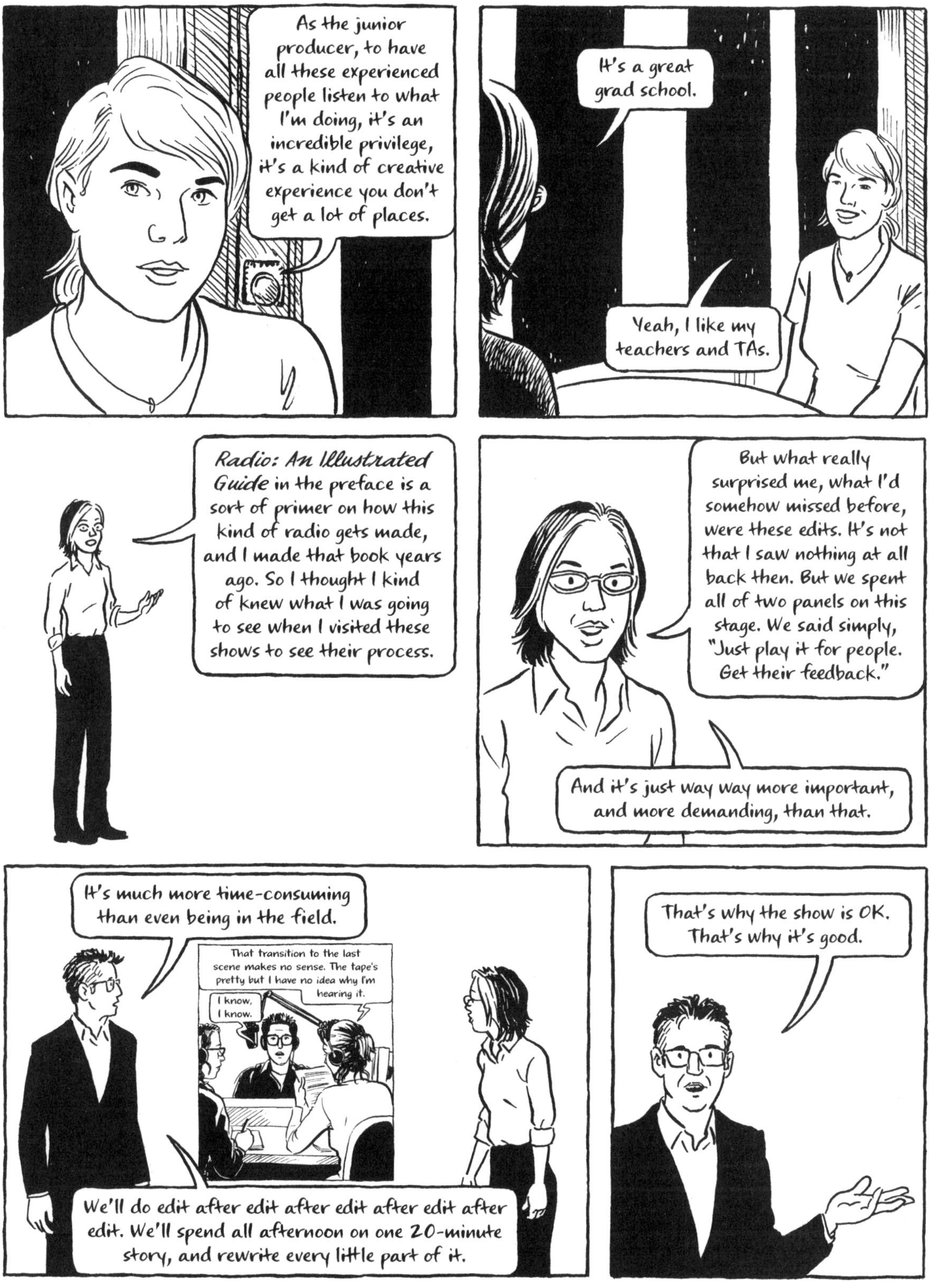
As the junior producer, to have all these experienced people listen to what I'm doing, it's an incredible privilege, it's a kind of creative experience you don't get a lot of places.
It's a great grad school.
Yeah, I like my teachers and TAs.
Radio: An Illustrated Guide in the preface is a sort of primer on how this kind of radio gets made, and I made that book years ago. So I thought I kind of knew what I was going to see when I visited these shows to see their process.
But what really surprised me, what I'd somehow missed before, were these edits. It's not that I saw nothing at all back then. But we spent all of two panels on this stage. We said simply, "Just play it for people. Get their feedback."
And it's just way way more important, and more demanding, than that.
It's much more time-consuming than even being in the field.
That transition to the last scene makes no sense. The tape's pretty but I have no idea why I'm hearing it.
I know, I know.
We'll do edit after edit after edit after edit after edit. We'll spend all afternoon on one 20-minute story, and rewrite every little part of it.
That's why the show is OK. That's why it's good.

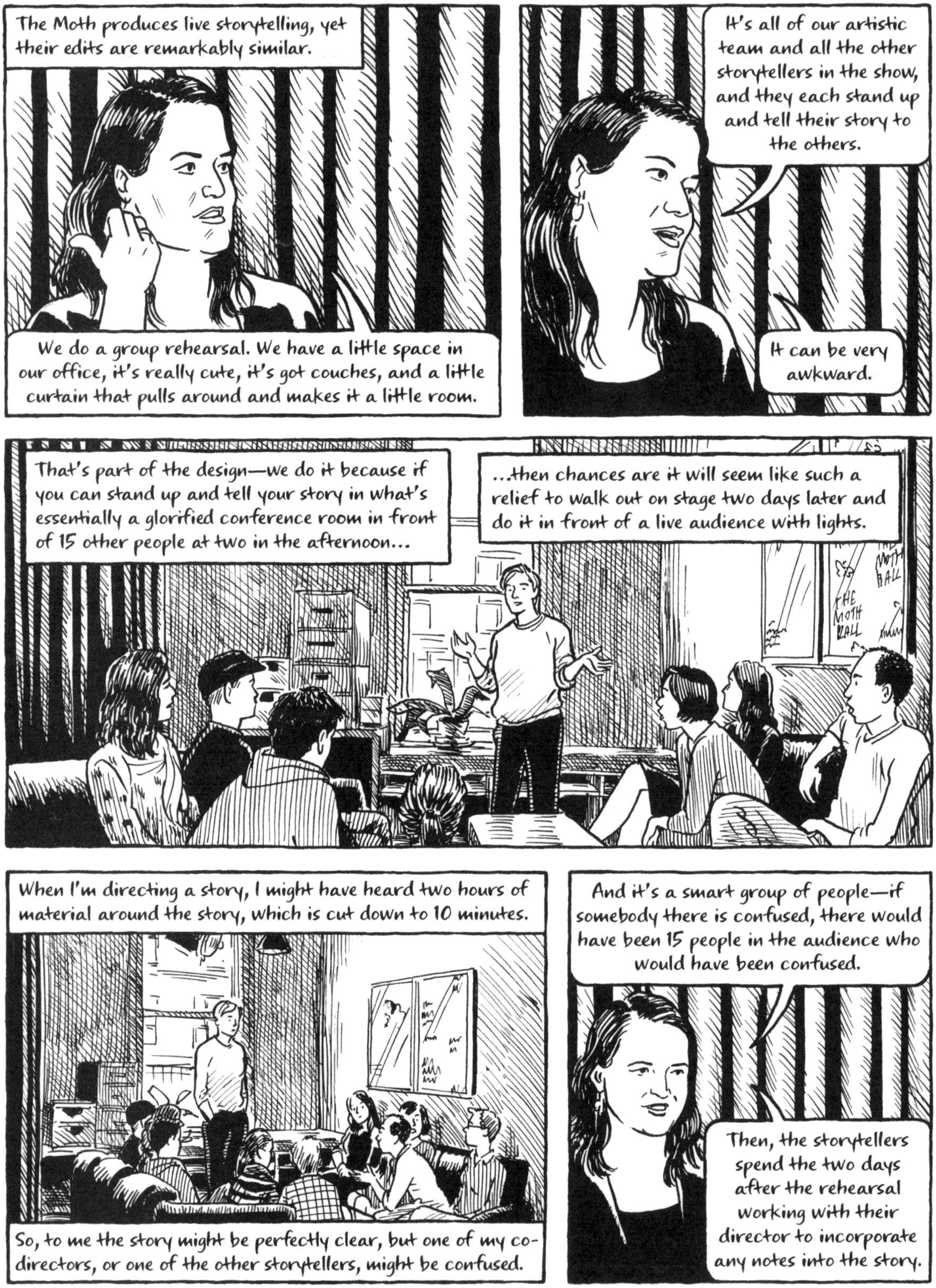

The Moth produces live storytelling, yet their edits are remarkably similar.
We do a group rehearsal. We have a little space in our office, it's really cute, it's got couches, and a little curtain that pulls around and makes it a little room.
It's all of our artistic team and all the other storytellers in the show, and they each stand up and tell their story to the others.
It can be very awkward.
That's part of the design—we do it because if you can stand up and tell your story in what's essentially a glorified conference room in front of 15 other people at two in the afternoon...
...then chances are it will seem like such a relief to walk out on stage two days later and do it in front of a live audience with lights.
When I'm directing a story, I might have heard two hours of material around the story, which is cut down to 10 minutes.
So, to me the story might be perfectly clear, but one of my co-directors, or one of the other storytellers, might be confused.
And it's a smart group of people—if somebody there is confused, there would have been 15 people in the audience who would have been confused.
Then, the storytellers spend the two days after the rehearsal working with their director to incorporate any notes into the story.

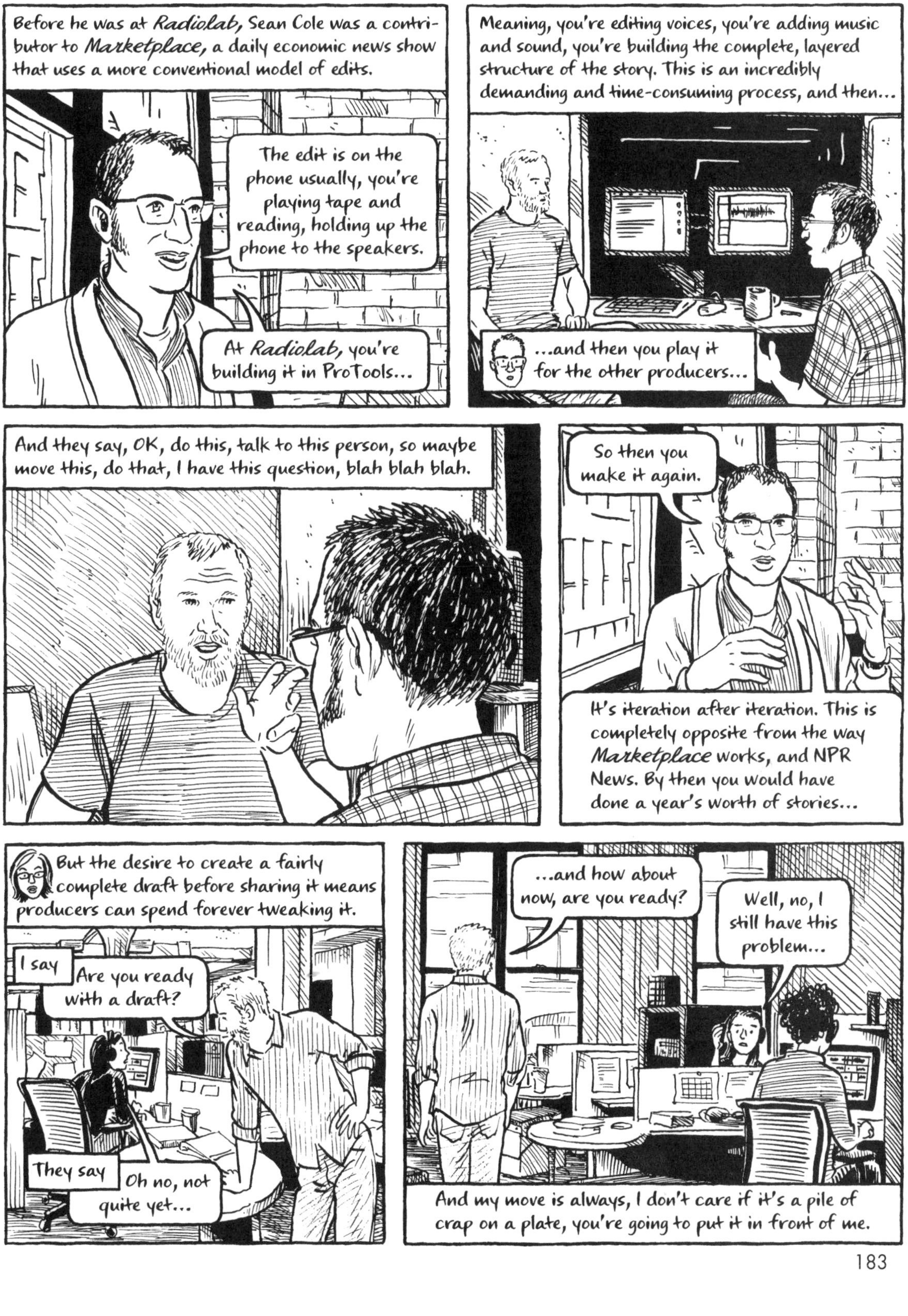
Before he was at *Radiolab,* Sean Cole was a contributor to *Marketplace,* a daily economic news show that uses a more conventional model of edits.
The edit is on the phone usually, you're playing tape and reading, holding up the phone to the speakers.
At *Radiolab,* you're building it in ProTools...
Meaning, you're editing voices, you're adding music and sound, you're building the complete, layered structure of the story. This is an incredibly demanding and time-consuming process, and then...
...and then you play it for the other producers...
And they say, OK, do this, talk to this person, so maybe move this, do that, I have this question, blah blah blah.
So then you make it again.
It's iteration after iteration. This is completely opposite from the way *Marketplace* works, and NPR News. By then you would have done a year's worth of stories...
But the desire to create a fairly complete draft before sharing it means producers can spend forever tweaking it.
I say
Are you ready with a draft?
They say
Oh no, not quite yet...
...and how about now, are you ready?
Well, no, I still have this problem...
And my move is always, I don't care if it's a pile of crap on a plate, you're going to put it in front of me.

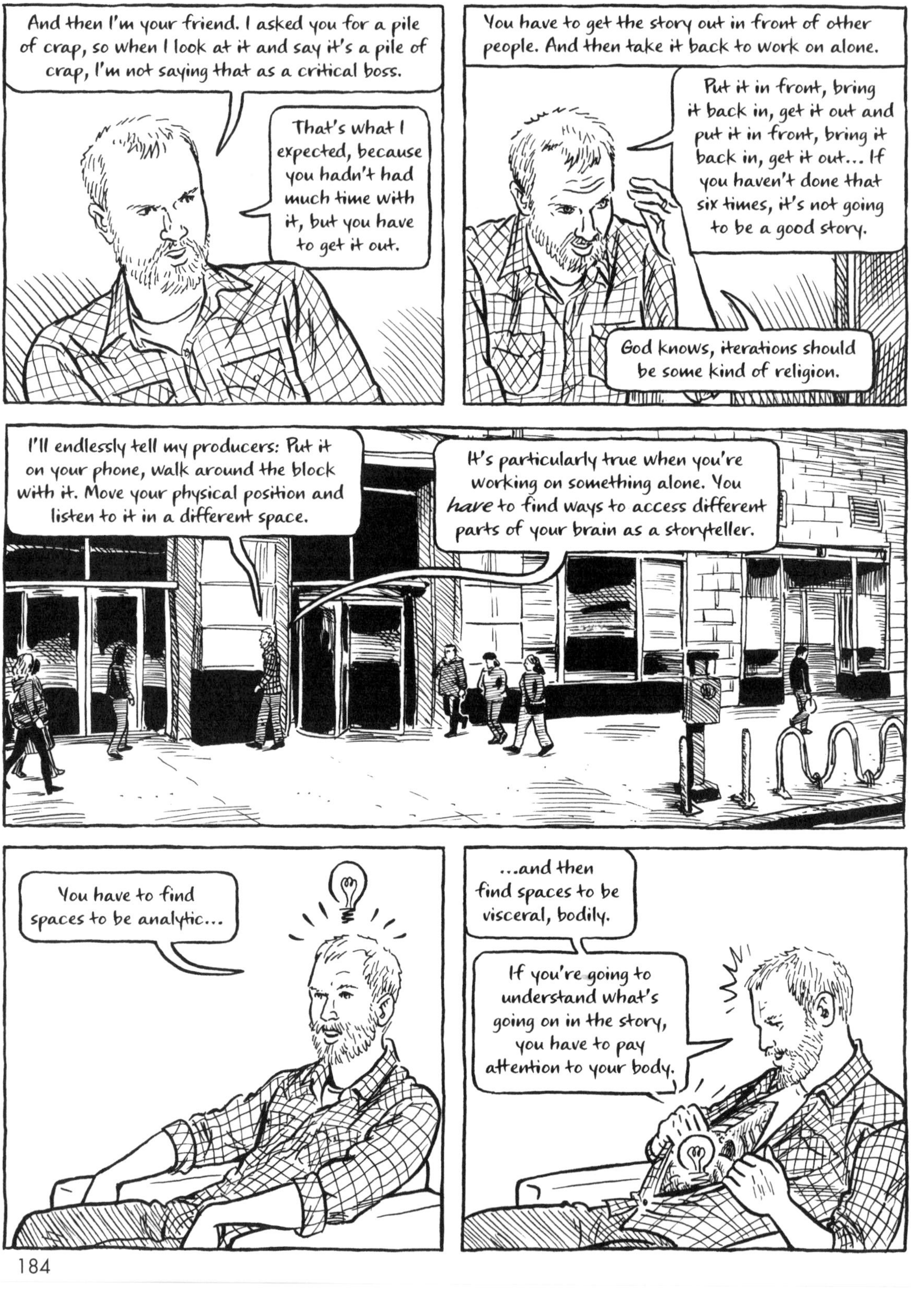
And then I'm your friend. I asked you for a pile of crap, so when I look at it and say it's a pile of crap, I'm not saying that as a critical boss.
That's what I expected, because you hadn't had much time with it, but you have to get it out.
You have to get the story out in front of other people. And then take it back to work on alone.
Put it in front, bring it back in, get it out and put it in front, bring it back in, get it out... If you haven't done that six times, it's not going to be a good story.
God knows, iterations should be some kind of religion.
I'll endlessly tell my producers: Put it on your phone, walk around the block with it. Move your physical position and listen to it in a different space.
It's particularly true when you're working on something alone. You *have* to find ways to access different parts of your brain as a storyteller.
You have to find spaces to be analytic...
...and then find spaces to be visceral, bodily.
If you're going to understand what's going on in the story, you have to pay attention to your body.

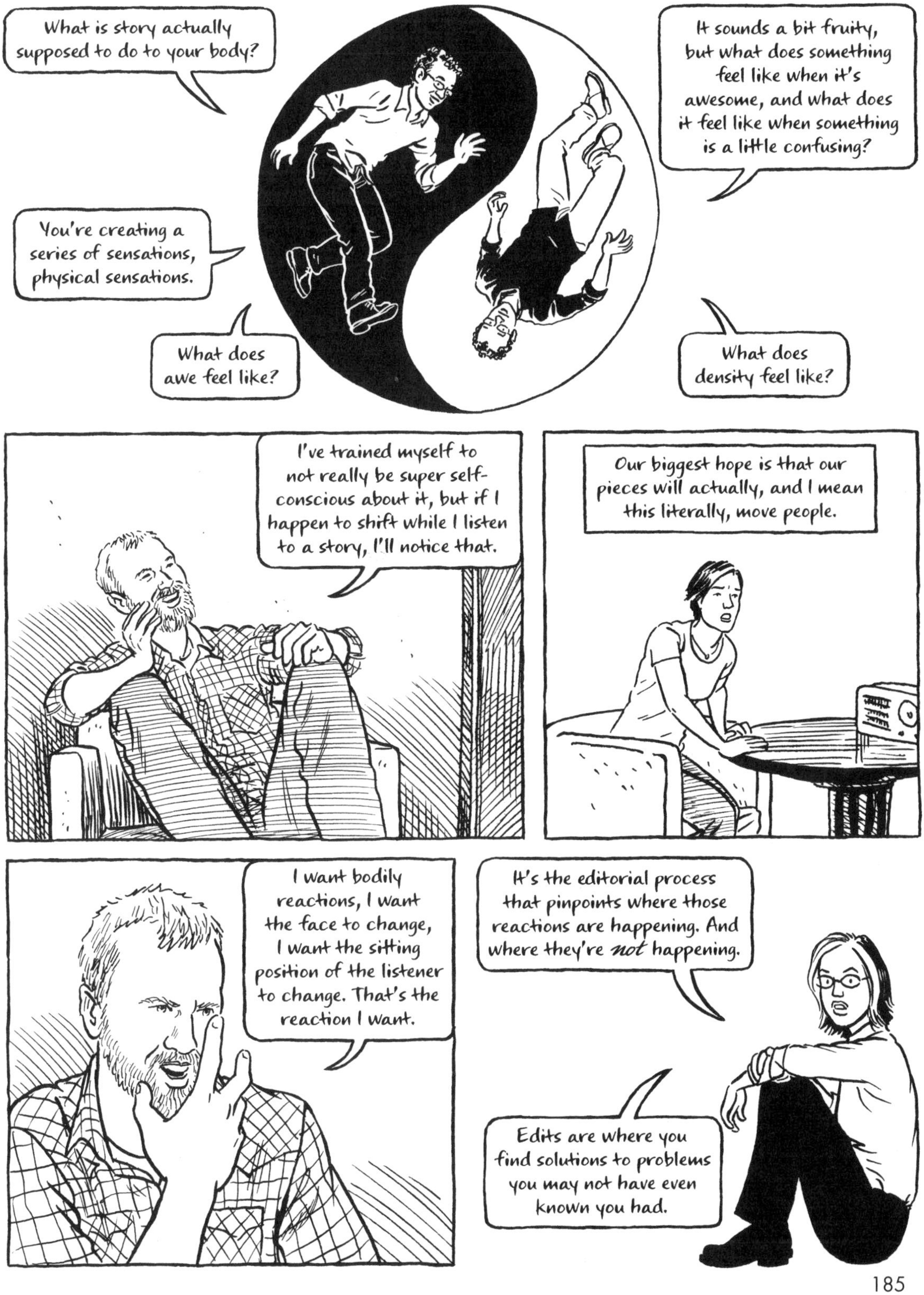

What is story actually supposed to do to your body?
It sounds a bit fruity, but what does something feel like when it's awesome, and what does it feel like when something is a little confusing?
You're creating a series of sensations, physical sensations.
What does awe feel like?
What does density feel like?
I've trained myself to not really be super self-conscious about it, but if I happen to shift while I listen to a story, I'll notice that.
Our biggest hope is that our pieces will actually, and I mean this literally, move people.
I want bodily reactions, I want the face to change, I want the sitting position of the listener to change. That's the reaction I want.
It's the editorial process that pinpoints where those reactions are happening. And where they're *not* happening.
Edits are where you find solutions to problems you may not have even known you had.

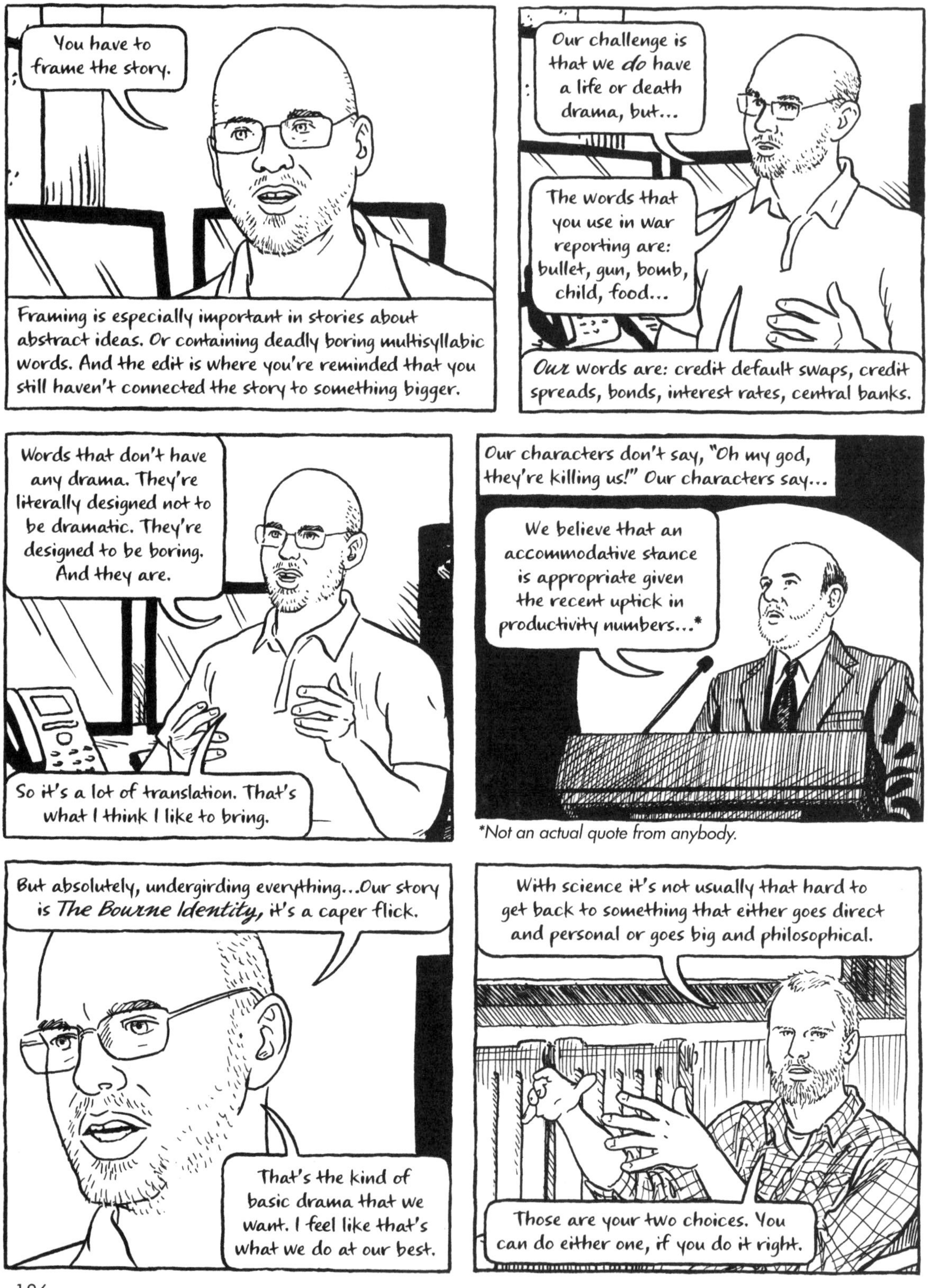
You have to frame the story.
Framing is especially important in stories about abstract ideas. Or containing deadly boring multisyllabic words. And the edit is where you're reminded that you still haven't connected the story to something bigger.
Our challenge is that we *do* have a life or death drama, but...
The words that you use in war reporting are: bullet, gun, bomb, child, food...
Our words are: credit default swaps, credit spreads, bonds, interest rates, central banks.
Words that don't have any drama. They're literally designed not to be dramatic. They're designed to be boring. And they are.
So it's a lot of translation. That's what I think I like to bring.
Our characters don't say, "Oh my god, they're killing us!" Our characters say...
We believe that an accommodative stance is appropriate given the recent uptick in productivity numbers...*
*Not an actual quote from anybody.
But absolutely, undergirding everything...Our story is *The Bourne Identity*, it's a caper flick.
That's the kind of basic drama that we want. I feel like that's what we do at our best.
With science it's not usually that hard to get back to something that either goes direct and personal or goes big and philosophical.
Those are your two choices. You can do either one, if you do it right.

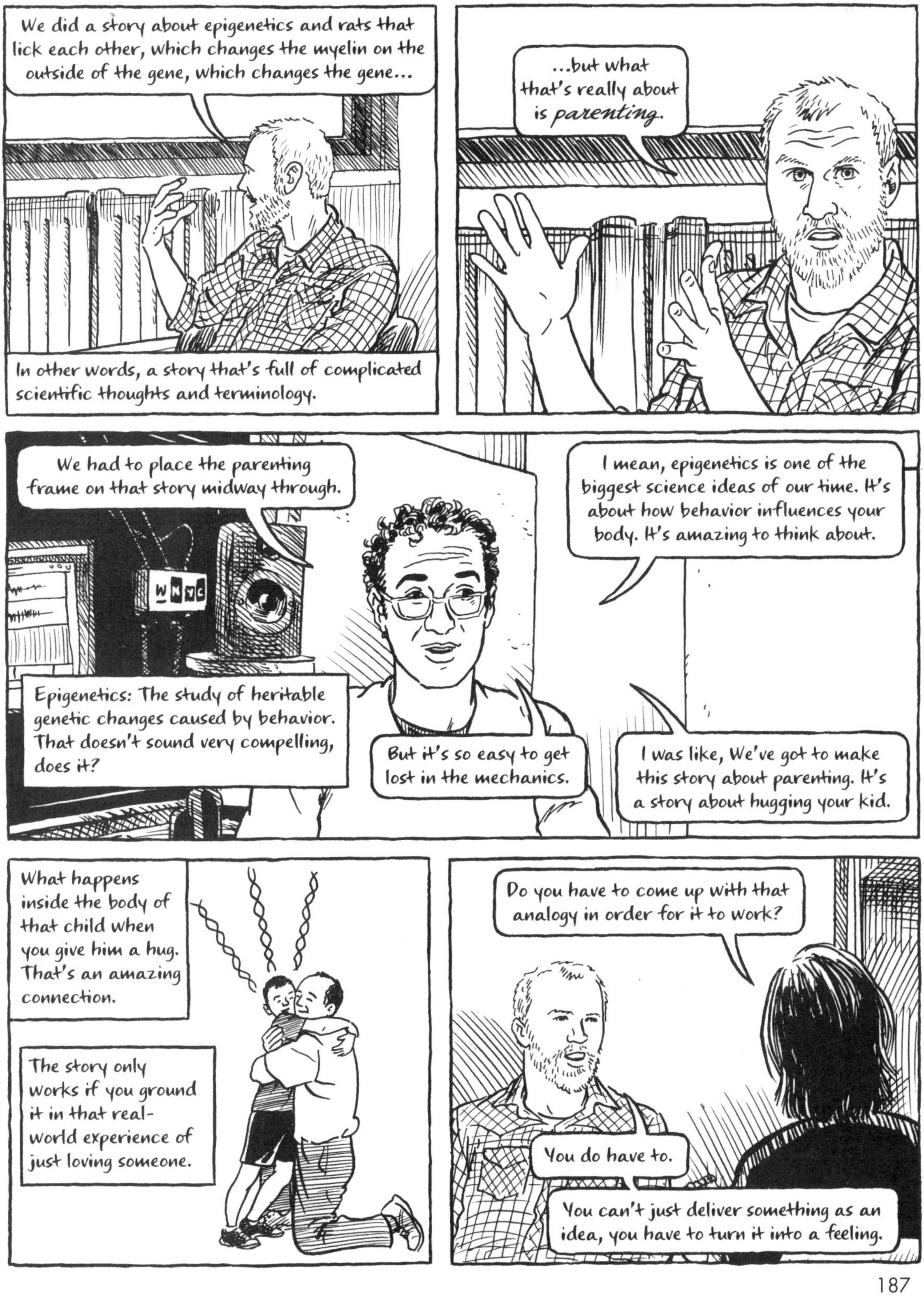
We did a story about epigenetics and rats that lick each other, which changes the myelin on the outside of the gene, which changes the gene...
In other words, a story that's full of complicated scientific thoughts and terminology.
...but what that's really about is *parenting*.
We had to place the parenting frame on that story midway through.
WNYC
Epigenetics: The study of heritable genetic changes caused by behavior. That doesn't sound very compelling, does it?
I mean, epigenetics is one of the biggest science ideas of our time. It's about how behavior influences your body. It's amazing to think about.
But it's so easy to get lost in the mechanics.
I was like, We've got to make this story about parenting. It's a story about hugging your kid.
What happens inside the body of that child when you give him a hug. That's an amazing connection.
The story only works if you ground it in that real-world experience of just loving someone.
Do you have to come up with that analogy in order for it to work?
You do have to.
You can't just deliver something as an idea, you have to turn it into a feeling.

YOU HAVE TO DEVELOP A THICKER SKIN. YOU JUST HAVE TO.

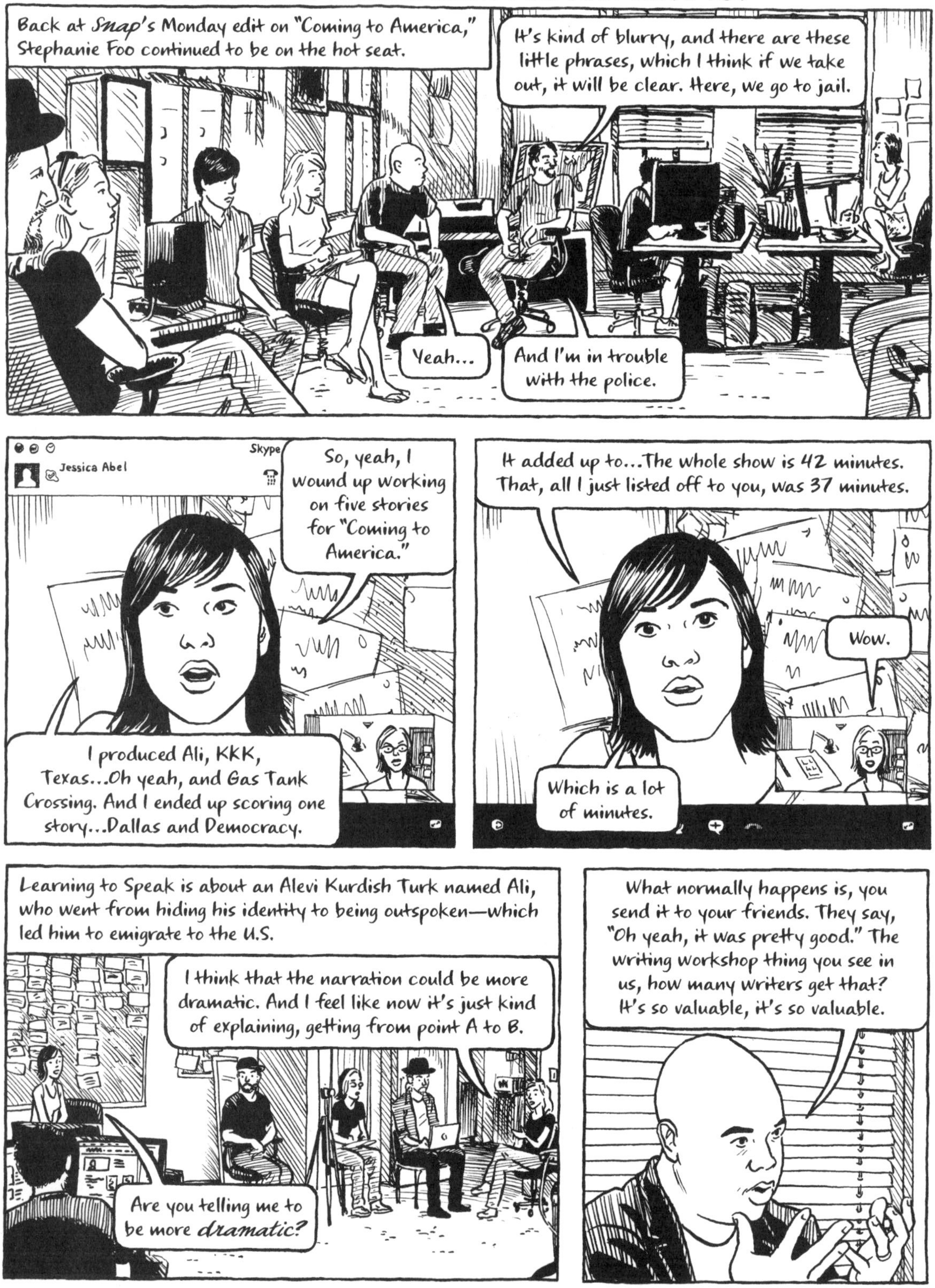
Back at Snap's Monday edit on "Coming to America," Stephanie Foo continued to be on the hot seat.
It's kind of blurry, and there are these little phrases, which I think if we take out, it will be clear. Here, we go to jail.
Yeah...
And I'm in trouble with the police.
Skype
Jessica Abel
So, yeah, I wound up working on five stories for "Coming to America."
I produced Ali, KKK, Texas...Oh yeah, and Gas Tank Crossing. And I ended up scoring one story...Dallas and Democracy.
It added up to...The whole show is 42 minutes. That, all I just listed off to you, was 37 minutes.
Wow.
Which is a lot of minutes.
Learning to Speak is about an Alevi Kurdish Turk named Ali, who went from hiding his identity to being outspoken—which led him to emigrate to the U.S.
I think that the narration could be more dramatic. And I feel like now it's just kind of explaining, getting from point A to B.
Are you telling me to be more dramatic?
What normally happens is, you send it to your friends. They say, "Oh yeah, it was pretty good." The writing workshop thing you see in us, how many writers get that? It's so valuable, it's so valuable.

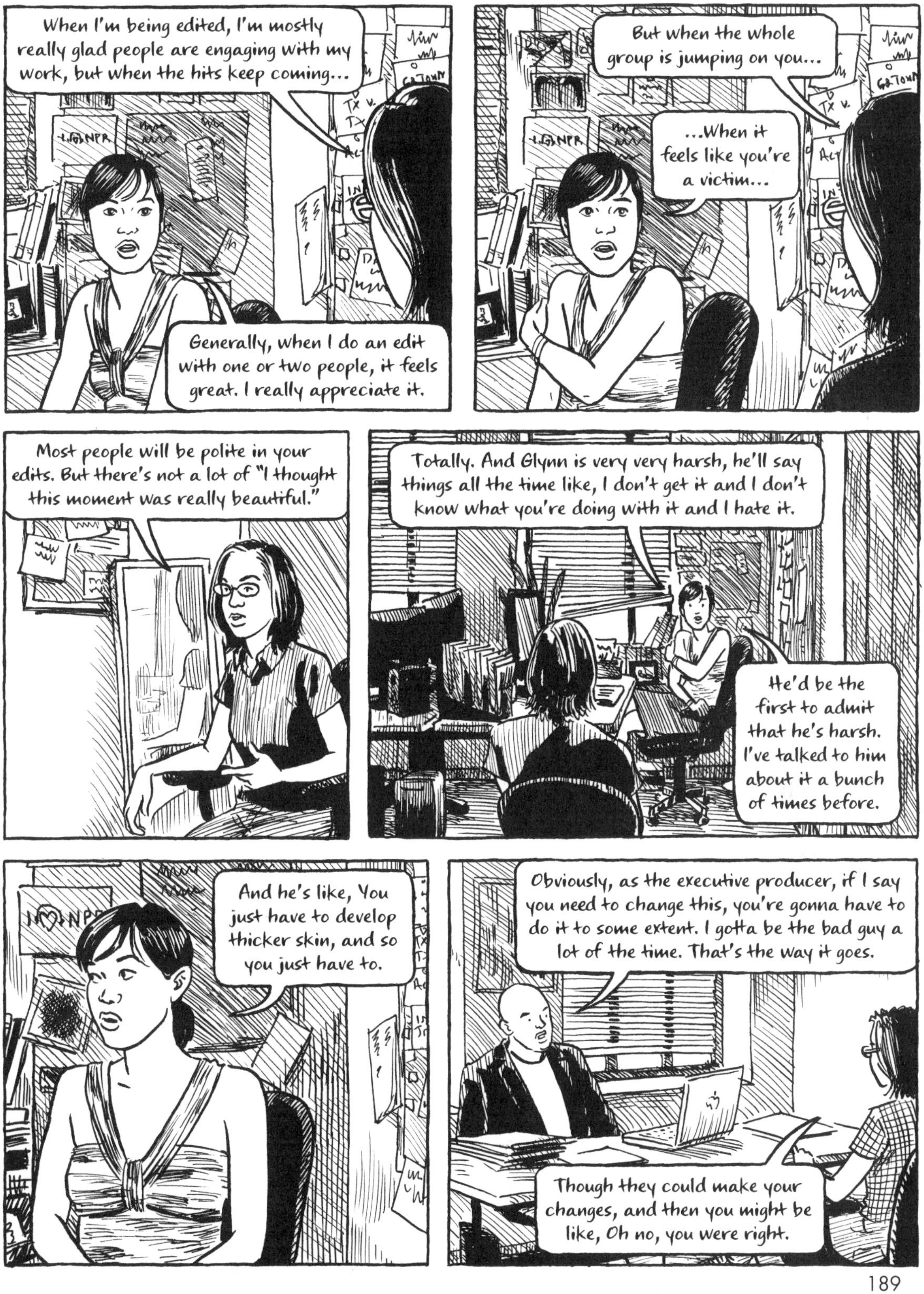
When I'm being edited, I'm mostly really glad people are engaging with my work, but when the hits keep coming...
Generally, when I do an edit with one or two people, it feels great. I really appreciate it.
But when the whole group is jumping on you...
...When it feels like you're a victim...
Most people will be polite in your edits. But there's not a lot of "I thought this moment was really beautiful."
Totally. And Glynn is very very harsh, he'll say things all the time like, I don't get it and I don't know what you're doing with it and I hate it.
He'd be the first to admit that he's harsh. I've talked to him about it a bunch of times before.
And he's like, You just have to develop thicker skin, and so you just have to.
Obviously, as the executive producer, if I say you need to change this, you're gonna have to do it to some extent. I gotta be the bad guy a lot of the time. That's the way it goes.
Though they could make your changes, and then you might be like, Oh no, you were right.

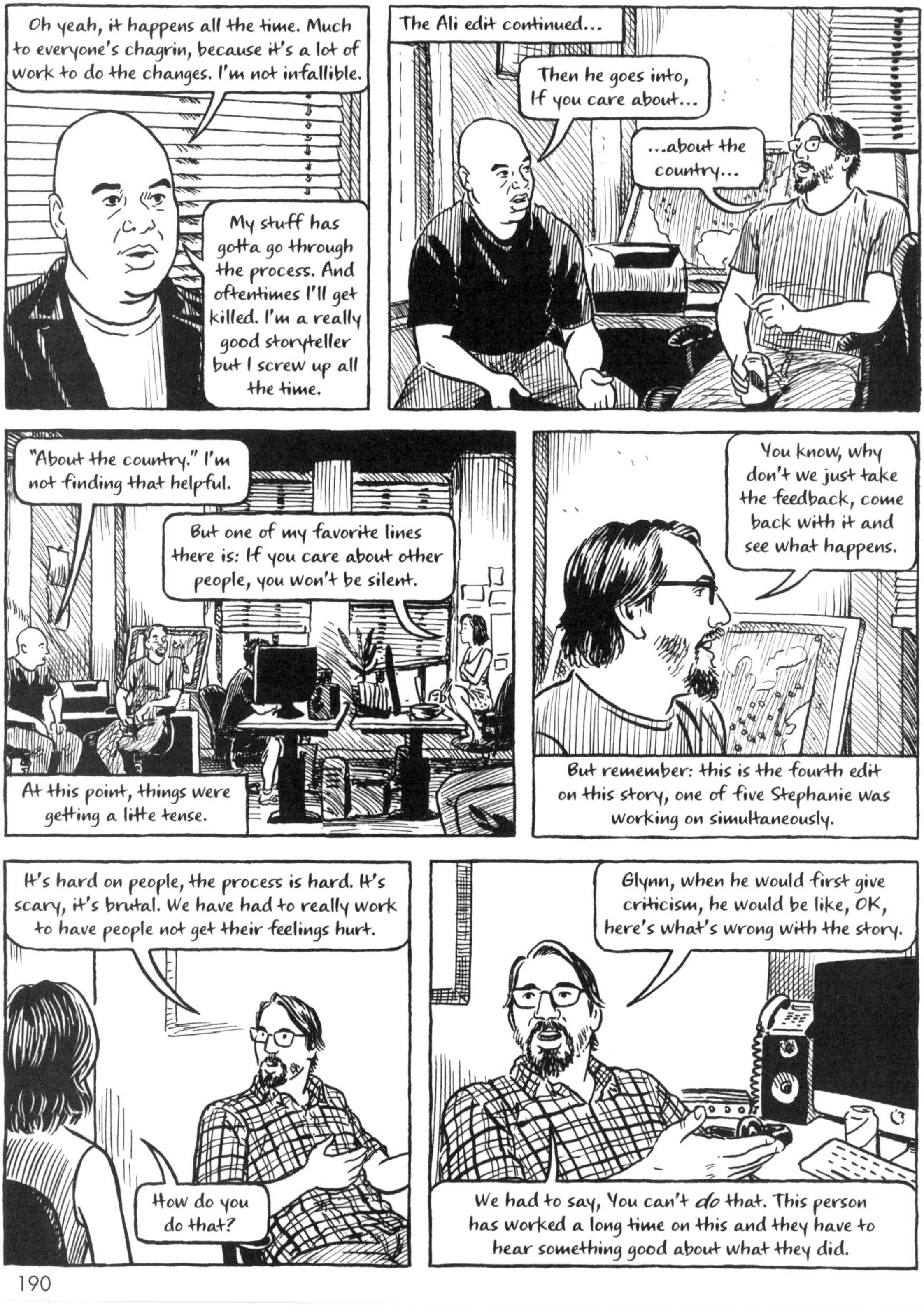
Oh yeah, it happens all the time. Much to everyone's chagrin, because it's a lot of work to do the changes. I'm not infallible.
My stuff has gotta go through the process. And oftentimes I'll get killed. I'm a really good storyteller but I screw up all the time.
The Ali edit continued...
Then he goes into, If you care about...
...about the country...
"About the country." I'm not finding that helpful.
But one of my favorite lines there is: If you care about other people, you won't be silent.
At this point, things were getting a litte tense.
You know, why don't we just take the feedback, come back with it and see what happens.
But remember: this is the fourth edit on this story, one of five Stephanie was working on simultaneously.
It's hard on people, the process is hard. It's scary, it's brutal. We have had to really work to have people not get their feelings hurt.
How do you do that?
Glynn, when he would first give criticism, he would be like, OK, here's what's wrong with the story.
We had to say, You can't *do* that. This person has worked a long time on this and they have to hear something good about what they did.

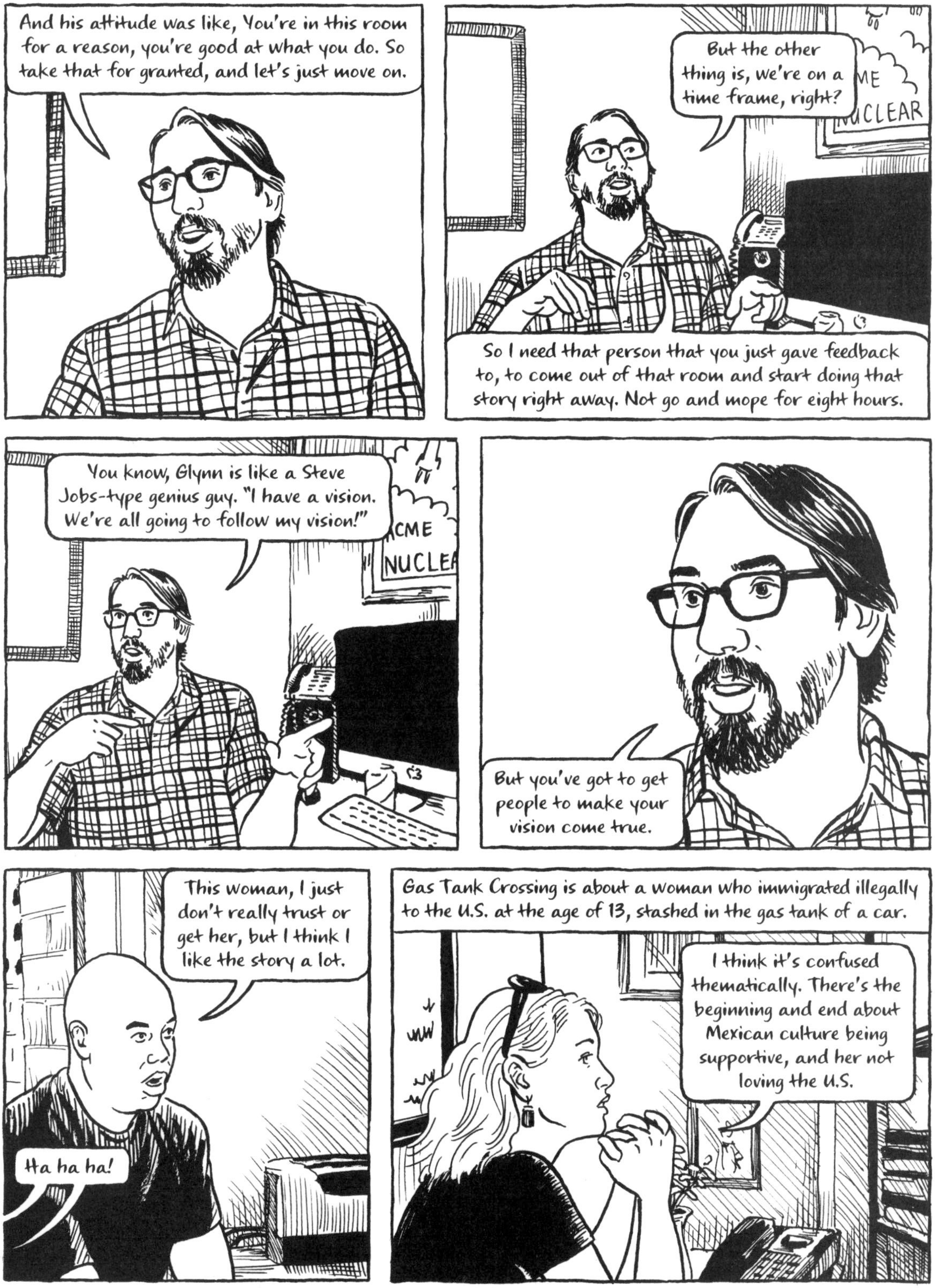
And his attitude was like, You're in this room for a reason, you're good at what you do. So take that for granted, and let's just move on.
But the other thing is, we're on a time frame, right?
ME
NUCLEAR
So I need that person that you just gave feedback to, to come out of that room and start doing that story right away. Not go and mope for eight hours.
You know, Glynn is like a Steve Jobs-type genius guy. "I have a vision. We're all going to follow my vision!"
CME
NUCLEA
But you've got to get people to make your vision come true.
This woman, I just don't really trust or get her, but I think I like the story a lot.
Ha ha ha!
Gas Tank Crossing is about a woman who immigrated illegally to the U.S. at the age of 13, stashed in the gas tank of a car.
I think it's confused thematically. There's the beginning and end about Mexican culture being supportive, and her not loving the U.S.

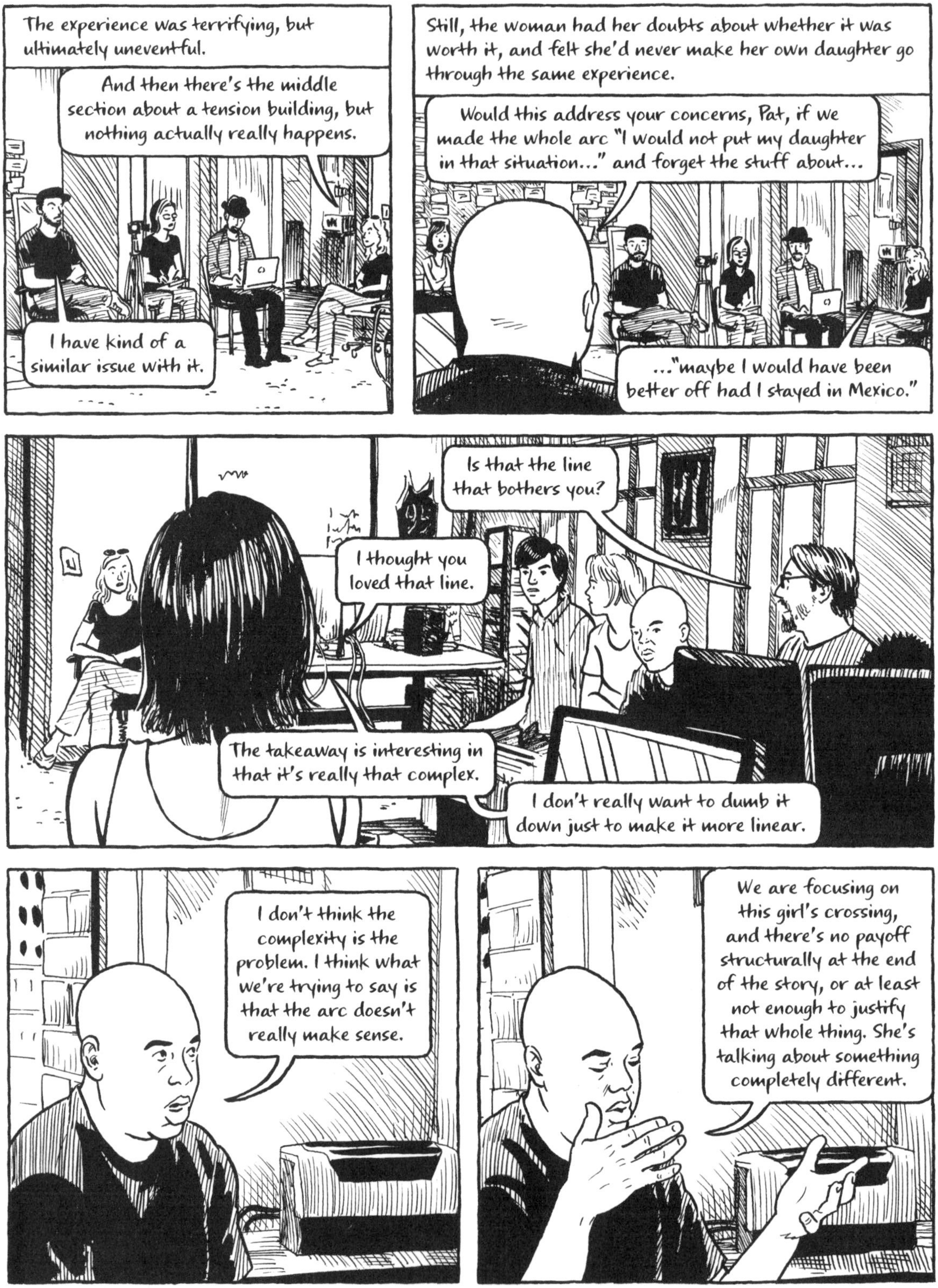
The experience was terrifying, but ultimately uneventful.
And then there's the middle section about a tension building, but nothing actually really happens.
I have kind of a similar issue with it.
Still, the woman had her doubts about whether it was worth it, and felt she'd never make her own daughter go through the same experience.
Would this address your concerns, Pat, if we made the whole arc "I would not put my daughter in that situation..." and forget the stuff about...
..."maybe I would have been better off had I stayed in Mexico."
Is that the line that bothers you?
I thought you loved that line.
The takeaway is interesting in that it's really that complex.
I don't really want to dumb it down just to make it more linear.
I don't think the complexity is the problem. I think what we're trying to say is that the arc doesn't really make sense.
We are focusing on this girl's crossing, and there's no payoff structurally at the end of the story, or at least not enough to justify that whole thing. She's talking about something completely different.

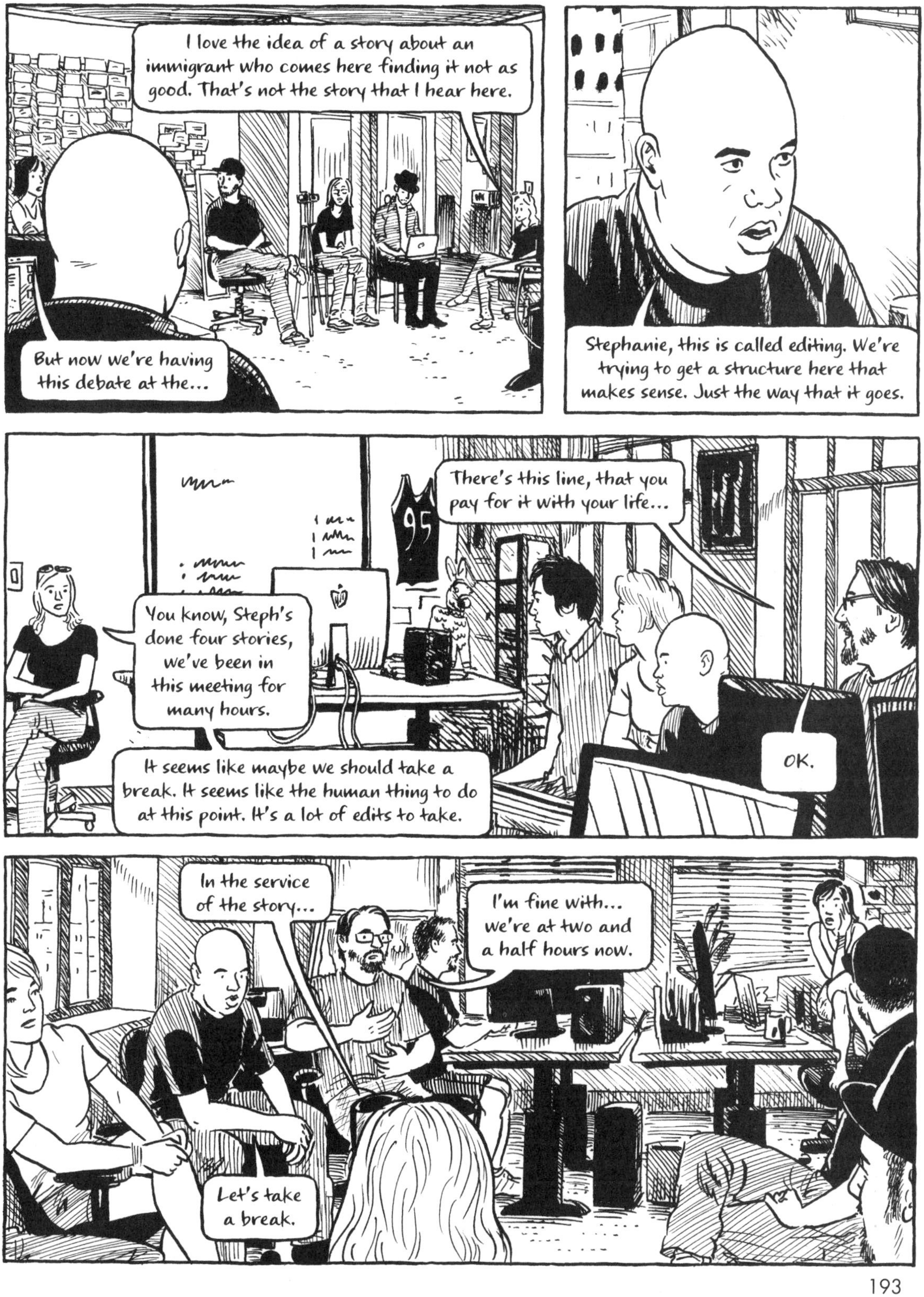
I love the idea of a story about an immigrant who comes here finding it not as good. That's not the story that I hear here.
But now we're having this debate at the...
Stephanie, this is called editing. We're trying to get a structure here that makes sense. Just the way that it goes.
There's this line, that you pay for it with your life...
You know, Steph's done four stories, we've been in this meeting for many hours.
It seems like maybe we should take a break. It seems like the human thing to do at this point. It's a lot of edits to take.
OK.
In the service of the story...
I'm fine with... we're at two and a half hours now.
Let's take a break.

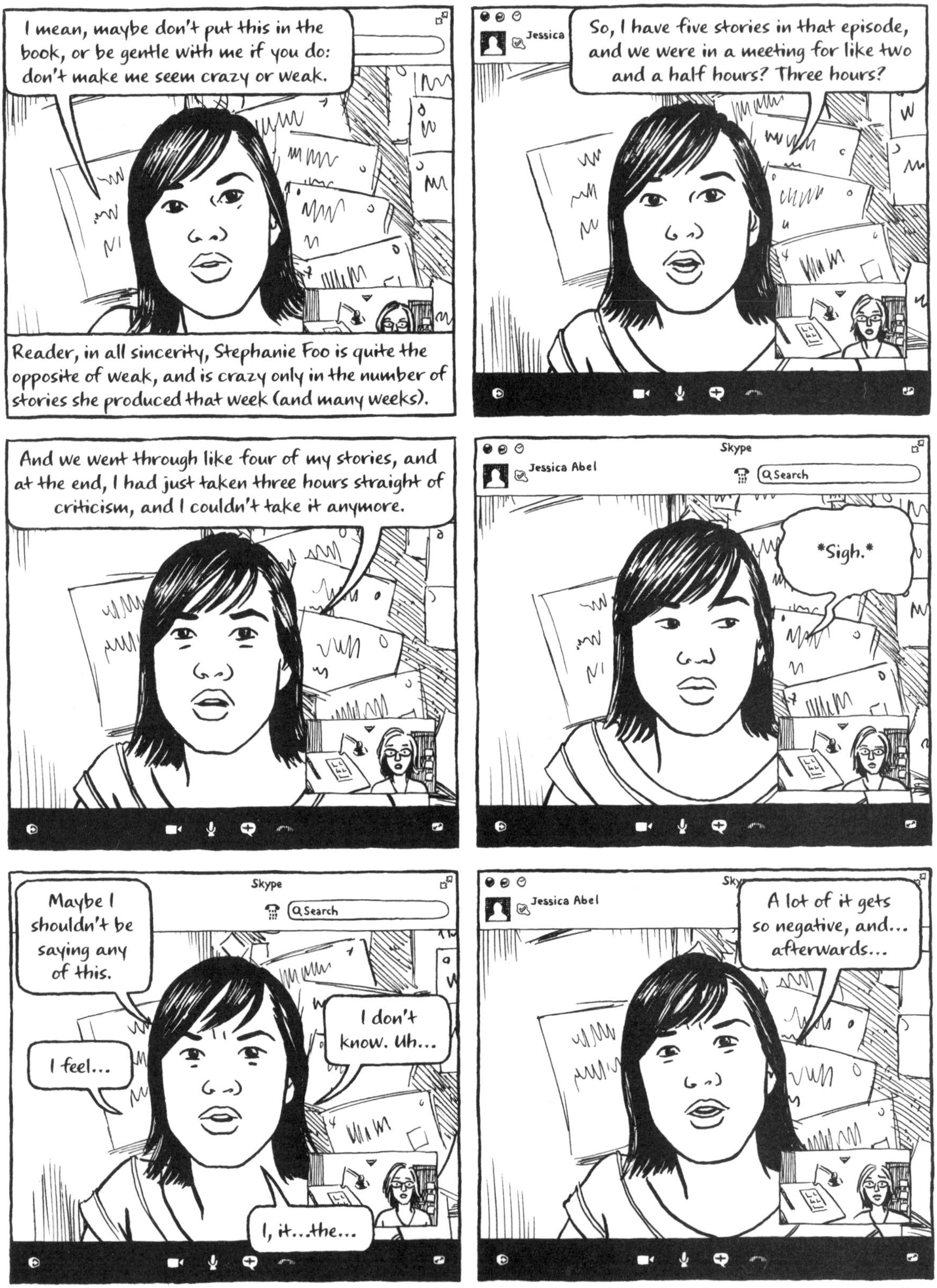
I mean, maybe don't put this in the book, or be gentle with me if you do: don't make me seem crazy or weak.
Reader, in all sincerity, Stephanie Foo is quite the opposite of weak, and is crazy only in the number of stories she produced that week (and many weeks).
Jessica
So, I have five stories in that episode, and we were in a meeting for like two and a half hours? Three hours?
And we went through like four of my stories, and at the end, I had just taken three hours straight of criticism, and I couldn't take it anymore.
Skype
Jessica Abel
Search
Sigh.
Skype
Search
Maybe I shouldn't be saying any of this.
I feel...
I don't know. Uh...
I, it...the...
Jessica Abel
A lot of it gets so negative, and... afterwards...

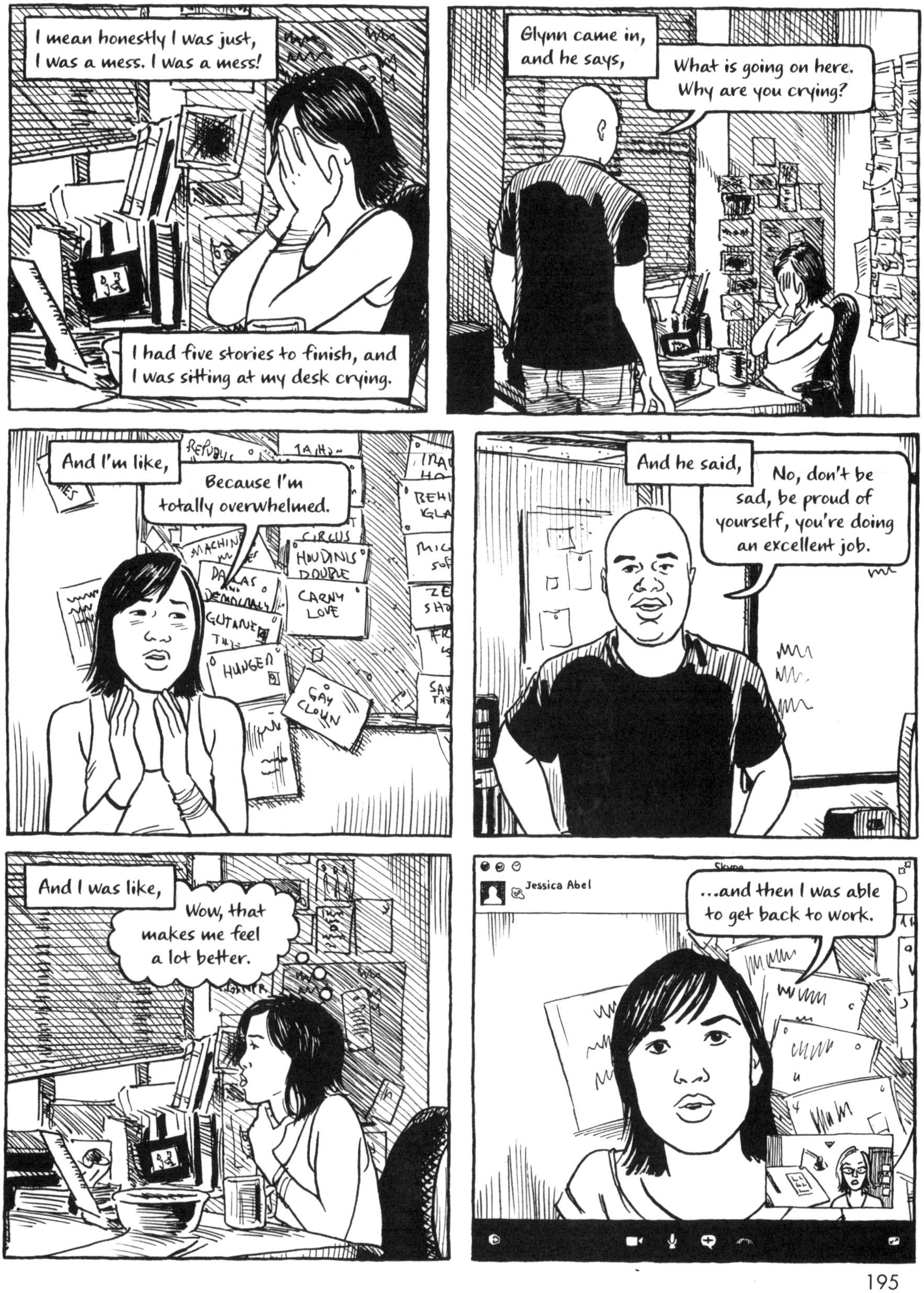

I mean honestly I was just, I was a mess. I was a mess!
I had five stories to finish, and I was sitting at my desk crying.
Glynn came in, and he says,
What is going on here. Why are you crying?
And I'm like,
Because I'm totally overwhelmed.
And he said,
No, don't be sad, be proud of yourself, you're doing an excellent job.
And I was like,
Wow, that makes me feel a lot better.
Jessica Abel
...and then I was able to get back to work.

WHAT THEY'RE SAYING IS, YOU FAILED.

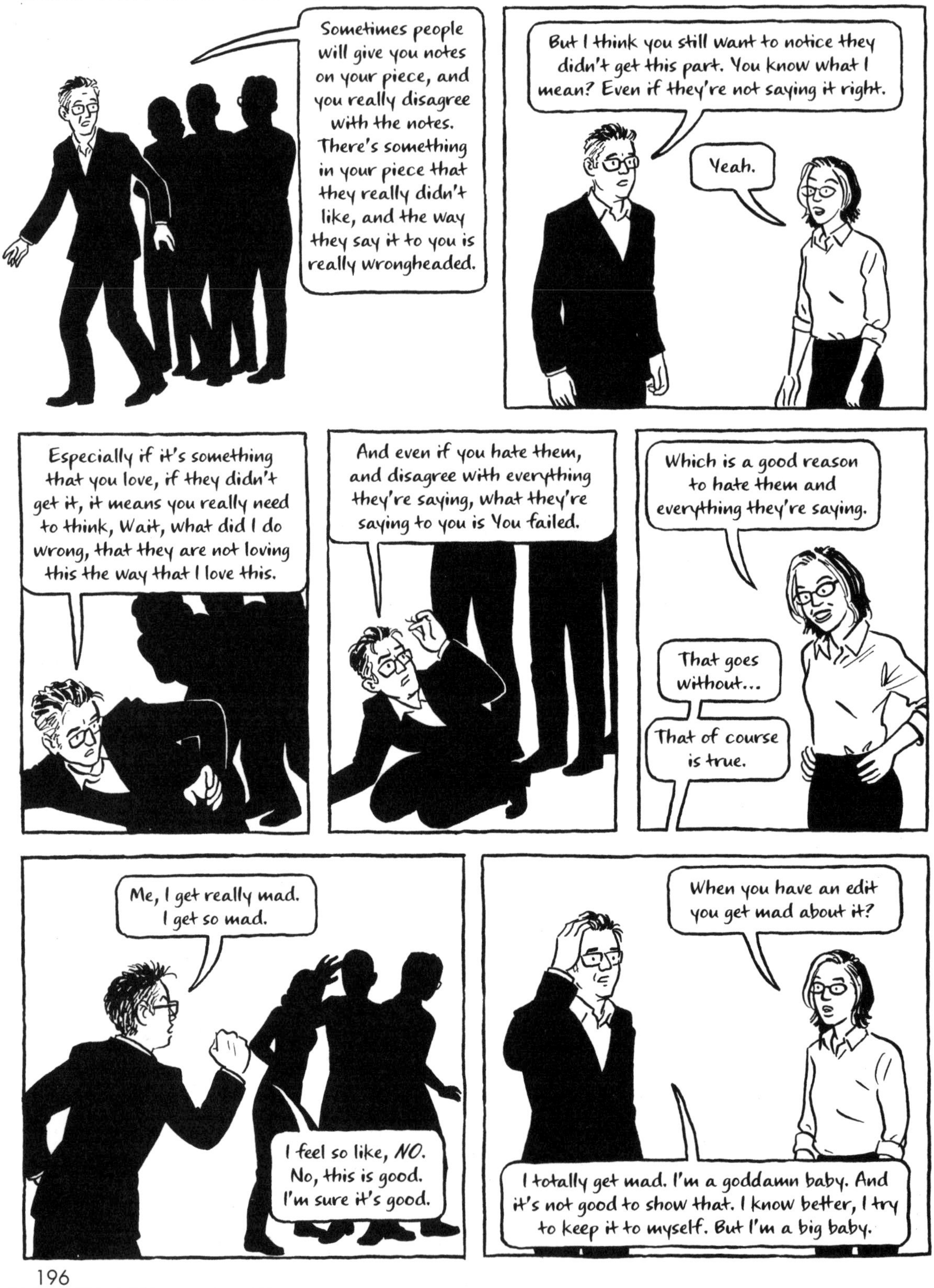

Sometimes people will give you notes on your piece, and you really disagree with the notes. There's something in your piece that they really didn't like, and the way they say it to you is really wrongheaded.
But I think you still want to notice they didn't get this part. You know what I mean? Even if they're not saying it right.
Yeah.
Especially if it's something that you love, if they didn't get it, it means you really need to think, Wait, what did I do wrong, that they are not loving this the way that I love this.
And even if you hate them, and disagree with everything they're saying, what they're saying to you is You failed.
Which is a good reason to hate them and everything they're saying.
That goes without...
That of course is true.
Me, I get really mad. I get so mad.
I feel so like, *NO.* No, this is good. I'm sure it's good.
When you have an edit you get mad about it?
I totally get mad. I'm a goddamn baby. And it's not good to show that. I know better, I try to keep it to myself. But I'm a big baby.

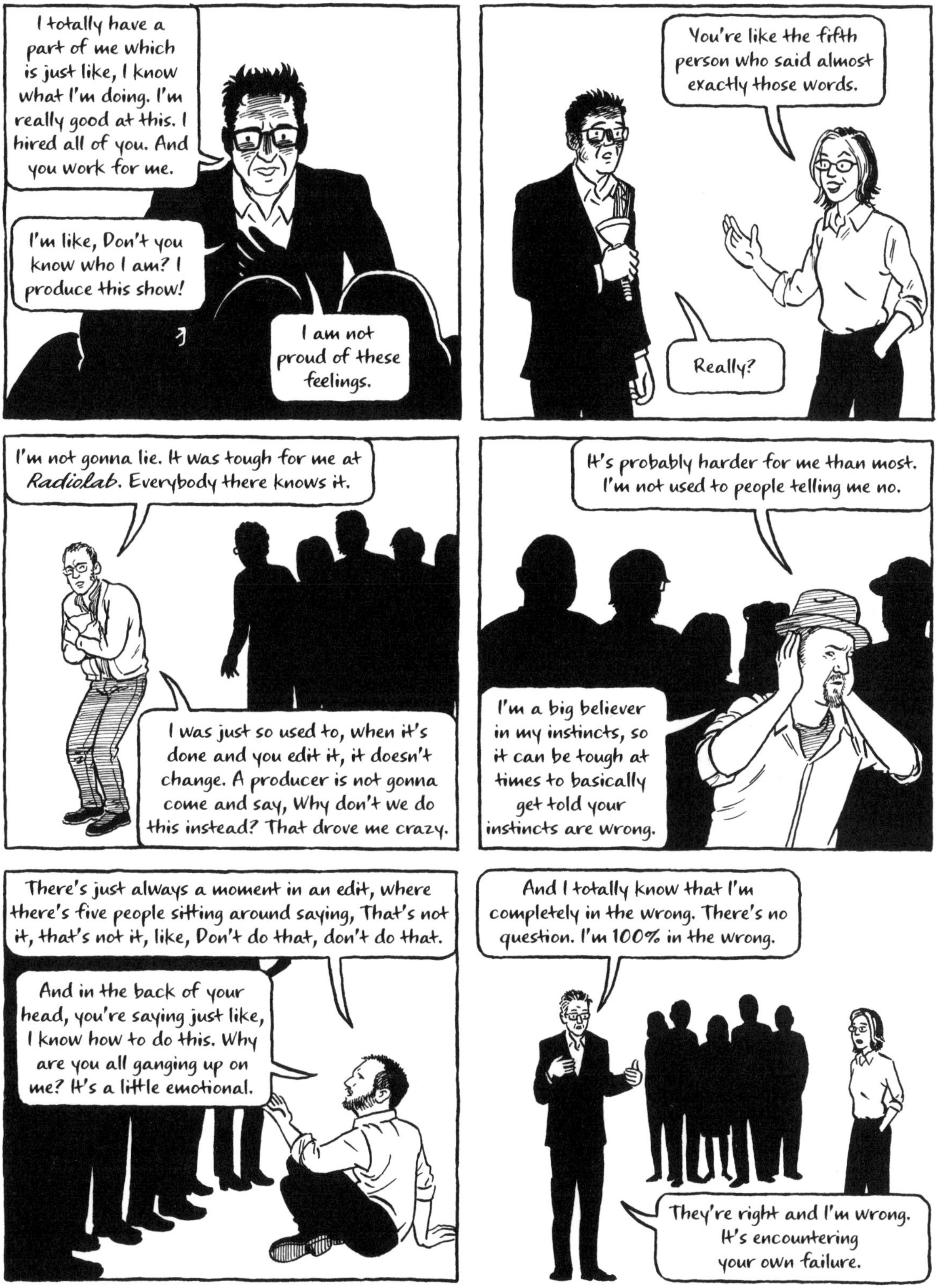
I totally have a part of me which is just like, I know what I'm doing. I'm really good at this. I hired all of you. And you work for me.
I'm like, Don't you know who I am? I produce this show!
I am not proud of these feelings.
You're like the fifth person who said almost exactly those words.
Really?
I'm not gonna lie. It was tough for me at *Radiolab*. Everybody there knows it.
I was just so used to, when it's done and you edit it, it doesn't change. A producer is not gonna come and say, Why don't we do this instead? That drove me crazy.
It's probably harder for me than most. I'm not used to people telling me no.
I'm a big believer in my instincts, so it can be tough at times to basically get told your instincts are wrong.
There's just always a moment in an edit, where there's five people sitting around saying, That's not it, that's not it, like, Don't do that, don't do that.
And in the back of your head, you're saying just like, I know how to do this. Why are you all ganging up on me? It's a little emotional.
And I totally know that I'm completely in the wrong. There's no question. I'm 100% in the wrong.
They're right and I'm wrong. It's encountering your own failure.

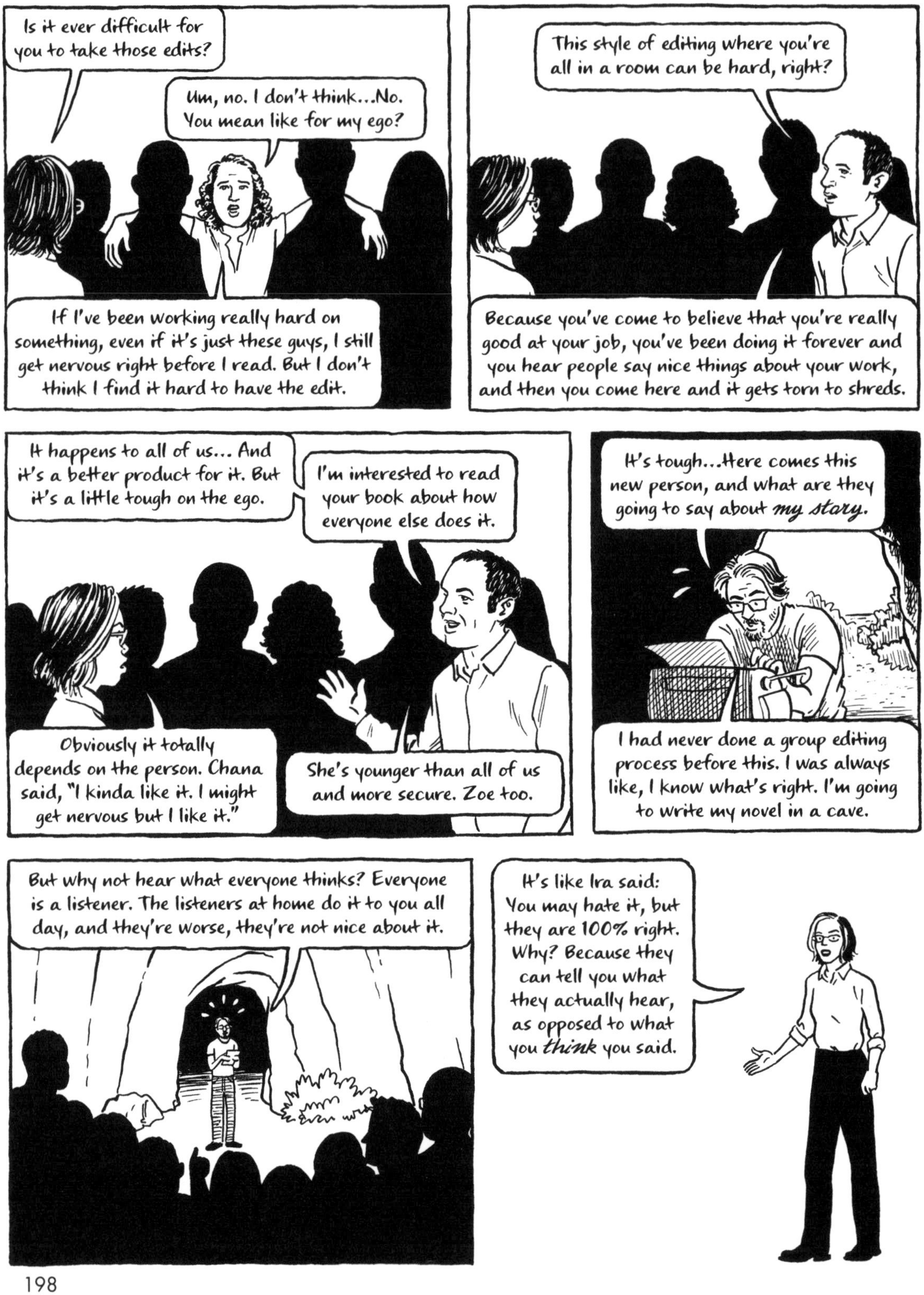
Is it ever difficult for you to take those edits?
Um, no. I don't think...No. You mean like for my ego?
If I've been working really hard on something, even if it's just these guys, I still get nervous right before I read. But I don't think I find it hard to have the edit.
This style of editing where you're all in a room can be hard, right?
Because you've come to believe that you're really good at your job, you've been doing it forever and you hear people say nice things about your work, and then you come here and it gets torn to shreds.
It happens to all of us... And it's a better product for it. But it's a little tough on the ego.
I'm interested to read your book about how everyone else does it.
Obviously it totally depends on the person. Chana said, "I kinda like it. I might get nervous but I like it."
She's younger than all of us and more secure. Zoe too.
It's tough...Here comes this new person, and what are they going to say about *my story*.
I had never done a group editing process before this. I was always like, I know what's right. I'm going to write my novel in a cave.
But why not hear what everyone thinks? Everyone is a listener. The listeners at home do it to you all day, and they're worse, they're not nice about it.
It's like Ira said: You may hate it, but they are 100% right. Why? Because they can tell you what they actually hear, as opposed to what you *think* you said.

GETTING LOST, AND GETTING FOUND

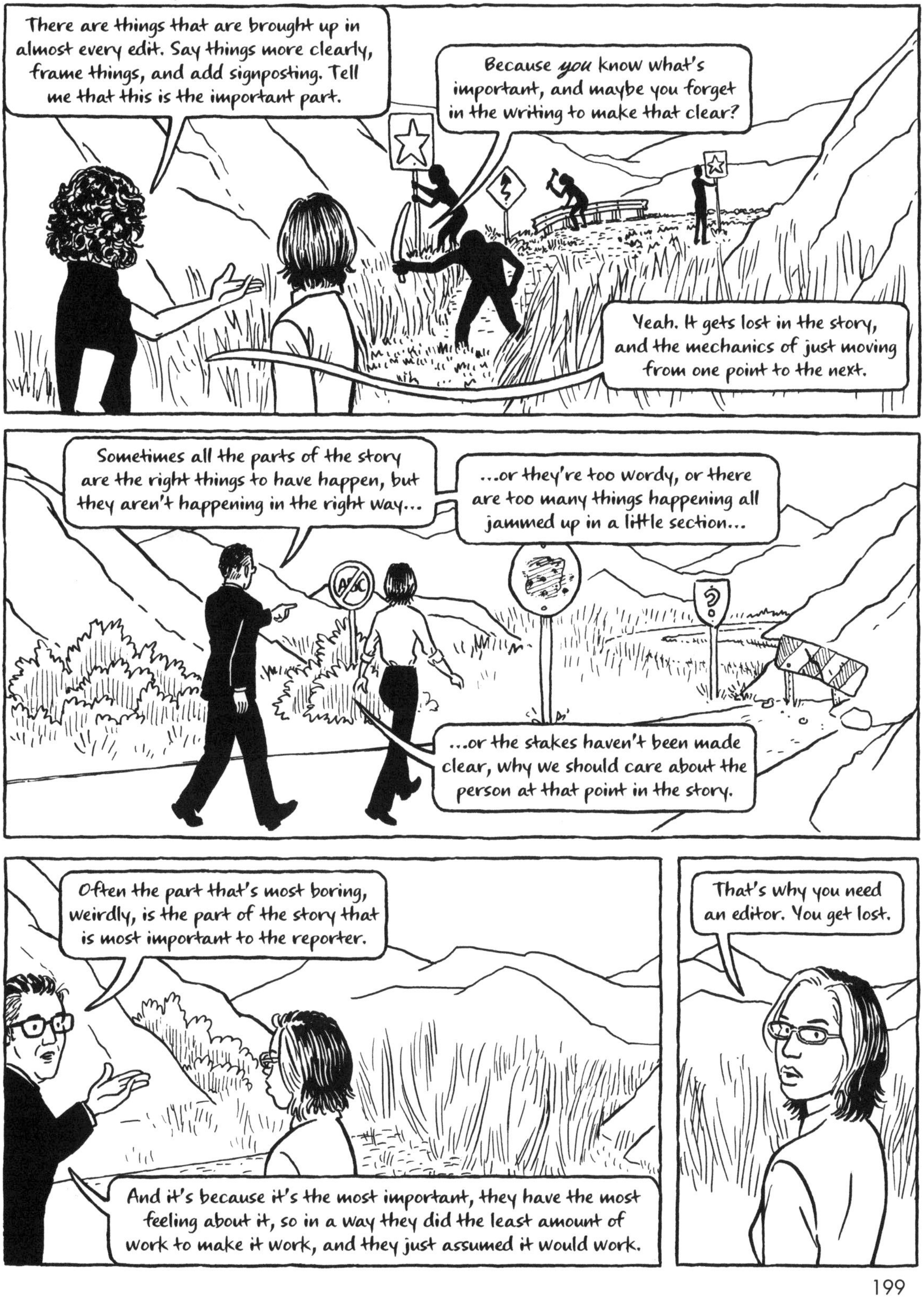

There are things that are brought up in almost every edit. Say things more clearly, frame things, and add signposting. Tell me that this is the important part.
Because *you* know what's important, and maybe you forget in the writing to make that clear?
Yeah. It gets lost in the story, and the mechanics of just moving from one point to the next.
Sometimes all the parts of the story are the right things to have happen, but they aren't happening in the right way...
...or they're too wordy, or there are too many things happening all jammed up in a little section...
...or the stakes haven't been made clear, why we should care about the person at that point in the story.
Often the part that's most boring, weirdly, is the part of the story that is most important to the reporter.
And it's because it's the most important, they have the most feeling about it, so in a way they did the least amount of work to make it work, and they just assumed it would work.
That's why you need an editor. You get lost.

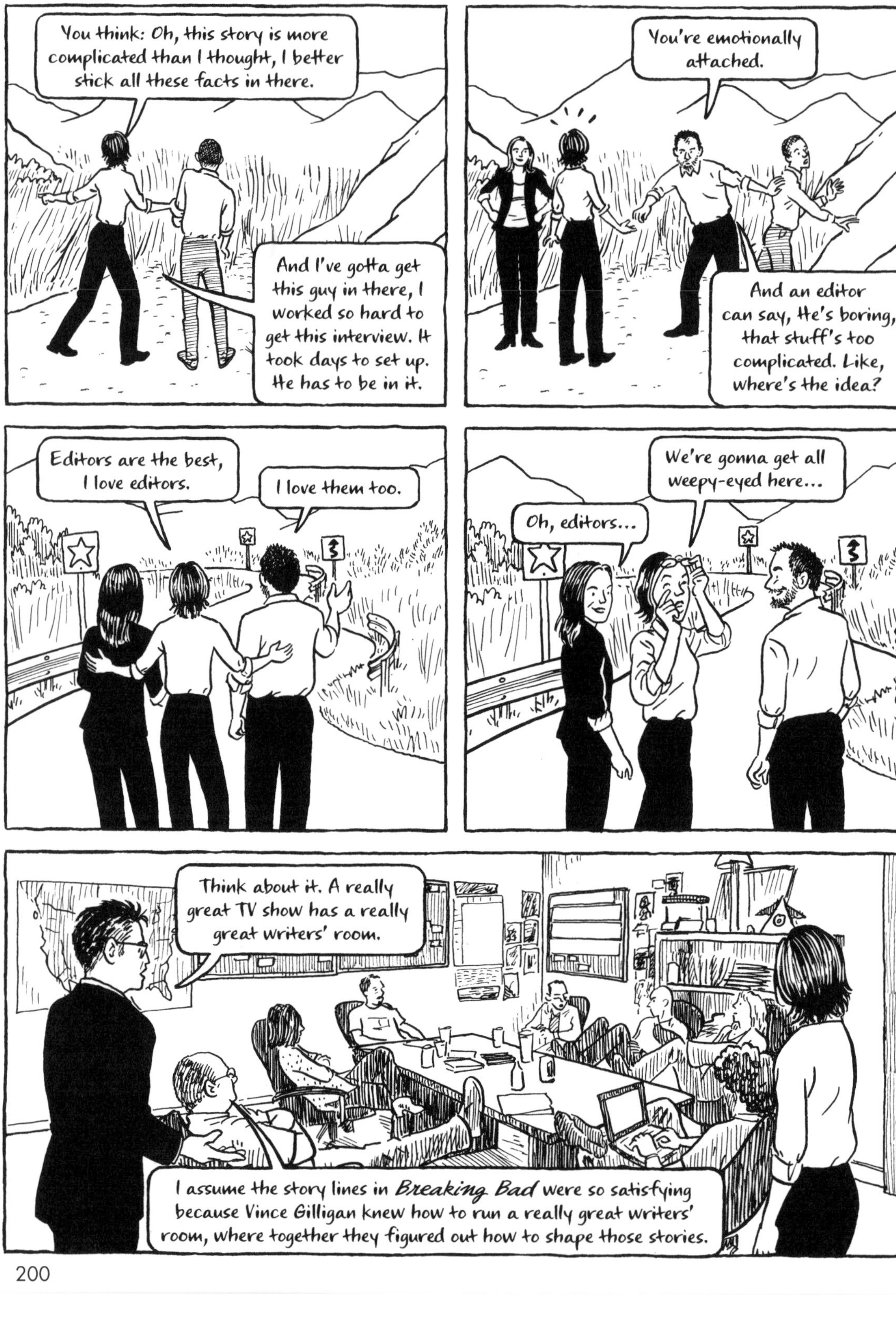
You think: Oh, this story is more complicated than I thought, I better stick all these facts in there.
And I've gotta get this guy in there, I worked so hard to get this interview. It took days to set up. He has to be in it.
You're emotionally attached.
And an editor can say, He's boring, that stuff's too complicated. Like, where's the idea?
Editors are the best, I love editors.
I love them too.
We're gonna get all weepy-eyed here...
Oh, editors...
Think about it. A really great TV show has a really great writers' room.
I assume the story lines in *Breaking Bad* were so satisfying because Vince Gilligan knew how to run a really great writers' room, where together they figured out how to shape those stories.

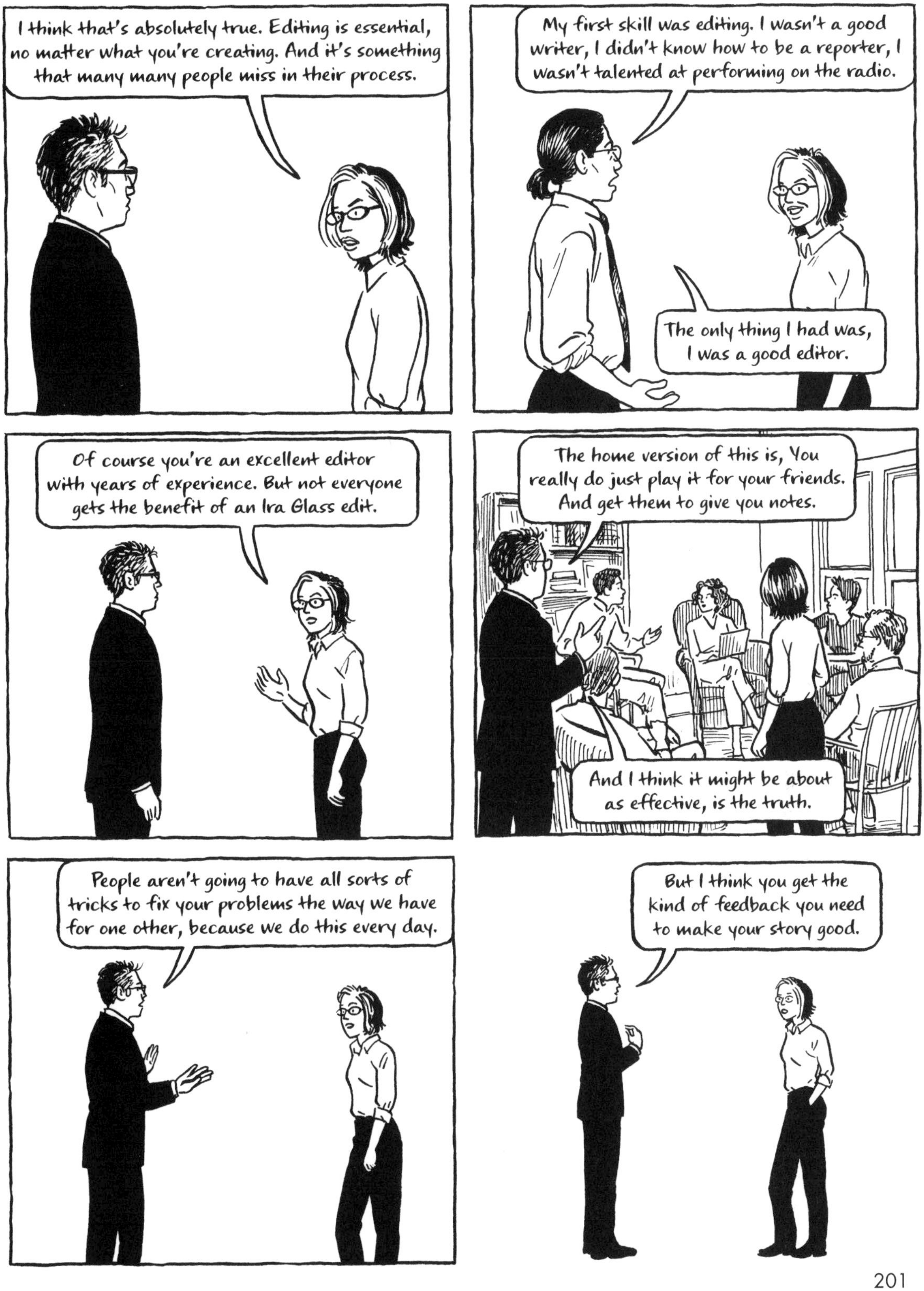
I think that's absolutely true. Editing is essential, no matter what you're creating. And it's something that many many people miss in their process.
My first skill was editing. I wasn't a good writer, I didn't know how to be a reporter, I wasn't talented at performing on the radio.
The only thing I had was, I was a good editor.
Of course you're an excellent editor with years of experience. But not everyone gets the benefit of an Ira Glass edit.
The home version of this is, You really do just play it for your friends. And get them to give you notes.
And I think it might be about as effective, is the truth.
People aren't going to have all sorts of tricks to fix your problems the way we have for one other, because we do this every day.
But I think you get the kind of feedback you need to make your story good.

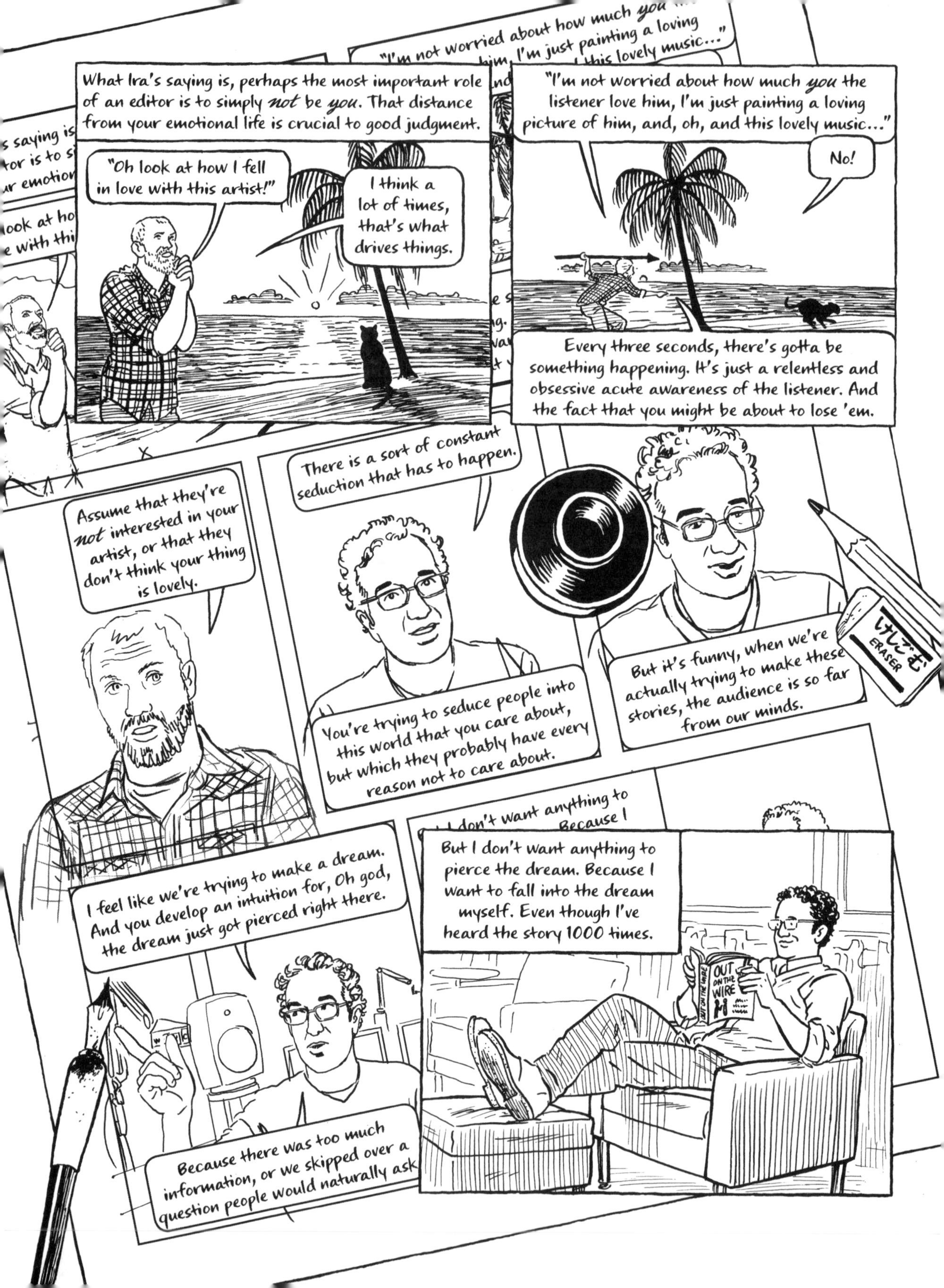
What Ira's saying is, perhaps the most important role of an editor is to simply *not* be *you*. That distance from your emotional life is crucial to good judgment.
"Oh look at how I fell in love with this artist!"
I think a lot of times, that's what drives things.
"I'm not worried about how much *you* the listener love him, I'm just painting a loving picture of him, and, oh, and this lovely music..."
No!
Every three seconds, there's gotta be something happening. It's just a relentless and obsessive acute awareness of the listener. And the fact that you might be about to lose 'em.
Assume that they're *not* interested in your artist, or that they don't think your thing is lovely.
There is a sort of constant seduction that has to happen.
You're trying to seduce people into this world that you care about, but which they probably have every reason not to care about.
But it's funny, when we're actually trying to make these stories, the audience is so far from our minds.
ERASER
I feel like we're trying to make a dream. And you develop an intuition for, Oh god, the dream just got pierced right there.
Because there was too much information, or we skipped over a question people would naturally ask
But I don't want anything to pierce the dream. Because I want to fall into the dream myself. Even though I've heard the story 1000 times.
OUT ON THE WIRE

Epilogue

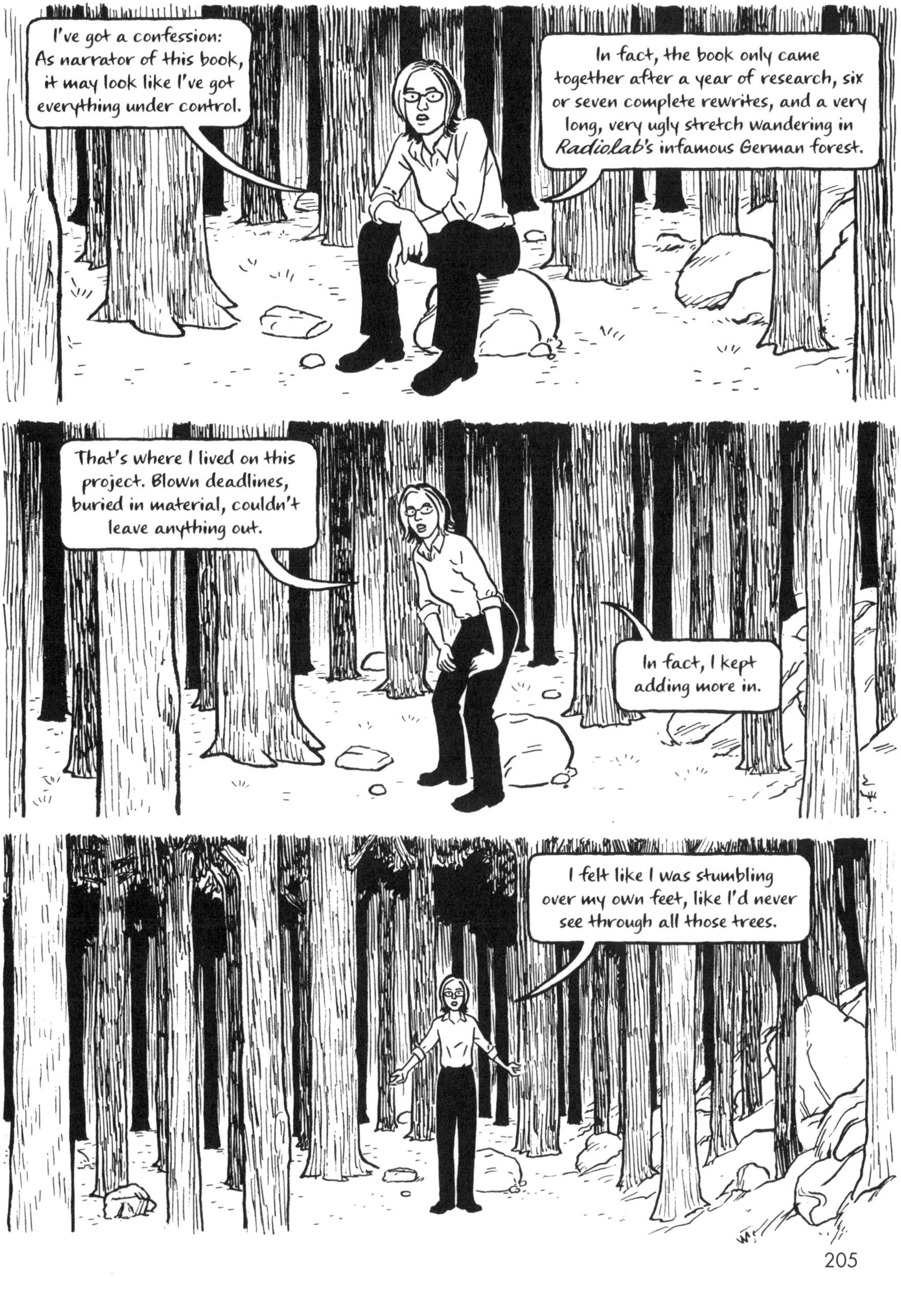
I've got a confession: As narrator of this book, it may look like I've got everything under control.
In fact, the book only came together after a year of research, six or seven complete rewrites, and a very long, very ugly stretch wandering in *Radiolab*'s infamous German forest.
That's where I lived on this project. Blown deadlines, buried in material, couldn't leave anything out.
In fact, I kept adding more in.
I felt like I was stumbling over my own feet, like I'd never see through all those trees.

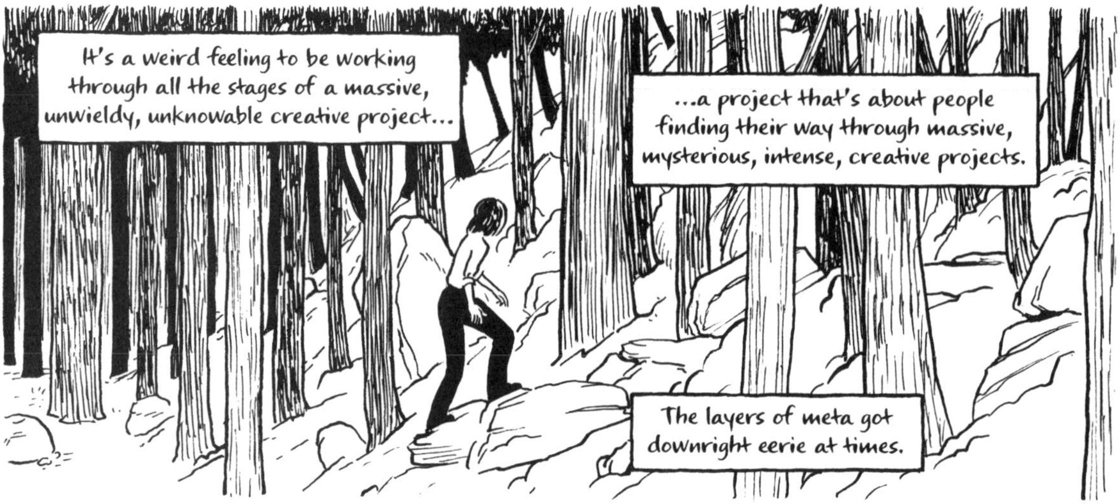
It's a weird feeling to be working through all the stages of a massive, unwieldy, unknowable creative project...
...a project that's about people finding their way through massive, mysterious, intense, creative projects.
The layers of meta got downright eerie at times.

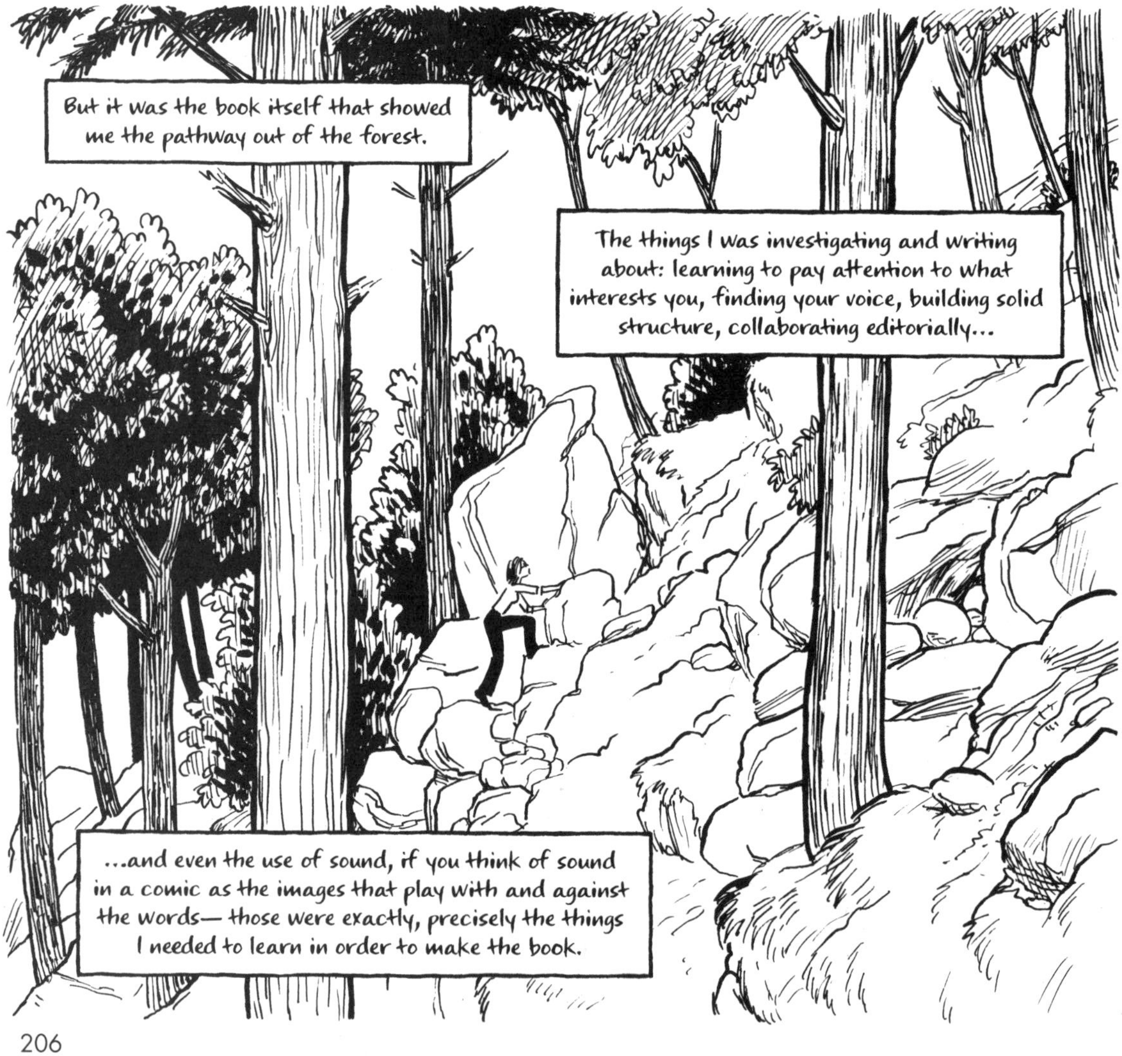
But it was the book itself that showed me the pathway out of the forest.
The things I was investigating and writing about: learning to pay attention to what interests you, finding your voice, building solid structure, collaborating editorially...
...and even the use of sound, if you think of sound in a comic as the images that play with and against the words— those were exactly, precisely the things I needed to learn in order to make the book.

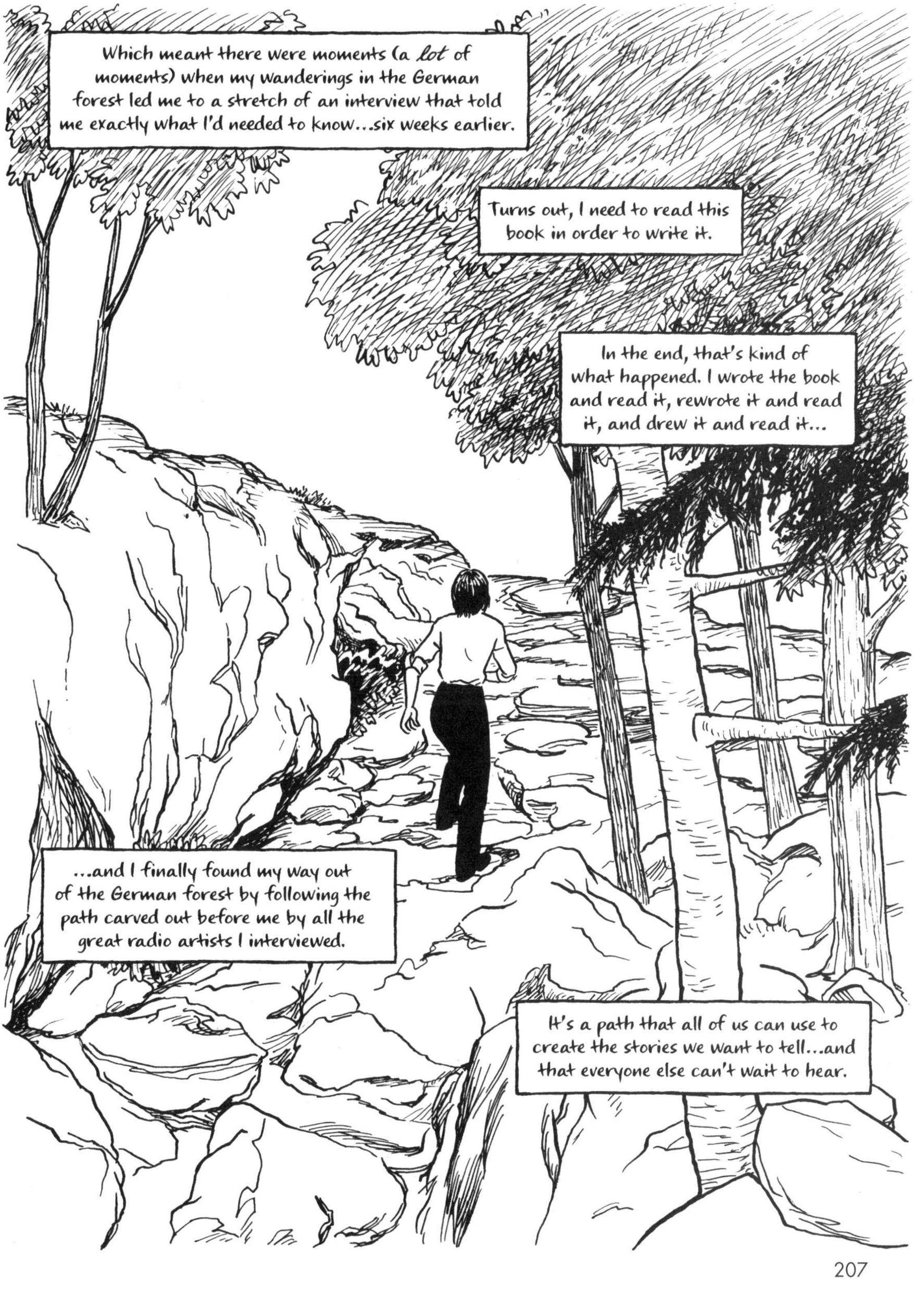
Which meant there were moments (a *lot* of moments) when my wanderings in the German forest led me to a stretch of an interview that told me exactly what I'd needed to know...six weeks earlier.
Turns out, I need to read this book in order to write it.
In the end, that's kind of what happened. I wrote the book and read it, rewrote it and read it, and drew it and read it...
...and I finally found my way out of the German forest by following the path carved out before me by all the great radio artists I interviewed.
It's a path that all of us can use to create the stories we want to tell...and that everyone else can't wait to hear.

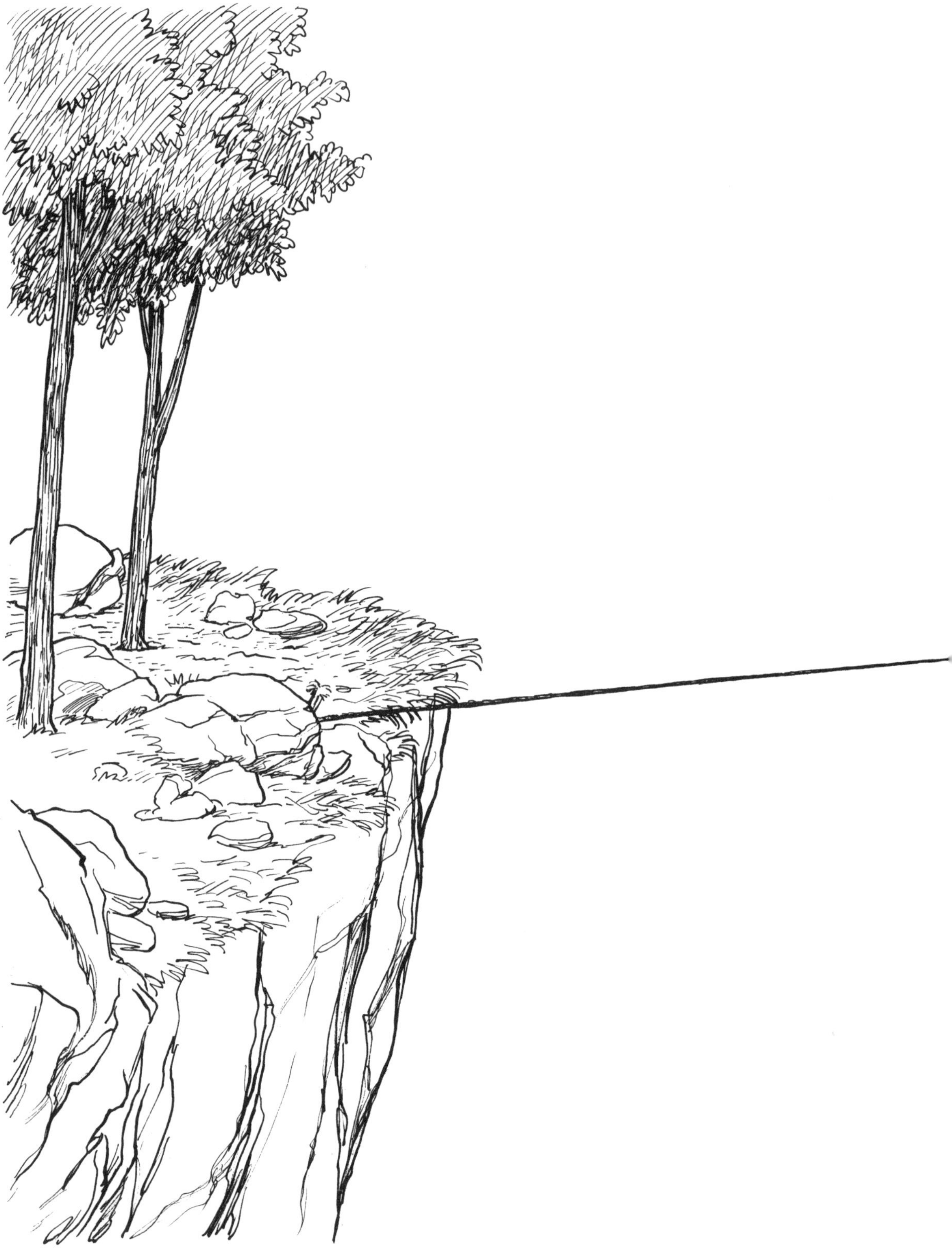

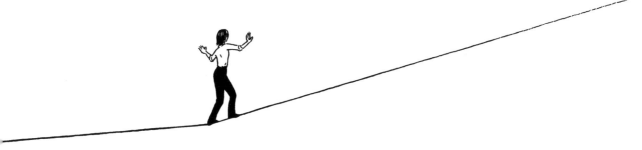

Notes

Except where noted below, quotes come from interviews I conducted or events I attended myself between February 2012 and June 2014. As will probably be obvious, locations for these interviews are often not as I depict them in this book—i.e., many interviews were over Skype, but I might show myself sitting in the same room with the person. Ira wore a snappy black suit on only one of the occasions we spoke, and that was just because some documentary film crew was in the office that day. Sometimes I depict someone in a historical "reenactment" or some other dramatization of what they're talking about. I had short hair in the summer of 2012, when I did many of these interviews. I take this artistic license for your sake, dear reader. Reading a comic that consists of people's faces on a Skype screen? Bo-ring.

About page numbers in the notes that follow: when you see something like this: 122:4, the first number is the page number and the number after the colon is the panel number. In other words, "page 24, panel 6" would read as 24:6.

PREFACE

1:1 *L'Atelier du son*, Thomas Baumgartner.
http://www.franceculture.fr/emission-l-atelier-du-son
This interview really did happen, but it was quite a bit longer. *L'Atelier du son*, May 7, 2013. http://www.franceculture.fr/emission-l-atelier-du-son-tomas-gubitsch-%20jessica-abel-2013-04-19
Radio France building referenced from a drawing by Stanislas in *Le Perroquet des Batignolles* vol. 1 (Paris, Dargaud, 2011).

2:3 In my studio at the Maison des Auteurs. I've been in residence here, as of this writing, for two years. It's a residency program for cartoonists and animators in Angoulême, France, and it's the reason I've been able to produce this book. My deep gratitude goes to the MdA, Pili Muñoz, and Brigitte Macias.
http://www.citebd.org/spip.php?article5209

4:1 Roman Mars and Sam Greenspan

4:2 Jad Abumrad

4:3 *Planet Money* made a T-shirt, and tracked the process from cotton seed to finished T-shirt. They funded this reporting with a wildly successful Kickstarter campaign.
http://www.kickstarter.com/projects/planetmoney/planet-money-t-shirt

Along with making radio and podcasts about it, they documented the process on Tumblr shown here.
http://seedtoshirt.tumblr.com/

4:4 Julia DeWitt

4:6 *Snap Judgment* at an edit

4:5 Radiotopia is a new collective of many of the best independent podcast producers, masterminded by Roman Mars of *99% Invisible* (see the Show Guide, page 223), and run by independent network PRX (http://www.prx.org/). Their first Kickstarter campaign, from which this screenshot was taken a week before it ended, was extremely successful, allowing them to invite three new podcasts to join their group, among other goals.
http://www.kickstarter.com/projects/1748303376/radiotopia-a-storytelling -revolution?ref=discovery

5.1 Sean Cole

5:5 Spices restaurant, 369 12th Street, Oakland, California. Snap treated me and the staff to the famous "Gangsta Casserole 'Murder Style.'"
http://www.spices3oakland.com
I also ate amazing dim sum and delicious Afghan food on the Snap dollar. It made it very difficult to concentrate on writing this book while I was transcribing that tape.

6:3 Justin Green, the author of *Binky Brown Meets the Holy Virgin Mary*, at the Comics: Philosophy and Practice Conference at the University of Chicago said, "The dirty little secret of comics writing is copy fitting. Maybe you need an arm holding a broken bottle in that space, so you axe an adverb."

6:5 Yes, you can still get *Radio: An Illustrated Guide*, for like five dollars. A big hunk of it follows, but there are about six pages of material in there that did not make it into this book.
http://store.thisamericanlife.org/ProductDetails.asp?ProductCode=RADIO%3 AANILLUSTRATEDGUIDE

7 And then 12 hours later . . .
Matt Madden, *99 Ways to Tell a Story: Exercises in Style* (New York: Chamberlain Bros., 2005).

8:5 The "journalistic comic" is called "Punk Pilgrimage," and ran in *NewCity* in 1995. Ira called me to propose doing *Radio: An Illustrated Guide* in 1998. I've posted the comic that inspired Ira to call me on my site.
http://jessicaabel.com/2014/12/03/punk-pilgrimage-fireside-bowl/

8:6 There are lots of researched nonfiction comics out there, lots more than there used to be. But it remains an underutilized form.

10:3 Those two textbooks:
Jessica Abel and Matt Madden, *Drawing Words & Writing Pictures* (New York: First Second Books, 2008).

Jessica Abel and Matt Madden, *Mastering Comics* (New York: First Second Books, 2012).

13–38 Excerpt from Jessica Abel and Ira Glass, *Radio: An Illustrated Guide* (Chicago: WBEZ Alliance, Inc., and Artbabe Army Publishing, 1999). The radio episode under consideration in this section is "Do-Gooders," *This American Life*, #126, April 9, 1999.
http://www.thisamericanlife.org/radio-archives/episode/126/do-gooders

19 You can find an archive of stories like this one at Brett Leveridge's website: www.brettnews.com. He also writes at Salon.com, among other places.

22 Philip Gourevitch, *We Wish to Inform You that Tomorrow We Will Be Killed with Our Families: Stories from Rwanda.* (New York: Farrar, Straus and Giroux, 1998).

39–41 Just to make sure this is perfectly clear: The people pictured in pages 39–41 are those that I've interviewed or mentioned by name in this book. They are not **by any means** all who are involved in producing the shows I name there. They're also not all still at the same shows since I interviewed them. Please see Show Guide, page 222, for further details.

AMUSE YOURSELF: IDEAS

48:4 Ira Glass commencement address to the CUNY Graduate School of Journalism, December 13, 2012.
http://vimeo.com/55563744

49:1 Alex Blumberg, Adam Davidson, Ira Glass, "The Giant Pool of Money," *This American Life*, #355, May 9, 2008.
http://www.thisamericanlife.org/radio-archives/episode/355/the-giant-pool-of
-money
Thanks to Clarence Nathan for pictures of himself. He reports, "I eventually lost the property through short sale and have relocated to Durham, NC."
He also said, "I thought about that statement and it was one of my more colorful ones. I feel it served the moment almost perfectly."

49:4 Calculated Risk.
http://www.calculatedriskblog.com

49:5-6 Background referenced from a photo by Shawn Hoke.

50:5 Referenced from a photo by Seth Wenig/AP Photo.

50:8 Background referenced from a photo by Flickr user mlouispink.

52:3 Tod Maffin, *From Idea to Air* (self-published ebook, http://todmaffin.com/shop/ideatoair).

53:1 The story the Workshop had under discussion was Jessica Kittams's "About One Acre." There used to be lots of funny quotes from the class about oxen and Mar-

tha's Vineyard in an earlier draft of this book, which was about eight times as long. Argh, comics.
http://transom.org/workshop/story-workshop/story-workshop-alumni/jessica-kittams-about-one-acre/

56–59 The idea of the XY Story Formula is delineated in Alex Blumberg's 2006 Transom manifesto. His lines on these pages are direct quotes from there.
Alex Blumberg, "Alex Blumberg's Manifesto," *The Transom Review*, volume 5/issue 2, September 1, 2005.
http://transom.org/?p=7003

57 David Kestenbaum picked up on Alex's formula and talked about it in the online comments in response to his own *Transom* article, quoted here.
David Kestenbaum, "The 4:30 FAQ," *The Transom Review*, volume 6/issue 2, April 24, 2006.
http://transom.org/2006/david-kestenbaum-430-faq-2/

57:3 David Kestenbaum, "E-Mail Encryption Rare in Everyday Use," NPR News, February 22, 2006.
http://www.npr.org/templates/story/story.php?storyId=5227744

59:3 Referenced from a photo found on Fotosearch.

59:4 Referenced from a photo by lewkmiller.

62 Robert Smith, "Does New York City Need More Taxis?" *Planet Money*, July 31, 2012.
http://www.npr.org/blogs/money/2012/07/31/157477611/does-new-york-city-need-more-taxis

63–64 This is a re-creation of Ira's discussion with Mike Shuster, based on Ira's recollection (and historical photos from NPR—thanks, Emerson Brown!).

65 "What Kind of Country," *This American Life*, #459, March 2, 2012.
http://www.thisamericanlife.org/radio-archives/episode/459/what-kind-of-country

65:2 Referenced from a photo by Alamy.

66:4–6, 67:1 Although the majority of Jay's dialogue is from my interview with him, these panels are quotes from a comment he made on Alex Blumberg's Transom manifesto (see note to pages 56–59), May 15, 2005, comment #30. The "interviewees" in 68:3 are fictional.

67:4, 68:1 Ira is talking about "129 Cars," *This American Life*, #513, December 13, 2013.
http://www.thisamericanlife.org/radio-archives/episode/513/129-cars

67:3 Referenced from a photo by Paul Sancya /AP.

67:4 (AND 68:1) Referenced from a photo by Jeff Minton.

69 Alex Blumberg was not in the room when I interviewed Chana, and to my knowledge has no interest in enforcing his XY rubric. It was just funnier if he said it than if I did.

70–72 "Trends with Benefits," *This American Life*, #490, March 22, 2013.
http://www.thisamericanlife.org/radio-archives/episode/490/trends-with
-benefits?act=1
Also see Chana Joffe-Walt's related article "Unfit for Work: The Startling Rise of
Disability in America."
http://apps.npr.org/unfit-for-work/

70:1 Referenced from a photo by Matthew Christopher Murray.

71:2–4 These are direct quotes from the story.

73–74 Reader, she married him. Thanks to Cynthia for photos of the cryptogrammic
mash notes, her postmistress, and herself and Howie at their wedding. 73:3, 5, 6,
and 74:1, 3, 4, 6 are direct quotes from the story.
Cynthia Riggs, "The Case of the Curious Codes," *The Moth*. Directed by Sarah
Austin Jenness. Recorded at a Moth Mainstage event at Union Chapel in Oak
Bluffs on Martha's Vineyard, August 13, 2012. Appeared first on *The Moth Radio
Hour* on February 5, 2013, and then on *The Moth Podcast* on July 16, 2013.
http://themoth.org/posts/storytellers/cynthia-riggs
This story was also reprinted in *The Moth: 50 True Stories*, Catherine Burns, editor
(New York: Hyperion, 2013), 252–57.

75–76 "What's Up, Doc?" with Sean Cole, *Radiolab*, November 6, 2012.
http://www.radiolab.org/story/248590-blanc/

THE HEAT OF THEIR BREATH: CHARACTER AND VOICE

79:1 I picture my self backstage at a simplified version of The Players in New York,
where The Moth holds many of its Mainstage events. I have never been backstage at The Players, nor front-stage, for that matter.
http://en.wikipedia.org/wiki/The_Players_(New_York_City)

80:4 Referenced from a photo by Rebecca Davis.

83–84 Jad plays a YouTube video that is an adaptation of a 2012 presidential campaign
speech by Ron Paul, read by an actor and with flashy graphics. Images at 83:6
and 84:1 are from this adaptation:
"Imagine," posted by WRB Ministries.
https://www.youtube.com/watch?v=uhxBM8ebECo

85:3,4 Referenced from a photo taken by Melikhaya Mpumela.
Joe is obliquely referring to his work in South Africa; in particular, "Thembi's
AIDS Diary." The image is of Thembi Ngubane, who died in 2009.
Thembi Ngubane and Joe Richman, "Thembi's AIDS Diary," *Radio Diaries*, 2006.
http://www.radiodiaries.org/thembis-aids-diary/
More information about this story appears on Thembi's AIDS Diary website:
http://www.aidsdiary.org/

87:1–2 Alex Blumberg's quote is from a comment on his Transom manifesto. See note to
pages 56, 58, 59.

88:4   Jad is referring to "Speed" ("Million Dollar Microsecond," with David Kestenbaum), *Radiolab*, February 5, 2013.
http://www.radiolab.org/story/267195-million-dollar-microsecond/

89:2   Johann Kraus © Mike Mignola. It's "ectoplasm" actually, not smoke. I've used the film version of the character, not the comics one, since Jad talks about the film.
http://en.wikipedia.org/wiki/Johann_Kraus

90:5–92:3   These are quotes from a talk that Jad Abumrad and Robert Krulwich gave at Oberlin College on March 6, 2008, which they recorded and distributed as a *Radiolab* podcast. They spoke in Finney Chapel.
Jad Abumrad and Robert Krulwich, "Jad and Robert: The Early Years," *Radiolab*, May 6, 2008.
http://www.radiolab.org/story/91820-jad-and-robert-the-early-years/

91:3   Referenced from a photo by Zenith Richards.

92:3–94   These are quotes from a talk Jad gave at the Third Coast International Audio Festival in 2005.
Jad Abumrad, "Music: A Force for Good (and Sometimes Evil)."
http://www.thirdcoastfestival.org/library/450-music-a-force-for-good-and-sometimes-evil
Photo reference for Jad in this sequence by the Third Coast International Audio Festival and Jared and Corin, Wikimedia Commons.

92–94   The story Jad discusses is from "There Is No Lord of the (Fire)Flies," *Radiolab*, February 18, 2005.
http://www.radiolab.org/story/91501-there-is-no-lord-of-the-fireflies/

93:4-5   Referenced from a photo by Chi Phat Ecotourism Adventures.

95:4   Robert and Zoe are referring to a series of stories they did in Europe, including a story on Barilla Pasta (that's what's pictured in panel 3, referenced from a photo by Barilla Pasta).
Robert Smith and Zoe Chace, "How a Pasta Factory Got People to Show Up for Work," *Planet Money*, August 10, 2012.
http://www.npr.org/blogs/money/2012/08/10/158565443/how-a-pasta-factory-got-people-to-show-up-for-work

96:1–97:3   "Razzle Dazzle"; producer: Jamie DeWolf; sound design: Renzo Gorrio, *Snap Judgment*, #316, July 13, 2012.
http://snapjudgment.org/circus-circus

98:3–100   "Rocky," by Julia DeWitt, *Snap Judgment*, #316, July 13, 2012.
http://snapjudgment.org/circus-circus

101:5   Referenced from a film still of Kenneth Branagh as Hamlet.

103:4   This quote is from Roman Mars, "The Feltron Annual Report," *99% Invisible*, #31, July 14, 2011.

http://99percentinvisible.org/episode/episode-31-the-feltron-annual
-report/

104:1   A quick visual quote from the excellent book: Brooke Gladstone and Josh Neufeld, *The Influencing Machine: Brooke Gladstone on the Media* (New York: W. W. Norton & Company, 2011).

106   The Kitchen Sisters: Nikki Silva and Davia Nelson.

I actually met Nikki and her family at Jay Allison's house on almost the first day I was reporting this book. I was so nervous to get started, and had so little idea what I was doing, that I didn't even try to interview her. Totally whiffed that one.
http://www.kitchensisters.org/

106:1   Referenced from a photo by Weluvradio, Wikimedia Commons.

KEEP OR KILL: STORY STRUCTURE

110–11   Faye Lane, "Fireworks from Above," *The Moth*. Recorded at a Moth Mainstage event at Arlene Schnitzer Concert Hall in Portland, Oregon, February 17, 2011. Directed by Catherine Burns. Appeared first on *The Moth Radio Hour* on November 18, 2012, and was on *The Moth Podcast* on February 4, 2013. 110:1, 3, 4, and 111:2–5 are direct quotes from the story.
http://themoth.org/posts/stories/fireworks-from-above
This story was also reprinted in *The Moth: 50 True Stories,* Catherine Burns, editor (New York: Hyperion, 2013), 385–91.

112:4   This refers to the writing section in *Radio: An Illustrated Guide* on page 29.

115–16   Joe Richman, Sue Johnson, and Samara Freemark, "Teen Contender," *Radio Diaries*, 2012.
http://www.radiodiaries.org/teen-contender/

115:2, 3, 5 AND 112:1   Referenced from photos by Ryan Garza.

115:4   Referenced from a photo by Sue Jaye Johnson.

117–18   The story under discussion is Lauren Ober's "Hunger Pains," *Transom Story Workshop*. 117:3 and 118:2, 3, 5 contain direct quotes from this story.
http://transom.org/workshop/story-workshop/story-workshop-alumni/
lauren-ober-hunger-pains/
Thanks to Lauren for the use of her photos from reporting the story.

119:2   Referenced from a photo by Mel Evans, AP.

119:4–6   David Kestenbaum and Jacob Goldstein, "The Friday Podcast: Gold!" *Planet Money*, October 15, 2010. 119:4, 5 contain direct quotes from this story.
http://www.npr.org/blogs/money/2011/02/07/130597201/the-friday
-podcast-gold

119:5   Referenced from an image by Peter Foley, Bloomberg, Getty Images.

120:1,2 Caitlin Kenney, "Keeping the Biggest Secret in the U.S. Economy," *Planet Money*, August 3, 2012.
http://www.npr.org/blogs/money/2012/08/03/157859194/keeping-the-biggest-secret-in-the-u-s-economy

120:5 United States Department of the Army, Psychological Operations (Department of Defense: Department of the Army, Headquarters, 1979).
http://books.google.com/books?id=O3rN-FbaNzcC&dq

122:1–3 These are quotes from Jad Abumrad, "Radio That's Close to Filmmaking," CNN's *The Next List*, May 9, 2012.
http://whatsnext.blogs.cnn.com/2012/05/09/jad-abumrad-radio-thats-close-to-filmmaking/

122:5–7 AND Quotes (visually and verbally) from David Fine, director, "American Hip-
123:1, 2, 5–7 ster Presents" *Radiolab*, #50, March 18, 2013.
http://americanhipsterpresents.com./#radiolab
The story Jad, Robert, and Soren are working on is "Inheritance," *Radiolab*, season 11, episode 2.
http://www.radiolab.org/story/251876-inheritance/

126 Sean is talking about his story, with Roman Mars, "Some Other Sign that People Do Not Totally Regret Life," *99% Invisible*, #59, July 25, 2012.
http://99percentinvisible.org/episode/episode-59-some-other-sign-that-people-do-not-totally/
Read the plaque, people!

126:7–127 Andy Christie, "The Ghost of Christmas Presents," *The Moth*. Andy told the version of the story that Catherine is referring to at a StorySLAM at the Bitter End with the theme "Gifts" on 12/29/2008. Later, a revised version was recorded at a Moth Mainstage show in New York City at The Players on April 15, 2010. It has not appeared on the radio hour but was on *The Moth Podcast* on December 24, 2013.
http://themoth.org/posts/stories/the-ghost-of-christmas-presents

127:2 Referenced from a photo by Erik Neumann and Carly Nairn.

127:4 Referenced from a photo by Librado Romero, *New York Times*.

127:6 Gustave Doré, illustration, *The Divine Comedy: Inferno*, Canto 21.

128:2 Referenced from a photo by Jikesh Kannan.

134:3–5 This is a quote from a comment Robert Krulwich made on his own Transom manifesto.
Robert Krulwich, "WHY I LOVE RADIO (and TV)," *The Transom Review*, volume 2/issue 9, November 1, 2002. Comment by Robert Krulwich: "Blocks, Triangles and the Mystery of Improvisation," #48, September 23, 2002.
http://transom.org/2002/robert-krulwich-why-love-radio/

134:4 The Talk of the Town interview with Martin Scorcese is in the November 27, 1995, issue of *The New Yorker*.

135:1 Referenced from a photo by Cristina Potters.

136–137 I take a scary walk with Zoe Chace and Robert Smith on these two pages.

138 Jay Allison is getting lost in the woods on this page.

139, 143 These are quotes from Jad Abumrad's 2012 keynote speech at the Third Coast International Audio Festival.
Jad Abumrad, "These Are a Few of My Favorite Things," October 7, 2012.
http://www.thirdcoastfestival.org/library/1227-these-are-a-few-of-my-favorite-things
The Wagner story he references is Jad Abumrad, "The Ring and I: The Passion, the Myth, the Mania," WNYC, March 2004.
http://www.wnyc.org/story/71011-the-ring-and-i-the-passion-the-myth-the-mania/

142 I stand on the cliff with Jad Abumrad and Kierkegaard, and then I base-jump with Jacob Goldstein of *Planet Money*.
Jad is referring to Søren Kierkegaard, *The Concept of Anxiety: A Simple Psychologically Orienting Deliberation on the Dogmatic Issue of Hereditary Sin*.

143 Jad leads me out of the woods.

139:1 Referenced from a photo by Kate Joyce Studios.

142:1 AND 3 These are quotes from Jad Abumrad's speech at the 2011 PRPD Conference (Public Radio Program Directors' Association). The audio can be found here:
http://www.prpd.org/conference/conference_past/2011_confaudiogen.aspx.
Jad also wrote a version of the speech as a Transom Manifesto, "The Terrors & Occasional Virtues of Not Knowing What You're Doing," July 26, 2012.
http://transom.org/2012/jad-abumrad-terrors-and-virtues/

143:3 Referenced from a painting by Ivan Shishkin.

THE DEEP SEA: SOUND

Throughout this chapter, I'm quoting lines from "Night at the Rock Bar," producer: Mark Ristich; sound design: Pat Mesiti-Miller *Snap Judgment*, #230, December 7, 2011.
http://snapjudgment.org/night-rock-bar
http://snapjudgment.org/fight-of-your-life

The songs Pat used in this story are:
"Statistica" (statistics) by Hadag Nahash
Album: *Hadag Nahash* on Hed Arzi Music
"Tubthumping" by Chumbawamba
Album: *Tubthumper* on Universal Records

"Equator" by Zero Cult
Album: *Vacuum* on Cosmiclead Records
"Grass" by Animal Collective
Album: *Grass* on FatCat Records
"The Product" (Instrumental) by Freeway & Jake One
Album: *The Stimulus Package* on Rhymesayers Entertainment

149:4 Referenced from a photo by Thomas Prouteau and Polina Fomina.

154:4 Referenced from a photo by Delbridge Langdon Jr.

155–58 "Out of Body, Roger," by Ann Heppermann and Kara Oehler, *Radiolab*, season 2, episode 4.
http://www.radiolab.org/story/91527-out-of-body-roger/
Images of the centrifuge at the Johnsville Naval Air Development Center (NADC) referenced from archival photos of NASA tests. Thanks to Timothy Sestak for helping me track these down. And thanks to Ann Heppermann for helping me get in touch with Timothy Sestak.

164:5 I like a man who casually tosses multiple references to comic books into his interviews.

YOUR BABY'S UGLY: THE EDIT

169–70 Chana's first story for *Planet Money* was, in fact, supposed to be the first *Planet Money* story ever. Which explains why there were so, so many people on the phone. Everyone was excited about this cool new project. As it happened, however, the global economy fell apart three days before the piece was supposed to go live on September 8, 2008, so, you know, they pushed it back until that November.
Chana Joffe-Walt, "How 6 Parts Nearly Delayed World's Biggest Airliner," *Planet Money*, November 1, 2008.
http://www.npr.org/templates/story/story.php?storyId=96378999

173:3 For a complete rundown of all the pieces on "Coming to America," see the Show Guide on page 222.
"Gas Tank Crossing"; producer: Stephanie Foo; sound design: Pat Mesiti-Miller, *Snap Judgment*, #315, June 29, 2012.
http://snapjudgment.org/gas-tank-crossing

173:4 Stephanie Foo and Mark Ristich, "Learning to Speak," *Snap Judgment*, #315, June 29, 2012.
http://snapjudgment.org/learning-speak

173:5–179 Stephanie Foo, "Texas vs. Texas," *Snap Judgment,* #315, June 29, 2012.
http://snapjudgment.org/texas-vs-texas
Thanks to Stephanie for sending me her photos from her interview with Joe Rowe.

The panels that run down the center of these pages are direct quotes from the rough cut of the story (this is not the version that ran on the air). Stephanie played the story first (as shown in 173:5) and then the group discussed it. The discussion is shown alongside quotes from the story for clarity, but in reality, they are using notes and their memory of the story to discuss it, and occasionally replaying short clips.

187   Jad and Soren are referring to the same story we saw them working on in Chapter 3, pages 122–23: "Inheritance," *Radiolab*, season 11, episode 2. http://www.radiolab.org/story/251876-inheritance/

188:5–6, 190:2–4   "Learning to Speak." See note to 173:4.

191:5–6, 192, 193   "Gas Tank Crossing." See note to 173:3.

Show Guide

99% INVISIBLE   http://99percentinvisible.org/

99% Invisible is a weekly podcast about design. At least, now it's weekly. When I spoke to Roman Mars, in July 2012, it was just before his first Kickstarter campaign, when he started ramping up staffing and frequency. At the time, he worked alone, with the long-distance assistance of one part-time staffer, Sam Greenspan. Since that time, Roman has become justifiably famous for his success in building an intensely loyal and generous fan base, and connecting to them directly for financial support. In his interview, Sean Cole talked about several stories he's made for the show, where he is a regular contributor.

Roman was also one of the earliest staff members of *Snap Judgment*, hired to help Mark and Glynn learn the essentials of tailoring their audio style to what was required for a radio show (like where breaks should fall, making sure vocals were clear, and so on). That's why he's in here talking about *Snap*. *99% Invisible* and *Radio Diaries* are founding members of a new narrative podcast collective called Radiotopia. (http://www.radiotopia.fm/)

THE MOTH   http://themoth.org/

The Moth is, at its heart, a live storytelling event (or collection of events). Founded by George Dawes Green in New York City in 1997, it now runs events all over the country, as well as doing a weekly radio show and a podcast.

The Mainstage is the "flagship" event, where directors solicit stories from tellers and then direct them intensively. This is primarily what Catherine Burns was talking about in our interview. She also refers to a "StorySLAM," in which storytellers work up their own stories and compete to win the accolades of the crowd. Stories from both the Mainstage and the StorySLAMs can make it onto the radio show and the podcast. For the radio, they are edited (extremely minimally) by Jay Allison, who is the radio producer for *The Moth Radio Hour*, and are introduced by Jay and the directors.

I spoke to Jay Allison in Woods Hole, Massachusetts, in April 2012. I spoke to Catherine Burns in September 2013, and I visited the Moth office in February 2014. Jenna Weiss-Berman (she of the Transom Workshop), showed me around and helped me with follow-up questions. The rest of The Moth's directorial staff includes Sarah Haberman, Sarah Austin Jenness, Jenifer Hixson, Meg Bowles,

Kate Tellers, Maggie Cino, and Inga Glodowski; with support from Kirsty Bennett, Whitney Jones, and Jenelle Pifer.

PLANET MONEY http://npr.org/money/

Planet Money is a podcast and radio program about money and the economy. Its creators are Adam Davidson and Alex Blumberg (the latter of whom was then also a staff member at *This American Life* but has now departed both *TAL* and *Planet Money* to start a new podcast company, called Gimlet Media).

I visited *Planet Money* in the summer of 2012, on July 25–26, and August 2 and 8, and followed up with several Skype calls. At the time, they produced two podcasts, and two or three segments for *All Things Considered* and *Morning Edition* a week, as well as blog content, and four hours a year for *This American Life*.

The main story I followed through the process was about offshore finance, by Chana Joffe-Walt, but in the end, that one didn't make it in. The other stories I reference are all noted as they come up.

The reporting staff when I visited consisted of:

Alex Blumberg

Zoe Chace

Adam Davidson

Jacob Goldstein (reporter and blogger)

Chana Joffe-Walt

David Kestenbaum

Robert Smith

And the rest of the staff:

Caitlin Kenney (producer)

Jess Jiang (producer)

Lam Thuy Vo (graphics and design for the website)

I divide it up like that because, officially, those are (were) their jobs. But one of the characteristics of this kind of radio is a DIY, follow-your-interests focus, and that means that basically everybody produces and basically everybody reports and is on the air.

RADIO DIARIES http://www.radiodiaries.org/podcast

Radio Diaries is also growing, thanks to a very successful Kickstarter campaign, and has moved into quarters down the hall from *This American Life*. When I interviewed Joe Richman, in June 2012, he was still working (with part-time assistance) out of his former apartment, a classic Lower East Side tenement, complete with bathtub in the kitchen. That was cool.

Radio Diaries grows out of the idea of giving ordinary people tape recorders and getting them to record their lives, which Joe and his staff then edit intensively into non-narrated pieces that run on *All Things Considered* (and are podcast). But they also do non-narrated histories using interviews and historical tape, and have even done a few narrated pieces, including for *This American Life*. They have begun producing more stories in more different varieties than ever, which you can find on their podcast. They are also founding members of the podcast collective Radiotopia, with *99% Invisible.*

RADIOLAB   http://www.radiolab.org/
Radiolab is a radio show about ideas, often scientific ideas, that uses experimental techniques and avant-garde sound to illuminate complex subjects. I visited *Radiolab* in February 2012. Sean Cole was on staff at that time, though he'd left shortly before I interviewed him in May 2013. I interviewed Jad Abumrad in November 2013 and June 2014, and senior producer Soren Wheeler and executive producer Ellen Horne in November 2013.

SNAP JUDGMENT   http://snapjudgment.org/
Snap Judgment is a themed weekly radio show that focuses on propulsive first-person storytelling, intensively edited and soundtracked. I visited *Snap Judgment* June 11–14, 2012, and had many Skype follow-ups in the subsequent three weeks. While I was following them, they were producing two episodes in a three-week period, listed below with all the individual stories on those shows.

The staff in June 2012 was as follows:

Host and executive producer
Glynn Washington

Executive producer
Mark Ristich

Senior producer
Anna Sussman

Producers
Stephanie Foo
Jamie DeWolf
Renzo Gorrio
Pat Mesiti-Miller (who is also "music editor")

Webmaster, video producer, and graphics designer
Will Urbina

"Assistant producer" (i.e., intern)
Julia DeWitt (she is now a full producer on the show)

"Coming to America"—*Snap Judgment*, #315, June 29, 2012
http://snapjudgment.org/Coming-to-america
"Pen Pals," producer: Stephanie Foo; sound design: Renzo Gorrio
"Gas Tank Crossing," producer: Stephanie Foo; sound
design: Pat Mesiti-Miller
"Texas vs. Texas," producer: Stephanie Foo
"International Gaydar," producers: Pat Mesiti-Miller and
Anna Sussman
"Learning to Speak," producers: Stephanie Foo and Mark Ristich

"Circus, Circus"—*Snap Judgment*, #316, July 13, 2012
http://snapjudgment.org/circus-circus
"Real Boy," producer: Glynn Washington; sound design: Pat Mesiti-Miller
"Circus Soviet," producer: Anna Sussman
"Razzle Dazzle," producer: Jamie DeWolf; sound design: Renzo Gorrio
"Rocky," producer: Julia DeWitt
"Big Mary," producers: Glynn Washington and Anna Sussman
"No Talent Circus–Chicken John," producer: Jamie DeWolf; sound design: Mark Ristich

I also focus on "Night at the Rock Bar," producer: Mark Ristich; sound design: Pat Mesiti-Miller, which appeared on a different episode, "Fight of Your Life," *Snap Judgment*, #230.

As a side note, for random reasons the two *Snap* stories I spend the most time on involve guns and violence. This isn't reflective of the majority of *Snap* stories, which cover the gamut of human experience. Just needed to put that out there.

THIS AMERICAN LIFE   http://www.thisamericanlife.org/

More information about participants in and dates for *Radio: An Illustrated Guide* can be found in the preface, on page 13. That book was published in September of 1999 as a pledge-drive premium, and has been in print ever since, available primarily via *This American Life*'s website: http://store.thisamericanlife.org/ProductDetails.asp?ProductCode=RADIO%3AANILLUSTRATEDGUIDE

I did follow-up interviews with Ira Glass in November 2013. Since I completed my research for this book, *TAL* has hired up some of the great producers you'll see here from other shows: Chana Joffe-Walt, Sean Cole, Stephanie Foo, and Zoe Chace all now work at *This American Life*. On the other hand, Alex Blumberg has now left *TAL* and also *Planet Money*, to begin his own podcast company, Gimlet Media. His first podcast, the story of his company, is called *Startup*. *TAL* has also started a new podcast which reports a single story serialized over many weeks, called *Serial*. As I write this, in December 2014, the whole podcast sector is growing and changing so rapidly it feels foolish to even try to catalogue the changes, but I call that a good problem to have.

In April 1999 (when *Radio: An Illustrated Guide* was written), *This American Life* was produced by Ira Glass, Julie Snyder, Alix Spiegel, and Nancy Updike, with help from Todd Bachmann, Jorge Just, Sylvia Lemus, and webmaster Elizabeth Meister.

TRANSOM STORY WORKSHOP   http://transom.org/workshop/

I visited the Transom Workshop on April 7–9, 2012.

Reading my sections on the workshop, you'd think instructor Rob Rosenthal is the kind of teacher who holds forth at length while students listen and take notes. Nothing could be further from the truth. The most remarkable aspect of the class was Rob's teaching method, which involves a lot of listening to students, and not a lot of talking. But because of the brutal editing required by comics, I wasn't able to depict this interplay.

You can listen to all the pieces from that spring's Transom Workshop here: http://transom.org/2012/story-workshop-pieces-spring-2012-2/

Rob Rosenthal produces a really great podcast series that goes behind the scenes with radio makers and analyzes their best work, called *HowSound* (http://howsound.org/).

There were nine participants in the Spring 2012 workshop, but only four were in the class I attended:

Lauren Ober (http://www.oberandout.com/)

Jessica Kittams (http://transom.org/workshop/story-workshop/story-workshop-alumni/jessica-kittams-about-one-acre/)

Jenna Weiss-Berman, who afterward worked at The Moth, was incredibly helpful to me in getting reference and filling in the information I needed about Moth stories. (http://transom.org/workshop/story-workshop/story-workshop-alumni/jenna-weiss-berman-knock-out/)

Andrew Norton (http://www.andrewnorton.tv) has produced a really wonderful series of short documentary videos (http://www.thisisradio.com/) featuring many of the producers who are in this book, and from which I cribbed for photo reference.

FURTHER RESOURCES

If you're interested in making radio yourself, you can find huge amounts of great information on Transom.org, about everything from how to mic an interview to how to write narration, to how to set up a home studio. It's an amazing resource. I learned a ton and I've never even tried to make radio.
http://transom.org/

Another very comprehensive site devoted to narrative journalism (and not only on the radio) is Nieman Storyboard.
http://www.niemanstoryboard.org/

This American Life also maintains a wrap-up of radio-making resources.
http://www.thisamericanlife.org/about/make-radio